We now inform your Honors, that we will not restore to the Schedule the Sum of £7000 which we permitted to appear in it at the second reading. NO! not even for your favorite Governor!

Thursday the 23d day of Augt. 1764.

Read the Journals of Yesterdays Proceedings.

The House (agreeable to Order) proceeded to take into Consideration the mefsage from the Council of yesterday, recommending a Provision therein mentioned to be made to the Tax Bill, and the same being read a 2d time.

Resolved this House disagree to the Request of the Council by their said Mefsage. —

Ordered that the said mefsage be referred to a Committee of the following Gentlemen to prepare a Proper Answer thereto, to inform them thereof, (vizt.)

Mr. Bee

Mr. Manigault   Mr. Gadsden

Mr. Rutledge   Mr. Drayton —

Mr. Manigault reported from the Committee appointed to draw up an Answer to the Councils Mefsage of yesterday, —

That they had prepared an Answer thereto, which they had directed him to Report to the House; and he read the report in His place and afterwards delivered it in at the Clerks Table, and is as folows, vizt,

Honble Gentlemen —

Your Endeavours this Sefsion to draw us into a dispute, have been so frequent, that we, cannot say. We are at all surprised at your Mefsage of yesterday, And as We know of no right you have, to provide for the principal Officer; or indeed any Officer in the Government; tho you may wantonly exert a power, to postpone the Payment of the Debts, due to the Creditors of the

Christopher Gadsden

The Writings of Christopher Gadsden
represents more than seven years of work
in searching among obscure documents,
letters and papers of memorabilia. Skillful
editing of the papers of Christopher Gadsden has been a painstaking task because
Gadsden was a prolific writer and poured
forth voluminous words in defense of any
cause in which he was interested. His
thinking, therefore, had great impact on
the local and national political and social
events of the revolutionary movement.
He led the democratic forces for revolution and independence, and was a ranking,
forceful advocate for independence and
national union in the Continental Congress. His power in these respects was
acknowledged, and had he not been forced
to return to his native state when hostili-
ties between Britain and America commenced, Gadsden would have been ranked
with such nationally remembered figures
as John Adams, Thomas Jefferson and
others. After the American Revolution,
he fought valiantly to stabilize the country.

Gadsden has been totally neglected in
history as a state and national leader, who
gave form to and reflected the political
thinking of his period. He was an important colonial and revolutionary merchant, and at the same time a builder of
his state and the American nation. As
president John Adams remarked, Gadsden "was of a breed of men born for the
public, not for themselves." In *The Writings of Christopher Gadsden* his stature
is revealed for the first time.

The Writings of Christopher Gadsden

CHRISTOPHER GADSDEN AS A YOUNG MAN
Attributed to Sir Joshua Reynolds

The Writings

of

Christopher Gadsden

1746-1805

Edited

by RICHARD WALSH

The University of South Carolina Press

Columbia, South Carolina   1966

Library of Congress Catalog Card Number: 66-28136

Copyright © 1966
By The University of South Carolina Press

Printed by THE R. L. BRYAN COMPANY
COLUMBIA, SOUTH CAROLINA

TO

B. J.

J. M.

B. R.

Abbreviations

DAB   *Dictionary of American Biography.*

HSP   Historical Society of Pennsylvania.

NYPL   New York Public Library.

SCHM   *South Carolina Historical Magazine.*

SCG   *South Carolina Gazette.*

S.C.A.D.   South Carolina Archives Department.

SCHS   South Carolina Historical Society.

Preface

Despite Christopher Gadsden's importance during the Revolutionary period, both as a merchant and a politician, relatively few of his letters have survived. Except for a small collection at Presbyterian College, Clinton, South Carolina, there is little of his correspondence to be found. His letters are widely scattered in the collections of his contemporaries. Had it not been for nineteenth-century historians George Bancroft, who transcribed many of Gadsden's letters, and Robert W. Gibbes, who saved some of them, there would be very few, indeed. Possibly many materials were lost in the burning of Gadsden's warehouse on his Charles Town wharf in 1783. His personal property was seized by the British during the occupation of the city between May 1780 and December 1782, and probably many papers were destroyed then. But one cannot overlook Gadsden's carelessness, of which there is ample evidence in the *Writings* published here. He often wrote in haste, ignoring punctuation and rules of grammar, at the same time inventing abbreviations. Also, he may never have kept a file of correspondence.

Yet for all this, the search for Gadsden letters and essays over the past five years has not been unrewarding. Those which have been discovered form a volume of documents on national and state history in the Revolutionary period; and his observations and reactions give insight into the minds of the men of his generation. As a member of one committee or another, Gadsden signed numerous letters; only those never before published, i.e., those that exist in manuscript only, are included here. Others are noted in the footnotes, such as those written as Member of the Committee of Correspondence to Charles Garth, published in the *SCHM*.

Gadsden's published essays in William Henry Drayton's *Letters of Freeman,* on the Cherokee War, signed *Philopatrios,* are not included herein, as they are available on microfilm.

Gadsden's "Diary," referred to in my previous articles in *Manuscripts* is a misnomer. The "Diary" consists of Gadsden's personal copies of *Common Sense* and a *Journal of the First Continental Congress.* Gadsden had these books interleaved when they were bound. On the blank pages, he made a few cryptic remarks, copied some letters,

vii

and repeated a portion of a speech by John Adams which can not be found in any edition of the *Journals of the Continental Congress*. Most of this material was written in shorthand. Because Gadsden's remarks were so few and brief, and because by far the largest amount of the material was copies of others' speeches or letters, the "Diary" is not reproduced in this collection. However, included is a piece of his "Daybook," consisting, unfortunately, of only one page. The remainder has been lost.

Every item used in this collection posed editorial problems. The nature of the materials has defied consistency all too often. At first it seemed that only complete modernization could standardize the collection, which consists of originals in Gadsden's hand, secretary's copies, transcripts of manuscripts, published letters and essays not available in the originals. Complete modernization was rejected. A compromise was made by preserving the eighteenth-century style and at the same time rendering these documents understandable to the twentieth-century reader. For the sake of the purist, transcripts of the materials have been deposited in the South Caroliniana Library, Columbia, South Carolina.

The following editorial course has been maintained: superscript letters have been brought down to the line; the thorn has been rendered "th"; and the ampersand has been changed to "and." Also, punctuation has been supplied where it was necessary for clarity, but sparingly for fear of misinterpreting meanings. Wherever there was doubt, the sentence has been allowed to stand. Dashes and colons ending sentences have been converted to periods or semi-colons and, chiefly in the earlier essays wherein Gadsden employs a highly Latinized style, words have been interpolated to reveal the intricacies of his thoughts. The complimentary closes to letters have not been changed, except for the addition of periods to abbreviations.

Gadsden's spelling and indiscriminate capitalization, typical of the eighteenth-century writer, have been unaltered. However, because of the peculiarity of his abbreviations, these have been spelled out or modernized, e.g. "act." becomes *account,* and "&c.," *etc.* Where the meaning of the abbreviation was obvious, it has been left untouched.

Latin phrases arise frequently in Gadsden's formal writing. They are drawn from the classics: Virgil's *Aeneid,* Ovid's *Metamorphoses,* Horace's *Ars Poetica* and *Epistles,* Juvenal's *Satires,* and so on. These translations, because of their brevity and apt contextual meanings, have been interpolated rather than placed in footnotes, and because such Gadsden publishers as printer Peter Timothy usually misspelled or garbled the translations, they have been corrected.

I returned to Charleston recently and tramped over the Gadsden place. His wharf at the foot of Calhoun Street had long since been gone; and in its place was a great shipyard. Company officials had never heard of Christopher Gadsden and his wharf, or his impact on history, but they were interested when I told them about him.

I walked over his "Middlesex," finding that when I was a student at the College of Charleston, I had lived within the sub-division! Behind me resided a man, who bears the Gadsden name, now Dr. Dick Gadsden of the Medical College of South Carolina.

With my little daughter, I sneaked into Fort Johnson, where Christopher Gadsden was stationed while the British were assaulting the Americans at Fort Sullivan. Nothing is there from Gadsden's time but one, uncared-for building erected in 1776, with a small marker. This historic spot is now a Marine Laboratory of the College of Charleston and is not open to visitors.

I had visited these scenes many times before, but on this trip, I could almost feel the spirit of Christopher Gadsden. I had already completed my manuscript, and it was in the hands of the editor. I wondered about this man who assisted in the birth of our nation. Would he have been pleased over my efforts to portray him for this generation? But any errors of interpretation or rendition in this book are surely not his nor those of the many good people who helped me.

R. W.

Georgetown University,
Washington, D. C.

Acknowledgments

The publication of these *Writings* of Christopher Gadsden has been brought about by a veritable army of cooperative men and women. A few of the many who deserve thanks are E. L. Inabinet and the late Professor Robert L. Meriwether, directors of the Caroliniana Library, University of South Carolina; Mr. Charles Lee, and the late Doctor J. Harold Easterby, directors of the South Carolina Archives Department; Miss Virginia Rugheimer of the Charleston Library Society; Mr. Paul Rugen, Assistant Curator of Manuscripts, New York Public Library; and Mrs. Kathleen Sloan of the University of South Carolina Press.

Especially, I am indebted to Mrs. Louise Jones DuBose, former director of University of South Carolina Press, for her enthusiasm and her interest.

The editor's students who transcribed documents or assisted in research were Doctor Philip Grant of Dayton University; Doctor Albert Abbott of Fairfield University, and Mr. Edward Hanlon; and the Reverend William H. Hogan, S. J., of Loyola University, Chicago, who translated the Latin in Gadsden's writings.

Constant encouragement has been found in the National Historical Publications Commission under its present executive director, Doctor Oliver Wendell Holmes, and especially under Doctor Philip Hamer, who formerly held the office. A grant-in-aid for research was supplied by the American Philosophical Society; and grants-in-aid of publication were given by the Georgetown University Alumni Giving Fund.

I am also grateful for donations to "Friends of The University of South Carolina Press," for use in the publication of the Gadsden Papers, from Mrs. Charles H. Woodward, Philadelphia, Pennsylvania; Miss Margaret S. Gadsden, Columbia, South Carolina; Mrs. Dwight H. Gadsden, Charleston, South Carolina.

Invaluable criticisms of this work were given by Doctor Joseph I. Waring; Doctor Charles L. Anger of The Citadel; Doctor Jack P. Greene of The Johns Hopkins University; and Doctor Richard Maxwell Brown and J. Joseph Huthmacher of Rutgers University; but none of these gentlemen is responsible for any errors in this compilation. To Mrs. Mary B. Prior, secretary of the South Carolina Historical Society, I am especially grateful for assistance, along with her constant interest and attention; the same must be said of the Reverend Brian A. McGrath, S. J., Associate Vice-President of Georgetown University.

R. W.

Contents

Contents continued

Contents continued

Illustrations

Introduction

Christopher Gadsden was "a man of deep and clear convictions; thoroughly sincere; of an unbending will, and a sturdy, impetuous integrity. . . . He possessed not only that courage which defies danger, but that persistence which neither peril, nor imprisonment, nor the threat of death can shake. Full of religious faith, and at the same time inquisitive and tolerant, methodical, yet lavish of his fortune for public ends, he had in his nature nothing vacillating or low, and knew not how to hesitate or feign."

In these words, Christopher Gadsden was described by Historian George Bancroft.

Bancroft said further: "As the united American people spread through the vast expanse of which their jurisdiction now extends, be it remembered that the blessing of union is due to the warm heartedness of South Carolina. 'She is alive, and felt at every pore.' And when we count up those who, above others, contributed to the great result, we are to name the inspired 'madman,' James Otis, and the magnanimous, unwavering lover of his country, Christopher Gadsden." [1]

Gadsden was born February 6, 1724, a son of Lieutenant (later Captain) Thomas Gadsden of the British merchant fleet, then port collector of Charles Town, and his wife Elizabeth. Two brothers, Robert and Thomas, and a sister Elizabeth, were older, Robert and Thomas dying before Christopher was born.

A year after Christopher Gadsden's birth his mother died. Three years later his father was married to Collins Hall, and in 1729 their son Philip was born. The same year, Christopher's sister Elizabeth died, and in 1731 occurred the death of his stepmother. Captain Gadsden then married Alice Mighells (1732), by whom he had at least two children, James and Thomas. [2]

---

[1] George Bancroft, *History of the United States* (11th ed.; Boston: Little, Brown & Co., 1857), V, 293.

[2] Biographical Sketches of Gadsden are to be found by Robert Lee Meriwether, *DAB*, XII, 82-83, Allen Johnson and Dumas Malone, eds. (New York: Charles Scribner's Sons, 1931); E.I. Renick "Christopher Gadsden," *Publications of the Southern Historical Association*, II (January, 1898), 243-5; David Ramsay, *History of South Carolina* (Charleston: David Longworth [for the author], 1809), II, 457-66; F.A. Porcher, *A Memoir of General Christopher*

In this ever-changing family, Christopher remained for a few years, and then was sent to England for schooling where he "acquired a knowledge of the learned languages, also, of French, Hebrew and Algebra."[3] When Christopher was sixteen years old he returned to Charles Town, and from there went to Philadelphia as an apprentice to the merchant, Thomas Lawrence. His father died August 16, 1741, leaving real estate, funds, and slaves to his three sons, Christopher and his brothers, James, and Thomas. Mrs. Alice Mighells Gadsden had died a month previously.

With the completion of his apprenticeship at 21, Gadsden went to England for a short while and returned to South Carolina on H.M.S. *Aldborough,* whose captain, Ashby Utting, was a family connection.[4] En route, the purser of the *Aldborough* died, and Gadsden was appointed to his place. Gadsden served in this capacity for two years and was at the siege of Louisbourgh,[5] afterwards returning to Charles Town to settle—as far as events and his own disposition permitted— becoming a merchant and land owner.

Just before his departure for the north, he had married on July 28, 1746, Jane Godfrey, daughter of the merchant, Samuel Godfrey. The following year their daughter Elizabeth was born. She was the first of several children born to the couple, including Christopher, Jr., (1750-1766), but only Elizabeth reached maturity.

Jane Godfrey Gadsden died in May 1755, and in late December, Christopher Gadsden married his second wife, Mary Hasell, a niece of the wealthy Mrs. Gabriel Manigault. For twelve years this union endured, but early in January 1768, Mary Gadsden died. Their children, who managed to survive the ills of childhood, were Thomas, Mary, and Philip.

On April 14, 1776, Gadsden married Anne Wragg, who survived him. She, too, was related to the Manigault family. They had no children.[6]

Gadsden (Charleston: Journal of Commerce [for the Society], 1851),; Edward J. Swords, *American Military Biography . . . Lives and Characters of the Officers of the Revolution. . . .* (New York: np, 1830), pp. 83-87. A "popular" sketch is in Helen Kohn Hennig, *Great South Carolinians* (Chapel Hill: University of North Carolina Press, 1940). Family relationships may be found in *SCHM,* XXXII (October, 1931), 301-13.

[3] Joseph Johnson, M.D., *Traditions and Reminiscences, Chiefly of the American Revolution in the South* (Charleston: Walker & James, 1851), p. 37.

[4] Letter from Commander W.E. May, National Maritime Museum, Greenwich, England, in possession of Louise Jones DuBose, formerly director of University of South Carolina Press, who is writing a biography of Christopher Gadsden.

[5] *See* letter to Henry Laurens, September 11, 1746.

[6] Mabel L. Webber, "Extracts from the Journal of Mrs. Ann Manigault," *SCHM,* XX (January, 1919), 61; XXI (January, 1920), 12; Webber, "John Rutledge and His Descendants," *SCHM,* XXXI (January, 1930), 7-25; "Chart of the Wragg Family," *SCHM,* XIX (July, 1918), 121. Personal letter from the Philip Gadsden family of Philadelphia, Pennsylvania, to Louise Jones DuBose. Genealogical Chart of Christopher Gadsden, Ms, SCHS.

Gadsden's business and political affairs might be divided into two eras, as described in his *Writings*. His career as a merchant began upon his return to Charles Town in 1748, and his public life commenced to take shape in 1757.

Charles Town, in 1748, was the center of trade extending throughout the British colonies and, by way of Great Britain and Cape Finisterre, to most of the civilized world. In Charles Town, besides his interests in wholesaling, retailing, and factorage, Gadsden engaged in money lending and land speculation. In addition, he managed stores at Cheraw and Georgetown with indentured servants in charge, and operated several plantations. He built a thriving business and he planned to expand it. He was financially indebted to no one on the eve of the Revolution.

Advertisements in *The South Carolina Gazette* of 1751 indicate the nature of the operations of the 27-year-old merchant:[7]

Just imported on the last Ships from London and Bristol, a large assortment of goods suitable to the present approaching seasons, also gunpowder, bar-lead, shot and bullets, shoe makers, spinnel, mahogany sconce glasses, violins, a great variety of men's and women's sadales, and most sorts of sadlery ware, matresses, garden seeds, linseed oil, red and white lead, yellow oaker and Spanish brown, an assortment of large china soup dishes and plates, &c double and single refined sugar, and sugar candy, best Scotch snuff, crown glass, 8 by 10 and 9 by 11; three gallon stone bottles, steel grates, with brass fenders; shovels and tongs; a good assortment of white plains and duffils, with a great variety of most articles that are usually imported here, to be sold wholesale or retail, by Christopher Gadsden.

Just imported in the Schooner *Nancy,* Capt. Richardson, from Philadelphia, exceeding good flour, in small cags, containing about sixty pounds each . . . an overseer very well recommended, may be inform'd of a very good place.

Christopher Gadsden.

Runaway from the subscriber, about 18 months ago, a negro man named Cyrus, and a negro wench named Berry with her two children, late belonging to the estate of Mrs. Williamson

---

[7] *SCG,* April 29, July 22, September 23, 1751. (Note the peculiar spelling). For information on Gadsden's stores, speculation in lands, and plantation affairs, *see* Robert Lee Meriwether, *The Expansion of South Carolina, 1729-1765* (Kingsport, Tennessee: Southern Publishers, Inc., 1940), pp. 94-95, 20n; *SCG,* January 4, February, 1768. His economic enterprises may also be traced in his newspaper advertisements, principally in the *SCG* and its successors, and, occasionally, in the *South Carolina Gazette and Country Journal.* His suits for debts are in Judgment Rolls, Court of Common Pleas to 1774. *See* Index under C.G. and documents, S.C.A.D.

deceas'd, who are well known about *Stono,* and are said to be harbour'd there or thereabout. Whoever secures the said negroes in the work-house at Charles Town, and gives notice thereof to Mr. Christopher Gadsden merchant on the Bay shall have £ 20 reward for the fellow, and the like sum for the wench and her children. . . .

Such advertisements were not to continue for many more years, as the routine of a merchant's life did not consume all of Gadsden's energy and interests.

In 1757, he first entered the Commons House of Assembly in South Carolina and before long was concerned with the Province's lack of military forces in the face of Indian attack and trouble from abroad. Before the year was out, sixty young men of Charles Town had formed the Volunteer Artillery Company with Gadsden in command, commissioned by the Governor. The *Gazette* account included the observation that "so zealous are they in what they have undertaken that there is already a Scarcity of Books' upon Gunnery." [8] At this time, William Henry Lyttelton was governor and before his term was concluded in 1760, both Gadsden and his battalion became active in the Cherokee War.

A supporter of Governor Lyttelton, Gadsden went as captain of the Charles Town Battalion of Artillery, a part of that "silken body" of planters and aristocrats, as misnamed by James Adair, on the first expedition against the unruly Cherokee.[9] Lyttelton's expedition was a tragi-comedy of blunders and cruelties against the Cherokees, ending in a general Indian uprising, massacres, and Provincial indebtedness. Perhaps it marked the beginning of the close of the empire for South Carolina, because a bitter result was a hot newspaper debate over the management of two succeeding expeditions, led, respectively, by Colonel Archibald Montgomery, and Lieutenant Colonel James Grant, both English officers.

Montgomery's military activities in 1760 were regarded as generally unsatisfactory by the Provincials, but it was Grant who became the chief target of their assaults. Grant, according to his antagonists, had seized the command over the ranking Carolina officer, Colonel Thomas Middleton. Among the leading proponents of Middleton's claims was Gadsden, who wrote under the pseudonym, "Philopatrios." He excoriated Grant for questionable strategy and false claims to victories. His ire was raised chiefly against the lieutenant colonel for branding the Rangers cowards. Gadsden intimated that Grant

---

[8] *SCG,* December 6, 1756; January 20, February 10 and 17, August 4 and 11, 1757.

[9] James Adair, *The History of the American Indians* (London: E. & C. Dilly, 1775).

xviii

and his regulars, not the Rangers, were the real cowards for not pursuing the Indians in 1761 to cut as many of their throats as possible, and force an end to their barbarity.[10]

At this early period, Gadsden's writing made him popular with the mechanics of the town, and many became members of his battalion of artillery. But while the writer won favor with the home folk for his barbs against the British, he likewise earned antagonism in royal circles. As Philopatrios, he displayed that excessive fervor of temperament which moved Josiah Quincy to describe Gadsden in a Commons House debate in 1773 as "plain, blunt, hot, and incorrect; though very sensible." [11] Later, the Carolinian was to characterize himself as "Don Quixote Secundus."

Tempers aroused over the Cherokee War and the Philopatrios writings had scarcely cooled before another assault on Provincial pride and principles was attempted. Called the "Gadsden Election Controversy," it clearly signaled the beginning of the movement toward independence in South Carolina.[12] Gadsden saw in this local embroilment the larger issue of British encroachment on the natural rights of Englishmen, the continuance of which, he felt, would result in separation of the colonies from the mother country. He believed that ancient rights did not stop at the shores of England but were likewise held by the settlers of the new world.

Trouble had begun when Lyttelton's successor, Governor Thomas Boone, instructed by the Board of Trade and Plantations, endeavored to revise and improve the South Carolina electoral system. The move by the Board was based upon the Act of 1721 which required church wardens to take oaths before a magistrate, prior to conducting each parish election. Few wardens bothered to comply, as was the case when Gadsden was elected from St. Paul's Parish in 1761. Governor Boone attempted to unseat him in the Assembly, to prove thereby the necessity of his proposed revisions in election laws. Because of this "irregularity," Boone unceremoniously refused to administer to Gadsden the customary state oaths. The House accepted

---

[10] *See* resumé of "Philopatrios" (pseudonym of Christopher Gadsden), "Some Observations on the Cherokee War," *SCG,* December 18, 1761.

[11] *Memoir of the Life of Josiah Quincy Junior of Massachusetts,* Josiah Quincy (Boston: Cummings, Hilliard & Co., 1825), p. 112. "In the course of the debate," Quincy continues, "he used these very singular expressions, for a member of parliament:—'And, Mr. Speaker, if the governor and council don't see fit to fall in with us, I say, let the general duty law [the Tea Act] and all, go to the devil, sir; and we go about our business'."

[12] Jack P. Greene, "The Gadsden Election Controversy and the Revolutionary Movement in South Carolina," *Mississippi Valley Historical Review,* XLVI (1959), 469-92. W. Roy Smith, *South Carolina as a Royal Province* (New York: Macmillan Co., 1903), pp. 340ff. *See* article "To the Gentlemen Electors of the Parish of St. Paul, Stono." Doctor David Ramsay surely had these events in mind when he asserted that Gadsden was the first man in the Province to advocate independence.

Gadsden's election, nevertheless, and criticized the Governor's stand. The House's stubborn refusal to recognize the chief executive's position, or to revise the electoral laws, brought an impasse. No legislation of any kind came from the Commons House for two years, and members refused payment of the "gubernatorial annual grant."

As chairman of the House Committee on this matter and an eager correspondent in the newspapers, Gadsden led the attack. Boone soon found himself overmatched by Gadsden and his political allies, Rawlins Lowndes, John Rutledge, and other Carolina leaders. No one supported Boone—not even William Wragg and Henry Laurens, who upbraided Gadsden and the Assembly for not paying Provincial creditors during the dispute.[13] The deadlock was only partially resolved by the Board of Trade and Plantations. Its suggestion to the King to recall and admonish Boone for his unconstitutional behavior was adhered to, but members insisted that the South Carolinians were wrong in withholding the Governor's salary. The controversy caused the Carolinians to review English history and precedent on the Rights of Assembly; and Gadsden began to assert openly his belief in the natural rights of British Americans.

The experience was peculiarly timely, as on the heels of the imbroglio came the first of the imperial crises, the Stamp Act. Gadsden attended the Stamp Act Congress in New York with John Rutledge and Thomas Lynch and, joining with other colonial leaders, he there affirmed his principles of the natural rights of British citizens, a philosophy that became the basis of American resistance. Gadsden considered appeals to the Crown based on the colonial charters— which he said the "Eastern gentlemen" wanted—as dangerous to these maxims. He thought the distinction between internal and external taxation an equivocation, because he believed that Parliament possessed no power to tax without colonial representation.[14]

Gadsden spoke against the Stamp Act "with irresistible impetuosity," [15] particularly emphasizing unity of the colonies, saying:

A confirmation of our essential and common rights as Englishmen may be pleaded from charters safely enough; but any further dependence upon them may be fatal. We should stand upon the broad common ground of those natural rights that we all feel and know as men, and as descendants of Englishmen. I wish the charters may not ensnare us at last, by drawing different colonies to act differently in this great cause. Whenever that is the case, all will be over with the whole. There ought to be no New England

---

[13] *Ibid.*

[14] *See* letters to William Samuel Johnson, December 2, 1765; April 16, 1766, and 6n.

[15] Bancroft, *op. cit.,* p. 335.

man, no New-Yorker, known on the continent, but all of us Americans.[16]

On returning from New York, Gadsden moved the radical "grand machine," whose chief cogs were the Charles Town mechanics, in resistance to the Act itself and to the Declaratory Act. Gadsden was the chief figure at every meeting under the "Liberty Tree" from that moment, through the Townshend Acts, to the final break. By 1773, he was correctly called by Lieutenant Governor William Bull one of the "Tribunes" of the people.[17]

As the leading radical, and defender of American rights which might be gained through economic boycotts against Britain, Gadsden was sent as a delegate to the First Continental Congress. There he exhibited a far greater radicalism than his colleagues; he was ready to sacrifice local to national interests. He constantly pleaded with his countrymen for unity of resistance to the British Empire, and was remarkable for his fiery enthusiasm which surpassed that of his friend and correspondent Samuel Adams.

Said Silas Deane:
"Mr. Gadsden leaves all New England sons of Liberty far behind. He is for taking up his firelock and marching direct to Boston; nay, he affirmed this morning, that were his wife and all his children in Boston, and they were to perish by the sword, it would not alter his sentiment or proceeding for American liberty. . . ."[18]

---

[16] *See* letter to William Samuel Johnson and Charles Garth, December 2, 1765.

[17] Robert H. Woody, "Christopher Gadsden and the Stamp Act," *Proceedings of the South Carolina Historical Association,* 1939, pp. 3-12. Richard Walsh, *Charleston's Sons of Liberty* (Columbia: University of South Carolina Press, 1959), pp. 32, 35 *passim.*

[18] Silas Deane's descriptive comment is in Connecticut Historical Society, *Collections,* II (Hartford, 1870), 175. *See* letter to Samuel Adams, June 5, 1774; for further discussion of Gadsden's economic thought, *see* Richard Walsh, "Christopher Gadsden, Radical or Conservative Revolutionary?" *SCHM,* LXIII (October, 1962), 195-203; *SCG,* June 22, 1769; his essays in William Henry Drayton's *Letters of Freeman* (London: n.p., 1771) and the summary below. *See* letters to George Washington, May 13, 1787; to Thomas Jefferson, October 29, 1787.
Gadsden's writings indicate the desirability of investigation of the American merchants as political radicals or conservatives, and they indicate a tendency toward natural law in economics and free trade. Perhaps this explains the motivations of those merchants who supported the cause of independence rather than remain within the empire. O.M. Dickerson's *The Navigation Acts and the American Revolution* (Philadelphia: University of Pennsylvania, 1951), p. 122 *passim,* minimizes parliamentary restrictive legislation and the tax acts as a cause of the revolution in the South. But Gadsden, in the minority among fellow tradesmen, had friends who agreed with him. They were Thomas Morris, William Brailsford, William Logan, Thomas Gadsden, and Thomas Legare (*Gazette of the State of South Carolina,* July 23, 1783; Senate Journal, January 30, 1783, fol. 56-57, S.C.A.D.) David Ramsay noticed them briefly as the "new Set" of adventurers in his *History of the Revolution of South Carolina from a British Province to an Independent State* (Trenton, N.J.: Isaac Collins, 1785), II, 75-76.

Gadsden was personally, and politically, responsive to those early measures of Great Britain relating to commerce of the colonies. His entire fortune had been invested in a wharf which he saw threatened by the closing of the port of Boston by Parliament in 1774. He felt that if it were to become an established legal precedent for Boston's trade to be thus reduced, Charles Town's trade would likewise suffer. Could not any colonial port be summarily closed over a real or imagined affront to parliament? he asked.

Historians have made Gadsden known to posterity as a man of unswerving devotion to independence, whose actions were motivated solely by political and constitutional principles; but it should be pointed out that economic factors also shaped his thinking. He felt rightly that prosperity depended upon the well-being of the planters. Gadsden termed this the "land interest." It was obvious to him that, if the planters had the wherewithal to buy, merchants benefited; if not, trade languished as profits from factoring and selling dwindled, and the merchants' coffers became depleted. Unlike his fellow merchants who were reluctant to move against the empire because its naval power offered commercial protection, and its wealth extensive credit, Gadsden discarded those benefits for economic independence. He believed British mercantile legislation was a positive hindrance, preventing merchant and planter alike from trading unshackled with all the world. In the early part of the conflict, he supported the production of American manufactures as a balance to agriculture.

His election to the Second Continental Congress saw him perform yeoman duty in the cause. He served on the Marine Committee and was unwavering in his advocacy of a Navy. His forthright statements supporting this essential project were circulated by John Adams, and may have helped form a favorable opinion among the delegates. But Gadsden alienated the powerful Rutledges who thought him "wrong headed" and too much inclined to cooperate with the New Englanders. Gadsden had already brushed with the Rutledge family over their excepting South Carolina's rice from the enumerated list allowing it to be shipped South of Cape Finisterre.[19]

In the Second Continental Congress, Gadsden was among the first advocates for a Declaration of Independence and foreign alliances. John Dickinson and his party, in a concerted effort to undermine this trend, and to bring about conciliation with the mother country, were particularly concerned with the South Carolina delegation. They found some of the members approachable, and brought about a temporary wavering. But, as John Adams recorded in his *Auto-*

---

[19] *See* letter to Dudley Saltonstall, November 27, 1775 and 2n.

biography, "Mr. Gadsden was either from dispair or success, never attempted, or, if he was, he received no impression from them." [20]

In February 1776, Gadsden returned to Charles Town, having been recalled by the Legislature to assist with fortifications in view of an expected British attack. Shortly after his arrival, he introduced a motion for independence in the Provincial Congress, and thereupon, his highly-dismayed, conservative colleagues marked him as dangerous. Those Carolinians, whom Gadsden tabbed "the old leaven," were willing to fight for their rights as Englishmen, but drew back from separation from the mother country. In the ensuing debate, Gadsden applied the reasoning of Thomas Paine's *Common Sense* to no avail.[21] He was defeated by the cautious planters' representatives who regarded the conflict as a civil war within the empire, and hoped for an acceptable accommodation with Great Britain.[22]

However, the course of events soon necessitated a permanent Constitution, and Gadsden was appointed a member of the committee to formulate it. With William Henry Drayton and the Reverend William Tennent, he began altering the old form. In the new Constitution of 1778, Gadsden was instrumental in securing the disestablishment of the Anglican Church, as advocated by Tennent, but was unable to have complete religious toleration allowed. For the most part, the Constitution was moderate. It set up a democratically-elected House and Senate, and provided for the election of a President by the Legislature; but despite the objection of the radical element it kept the old Council and high property qualifications for office holding.[23]

No faction was happy with the results, and Gadsden, as the guiding spirit and chief framer of the instrument, was soon placed in a cross fire of criticism between radicals and conservatives. John Rutledge resigned his position as President of the State in protest to the passage of the Constitution and the oath it prescribed. Vengefully, conservatives chose Rawlins Lowndes as Rutledge's successor in the close election over Gadsden, who was shelved into the vice-presidency.[24] The first ballot showed Lowndes to have 54 votes and Gadsden 48; and only on the second vote did Lowndes gain a clear

[20] *Autobiography and Diary of John Adams,* L.H. Butterfield *et al.* eds., 4 vols (Cambridge: Harvard University Press, 1961), III, 317.

[21] Gadsden's copy of *Common Sense* and the *Journal of the Continental Congress,* marked by his under-linings and annotations, are in the College of Charleston Library. *See* Richard Walsh, "Christopher Gadsden, The Challenge of His Diary," *Manuscripts* (Summer, 1957), pp. 139, 187; and "The Gadsden Diary Deciphered," (Spring, 1964), pp. 17-23.

[22] McCrady, *South Carolina in the Revolution,* pp. 235-45. William M. Dabney and Marion Dargan, *William Henry Drayton and the American Revolution* (Albuquerque: University of New Mexico Press, 1962), p. 142.

[23] *Ibid.*

[24] Raymond Starr (ed.), "Letters from John Lewis Gervais to Henry Laurens, 1777-1778," *SCHM,* LXVI (January, 1965), 29, 32.

majority. When it was proposed that Rutledge be thanked for his services, another contest ensued, proving that Gadsden still had a strong following. In June 1778, Gadsden "was used pretty ruffly" by a "rather Crusty" radical mob, under the leadership of John Budd and "jobbers and trimmers," (as he branded them). Gadsden had promulgated—they accused, "contrary to law"—a proclamation temporarily halting the act which would place the numerous Tories in the Province under a loyalty oath. During the attack, Gadsden noticed regretfully that many of the radicals were his former friends, the mechanics who "ought not to be there." He became apprehensive because of their disregard for legal processes, and their disrespect for the Council which had issued the order on his advice. Despite the "whole herd of contemptible *exportable* Tories," as he called them, Gadsden declared to Peter Timothy, "We have too many amongst us [who] want to be running upon every Fancy to the Meetings of the Liberty Tree." [25] Gadsden, who styled himself later as the "Steady and Open Republican," had become fearful of the tyranny of the mob.

Another blow to his political fortunes was afforded by the "old leaven" in 1778 when Gadsden questioned General Robert Howe's right to command American forces in South Carolina. General Howe, a Continental officer, had come to South Carolina during the battle for Charles Town Harbor, and after General Charles Lee's departure for Long Island, had assumed command without explicit written orders. Howe was a man of burning ambition and wrote Henry Laurens, president of the Continental Congress, "I have been long upon the Brigadiers list and pant to get higher." [26] Gadsden, at the time, was busy preparing the defences at Fort Johnson and later at Sullivan's Island, where he built a bridge to the mainland as a route of retreat in case of another attack. He learned of Howe's manipulations, but was cautioned by his friends not to challenge him. Finally, however, he brought the matter to the attention of the Assembly which refused to investigate. Forthwith, in a fit of anger, Gadsden resigned his command. To his mortification and the delight of his enemies, the Continental Congress had agreed with Howe's explanation, and accepted Gadsden's resignation without bringing it to a vote. [27] A duel between the principals, Howe and Gadsden, resulted in injury to neither; and it was satirized by Major John André in the Loyalist press. [28] With this affair added to his already unpopular status, Gadsden's political future immediately became obscured.

---

[25] John Lewis Gervais to (?) June 26, 1778, Gervais Papers, SCHS. *See* letters to Peter Timothy, June 8, 1778; to W.H. Drayton, June 15, 1778; to Thomas Bee, October 5, 1778.

[26] Robert Howe to Henry Laurens, June 9, 1777, "Laurens Letter Book 16, 1777-1778," fol 82, SCHS.

[27] *See* letters to W.H. Drayton, June 1; July 4; September 22; September 9, 1778.

[28] Johnson, *op. cit.,* p. 42.

The occurrences of 1778 wrought some change in his sentiments, but he was still the scourge of those who would not support independence. During General Augustine Prevost's raid, Gadsden threatened to hand over the timid—among them, John Rutledge—who would surrender Charles Town to the British.[28] This was the year Gadsden called himself, "Don Quixote Secundus," but in his essays he continued to describe himself as a man of true independence.[29]

Some months following his attack on Rutledge, when the British were overwhelming Charles Town, it devolved upon Gadsden as lieutenant governor to surrender the city May 12, 1780. Because Governor Rutledge had gone into the interior where he hoped to recruit men and supplies to continue the war, Gadsden was in charge. He was, after the capitulation, paroled, along with scores of others, and expected to remain in Charles Town with his family. However, in September he and sixty-two of his fellow patriots were seized and sent to prison in San Marcos Castle, St. Augustine, Florida. There Gadsden refused parole when his captors offered it, he accusing them of having violated their faith by their action, saying that he would "never deal" with them again.[30]

Thereupon, he was confined in the dungeon of the castle and "never saw the sun for about eleven months." His energies persisted, nevertheless, and he set out to learn something of the oriental languages.

In June 1781, prisoners were exchanged, and Gadsden was sent to Philadelphia. There he and the other patriots remained about six more months while the war continued.

By mid-January of 1782, the British military position had declined to such an extent that Governor Rutledge was enabled to call a meeting of the General Assembly, at Jacksonborough, a place on the Edisto River, about twenty miles west of Charles Town which was occupied by the enemy. Gadsden had returned home the previous November, and attended the session where he was elected Governor by two votes.[31]

He declined the honor for reasons of health, and because it was necessary that he rebuild his personal fortunes so greatly depleted during the war. Also, from his writings in 1784, it may be inferred that he was becoming disillusioned with the course of government and believed that his own contributions had already been made. Gadsden returned to private life, but still he maintained correspondence with the great leaders of the land. He continued to publish his opinions and interpretations of local, national, and international

---

[29] *See* letter to William Henry Drayton, June 15, 1778.
[30] Johnson, *op. cit.*, p. 43.
[31] Robert W. Barnwell, ed., "Correspondence of Hon. Arthur Middleton," *SCHM*, XXVI (October, 1925), 193-4.

happenings. As usual, his zeal for a cause offended both friend and foe, but it emphasized his consistent determination not to court popularity. Francisco de Miranda, exiled South American revolutionary who visited Charles Town in 1783, characterized him as "one of the most original personalities I met here. . . ."[32]

By the early 1780's Gadsden was despised by the "democrats" for ameliorating some of the Tory sufferings, and for his public censure of Alexander Gillon who led the superpatriotic, anti-Tory, anti-aristocratic "democrats," whom he accused of provoking class warfare and rioting. In 1783, the mob hanged a Tory in effigy on Gadsden's wharf, and later one of his warehouses was burned under suspicious circumstances. Gadsden denounced Gillon for secretly directing the violence.[33]

The spector of anarchy haunted Gadsden during these years of turmoil and wrath. He exhorted men to republicanism in his essays; he pleaded for lawfulness in the eyes of foreign nations; he wanted liberty with order. The post-Revolutionary struggle with Gillon and mob rule brought about the most hard-fought victory of his life. He waged it against former friends, the now Gillon-guided-mechanics.

In 1787, Gadsden fervently supported the new Federal constitution which became almost an object of reverence to him, voting for it in the ratifying convention. He was present at the State Constitutional Convention of 1790 where, according to a letter to his son-in-law Thomas Morris, he indicated that he favored an extension of representation to the back-country, an inevitability which his fellow low-countrymen found hard to accept.[34] This concession to democracy, born out of the need for compromise, was the last liberal act of his days.

His politics had continued to move to the right after the Revolution, perhaps a natural attribute of his advanced age, but there were other factors. He deplored the debtor economy, not only be-

---

[32] Miranda said: "He [Gadsden] is close to eighty years old [*sic*] and nevertheless is learning the Hebrew language. He built a very long wharf over the river Cooper (from which the British troops embarked, protected by two batteries on the flanks, when they withdrew from this city), despite the disapproval of most of the intelligent people, who doubted very much that it could be executed. While I was here, fire spread from a near-by rum warehouse to the wharf, and though everybody gathered immediately with fear and surprise at such terrible and dreadful spectacle, the General gave his orders and took necessary measures with the greatest serenity. A man of unusual fortitude and presence of mind!": *The New Democracy in America: Travels of Francisco de Miranda in the United States, 1783-1784,* Judson P. Wood (trans.) and John S. Ezell (ed.), (Norman: University of Oklahoma Press, 1963), p. 29.

[33] *See* articles "To the Public," May 6, July 17; "To the Public in General and Commodore Gillon, in Particular," August 5, 1784. *See also* John Lewis Gervais to Henry Laurens, April 15, 1784, South Caroliniana Library; (Philadelphia) *Pennsylvania Packet and General Advertiser,* October 23, 1783.

[34] *See* letter to Thomas Morris, May 30, 1790.

cause it had affected his own financial situation but also because it offended his sense of what was right and proper. In 1792 he wrote to his friend Thomas Pinckney concerning worthless bonds and pressing demands from "the northern lads," the New York bankers Herman Le Roy and William Bayard.[35] He despised the Jay Treaty,[36] but remained an avid Federalist, even when his contemporaries deserted the party. He defended George Washington's administration against Thomas Paine whom he called a "pull-down" politician who had out served his usefulness to the republic. He opposed the excesses of the French Revolution, and was deeply concerned about French intervention in the internal affairs of the United States. To him the Virginians and Jeffersonians were "Francophile caballers," and he therefore campaigned in the press for Adams for the presidency in the election of 1800.[37] Hoping to counteract the egalitarian spirit of the times, Gadsden reprinted and circulated at his own expense the reactionary pamphlet, *A Good Twelve Cents Worth of Political Love Powder,* by Parson (Mason) Weems, a work seeking to prove that inequality was the natural order of life. To Gadsden's utter disgust, the Republicians, whom he called "madmen," carried South Carolina, and Jefferson won the presidency. However, his striving for order and unity, along with his nationalism —a constant thread through his life—would not admit revolt against the liberals. The new President, he maintained, deserved all of "our support." [38]

To some, Gadsden's public life is inconsistent, but beyond temporary expediency there was his constant devotion to the rights of Englishmen prior to the Revolution, and, subsequently, his adherence to constitutionalism. An attack on these maxims from any quarter he felt must be opposed, whether it came from such an unenlightened and haughty royal Governor as Thomas Boone or from "caudillos of the rabble," as Miranda termed Gillon and his friends. Like John Adams and many of the founding fathers, Gadsden was a realist. He was a believer in "mixed government" which, representing the wealthy and the needy, would maintain a balance between aristocrats and democrats, would contain their quarrels, compromise their interests, and limit their passions.[39]

Gadsden died in Charleston, (the city's name having been changed from Charles Town in 1783), on August 28, 1805, following a fall

[35] *See* letter to Thomas Pinckney, April 17, 1792.
[36] Washington Papers, Vol. 273, May 31–July 23, 26, 1795. Library of Congress; *American Daily Advertiser* (Philadelphia), August 24, 1795.
[37] *See* letter to John Adams, March 11, 1801.
[38] *See* letter to John Adams, March 11, 1801; *SCG* and *Timothy's Daily Advertiser,* October 8, 1800.
[39] Wood and Ezell, *op. cit.,* p. 31; George C. Rogers, *Evolution of a Federalist: William Loughton Smith of Charleston, 1758-1812* (Columbia: University of South Carolina Press, 1962), p. 352. *See* letter to John Adams, July 24, 1787.

near his home on Front Street. Funeral services were held in St. Philip's, with burial close to his parents in the "western church yard," [40] by his request, which also stipulated that his grave not be marked.

---

[40] *City Gazette* (Charleston), August 29-30, 1805; *Charleston Courier,* September 10, 11, 1805.

The Writings of Christopher Gadsden

To Henry Laurens

Henry Laurens (1724-92), a wealthy merchant, plantation owner, and statesman, was a fellow townsman of Gadsden, and they were intimate friends for many years. The Cherokee War opened a breach which was never closed, although the two maintained a courteous relationship in their business and political dealings with each other. Laurens was more conservative and deliberate than Gadsden. Laurens was president of the Provincial Congress (1775) and the Council of Safety (1775). Elected a member of the Continental Congress, he was shortly afterward made president of the body (1777-78). Laurens was appointed to treat with The Netherlands but was captured by the British en route to that country and imprisoned in England in the Tower of London (1780-81). After being exchanged for Lord Cornwallis, he was made a commissioner for signing the Treaty of Paris (1782). He returned to South Carolina and died at his Mepkin plantation in 1792, never having recoverd from the illness resulting from his confinement in the Tower. See David Duncan Wallace, The Life of Henry Laurens (New York and London: G. P. Putnam's Sons, 1915.)

Aldborough in Louisbourgh Harbor,[1]

11th September, 1746

Dear Harry,

The enclosed Letter I received from your Father, when I came from Carolina to deliver to you in Boston where I thought we shou'd have touch'd. We arrived here the 26th ultimo. To morrow we are to Sail to New Yorke to convoy some vessels bound there and from thence we are to proceed as soon as possible to our Station again. I left the letters I received from you and recommend your Business therein mentioned to Jo Pickering[2] when I left Charles Town.

As this Letter will come with the fleet, it will be needless to write you any News, or indeed do I know of any worth mentioning. This

---

[1] SCHS. A version of the letter was published in the *SCHM*, IX (October, 1908), 228-9, under the heading "An Interesting Letter of 1746."

[2] Joseph Pickering, Esq., was a Charles Town lawyer. "Correspondence of Henry Laurens," annotated by Joseph Barnwell, *SCHM*, XXIX (January 1928), 34.

is a very pretty Place but a bitter cold one. The *Kingsale* and *Hind* brought in 7th Instant a ship they took in Canada River worth £10,000 Sterling. We have a Rumour here that the French Fleet and Transports are on this Coast; if so, we stand a fine Chance for a Golden Chain or a Wooden Legg, for we can't well miss them in our Passage to New Yorke.

A little before I left Carolina, I remitted Mr. Crockatt[3] on my own account an undoubted good bill for one hundred pounds sterling, which trouble my Intimacy with you induced me to give him; I have wrote to him by this opportunity. I believe I shall have Occasion to draw on him for twenty or thirty pounds when I get to New Yorke which I begg you'll acquaint him of.

Dear Harry:

I am out of your Class, for I was married a few Days before I left Carolina to Miss Jenny Godfrey,[4] but never more than at present.

I begg you'll informe me in yours the Prizes of Goods from Time to Time of Carolina Produce, or of Prize Goods. I may Sometimes have the opportunity to purchase some to advantage.

Yr. Sincere Friend & Most Hble. Servt.

Christ Gadsden.

---

[3] James Crockatt, a merchant-lawyer of Charles Town, was one of three managers of the "Friendly Society for the Mutual Insurance of Houses against Fire," which had been organized in 1735. He was elected "Merchant-Director" of this fire insurance company in 1736. *SCHM,* VIII (January, 1907), 46-53.

[4] Jane Godfrey, daughter of a merchant, Samuel Godfrey, and Gadsden were married July 28, 1746. She was described in the *South Carolina Gazette* (August 4, 1746) as "an agreeable young lady, of distinguished merit, with a good fortune."

ADVERTISEMENT FOR GADSDEN'S WHARF AT CHARLES TOWN

To Thomas Lawrence

Thomas Lawrence (1684-1754) was an influential merchant of Philadelphia under whom Gadsden had served his apprenticeship (c. 1740-1745). Prominent in civic affairs, Lawrence was Common Councillor and alderman in Philadelphia prior to his serving as mayor for five terms. He died April 25, 1754, and is buried at Christ Church, Philadelphia. Among other pursuits, Lawrence dealt in the Pennsylvania fur trade and held partnerships with such men as Edward Shippen and the great "lawmaker," James Logan. His mercantile interests were widespread. Pennsylvania Magazine of History and Biography, X, 71, XIX, 290, XXVII, 308, 315, XXIV, 499, XLIII, 241, VII, 231-2, I, 404.

Chas. Town, S. Carolina,[1]

15th February, 1753

Dear Sir:

Your favor of the 30th Nov. last in care of Capt. Abbercrombie [2] covering Invoice and Bill of Lading for Seventeen Barrels of Flour came duely to hand for the amount of which I have given you credit accordingly.

Your affair with Bullard,[3] I shall be particularly careful of and as soon as the first of the year comes about which is now at Hand shall be very pressing with him for part of his bond or the Interest at least, and at the expiration of the two years you may depend on my doing every Thing in my Power immediately for your Interest. I make no manner of doubt of getting Money for you, and think you may rest Satisfied that you'll at last recover this long winded debt.

---

[1] HSP, Martha Morris Lawrence Collection, 1684-1759, Letter Book. *Guide to the Manuscript Collections of the Historical Society of Pennsylvania*, 2d. ed. (Philadelphia: The Historical Society of Pennsylvania, 1949), Nos. 1157, 1467.

[2] Captain James Abercrombie of Philadelphia, master of the ship *St. Andrew, SCG,* January 22, 1752.

[3] Edward Bullard was owner of the plantation *Rat-Trap* on the Ashley River. H. A. M. Smith, "Charleston and Charleston Neck," *SCHM,* XIX (January, 1918), 26.

I shewed Mrs. Rutledge [4] the account received from Mr. Bowers' and Company and paid her fifteen pounds this Currency equal to the three pounds Proclamation being the sum allowed her with which she is satisfied.

For these two years past, I have lived in a very inconvenient House which has been the occasion of all my Family's and my own sickness almost contintally.[5] During that time, about three months since I moved into a much better and airier House since which I thank God I have my Health exceeding well.

Pray my Compliments to Mrs. and Miss Lawrence and all your family.

I am Sir Yr. most Hble. Servt.

Chris Gadsden.

Chas. Town, So. Carolina,[1]

6th July, 1753

Dear Sir:

I wrote you the 19th May last, since which have received three hundred and fifty pounds our Currency equal to fifty pounds Sterling of Bullard on your account which I did all in my power to get you a good Bill for in Order to have sent by this Opportunity; they are exceeding scarce now as they generally are this time of year; however I am promised one in six or eight Weeks in which time I hope to get much more from Bullard. I wrote you in my last and shou'd be much oblig'd to you to let me know what you wou'd chuse I shou'd send if I can't get Bills.

I have several Times forgot to acquaint you that I make myself still in Debt of the Exchange of Mr. Bower, £7:3:8 Our Currency, owing to the Distinction I made in settling with Mrs. Rutledge, which I observe you have not made the distinction between Philadelphia Currency and Proclamation; if there is no Difference between them, then I have rec'd so much more of Mrs. Rutledge than I shou'd have done, and which ought to be refunded; or if any Settlement is right then I am still so much in the Exchanger's Debt. The Bond

---

[4] Sarah Hext Rutledge (1724-1792), mother of John, Edward, and Andrew, was the widow of Dr. John Rutledge. Mabel L. Webber, "John Rutledge and his Descendants," *SCHM*, XXXI (June, 1930), 7-25.

[5] Philip Gadsden, "a child," evidently Christopher Gadsden's son, was buried May 19, 1752. A. S. Salley and D. E. H. Smith, *Register of St. Philip's Parish, 1720-1758* (Charleston: Colonial Dames of America, 1904), p. 220.

[1] NYPL, Emmet Collection. Copy in the Letter Book of Thomas Lawrence, HSP.

was for Proclamation Money, the Account for Philadelphia Currency; pray set me to rights and you'll much oblige.

Yr. Most. Hble. Servt.

Christ Gadsden.

P.S. I can get nothing faster out of Bullard in regard to what you desir'd me, to enquire about, than what I wrote you some Time ago; he says after that settlement he never collected any Debts or did any thing else in these affairs. Praying compliments to Mrs. Lawrence and Family.

[Charles Town], July 21, 1753 [1]

Dear Sir,

On the other side is Copy [2] since which [I] am favored with yours of the 15th Ultimo and according to your Direction therein have sent Messrs. David Barclay and Son [3] on your Account first Bill of Exchange for Sixty pounds Sterling Charles Mayne [4] Esq. in my favor Jno. Mayne Esq. in London dated the fifth Instant and which I have endors'd. Inclosed you have second Bill.

I have as yet received only fifty pounds Sterling from Bullard so that I am ten pounds in advance for you. Bills of Exchange are extremely Scarce and it was a great Favor done to me that I procur'd this. I dun him very closely and make no Doubt of having about fifty pounds Sterling more in a few weeks.

Pray my Compliments to Mrs. Lawrence and family. I am

Yr. Most Hble. Servt.

Christ Gadsden.

P.S. I sent first Bill [in care of] the Snow Katherine Capt. Harris for London.

---

[1] Thomas Lawrence Letter Book, HSP.

[2] *See* "Letter to Thomas Lawrence," July 6, 1753, which appeared on the reverse and is the "copy" to which Gadsden refers.

[3] David Barclay was a London correspondant of several merchants of Charles Town, including Henry Laurens. Joseph W. Barnwell, "Correspondence of Henry Laurens," *SCHM*, XIX (January, 1928), 28.

[4] An advertisement for the London-Charles Town firm of the Maynes is in *SCG*, December 2, 1756.

[Charlestown] Oct. 13th 1753 [1]

Dear Sir:

The Foregoing is a Copy of my last since which am favor'd with yours of the 22d August together with a Barrel of Rice for which am much oblig'd to you.

I have not as yet rec'd any more from Bullard tho' I have ply'd him very closely, but as his Bond will be all due next Spring it will then be in my power to be more pressing than I can at present and make no doubts of getting the Money at that Time; as for that in the Interim, you may depend on my losing no Opportunity that Offers.

I beg you'll set me to rights in regard to the Paragraph in my last Letter that you have received relating to Mrs. Rutledge's affair.

Pray my compliments to Mrs. Lawrence and family. I am S. Yr. Most Hbl Servt.

Chris Gadsden.

P.S. I have sent a barrel of Potatoes by Capt. Read [*sic*] [2] which I beg Mrs. Lawrences acceptance of.

------

[1] Thomas Lawrence Letter Book, HSP. The letter, apparently written from Charles Town, is addressed "To Thomas Lawrence of Philadelphia, by the favor of W. I. Griffith."

[2] Captain James Reid was one of the commissioners of Pilotage and Bar of Charles Town Harbor, with John Torrans, Henry Laurens, Thomas and William Savage, and George Abbot Hall. [John] *Well's Register and Almanac for 1775* (Charles Town: John Wells, 1775), p. 94.

To William Allen

William Allen (1704-1780) was an important merchant and industrialist in Philadelphia, and one of Pennsylvania's early iron-makers. He was also a noteworthy colonial statesman, being leader of the "Gentlemen's Party" of Philadelphia which was supported by the Anglicans and Presbyterians of the city. As a political ally of Benjamin Franklin, Allen opposed the Quaker party because of its pacific tendencies during the French and Indian War. He became Chief Justice of Pennsylvania in 1751, and held the office until 1774, when he resigned. Although Allen was an advocate of colonial rights, he had become disgusted with American radicalism and the desire for independence from Great Britain. He left Pennsylvania in 1778, dying in London in 1780. Besides his interests in trade and industry, Allen was a great philanthropist and patron of the arts. In this last respect, he was a benefactor of the artist Benjamin West. Allentown, Pennsylvania, was named for William Allen, who had extensive real estate holdings in the area. Edward F. DeLancy, "Chief Justice William Allen," Penn. Mag. of Hist. and Biog. I (1877), 202-11; Theodore Thayer, "The Quaker Party of Pennsylvania," ibid., LXXI (January, 1947), 20-21.

Charles Town So. Carolina,[1]

27th October, 1757

Sir:

By the direction of His Excellency Governor Lyttleton, We have the Honour of addressing you with this, to request Your Assistance in procuring and forwarding to this place a Quantity of Cannon Shott and other Military Stores for the Immediate Service of this Province, the particulars of which are sett forth in a Schedule here

---

[1] Lyttelton Papers, William L. Clements Library, University of Michigan. This document concerns the procurement of supplies for recently constructed Fort Lyttelton at Port Royal. On the reverse side of the letter appears the annotation, "Letters concer'g Indian affairs and also the building of fort Lyttelton Anno 1757." Information concerning the Fort may be found in John Richard Alden, *John Stuart and the Southern Colonial Frontier* (Ann Arbor: University of Michigan Press, 1944), p. 81, 19n.

Inclosed. For the purchase and Importation of these Articles Our General Assembly have Granted One Thousand pounds Sterling and if We are rightly informed We may have the whole purchased in Philadelphia and transported to this place for that sum Including your Commission, Freight and other incidental Charges, amongst which you will please to reckon a premium of Insurance to be made by you, unless a Convoy is order'd for the Vessel in which the same may be Ship'd, but if Contrary to our Expectations the cost and Charges of the several Articles will Exceed the said Sum of One Thousand pounds sterling you will in that Case make a proportionable diminution of the smallest fixed Shott, so as to keep the whole Confined to that Sum or within the Same. For your Reimbursement of this Expense be pleas'd to Value at Thirty days Sight on Mr. John Nutt [,] Merchant in London, expressing the Amount to be Charged to the Account of Messrs. Austin and Laurens,[2] of which they will advise, and you may rest assured your Bills will be duly honoured. If there is not a Convoy appointed for this Service, of which We presume you will be informe'd by His Honour the Governor of Your Colony to whom Governor Lyttleton has wrote in this Head. We must then desire you to Ship said stores in the first Good Vessel for this port with Invoice or Account of the same directed to us for His Majesty's Service, and if you think proper to make the Shipment in a vessel of your own, or one belonging to your Friends, we will do our utmost to promote the Interest of such vessel in procuring a Freight from hence to Europe, and we can assure you, here's a prospect of very good Freights the Ensuing Season as our crop of Rice is far from being Short and very few Ships yet in our Harbour.

We are with perfect Esteem & respect

Sir Your most hum. Servts.

> B.S.
> C.G.
> H.L.[3]

To the Honble. William Allen Esq.
> Philadelphia

[Enclosure]

Schedule of Warlike Stores, to be Imported from the Northward for the use of this Province, By order of His Excellency the Governor,

---

[2] (George) Austin and (Henry) Laurens was a mercantile firm of Charles Town. Rogers, *Evolution of a Federalist*, p. 14.

[3] B. S. is Benjamin Smith, speaker of the Commons House of Assembly, 1755-1763. H. L. is Henry Laurens. A. S. Salley, Jr., "William Smith and Some of His Descendants," *SCHM*, IV (July, 1903), 239-57.

which schedule is Concurr'd to by the Commissioners of Fortifications

Three Hundred Shott for	Two	⎫
Five Hundred ditto	Three	
Three Hundred ditto	Four	⎬ Pounders
Three Thousand ditto	Twelve	
Three Thousand ditto	Eighteen	⎭

Five Hundred Cross Barr Shott, for twelve and Eighteen pounders
One Thousand Weight of Match
Six Iron Cohorns of Five Inches and a half Calliper
Twelve Hundred Tin Tubes for firing Nine, Twelve, and Eighteen
 pounders

NB The Remainder of the Money is to be Laid out in Twelve and
 Eighteen pound Shott

Charles Town 27th October, 1757

                            B.S.
                            C.G.
                            H.L.

To Governor William Henry Lyttelton

William Henry Lyttelton (1724-1808) replaced James Glen as governor of South Carolina June 1, 1756. Scholar, writer, and favorite of the Lords of Trade, Lyttelton expelled William Wragg from the Council, dealing a blow to the body, as on the eve of the Revolution it had become increasingly a group of Royal placemen. Lyttelton marched against the Cherokees in 1759. He took some thirty headmen virtually as prisoners, although the Indians were negotiating for peace, and precipitated the Cherokee War. Soon after his return from this tragi-comic campaign, he accepted the governorship of Jamaica, January 1760, with the result that the full force of his errors fell not upon him but his successor, Lieutenant Governor William Bull. Meriwether, Expansion of South Carolina, pp. 213-40.

Congarees, October 31, 1759 [1]

Sir:

We whose names are Subscribed are come to this Place to attend your Excellency as Volunteers on your Expedition against the Indians [2] and are ready to do any Duty you may please to command us.

---

[1] Lyttelton Papers, William L. Clements Library, University of Michigan.

[2] These volunteers accompanied Governor Lyttelton on the ill-starred expedition to Fort Prince George, a journey which began the Cherokee War in earnest. They had assembled with the governor at the Congarees. Adair, who intimates that the group was drawn from the Charles Town aristocracy, by calling them "that silken body," is apparently wrong, for they appear to have come from all classes, and included among others the great merchant, Barnard Elliott, and the blacksmith, Tunis Tebout. Adair, *op. cit.,* pp. 250-51; Meriwether, *Expansion of South Carolina,* p. 219.

Gadsden's group probably included the names of some of the first members of the Volunteer Company of Artillery, who engaged in the Lyttelton expedition as its first campaign. The Company was enlarged to a battalion in the Revolution, was captured and its members imprisoned by the British at the fall of Charles Town in 1780. A. S. Salley, ed., "The Diary of William Dillwyn," *SCHM,* XXXVI (January, 1935), 33; *SCG,* December 9, 1756.

We are your Excellency's most Obedt. and most hum. Servants

Tho. [*Illeg.*]
W. Moultrie
John Ainslie
Tho. Middleton
Geo. Logan
James Coachman
W. Withers
Edw. Lightwood Junr.
Francis Marion
Tho. Coulliette
Charles Odingsells
Benj. Cayne
John Freer Junior
John Martin
Champn. [?] Williamson
Joseph Berry
James Lydell
Thos. Williamson

Christ. Gadsden
Tunis Tebout
Jno. Braund
John Remington Jr.
Barnard Elliott
Newman Swallow
Saml. Winborn
Herbert Heriot
Alexander Tyffe
James Reid
Thos. Farr Junr.
John Dunbar
Jno. Harvey
John Ward
R. Izard Junr.

} Artillery Men

The Philopatrios Essays on the Cherokee Wars

I, December 18, 1761

II, Some Observations, 1762

(Summary)

An Abstract [1]

These two essays, written under Gadsden's pseudonym "Philo-patrios,"[2] are critical of Lieutenant Colonel James Grant's conduct in the two campaigns against the Cherokee in 1760 and 1761. The essays contain a spirited defense of the Provincial Rangers whom Grant accused of cowardice in the battle of June, 1760. Gadsden seeks to prove that Grant was responsible for the failure of Colonel Archibald Montgomery's expedition, and that he was in command of it. In the 1761 phase of the war led by Grant, Gadsden blames him for the fall of Fort Loudoun which he failed to relieve. Gadsden charges him with lack of aggressiveness, saying that Grant, instead of vigorously pursuing the enemy and "cutting as many throats" as possible, burned corn-fields and destroyed towns in the friendly Middle Settlements.

Gadsden further accused Grant of claiming victories he had not won, dangerously thereby misinforming the Province. Gadsden concluded that the war was "without advantage" to South Carolina, and that the Treaty of Peace of 1762 was an invitation to further

---

[1] The original manuscripts of Philopatrios Numbers 1 and 2 are a part of the "South Carolina Miscellany," in the Presbyterian College Library, Clinton, South Carolina. "Philopatrios Number 1" is in the *SCG, December 18, 1762,* Historical Society of Wisconsin; a photocopy is in the South Caroliniana Library. "Philopatrios Number 2" is a pamphlet entitled: *Some Observations of the Two Campaigns against the Cherokee Indians in 1760 and 1761 in a Second Letter from Philopatrios* (Charles Town: Peter Timothy, 1762). *Some Observations . . .* is deposited in the Library of Congress and the Harvard College Library. Two copies are contained in the microcard collection, *Early American Imprints,* Clifford K. Shipton, ed. (American Antiquarian Society, Worcester), Items nos. 9242, 9243. *Some Observations* also contains printer's corrections of the newspaper essay Philopatrios Number 1.

[2] In his essay addressed to Peter Timothy (March 12, 1763), Christopher Gadsden asserted that he signed the *Philopatrios* letters. The opposite view to *Philopatrios* was taken by Henry Laurens writing as *Philolethes. See* Laurens Papers, SCHS. For further information on the Cherokee War, *see* Meriwether, *op. cit.,* pp. 213-40; David H. Corkran, *The Cherokee Frontier, 1740-1762* (Norman: University of Oklahoma Press, 1962), pp. 142-272.

attack because of its mildness, its concessions, and the gifts bestowed upon the Indians. The conflict, availing nothing, had cost the Province some £100,000 sterling.

Gadsden writes at some length on the low state of morale among the South Carolina Militia, because of Grant's ordering its return to Fort Prince George in the middle of the campaign, and before he began his "corn-pulling" tactics in the Middle Settlements. While the Militia waited for the lieutenant colonel to arrive at the fort, Gadsden alleged that the troops, victimized by exorbitant prices of sutlers whom Grant had hired, derived no profit or advantage as common soldiers from the campaign.

Gadsden, as a partisan of Colonel Henry Middleton, contended that Middleton, who outranked Grant, should have been in command instead of the glory-seeking Briton.

An Advertisement
December 11, 1762

This bogus advertisement, supposedly written by Governor Thomas Boone but headed with the true author's prophetic quotation, "The times are being changed and we are being changed with them," was the opening shot in the Press War over the Gadsden election controversy. It can be assumed that Gadsden wrote this by stylistic evidence, his use of the Latin phrase "tempora mutantur," and the fact that his election from St. Paul's was the center of the political storm. He had used the "tempora mutantur" in A Second Letter from Philopatrios.

Gadsden, with Rawlins Lowndes and John Rutledge from the Committee on elections, formulated and directed claims by the Commons House that it had the sole right to determine membership. Boone's high-handed actions inspired the opposition and spurred it on with such answers to remonstrances by the House as "Your deference to the Crown should be more conspicuous" and "I applaud myself for having checked constitutionally, so dangerous an usurpation." Gadsden's phony advertisement is therefore pregnant with Popean satire and sarcasm. He apparently chose the signature "Auditor Tantum" because the House accused Boone of acting upon the hearsay of its proceedings, not upon fact. See Greene, "The

15

Gadsden Election Controversy . . .," *p. 480 30n* , *SCG, Dec. 11, 1762, and supplement, contain the above advertisement, and messages for both the Commons House and the Governor. Gadsden's communication "To the Gentlemen Electors of the Parish of St. Paul, Stono," immediately follows.*

Tempora mutantur et nos mutamur IN illis [1]
[*The times are being changed and we are being changed with them*]
Shortly will be Published,
Cum Notis variorum, [*with notes of various things*]

The rights and privileges of the people of this province, proved to be ultimately *permissive*, not *inherent* as lately determined with the greatest accuracy and precision, by a most profoundly learned, critical and eloquent political orator, thoroughly acquainted with the British constitution, before a large and respectable audience; wherein (unexceptionably to corroborate and support that useful point) the said never-to-be-too-much admired and heart chearing doctrine, will be shewn to be inseparably allied, not only in the *generality* but the universality also to the truly orthodox, miraculously enlightening, and deeply erudite positions of the *divine right of Kings, passive obedience, and non-resistance,* in these latter, ungracious times, most prophanely and deplorably scoff'd at and exploded, to which it will be compared, and all these hopeful and comfortable subjects thereby greatly elucidated, and if possible, more closely constricted to the entire stopping, beyond all manner of doubt, the mouths of all wicked gain-sayers.

To which will be added, by way of appendix, a detail of the many and wonderful emoluments that may redound to the good people of this province, by another altogether new and important discovery of the same great master of criticism, "That the foundation of the present *Election* of any *Member* of *Assembly* is in a *particular* oath of the *Church Warden,* and not in the choice of the freemen of the *parish;* "or, in other words, that the *least part* of the mode of a thing is *more material* than its whole essence"; or to use his own most concise and emphatical expression, that "the mode in the present case" (he must mean that part only which is contested) "is the essence."

By *Auditor Tantum* [*Only a Hearer*]

N.B. If the author (no less a mathematician, philosopher and metaphysician, than a politician) meets with encouragement by the sale

---

[1] *SCG* Supplement, December 11, 1762.

16

of the said treatise, he will, incontinently, oblige the public with as clear a confutation of several very important *vulgar* errors in each of these sciences.

To the Gentlemen Electors of The Parish of St. Paul, Stono

As explained in the Preface, the controversy resulting from Governor Thomas Boone's refusal to administer the Oath of office when Gadsden was elected to the Commons House in 1762 brought forth an immediate and bitter contest between the body of legislators and the chief executive. One result was that the House declined to pass any bills until Boone had left the Province in March, 1764.

In the essay which follows, Gadsden defends the tactics of the House, against the criticism of Henry Laurens and, more specifically, that of William Wragg. While the two gentlemen agreed that the Governor had acted unconstitutionally, they deprecated the refusal of the lawmakers to pass certain recommended measures. Particularly, Laurens and Wragg noted the House's failure to authorize payment to creditors for supplies furnished during the Cherokee War, Laurens, himself, being a creditor. The two also called attention to the fact that the House had not awarded the bounty payments promised to the recently arrived German immigrants.

Gadsden met the immediate objections of Laurens and Wragg, but transcended them by citing precedents of English legislative bodies. This essay is one of the earliest appeals published in America in support of the natural rights philosophy.

February 5, 1763[1]

(Published by the particular desire of some of the said electors.)

Gentlemen,

The unmerited as well as unrequested honour you have twice successively conferred upon me, by choosing me as one of your representatives in [the] general assembly, and each time in so dis-

[1] *SCG*, February 5, 1763.

17

tinguished a manner; the first by a very large majority; the last by the almost unanimous votes of an [uncommon] number of electors, demand my highest acknowledgments.

My sense of these obligations [has] been always endeavoured to be demonstrated in the best and most effectual way I could think of, that of paying a constant and zealous attention, to the utmost of my slender abilities, to the important charge you have delegated to me; and have never yet given my vote (and hope never shall) for anything but what, upon the maturest deliberation, appeared to me reasonable, just and necessary; and, next to my own consciousness of the rectitude of my intention, that of my actions appearing to all mankind, more especially to you, to have proceeded from sound, honest and well-weighed principles, is my highest ambition.

To you I must think myself more particularly accountable for my behavior in the character you have placed me in: I hope it will be thought therefore no impropriety if to you, gentlemen, I address myself on the following occasion, where I think that character not a little concerned.

You need not be informed that I voted for every step taken by the assembly, in the unhappy difference between the governor and them, and for none more readily than the last, the resolution they were drove to the necessity of coming into, that of entering into no further business with his excellency, until he shall have done justice to the house on the important point in dispute.

This last step, by a letter with Mr. Wragg's name [2] at the bottom, printed in the weekly Gazette of the 5th instant, must appear to all mankind (if there rightly stated) to have been intended to be taken from such principles, that none but a set of obstinate men, determined to act contrary to reason, and several of the plainest passages of the election-law itself, could have thought of.

To prove this was not the case, by endeavouring to remove any prejudice that may have been conceived from that letter, against that resolution of the house, is the intention of this to you and if I am so happy as to succeed in this attempt, which I am far from despairing of, it will then clearly appear, not only that I have not, by voting for that important step, abused the generous confidence you have placed in me, but also, that the step taken was absolutely necessary, and the only step that a *free* assembly, *freely* representing a *free people,* that have any regard for the preservation of the happy

---

[2] Biographical sketches of William Wragg are in Ramsay, *History of S. C.,* II, 532-8, and *DAB,* XX, 541-2. Wragg was a planter, a member of the Commons House who defended the pro-British position on the eve of the Revolution.

constitution handed down to them by their ancestors, their own most essential welfare, and that of their posterity, could *freely* take. had they not taken it, all besides would have been to no purpose, be mere blustering, and nothing else: Here, and only here, the shoe pinches, and must bring about a careful examination into what occasioned it (which is all we want, the remedy will follow of course). This examination, without that step, might have been easily evaded, and the point totally lost for ever.

A fair stating of the case, and examination of the force of the writer's reasons, is the more necessary, because his learning, reading and abilities are so conspicuous, that a prepossession in favour of what he declares "his judgment to incline to," is in several respects unavoidable. His experience in all branches of the law and equity; his thorough knowledge of the British constitution, and of course of all parliamentary matters, joined to that quick and penetrating judgement, immediately perceiving the true turn and gift of an argument, he is so remarkable for, all conspire to make it the more difficult to persuade many that he can be mistaken, especially in this dispute; because 'tis well known, that gentleman, sensible of its importance, moved, himself, that he might be up on the committee that drew up the report, and was present at every transaction.

I readily acknowledge the writer's superior abilities; yet what I take to be the cause of truth obliges me, in this instance, to oppose his representation of this matter, not thereby meaning to insinuate that my talents are equal to his; far from it, I only think the present point a plain one, level to the meanest capacity, and being so, any [talents], even mine, may be able to decide it, as well as that of the most *distinguishing* genius in the world.

As 'tis generally believed the house would have been unanimous, had not this gentleman "been inclined towards a negative," I cannot but say I wished to see his opinion in print. The same arguments made use of in the letter, were used by the writer when (what I take to be) the *real* matter was before the house. Upon that, as well as now and then upon other occasions, I have thought him mistaken, and have even ventured to point out where, but have always found that, for want of a good memory to retain a long argument, I had only misapprehended him, and by my presumption gave him the trouble to make farther distinctions, which I have again mistook: But now, as his letter is *printed,* you will be the best judges whether my arguments, in opposition to this matter obtained therein, are justly founded or no.

In order that my observations on this letter may appear to be properly made, it will be necessary to consider only the transactions

19

that passed in assembly previous to the last resolution taken on the 16th December, which must be supposed to be still depending.

To begin then. On the Saturday the writer mentions (the 11th) it was ordered by the house, as appears by the journals of that day "that the messengers do summon all the absent members (either in town or country) to attend on Thursday next, at ten o'clock in the forenoon, on the service of the same, upon business of the *utmost importance.*"

There must have been *some* motion that occasioned this order (though none is entered on the Journals) but that it could not be *the* motion the writer mentions, I am well convinced; I certainly heard none such, though never absent during the whole proceeding. Had that motion been made, it must and would have been opposed by many, unless it can be thought that, at that particular moment, the house was determined to do, what, at every other, they took the greatest pains to avoid.

By the writer's stating of the motion then, he appears to have forgot all the proceedings previous thereto, but particularly,

1st. The privilege the house claimed, and his excellency denied.

2dly. The satisfaction the house expected, and could not obtain.

3dly. If he had reflected on both, or either of these he must have discovered whence the inlettering [?] was said to come, and of consequence the extent of the intended resolution.

First. The privilege the house claimed, and his excellency denied, is expressed in these words in the Remonstrance, "That essential, fundamental privilege of solely examining and determining the validity of the election of their own members."

In the Reply to the Governor's Answer, it is called "their birthright to be constitutionally represented in general assembly by *free* men of the province, first elected solely by *free* men, and those elections, as far at least as they relate to the elected taking their seats, (the Only point we *are extending fully*[)] finally and solely determined by the collective body of *free* men so elected."

That the house confined themselves to this point, and this *solely,* is apparent, not only from the above plain passages, but from many others plain; and a single paragraph can be produced (when continued with any degree of fairness, candour and knowledge of

20

the dispute) in the least contenancing the writer's general assertion, where the house have said, or meant to say, the governor "had no right, under the election act, or by his commission to interfere in, or take cognizance of, Any Matter Relative To Elections." Nothing they so carefully avoided. Are there not SEVERAL matters relative to elections, that the election–act authorises Any person in the province to interfere in, and of course they could not be so absurd as to say, his excellency might not, in such matters. Besides, the house tells his excellency expressly, that they "had not occasion to take notice of any matters relative to election" (which are certainly matters relative to elections). "If we had, we should Undoubtedly have inserted the proviso your excellency mentions," which proviso too 'tis well known the letter–writer himself moved for, when this very reason was given against his motion by the gentleman that opposed it. This being attended to, it follows of course:

2dly. That the satisfaction the house expected, and could not obtain, must have related to his excellency's denial of that particular privilege, and to nothing else, because the house confined themselves to their claim to that only. The writer must strangely have forgot what passed, with regard to this matter, at the debating of the Remonstrance, or he never could have asserted, that the house expected such *formal* acknowledgment from his excellency as he mentions. The Remonstrance (to which the Reply closes with referring) is so very modest, that even had his excellency been pleased to give the common answer that is *almost always* given to every speaker when first presented to a governor, I verily believe the whole affair would have dropt. Nothing evinces this more clearly than the following motion's being lost, the only one that was throughout the whole affair. Nay, every other passed almost unanimously. It was put to the question, whether the following words would be added to the end of the Remonstrance: "And we also humbly hope that your excellency will quiet the minds of the people, by acknowledging Their just right to the particular privilege herein mentioned," passed in the negative. This I hope, is sufficient to settle this matter.

And

3dly. As the interfering came only from his excellency, satisfaction can only be expected from him. The intended resolution could not then be supposed to mean to extend to the council, with whom the house had not, nor could have, any difference about this matter (wherein they think, the council never were consulted). Therefore,

21

while the assembly is permitted to exist, there is no reason why they and the council should not do what business they can together; and also, that the house continue to do any matters peculiarly relating to themselves. This is sufficient to shew, the motion could not be intended, that the house should not proceed "upon any farther business," in the *universality,* but, any farther business *with his excellency,* in the *particularity.*

Having now ('tis to be hoped) pointed out three very material mistakes in the motion mentioned in the letter, let me now beg leave to give my stating; and, that the difference between the two may be perceived at one glance, let them front each other.

LETTER	MINE
On Saturday a motion was made for not proceeding upon *any further business,* as the governor had not given the satisfaction that *was asked of him, by acknowledging* that he has no right, under the election-act, or by his commission, to interfere in, or take cognizance of *any matters relative to elections.*	On Saturday last a motion was made for not proceeding upon any further business *with his excellency* 'till the house shall be satisfied that he will allow them, without any molestation whatever, their essential and inherent right of solely examining, and finally determining, the election of their own members.

As all the proceedings relating to these matters are now published, I beg leave to refer thereto, to see which of these two statings are most conformable to their plain, obvious and uniform meaning, particular regard being had to the claim, and manner thereof, in the Remonstrance, because the assembly conclude their Reply to the governor's Answer by referring thereto. That even alone will shew us what *satisfaction* the house expected.

If the stating of the motion in the letter be right, there is no manner of occasion to proceed any farther, or indeed so far, for any the least appearance of reason whatever would be sufficient to shew the assembly must have been very much to blame, to insist that his excellency had no right to interfere in *any matters relative to elections,* and of course more so, for obstinately persisting in their expectation, that his excellency should *formally* acknowledge to them that he had no such right. If the writer understood the point in dispute in that manner, none besides himself in the house (and I believe it may with safety be added Out of the house too) did so understand it.

That the motion must have been in substance as I have stated it, and no other, is evident from the slightest inspection of all, or any of the papers published, preceding the resolutions taken in consequence of the motion.

This matter now being brought to a point, I am so far from thinking that the reasons that the writer has given can be of any weight, that had even those he thought proper not to give (for only *some* are given) appeared too, the whole would hardly have been sufficient, in my opinion, "to incline my judgment towards a negative upon it."

The house thought and said, *"that our* All *was at stake,"* upon this unhappy occasion; or in other words, if we lost the point in dispute we should lose our *all;* and we most certainly should, for what would an assembly be without it, but an outsider shew only, a mere piece of state-mockery; and without a free assembly what security would the people have for their lives, liberty and property? Just as much as there is in Turky, as all depends there on the will of their governor, so should we find all here, too soon depended upon the will of ours! 'Tis a joke to talk of individual liberty of *free* men, unless a collective body, freely chosen from amongst themselves are empowered to watch and guard it; and if this body lose their *collective* freedom, the *individual* must follow of course; therefore every matter that comes in the least competition with this grand point ought to be disregarded; better that some, or every individual, should suffer any temporary inconveniences or hardships, than to run any risk of sapping this great rock of their lasting salvation in this world, that of the freedom of parliaments or assemblies.

From hence it must appear, that, for my own part, I think it altogether needless and unnecessary to enter into any examination of the writer's reasons; however, they shall be touched upon, in order to shew, that he has been as forgetfull in drawing them up, as I think, he has the purpose he produces them for. That they cut either way is as evident as that if either side was wantonly and unjustly the occasion of this unhappy dispute, that side, and that alone, is, and must be answerable for all the consequences, in the eye of every impartial judge.

The gentleman then *forgot,* in his first and most laboured reason, to his constitutents, that he had taken notice only of one part of the stating of the account shewn him by the treasurer, relative to the township fund. That of the money *paid* away, which is truly as he represents it, £54,000 and upwards, or more particularly [the sum is] 54,164 : 74 : 0.

Had he not overlooked the other part, that of the money *received*, he must certainly have acquainted them at the same time, that the sum was—78,257 : 0 : 0.

And then his constitutents might have discovered themselves (supporting it had not been pointed out to them) a balance of—24,092 : 6 : 0. then actually remaining in the Treasurer's hands, ready to answer the purposes that fund is appropriated to, "the encouragement of settling protestants amongst us, for the better strengthening the province."

I believe most gentlemen in the province think, this sum alone will be more than sufficient to answer the demands that may be expected upon the fund for one twelve month at hand, and would gladly compound to see it paid away in that time.

But, when we farther considered, that this is the most increasing fund we have; and on the other hand, when we turn our minds, as the subject naturally leads us, to reflect on the long and terrible wars in Europe, and the great want of men there, thence occasioned, not only in the military way, but to carry on the laborious part of all branches of trade and manufacture, and the great and certain encouragement given upon the spot, by great bounties and advancement of wages to the effective poor of all denominations, certainly these considerations must make the writer's reasons on this hand vanish into nothing. Besides, may not even the doubting and much more so the denying, of such an important point as the assembly's having the right to be "the sole judges of the validity of the election of their own members," by one of his Majesty's governors, that may be called the *sine qua non* of a body of a people, to renominate them really free, be too alarming as to be expeditiously and universally spread every where? Our crowded doors, while our Remonstrance and Reply were debating, sufficiently demonstrate the consternation the people are in on this occassion.

Now, supposing the assembly had tamely submitted to proceed on any farther business with his excellency, while this point was so repeatedly denied them, such a precedent must have been construed as giving up the point by all the discerning part of British subjects, and if so, 'tis more than probable, many more of her best and oldest inhabitants would be for *leaving* the province, than there could be expected of new settlers to venture into it, after such an event was generally known; so that the *real* motion passing upon the question in the negative, "might, and probably would, be the means of preventing," not "our keeping, our faith with *such* persons as are daily expected" *with regard to the bounty.*[3] Should any arrive before the thing is spread abroad, there is more than enough remaining in the fund itself to answer their purpose, in the opinion of every man in the province, I believe, but the letter writer. But that "dishonour to us, would" in all probability occasion an "effectual stop that would be thereby put to the future importation of others, who would never after" such a precedent "be induced to trust" their inherent and natural privileges into such dastardly hands. Can we suppose any free born men of Britain or Ireland, would be such fools, like Esau of old, to sell their birth-right for a mess of pottage, a little pittance of a bounty, which too they must undergo the fatigue of a long and dangerous voyage to come at. The writer's prime and most formidable reason being that, I hope fully answered, let us go to

The second; and here 'tis observable, that the gentleman has *forgot again,* to inform his constitutents that our Agent, by his letter of the 14th *August* last, has acquainted us, that "he had but faint hopes of success in his present suit for, that all the money already provided by parliament, had been distributed among the several agents of the other different provinces, excepting £10,000 agreed upon by them (to be taken out of their several dividends, each one 20th part) to be left in the treasury, to answer the demands of the *Massachusets,* if they are able to furnish their agent with the proofs, they expect to entitle him to it; if not, then each to have this one 20th part for his respective province; so that he is afraid, it could hardly then be called treasury money, but being in the treasury, he thought himself to take notice of it, and the lords must do therein as they think proper."

In regard to any future monies that may be granted. As the agent, in the same letter tells us "the lords of the treasury" have come to a determination to let a report of a number of men raised in each province direct their distributions, without regard to *any other circumstances;* "which rule he is told will not be departed from." There is no doubt his excellency *can,* and as little that he *will,* furnish general *Amherst* with the proper proofs, of the number of men we have furnished at different times, to induce the general to supply the certificate required.

There cannot be any reason to suspect, that his excellency, through a resentment to a particular assembly, which he may get rid of at

---

[3] The Act of July 25, 1761, was one of several attempts to encourage immigration to South Carolina. It provided £4 sterling, passage money for settlers from Europe who were specified as "Poor Protestants," and £20 sterling for tools and provisions: Warren B. Smith, *White Servitude in Colonial South Carolina* (Columbia: University of South Carolina Press, 1961), p. 65.

any time, would neglect the general interest of the province. This, I am persuaded, no man in it ever entertained the least suspicion of; we have all the reason in the world to think the contrary; numbers of facts demonstrate it; our agent's letters, and many other circumstances known to every body, manifest how early and indefatigable he has been in his endeavour, even through his private friends, to obtain this very bounty. By his application too, in the same manner, both in Europe and America, he hath procured us men of war to protect our trade, and guard our coasts. All these things considered, it must give every thinking man the greatest concern, to find that we are obliged to differ with a penitent man that has shewn himself so willing to serve the province in these and several other matters that certainly were thought capital and material, till the unfortunate accident happened that gave life to this unhappy difference. His excellency's own officer's asking what surely he had no right to ask (and what is well known could have been no strange matter to him) whether the church warden that returned a writ was particularly sworn to the due execution thereof? Could but that question have been previously prevented too, in any or the like manner as the same question was most justly prevented to be put by the majority of the last assembly, in all probability we should have been a happy people still, under a governor we received with the greatest cordiality, and had the highest opinion of. But matters are otherwise with us now, and though we are ready to acknowledge with gratitude all favours received, yet we can by no means think, that because a gentleman has given us roast meat, he has therefore a right to beat us with the spit.

The Third reason relates to the transportation of provisions to fort Prince George, and is, I think not a little unlucky because the bearing of this expence is well known to be peculiar to this province, and his excellency's great attention to our interest, very soon after his arrival amongst us, discovered it to be so, and induced him in February last, to take notice of it in a message to the last house, and then very generally promised (unasked) to "represent the disadvantages we labour under to the commander in chief, and request, in behalf of the province, the same favour and indulgence" the other colonies had, that is an exemption from this burden. The general's answer to his excellency's kind application was as follows: "I hope the assembly of *South Carolina* have not reason to complain of that province not having, upon every occasion, received the same favour and indulgence granted to other colonies; but as to the expence of transporting provisions to the outposts, I cannot consent to its being charged to the crown. *It is True, in the Northern colonies that expence is defrayed by the king;* but that has been owing to the great number of troops occupying those posts, and the impracticability of the provinces being able to subsist them; and I make no doubt the colonies Will Be Required to take the expence on themselves, as soon as the service will admit of the several garrisons being reduced."

The last house being acquainted herewith, resolved to make provision for this expence to the first of this month. Thus stands this affair; and as this province has not lately "received the same favour and indulgence granted to the other colonies," that is, any part of the last bounty granted by parliament, notwithstanding the immense expence it has been at in the *Cherokee* war (above £100,000 sterling) if this matter is discontinued, we shall only then be on the same footing, in this respect, with the other provinces who *have received* their several proportions of that bounty; and are therefore *better enabled* to bear such extraordinary expence. Surely it will be time enough to take this spontaneous peculiar engagement upon us again, when the other *"colonies* Will *be required* to do the like," or, at least, when we are again in *status quo,* with respect to the privilege denied us.

Besides, the resolution of the last house being *unlimited,* with regard to the sum provided, "I had the public treasurer to advance out of Any *money in his hands,* Any *sum that May be wanted,* for defraying the charge of transporting provisions to the out-posts, to the *governor's order,* 'till the first of *January* next." There could be no doubt his excellency would be polite enough before the first of *January* (upon our refusing to consider his message, sent perhaps to try us) to draw upon the treasury for a sufficient sum to answer this purpose, to avoid being blamed for *reducing himself* to "the necessity of withdrawing the garrison of fort *Prince George,* and thereby abandoning the back [country] settlers to the rapine or drunken frolicks of the Indians." The words "any sum that may be wanted," as they stand in the order, are at least as *pliable,* and *indisputably* more in his power, than the "every such portion in the election-act." From hence it appears that not the least risque was taken of the above-mentioned danger, though the house "did not take into consideration the message sent to us by the governor, relating to this transportation of provisions thither, and engage still to continue that expence which we have hitherto borne."

The Fourth Reason Comes Next. Present inconveniencies and hardships will arise to *some few* individuals, by not discharging the debts due to them, "and not making such provision as the exigencies of government may require:" but this reason proves too much, and therefore ought to prove nothing at all because this must always be the case in such a situation as the present, and of consequence would be an argument for making the All of the whole people, on every occasion, submit to the *partial* and *least essential* interest of a *few*. The necessity of the step is apparent; the public creditors must see it so, and know that it is taken for their general good. This, (when matters are settled again) or any future assembly may, should the tax bill be delayed much beyond the usual time of passing it (which, by the bye, is not yet done by several months) consider the particular sufferers, and make them some satisfaction, if, perhaps, they should be permitted so to do. For if the point in dispute is lost, God knows which such an assembly (if it can be called one) as shall succeed may do; everything to be sure that they are bid, which no doubt must turn out wonderfully to the emolument of the public, especially if they should obligingly pass the militia law, *so much wanted, suited* to the *extraordinary* exegencies of this government.

The Fifth And Last Reason, I must confess I am entirely at a loss what to make of, or to find what use it could be . . . to the writer's constituents, to enable them to "be obliging enough to point out his errors:" Certainly it could be of none to assist them to find out the "inconclusiveness of the argument." What *argument*? Has not all his reasoning been entirely on one side the question, and not a syllable said or hinted at on the other, save that "we happened to be displeased with his excellency's conduct"? What *conduct* with regard to us? Has he told them? How were they to know it then? By *rumour?* Will any men of sense and thought depend on such a matter of so great moment? If a person of the writer's penetration and quickness of judgment, who was himself extremely active in the matter, and never absent a moment during the whole proceedings has shewn himself so *egregiously* mistaken in the very foundation of the dispute, is it possible that common rumour could or would be regarded? So far from its being "impossible for his constituents to be unapprised of the nature of the dispute," it was very improbable they should have known anything about it, but by the authority just mentioned; because it is well known, that the proceedings of the present assembly (which were published as expeditiously as possible) were not printed, and the papers distributed even in *Charles-Town,* till the Wednesday afternoon after the date of the writer's letter, that is, Only the day before the matter was to be debated; so that it was hardly possible that his constituents in *John's* island could have seen them; and as to any copy of the assembly's Reply to the governor's Answer, they could not, because that Reply itself was presented to his excellency but on the very Saturday the gentleman mentions; and as soon as the governor's verbal answer was received, an immediate stop was put to the publishing the preceeding matters, that the whole might come out together; and, in order that the expectations of the public might be gratified as soon as possible, the very rough copy of our Reply, from which that presented to the Governor had been taken, was carried immediately, by two members to Mr. Timothy's, and he charged to print them without a moment's loss of time.

This being the state of the case, let us only suppose, if the gentlemen of *John's* island had sent a constitutional answer to their member's "constitutional method of addressing them," what must have been that answer? Why? Oppose the motion by all the means in your power; the assembly are mad surely, they are going to "involve the province in difficulties, and reduce individuals to a state of misery," when they have no reason "to be displeased with his excellency's conduct," whom every man in the parish would think extremely weak indeed, "to acknowledge that he has no right, under the election act, or by his commission, to interfere in, or take cognizance of, *any matters relative to elections*," when any person in the province has the right to do so in several matters, by the plainest words of the law itself.

I must here beg pardon of the gentlemen of *John's* island, for presuming to say what they would have wrote; but, from the situation they were in when they received the letter, and from the well known abilities, and the visible candour of the gentlemen who wrote it, I cannot help thinking, if they had sent any, it must have been such a one as just mentioned. What prevented them I don't pretend to say, but I think it very fortunate for the province that they sent none, for there is no knowing what might have been the consequence, had such a letter, signed by a whole parish, arrived critically at their member's house on Thursday morning (it could not much sooner). There is no doubt the gentlemen must then, if possible, have been "rendered more firm in opposing such a step." The house to have been told, just at the opening of the debate, that a whole parish had unanimously desired him to oppose the motion, with all his power, might have staggered many, and the letter being perhaps unluckily left at home, the mistake in stating the motion might not have been discovered, though, no doubt if the gentleman had perceived his error in time, that he would have ingenuously acknowledged it, and immediately set all to rights again; but had he not happened to make the discovery soon enough, it would have been to no purpose afterwards. Repentences would then have come too late.

Having now gone regularly through the gentleman's five reasons, let me finish my remarks on his letter, by taking notice of the following extraordinary passage. "His excellency's conduct, which we happen to be displeased with, for ought we know, may, in his majesty's judgment, merit his *highest* commendation." This appears to me a very extraordinary expression indeed! which begging the writer's pardon, I think now quite out of time and place too; had it escaped him seven years ago indeed, *upon such an occasion,* his then station might have made it appear a little less remarkable. A governor under the *present* happy establishment, "to merit his majesty's highest commendation" for denying that an assembly "have the sole and inherent right of judging of the validity of the election of their own members!" Is not a parliament or assembly supposed by the constitution to be an *independent* branch of the legislature? Is it not then a flat contradiction in terms to suppose this and at the same time suppose, that a governor can be any, much less the ultimate judge of the matter?

Thank God! we have as good a king upon the throne as ever graced it, who has given the earliest and most endearing signs of his tenderest regard for the liberties and privileges of his subjects, and has thereby manifestly shown, his inclination is, to reign solely *in* the hearts of *free* people, not over a parcel of *slaves; free* men I *say,* who have an *inherent* not *promissive* right to be so. And does not the act of settlement shew this, where it *says,* that "the laws of England are the birth-right of the people thereof." Does not the act too, declaring the rights and liberties of the subject, and settling the succession of the crown, expresely accuse King James the 2d of having "violated the freedom of elections of members to serve in parliament?" And does not the same act expressly declare, "that elections of members of parliament ought to be free?" How can they be so, if any but the people or their representatives are judges of the pretensions of any to be such? This right is so unalienable and inherent in the people, that they can be no longer denominated a free people when it is parted with; because all their *freedom* as British subjects most essentially depends upon it. The parliament of Great-Britain, and the general assembly (or parliament) of this or any American province, though they differ widely with regard

30

to the extent of their different spheres of action, and the latter's may be called a sphere within the former's, yet they differ not an iota when only the point in dispute is disregarded. 'Tis, in fact, so much the *sine qua non* of any real parliament or assembly, that without it, what might be *called,* such, would be just like the French parliament, a mere *rex et praeterea nihil* [king and a windy promise].

Will it be asserted by any friend to the natural liberties of British subjects, that, in order to retain those liberties, a man must never stir out of Britain, where they are *indisputably* and essentially his; or that the moment he sets foot on American ground, he has bid farewell to the *dearest* of them? If this had been the doctrine formerly, the sons of Britian would have been thinly, very thinly, scattered on this side the Atlantic ocean. It might indeed have been *then* fixed on, *very properly,* as a place to transport her convicts to, but surely no free men, on such conditions, would have ever thought of coming to America. Those nations only, who were already enslaved, therefore could lose nothing by the bargain, would certainly have been found almost, if not altogether, the only adventurers this way.

That the being *freely* represented in parliament, by men altogether first and last of the people's *own* chusing, without any interfering whatever, is the most essential and inherent right the British subjects residing in Great-Britain are possessed of, I believe none will be so hardy as to deny. That none of the British subjects residing in America have given their votes for any member of parliament of Great-Britain, cannot be denied also. Are then the British Americans to be represented nowhere? Shall their several hundred thousands, by which industry and spirit the nation has been greatly assisted to arrive at that conspicuous figure she now so extensively makes, Taken Collectively, be deprived of that birth-right and most characteristical privilege, that Every, even the lowest Individual Man, of her *domestic* subjects, *may be,* and most of them *actually are,* intitled unto, that of voting for a member of parliament?

What difference can there be between the subjects residing in Britain and America, but that of latitude and climate? Have these any natural or rational connection with the matter? How can, or ought, they then to affect it?

Again, if the British subjects in America are permitted to send no members to the British parliament, but may be capable, or have a natural right, to be represented somewhere, which surely will not be disputed, the next question is, where can that somewhere be, but in America? If they but have this capacity or right, 'tis not a farthing matter with regard to the argument, whether they send

31

their representatives to one general assembly to all parts (supposing that practicable) or whether, as at present, each colony has an assembly of its own. In all cases, whether the sphere of action for parliaments or assemblies be ever so extensive, or ever so much limited and contracted, by divisions and subdivisions, still the *smallest* within its own sphere *must be free,* and in order to be so, be the *sole* judges of the elections of its *own* members, or else it can be no *free* assembly at all, but a *mockery* of the people.

Now let us see how this reasoning can be farthar supported by fact, in regard to ourselves.

First, we have a charter, by which "the natural rights of free men of this province, to be represented in general assembly, is confirmed to them." (See our Reply, *etc.*)

We have also a law now in force, passed in December 1712, entitled "An act to put in force, in this province, the several statutes of the kingdom of England or South-Britain therein particularly mentioned; wherein, after such particular English statutes are expressly taken notice of by their titles, that are to be of force here, beginning with the Great Charter of Henry the Third, and ending with an act passed in the eighth year of queen Anne." That act, in its third, and part of its fourth section, goes on, and says thus:

III. And be it further enacted, by the authority aforesaid: that all the statutes of the kingdom of England, *relating to the allegiance of the people to her present majesty queen Anne, and her lawful successors,* and the several public oaths, and subscribing the tests required of the people of England in general by any of the said statutes as relates to the above mentioned particulars of the allegiance of the people to their soverign, the public oaths, and subscribing the tests required of them, and the declaring and securing the rights and liberties of the subjects, *are hereby enacted and declared to extend to, and to be of full force in this province,* as if particularly enumerated in this act.

IV. And, for the better putting force and execution of all and every the before enumerated statutes, paragraphs, sections, or numbers of paragraphs of statutes, be it further enacted, by the authority aforesaid, and it is hereby enacted and declared, *that the general assembly, for that part of this province that lies south and west of Cape Fear, and the several members thereof, shall have the* Same Power *and authority in* Any *matter or thing*

32

Relating TO *the said statutes, that is given by the same to the* Parliament Of England, *or the members thereof.*

Nothing can be more express than the above words of our act; they manifestly allude to the act of settlement, and that other act already mentioned; and refer likewise to so much of All Other Acts Then Passed In England, wherein the rights and liberties of the subjects are declared, and better secured.

Now certainly it must be granted, that nothing Can Concern the security of the rights and liberties of the British subjects more *essentially,* than those laws that relate to the securing of the Freedom of parliament, which is the essence of the thing; to which *every particular manner and form* appointed is intended to be subservient, and ought to be so, not to be construed into a destruction of it.

The last mentioned statute then, which may be called the basis of the present establishment, says expressly, "that elections of members of parliament ought to be free." This must at least be called free, in *the first step,* the choice of the electors; and with regard to *the last step,* that is an examination of the returns or credentials of all that pretend to a seat in parliament, can any act more plainly and carefully secure it solely to the collective body of *free men elected in parliament,* than the statute of the 7th and 8th of William the Third, wherein it is enacted, "That in case any person or persons shall return any member to serve in parliament for any county, *etc.* contrary to the last determination of the house of commons of the right of election in such county, etc." that such return so made, shall, and is hereby adjudged, to be a false return, "and that the clerk of the crown is not to alter any return without order of the house of commons, *etc.*" which certainly implies he may and is to alter it with such order, and that they, and only they, have to do with them.

Will any person here say, that those parts of these acts here quoted, by a fair and equitable construction, are not, and ought not to be, of force here, by virtue of our own law just mentioned, so far as to corroborate and ascertain these two grand and natural points, which is all we want?

1st. That our assemblies ought to be freely chosen by the people.

2dly. That the returns ought to be *solely* examined by such assembly so chosen.

That is, that our assemblies ought to be free first and last. Our writs are issued in the same manner, as near as may be, as writs

33

are in Great-Britian from the chancery, that is from the governor and council, who (by virtue of that very law of ours just now quoted) Unitedly form that court here, and solely issue them out, on account of their exercising that character, and upon no other.

From the statutes of Great-Britain let us pass to the laws and customs of parliament, which if we were now, as we have been *always* heretofore, allowed to quote as rules to us, the matter in dispute would be very quickly decided in our favour; but these, it seems, by the present doctrine, we have nothing to do with. What? a son not have a right to imitate his good parent, when nature tells him it ought to be his chief pride, as it most certainly is his chief duty!

If we were but allowed to put on our election-act, which relates *only to the manner and form of an election,* the same equitable construction that the parliament does, no more could be said. They, 'tis well known, regard only the *end;* if that, a free election, appears manifestly to have been obtained (as is indisputably in our case) that is all they want to fix the right of the elected to his seat, whether the *manner* and *form* thereof, that is, whether the sheriff has been sworn or not sworn, the return properly or improperly made (though numbers of acts of parliament point out these particulars) is totally disregarded; the sheriff indeed, may be punished for his neglect, but not the innocent member. This right, 'till the present remarkable era, we always thought we had. But, it seems, the times are so strangely altered, that we must prove our right, inch by inch, to everything, or expect nothing; and these proofs too must *doubtless* be drawn from precedents under *his majesty's governors,* or else we may be *sure,* under the present rigid discipline, they will be said to prove nothing at all. Let us then try what we can do to prove that we have a right to imitate our political parent the parliament of Great-Britain.

Amongst the reasons then given for repealing two, even of our election acts (passed only about three years before the present) that of their being "contrary to the laws and customs of parliament in Great-Britain," was assigned. Does not this tell us negatively, at least, that we ought to make those laws and customs our guide?

In governor Nicholson's time, in the very first assembly that were convened by virtue of the present election-act, and very soon too after their first meeting, a very critical case happened, much to our present point, wherein that gentleman, *who passed that law* "made some difficulty in suffering one Mr. *Akins* [Atkin] to take the state oaths." [4] As soon as that assembly were informed even of that hesita-

34

tion in the governor, they immediately desired his excellency to qualify Mr. Akins, acquainting him at the same time, the message, of the house "being unanimously of opinion, that they were the sole judges of their own privileges, and of the qualifications of their own members." He sent them for answer, that *"he was heartilly sorry* that he could not comply with their message," "As You Are," says he, "to maintain your rights and privileges, so am I, under an oath as governor, to maintain his majesty's royal prerogative. I Thank God! *I never desired to abridge you of any of your rights and privileges,* nor ascertain his majesty's prerogative *beyond its due bounds."* In the same message he tells them, that as "Mr. Akins had a bill of indictment found against him by the grand jury," till he was acquitted of that matter, "he thought he was not qualified for him to give him the oaths, except you can shew me any person under his circumstances to be a member of the house of commons of Great-Britain; and, when you have satisfied his majesty's honourable council and myself, in this point, I shall then readily administer the state oaths to him." At the same time, his excellency *condescended* to send to that house the *particular* instruction which he thought had him under that difficulty. This *condesension,* together with the *thing itself,* apparently proceeding from no design to injure the house in their privilege; and it appearing also that his excellency had not taken that step hastily and inconsiderately, but had thought it of importance enough to consult his council thereupon, the house could do no otherwise than satisfy his excellency's scruple by pointing out such a precedent as he wanted, to justify himself on this occasion, which they did, and his excellency gave up the affair. What could they desire more, than to be allowed to follow the precedents of the house of commons? I believe neither that house, nor any since would permit any member to keep his seat amongst them, however regularly returned (as Mr. Akins was) if, by a fair precedent from the journals of the house of commons, applicable to our situation, such a member could be proved unqualified. This instance plainly shews too, how unwilling the assembly of this province, *even in the*

---

4 Francis Nicholson served, 1721-1725; Robert Johnson (2nd term), 1730-1735; James Glen, 1743-1746. Nicholson, despite a stormy career elsewhere, was looked upon as a model governor by South Carolinians: Ramsay, *History of S. C.,* I, 96-104. The case Gadsden uses, that of Edmund Atkin who was elected from St. Thomas and St. Dennis in 1725, is not so clear-cut as he would have his readers believe. Nicholson refused the State Oath because of a Bill of Indictment pending against Atkin. When the House objected, Nicholson asked for precedent. The House obliged him. But whether Nicholson acknowledged this is not known, because Atkin may have been cleared of charges before the Governor gave him the Oath: Jack P. Greene, *The Quest for Power* (Chapel Hill: University of North Carolina Press, 1963), pp. 191-2. Gadsden consistently spells the name "Akins."

most delicate point, has been to differ with his majesty's governor, when it could possibly be avoided, without giving up their all.

To this gentleman Mr. Johnson succeeded in this government, and after him Mr. Glen, neither of which ever made the least attempt to interfere with the assembly in the great point in dispute, or gave the least room to doubt, that they even suspected they had not the *sole* right thereto.

After Mr. Glen came Mr. Lyttleton, the present gentleman's predecessor; under him a case happened (Mr. Pinckney's) that, besides several other, contained *all* the circumstances of the present, relative to the oath, and those circumstances not conjectured from hearsay, or any positive telling of any officer (such busy tale-bearers that gentlemen never listened to) but established beyond contradiction. A regular petition against the election was laid before the house, that regular petition regularly committed to the committee of privileges and elections, and by the state of the case reported to the house, with their opinion *too,* that the election ought to be *void;* but the house thought and determined otherwise; yet Mr. Lyttleton, who 'tis well known was apprized of the whole of this matter, never attempted to interfere with the house, he being convinced most certainly that the judgment of the election of their own members solely belonged to that house; and how could *he* think otherwise, after having the honour to serve in the British parliament, and thereby being made *a competent* judge of these matters.

After laying before you a more particular state of the occasion of the differences between his excellency and us as briefly as may be consistent with perspicuity, I will then proceed to give you, as near as I can recollect, what further occurred to me on this matter, in order that you may have All "the reasons that inclined my judgment towards" an affirmative upon the grand motion, as I have stated it.

Having already acquainted you that my vote was given for every matter in the Remonstrance, the Report, and the Reply to the governor's Answer. The reasons mentioned in those papers being already published, need not be inserted here.

But, still, 'tis necessary that some apology be made for my not taking previously "the constitutional method of addressing you upon it," which most certainly would not have been done, had the case been as doubtful as it was important; but it appeared to me quite the reverse, and that the step proposed to be taken, was the *only* proper and effectual step, that a free assembly, freely representing a

The SOUTH-CAROLINA GAZETTE.

[Numb. 1973]　　M O N D A Y, O C T O B E R 11, 1773.

CHARLES-TOWN: Printed by T. POWELL & Co. Printers to the Honourable the COMMONS HOUSE of ASSEMBLY, at the Printing-Office on the BAY, near the EXCHANGE.

CHRISTOPHER GADSDEN,

Gives Notice to his Friends in the Country,

THAT he is ready to serve them as FACTOR, upon the usual Terms, and will be much obliged to them for their Friendship.—They may depend on his exerting himself to the utmost for their Interest.—He has great Plenty of Stores, and such Gentlemen whom it may not suit to employ him in that Capacity, yet if they will order their Crops to be landed on his Wharf, may depend that their Factors, be they who they may, shall not be obliged to fill the same, or any Part thereof, contrary to their Judgment, for Want of Storage, as is frequently the Case.

N. B. He will be much obliged to Gentlemen whose Wharf Accounts have been delivered in, to discharge them as soon as possible. *Octo er 9, 1773.*

free people, could freely take. I always looked upon the matter in dispute, "that the assembly are the only judges of the election of their own members, so far as to entitle them to take their seats," to be the most fundamental privileges you have, and if ever lost, which God forbid! that all will be lost, because all will then depend solely upon the absolute will and pleasure of a governor, which, in the British definition of the matter, is *exacty the same* as losing all.

These being my sentiments, *Gentlemen,* I could not with any propriety consult you thereupon. What ask you whether I should give up what you sent me purposely to defend? What must you have thought of me if I had not? I look upon the indisputable possession of this point so absolutely and unalienably to belong to the representatives of the people, that it is not even *in their own power* to give it up, supposing that any past assembly had, or any future assembly should be base enough to *attempt* it; indeed, any such pernicious precedent being shewn, it might, under a wicked governor, countenanced by a bad administration at home, which thank God is far from being the case at present, be made use of as a precedent to *take it* from them, but give *it up* they cannot, their constitutents never gave them *that power,* therefore such an act must be void of course.

I by no means think the people that have done us the honour of choosing us to represent them, have delegated to us All the power they had, by no means: In this case, as in others similar thereto, the giver always retains *more* than he gives. We have the power to *defend* this darling-point, but without the greatest absurdity, it can never be imagined they did, or even could intend to, impower us to give it up.

Nothing astonished me more, than to see the heavy charge against the last assembly, who had neither time nor opportunity given them to examine into the merits of that election that occasioned this unhappy difference; therefore could not make any, much less "an undeniable infraction, of the election–act" by such no examination. His excellency's objections against the last house related only to two things:

To a writ presented to him without a return;

To his being positively told, by *his own officer,* that the church-warden had confessed he had not been sworn.

Upon comparing the last three or four lines of his excellency's *only* (written) answer, with the single place therein where the first

37

of these objections is mentioned, and that only incidentally in a parenthesis, it plainly appeared, that his *whole* stress was laid on the point he was positively told (which certainly cannot be called positive evidence, as it undoubtedly came from a second hand.) Indeed no stress could be laid on the first. For what can be more unreasonable, than to suppose, that after (all due notice) an election has been fairly and publickly carried on, in the presence of such numbers, that it ought to be invalidated in any degree, because a church-warden, either ignorantly or designedly, made an imperfect, or no return at all, especially when no manner of form is assigned any where by the act for a return, the attendance of that officer upon the assembly with the list of votes, as required by the act, easily setting to rights any difficulty that may happen in this respect.

Writs would frequently have been presented to the assembly without any return at all, had they always come there in the manner first returned (of late years) to the clerk of the council, and the returns themselves often been very lame, or perhaps been wholly unintelligible, if that gentleman, more experienced in such matters than the generality of church-wardens usually are, or can be expected to be, had not lent his assistance to make them, *after* they were brought to his office; and why this usual assistance was not given in Mr. Gadsden's case; nay, why his excellency's own officer that presented that writ to him without a return should tell the church-warden "there was no occasion for any" is as remarkable as his *particular* curiosity in asking him whether he was sworn or no. A writ brought to the clerk of the council without a return, 'tis Very Certain, could be no curiosity to that gentleman, neither could it be any news or matter of astonishment to him, whatever it might be to his excellency, to be told, that the church-warden had not been particularly sworn to the due execution of that writ; besides whether it was shown to his excellency or no, 'tis very certain, the writ contained a little piece of paper, when first sent to the house the 10th of September last, wherein was wrote,

"Christopher Gadsden, Esq; ....76 votes
Samuel Wainwright, ...17 votes
Edward Perry, Esq; .... 1 vote" [5]

---

[5] Samuel Wainwright was a barrister and planter who appeared before the Court of Ordinary: "Abstracts from the Records of the Court of Ordinary, 1764-1771," Mabel L. Webber, comp., *SCHM*, XXXI (January, 1930), 63-64. Edward Perry, Esq., was a planter of St. Paul's. He died May 22, 1799: "Marriage and Death Notices from the *City Gazette*," *SCHM*, XXV (July, 1924), 154.

By this paper it plainly, though perhaps not formally, appeared who was elected, and this paper, 'tis well known and remembered too, that the speaker then reported to the house.

No return being on the writ, the church-wardens were sent for to attend the house the 15th, when they accordingly came. Then "a motion being made, and the question put if that writ of election be given back to the church-warden to make a return *thereon*," it passed in the affirmative. Accordingly it was delivered to the church-wardens, and they made the return *thereon,* which was received and reported to the house the same morning, by the speaker, who at the same time acquainted the house, "that the church-warden had also returned a paper, intitled, the list of the names of those who gave in their vote for a representative for the parish of St. Paul June the 22d and 23d 1762, by which it appeared, that there were 94 votes taken at the election, and also the several votes or pieces of paper that were taken at the said election." After this, "a motion was made, and the question put, if the church-wardens of the said parish be now called in, to answer Such Questions as shall be asked them *by the house*," carried in the affirmative, 14 against 13; then the church-wardens being called in accordingly, the following question was proposed, "whether upon their receiving the writ of election to which they had this day made a return, they were sworn to the due execution thereof, by a majistrate of the county, before they proceeded in the execution of the same?" Upon this they were ordered to withdraw; and the previous question was put. If that question be now put, it passed in the negative.

Here this matter rested till the afternoon, to which the house adjourned. In the interim, I had notice of my being returned, and thought it my duty to attend the house as soon as they met, and being called in, Mr. Speaker acquainted me of my being returned to serve as a member in that general assembly for the parish of St. Paul, and desired to know if I would qualify myself as a member of that house. I answered in the affirmative, and after having the usual oath appointed by law properly administered to me, two members were ordered to attend the governor, and see me take the state oath before his excellency. Accordingly we waited on the governor, who was pleased to say, that he desired the attendance of that house immediately in the council-chamber, when he would assign the reasons why he would not qualify Mr. Gadsden. That house immediately waited on him, when he expressed "his disavowal so undeniably an infraction of the election-act," as he was pleased to call the proceedings upon this occasion, and dissolved them, by his speech on the 13th September where from the above passage is taken.

This is the plain, simple fact, *Gentlemen,* without the suppression or addition of any thing whatever, excepting the paper inclosed in the writ, and the list of names of the voters and votes themselves, delivered in by the church-wardens to the house. These facts I had from Mr. Speaker himself, and from many other gentlemen who were members of the last assembly. Those particulars not being entered on the journals, must have been owing to the clerk's not thinking it necessary, as he could not possibly imagine any thing like what did, could have happened, that house not having the least surmise of his excellency's being displeased at their proceedings, till they felt the utmost effects of it, "in a mode not" apparently "conformable to the Best example." And whether a dissolution, at such dangerous and critical times, just too, upon the back of three other unavoidable ones, that had, very unfortunately for the province, at short intervals preceded each other, without any attempt to prevent it or to accommodate matters, can be "attributed to the precaution which was thought necessary to be taken, but two months before: "That the day for the assembly meeting should not be postponed beyond a period that one may be almost answerable for," I will not presume to determine.

Here is no appearance of any examination into the merits of the case; nor could the house have done it without giving all parties a hearing.

The question proposed, and prevented, was so manifestly contrary to that known, maxim of law and reason, "That no man ought to accuse himself, unless it be before God," that that alone was sufficient for the majority to prevent it, by the previous question; and of course, as all things are, and ought to be, carried in any house of assembly by the votes of the majority, which alone constitute the act of the *house,* that question proposed was not *such* a question as *the house* thought proper to ask, and therefore could not be *"such a question"* as "the church-wardens were called in to answer." Let it but be considered too, that this extraordinary question was founded entirely on *hearsay,* and that at second hand, and that absurdity of giving any attention at all to it will more glaringly appear. When I first heard a question "of this kind, appearing to me to have a manifest tendency to introduce the utmost confusion," being proposed I could hardly believe it; but when informed that Mr. Wragg proposed it, it astonished me, I confess, beyond my shallow understanding, to discover upon what principle of law, equity, reason, or public utility, such a question, in such circumstances, could be built.

All that in any degree can be said to have been finished by that house, was merely the formal part, so as to admit the member returned to take his seat; nor could they have done otherwise, without violating their own constant customs, founded on those of parliament. And, in order to put this matter in the strongest light, let a case be imagined, in which the act (when proved) has fully and clearly determined. Suppose any member, by motion, had informed that, or any house, that he heard one say, that a person elected and returned by the proper officer, had positively confessed to him, that he had bribed many, frightened some, and forced others of the electors, to vote *for* him; and had, besides, menaced and despitefully used and abused all that voted *against* him. The plain, just and natural construction of the 14th section of the election-law, relative to such a case as this, is, that such a person elected would still have a right to sit and vote in the house, 'till such matter was *proved;* for the being "rendered uncapable," "*after* conviction of illegal practices, Before the said house," as the act says, to sit or vote therein; surely implies, that *before* such conviction he was not "*uncapable,*" that is, *capable* to sit and vote therein; and is not this *highly* consonant to reason and equity; for any man whatever may be *accused,* even by *legal* evidence, of the most attrocious crimes, of which he may be innocent; and, if guilty, he is not obliged to accuse himself, nor will any good judge *suffer* any leading, ensnaring questions to be asked a man, so as to make him do so.

The member's being admitted to take his seat, by no means prevented the merits of his election being enquired into, upon any proper *positivo* application to the house, according to their known and usual form, by petition. Not an instance can be produced, of any of our assemblies, discountenancing such an application. Shall every court whatever, nay every little corporation, be indulged in having it in their own power to disregard any business that does not come before them according to their well known and established forms; and shall this be denied to a branch of legislative body? This was all that was wanted.

As the merits of the election were never examined into, it cannot be said what weight that house would have put on the governor's objection; therefore it can not be certainly known whether they would have actually disagreed, even in opinion with his excellency, in regard to the construction and force of that part of the act relating to the oath, though there is not much doubt they would have done so in both. But this is conjecture only.

The *construction* and *exclusive force* of the passage of the law relating to the oath, as understood by his excellency, gave rise to this unhapply affair.

With regard to the first of these, his excellency thinks the church-wardens, and such other proper persons occasionally employed to execute writs of election, are also required to take the particular oath mentioned in the act.

This assembly are of opinion, that only the latter persons are so obliged; and they farther think, the construction is *very immaterial* (considered merely in itself) because, on which [*illeg.*] that is determined in the force of the passage cannot be made appear to have such an extensive influence upon the whole act, so as that the true intent and meaning thereof cannot be attained, unless that is rigidly complied with, it ought not to be supposed that *merely* the not taking the oath should be of such consequence as to overset an election.

The difference in the construction seems to depend altogether upon a very slight alteration in the pointing of the part of the act in dispute; either removing an improper parenthesis entirely away, or placing the first stroke of it before the words "to which," a little preceding it, in the same sentence; an error that might easily have happened because this pointing of an act is not done by the legislature, but Only by the printer, or perhaps by a single member, (the secretary's office has been searched to no purpose, to see whether the original act is, or is not so pointed).

That this might be the case too will further appear more probable, from a due consideration of the nature and extent of the duty of the two sorts of persons just mentioned, that can be employed to execute a writ of election.

With regard to the one it ought to be considered that the duty of a church-warden here is very different from that of such an officer in England, where it is *merely ecclesiastical*. Here it is not so, but lay also.

A view of the two oaths together (that taken in England and that here) and observing where we have retained the expression of the one, and where dropt it, with a few remarks will, 'tis apprehended, set this matter in a clear light.

[*England*]

You shall swear truly and faithfully to execute the office of a church-warden, *within your parish,* according to the best of your skill and knowledge; and present such things and persons as to your knowledge are presentable by the ecclesiastical laws of this realm.

[*South Carolina*]

I A.B. do swear, that I will truly and faithfully execute the office of a church-warden *within this parish,* for the ensuing year, according to the Laws And Usage of this province, to the best of my skill and power, and until I shall be thereof duly discharged.

If the duties were entirely the same, why might not the general expression "within this (or your) parish" without any farther explanation, be sufficient for the church-warden of every parish here, as well as for the church-warden of every parish in England? But it could not have been thought so in 1706, when our oath was appointed by the church-act; nor can it be thought so since, because neither before, at, or since the passing of that act, has the duty of a church-warden here been confined to ecclessiastical matters, by the laws and usage of this province.

This being duly considered, it cannot surely appear strange, that an additional particular injunction, naturally derived and flowing the *same, not a different,* cause, the *general* (ecclesiastical as well as other) laws of the province should be obligatory on the church-warden, by virtue of the general oath of office they annually take to execute their duty, according to the said laws and usage, supporting such general oath (which *must be antiscedently* ordered) had been appointed one, or one hundred years before.

These things being previously understood, the words of the second paragraph of the act "to which every such person shall be sworn, by any one justice of the peace for the county (who is hereby required to administer such oath without fee or reward)" appear to be merely incidental, and to relate to the *such* other proper persons, *etc.* just mentioned before, and these emphatical words "every one of whom," in the same clause a little preceding, when both the church-wardens, and such other proper persons, are indisputably meant, support this interpretation. If they were not so, the word "and" ought to be in the room of the words "to which every person," in order to refer *plainly* to "the every one of whom, *etc.*"

Besides the apparent inutility of making an officer take two oaths for the same thing, and the general practice of the church-wardens being in favour of this *construction,* 'tis certain no particular oath is required in any other act, though numbers have passed since 1712, imposing various duties on them.

With regard to the *such other proper persons,* 'tis well known they are very rarely, and only *accidently* appointed *to execute* any writ of election at all; many entire assemblies happening without any such appointment; therefore any directions to them are *naturally and properly* incidental.

Nothing further can be wanting now, to make our construction appear in its *full* light, than to quote that part of the second paragraph of the law which relates to this matter, and to remove the first stroke of the parenthesis just now mentioned, where it's thought it ought to be, "all writs, for future electors of members of assembly, shall be issued out by the governor and council for the time being, and shall bear date forty days before the day appointed for the meeting of the said members, and shall be directed to the church-wardens or church-wardens of the several parishes hereafter named; or in case there should be wanting church wardens in any parish, then To Such other proper persons as the governor and council shall think fit to nominate in the said writs, to manage such elections; *every one of whom* are hereby empowered and required to execute the said writs faithfully, according to the true intent and meaning of this act (to which every such person," that is, *such* other proper person just mentioned, "shall be sworn by any one justice of the peace for the county, who is hereby required to administer such oath without fee or reward) and shall give public notice in writing of all and every such writs, *etc.*"

With regard to the extensive force of the point in dispute (supposing the above construction, however natural, was given up) if his excellency's opinion must take place, it certainly makes the act, *Felo de se* [*a suicide*] with a witness, by defeating the *very end* for which it was enacted; and of course must be contrary to the good Old rule, that "all acts of parliament and letters-patent must be construed, *one part with another,* and all the parts of them together; and the words are to be taken in a lawful and rightful sense, and Applied To The Advancement Of The Remedy, *etc.*"

A more dangerous, as well as more insignificant part of the whole act could not possibly have been pitched upon, than this particular oath, to make the *sine qua non* of an election; because for a failure in the most material of the other parts, the church-warden is fineable, and, in all subject to be defected by numbers (as may be seen from the nature of his duty laid down in the 2d, 4th, 5th, 6th, 12th and 15th sections of the act). But with respect to the oath, *himself alone* may be conscious, no particular person being appointed to administer it; nor is he obliged to declare that he took it, or fineable if he does not; neither can we suppose any *future* church-warden otherwise punishable for that most material neglect, because the *present* found "no harm come to him on that account," notwithstanding his excellency was positively told he confessed he was not sworn unless such positive telling, though sufficient, at second hand, to govern an assembly's actions, may be thought highly improper at *first* to govern any body's also.

Nor is this all; for it determined, besides, by his excellency, that the church-warden is under no tie at all from his general oath of office, to execute this important business; and yet "we have as much right to declare a negro duly elected, as a qualified person returned by a church-warden not sworn." Is not this risking the whole freedom of our elections, upon the integrity of one or two men in each parish?

Has it not, besides, a manifest tendency to make the electors very regardless of going to elections at all? For, to what purpose should they go? Can we then think the makers of that law ever intended any such thing, without supposing them knaves or fools? But the law has given this oath no exclusive efficacy; if it had 'tis reasonable to think it would have declared it *in plain terms;* but it is altogether silent in that respect, which is the more remarkable, because in its 14th section it expressly says, that if a person chosen to be a member shall be proved, *before that house,* to have been guilty of violating the freedom of elections by arrests, menaces, threats, bribery, etc. he shall, after conviction, by a vote of the said house, be rendered incapable to sit or vote as a member thereof. Why is this so expressly declared, and a total silence with regard to the oath, but because the bad tendency of the one, to destroy the freedom of elections was clearly foreseen, and therefore prevented; and the danger of laying such a stress on the other, as clearly forseen, and therefore no such stress was laid. It cannot require a moment's time to decide, nor will it bear any comparison, which is the greatest offence against the design of the act; the officer's neglecting or omitting to take the oath, or a person's arresting, threatening, and bribing the electors; without the former, the freedom of an election may still clearly and effectually be obtained, which, by the latter, cannot so much as be supported because it must ultimately depend merely upon the honesty of such officer.

With regard to the general writs of the present assembly, 'tis remarkable, that the church-wardens of every parish excepting Prince William's, have taken the *particular* oath, and had that oath certified too on the back of their respective writs; but then, whether this was particularly directed by his excellency, or the church-wardens did it of themselves; in either case, as it is not directed by the act, but purely optional, the order, or compliance, or both, may be omitted at any time. With regard to the church-wardens of Prince William's parish, it does not appear, by their return, that either of them was sworn; notwithstanding which no notice has been taken of it to the house; but that may be owing perhaps to that writ's going through the proper officers hands, the chancery's, and not the governor's own. Or, very likely the gentlemen returned in that writ were greater favourites with his excellency's own officer than Mr. Gadsden was, is, or desires to be.

As his excellency alone is neither lord chancellor, or can by law compose that court of himself, it must be not a little surprising to find, that *his* own *officer* should have presumed to meddle with the writ at all, and I am entirely at a loss to know how he came *legally* by it, for let the return be ever so much strained, so as not to mean a return *immediately* to the assembly, surely, if it must not mean *to them,* Only *because* the writ of precept was not issued BY them; tho' *they alone* by law are provided with the power and means of examining into the validity of such return, it cannot, by any straining whatever, be tortured to signify to the *governor alone,* because *the governor alone,* neither issued the writ, nor is by law furnished with the power or means to examine into the validity of the return made by virtue thereof. Besides, 'tis well known, 'till very lately, the church-wardens made their returns themselves to the house in *propiis personis,* and that the omission of this custom has been *only* winked at, in order to ease those officers, it being unnecessary to keep *all* of them in waiting, merely on the contingency of an election's being disputed, a thing very rarely happening, and when it does, the presence of a particular one (or two at most) would be sufficient. If they shewed their returns, or either *themselves,* to the governor and council first, it was merely out of form, to shew they had received and executed the writ, issued by them *united* in their character of [a] court of chancery, the manner of *the execution* being to be examined by the assembly *alone.*

Nothing further seems to be wanting with regard to the thing, but a short comparison of the different offices that may arise, according to his excellency's or the assembly's opinion takes place in order to shew, which tends to conform and which to dispense with the law.

In the assembly's opinion, then, a full and certain force is given to the matter, which surely ought to be the case, if so much stress is to be laid thereon, as his excellency has determined shall. They think the church warden's general oath of office obliges him to execute the writ of election and he is obliged to take [the oath], under a penalty; if this oath has been omitted, it may easily be known and remedied in time, and the electors, who in some parishes come thirty, forty and even fifty miles to an election, [will] be assured their fatigue and trouble would not be taken to no purpose.

If his excellency's construction takes place, then it may be said, that the foundation of all our elections depends entirely upon the church-warden's taking that particular oath, for it so very rarely happens, or has happened, that "any such other proper person" is appointed to execute a writ, that it is not worth notice. This oath too, he is not fineable for not taking, and if he has been improperly influenced, or has any objection to any of the candidates, he may omit; and as he is not obliged to satisfy any elector whether he has taken Or No, it can be *certainly* known only by enquiring *of every individual* magistrate *throughout the county* (which contains *several* parishes) a task so ungrateful, as well as difficult in itself, that it is not probable any person would undertake it upon a bare suspicion of a church-warden. This security from detection will certainly be another great encouragement to any distant church-warden, to gratify his own private views, he being under the tie of no oath whatever, the general oath of office being, according to his excellency's opinion "widely different" from the particular one appointed by the election law, and this he may omit without any fear or punishment, so that, when the election is over, if the church-warden likes it, all is right, if not, then he has only to confess he was not sworn, and of course 'tis set aside.

The present assembly, after taking all the steps in their power, and that with more temper too than could have been imagined, upon so unexpected and violent an attack, were reduced to the necessity of taking the last step, or give a precedent that must have justly made them appear extremely pusillanimous indeed, and such a precedent, too, as might be very easily transferred, upon the like occasion, or no occasion, to the other colonies. For,

As any assembly "might determine an election contrary to law," and as "the enforcing obedience to laws in general is, by our form of government, entrusted to the king, or his representative," 'tis very obvious, how dextrously any state-physician may apply these two grand and *experienced* catholicisms to his own particular patients, especially when his *undeniable* infallibility alone is to be the judge of the propriety and necessity of the application.

From the nature of this important matter to us, which is now laid before you as fully as I am able to do, or can recollect, you must be convinced it can be *constitutionally* decided only by a British parliament; and if we should be drove to the necessity of petitioning them, there is not the least doubt, if we can get the matter properly represented, that we shall have redress.

If we petition elsewhere, the petition ought to be of another nature to remove the cause; not For this essential right, that must stand or fall with the British constitution itself. The rights and liberties of English subjects, are well known to be their birth-right; they must be tried and condemned by *their peers,* before they *can* lose either.

'Tis greatly to be wished, that all or most of the colonies, besides having their particular agents to represent the private and peculiar

47

matters of each province, would unite, if possible, in appointing one common agent, to represent the *general matters* of the whole, such as might relate to any encroachment upon the *natural* privileges they are *all* entitled unto as British subjects: (the many *un-civil* representations, of late, to the ministry, seems to make such a step still more necessary.) If this could be once happily brought about, and every particular agent ordered to assist the common agent, upon any such emergency, to the utmost of his power (or, at least, if no common agent could be fixed on, to unite among themselves) the greatest of the great men on *this side* the water would be perhaps a little more cautious, how they first causelessly trampled on the people's liberties, and afterwards contemptuously told them, that they relied solely and absolutely on the inefficacy of any thing they could do or say to sully their character or conduct. Under so many guardians, simple truth would have some chance of coming to light, as she would not then be obliged *solely* to depend on the health, integrity, interest, abilities, and industry of one agent, but would have the assistance of these qualifications in many; and in such a case, it does not seem altogether incredible, that we might hear, *now and then,* of an instance of [a] governor being severely and publickly censured, for *too bare-faced* stretch even of the prerogative, and then of course the lords of trade and plantations would be convinced, that American assemblies were not *always* turbulent, refractory and undutiful; and by this means too, we might at last attain the summit of all our wishes, to be tho't as quiet and loyal subjects as any his majesty has, utter abhorrence of absolute monarchy, and no friends to republicanism, but most ardent lovers of that noble constitution of our mother country (which may Heaven preserve entire 'till time is no more) by which, and only which, we desire, and have a right, as near as may be, to be governed.

What is the grand cause from whence spring many of the complaints against American assemblies? The history of the colonies will tell us. Instances of inexperienced governors can be produced, who (dizzied with a little power, not giving themselves time to attend to the plainest and most essential fundamentals of the constitution, impatient of the least contradiction, and depending solely and absolutely on their own interest and connections to bear them out in every thing) have been too apt to attempt such dangerous innovations as assemblies could not submit to, and of course must differ with them or betray their trust. Such governors too, if they happen to be of warm disposition and an arbitrary turn contracted perhaps from a larger acquaintance in the military than the civil life, are more apt to be surprised and duped into such wrong measures, by the sly insinuations, and misrepresentations, of artful flatterers of specious talents, with voluble time serving tongues and vain heads, always ready, with the utmost expedition, to carry or notify to them *all,* and perhaps, *more than all* that stirs, in order to magnify their own importance.

Weak servants are very apt to judge of their masters by themselves, a greater stretch of power they want; if then they can kill 2 birds with one stone, by acquiring a greater power to themselves at the same time obtain it for their masters, nothing to be sure, in their opinion, can contribute so much to secure and enlarge their interest, and so effectually recommend their own extraordinary abilities, as such notable management. This is but too often the case, and had assemblies but the same chance of introducing their story as *early,* and with as great advantages, as governors can theirs, there is no doubt, they would not be so often looked upon in the bad light they seem to be at present.

Would but all governors permit us, who reside in America, to enjoy the same privileges, that our fellow-subjects residing in Great-Britain do, we claim, we *pretend to* no more. Would they listen to no vain or subtle proposals from busy tale-bearers, to sap the very foundation upon which such privileges stand, they would find no people more docile, more tractable. As a specimen with regard to ourselves, take the complaisant resolution of the last assembly respecting the transportation of provisions to Fort Prince George. Could any people shew themselves more devoted to carry on his majesty's service, even in a matter they knew to be peculiar to themselves, more obliging to and confident in a governor, than that assembly upon that occasion?

Pardon me, *Gentlemen,* for this digression. 'Tis well known how dangerous precedents are, especially of the nature of that in dispute. Let me remind you of what an English parliament thought of them upon a very similar occasion. They told King James I: "That if the chancellor" (which with us is, as has been said already, the governor And Council, not the governor or council, who, by virtue of acting in that character alone, issue our writs and receives the returns) "only could examine returns, then, upon every surmise, whether it were true or false, the chancellor might send a second writ, and cause a new election to be made; and thus the *free* election of the county should be abrogated, which would be too dangerous to the common-wealth, for by such means, *the King and his council might make any man, whom* They *would, to be of the parliament house,* Against The Great Charter And The Liberties Of England."

And in a famous remonstrance, printed and directed to the king in 1604, they roundly assert, "That the prerogative of princes *may* easily, and *do* daily grow and encrease— but the privileges of subjects are, for the most part, *at an everlasting stand; they may,* by good providence and care, *be preserved,* but being *once lost,* are not to be recovered but with much disquiet and disorder."

If an English parliament thought *thus,* what must be the case with us, should such a misfortune happen? Would they not be lost, without a miracle, for ever? How watchful ought we then to be? How careful of shewing precedents?

I am most sincerely sorry for this unhappy dispute, and not a little so I assure you, Gentlemen, that my name should so unluckily happen to be mentioned in it, notwithstanding I am well assured, and convinced too, that the Thing, and not the Name, was aimed at By *his excellency.*

However, as the thing appears to me ultimately to have turned upon the sole wrong placing of a single scratch, a mere law-quibble, it would have made me *happier* I confess, and been at the same time of not the least prejudice to the cause, if either the famous Mr. John and Nokes or Mr. Thomas Styles, those renowned and experienced critics in such profound *points* and subtleties, had luckily been at hand, so as to have claimed in time their undoubted right of precedence in such a dispute, and thereby have obtained, if possible, that either of their names might have been inserted therein instead of mine.

Having now endeavoured to lay the argument before you, give me leave to conclude this long epistle with assuring you, that I will endeavour to discharge the trust you have honoured me with, to the utmost of my power, and above all things take care not to go *beyond it.* If my vote will not be of service to *preserve* your privileges, I will never *assume* to myself the right (that my conscience tells me you can never have given me), that of voting for the giving any one of these up.

CHRISTOPHER GADSDEN.

Farm,[6] 25 January, 1763

---

[6] In his will, Thomas Gadsden, father of Christopher, had left him a farm near Dorchester. As that community was the border of St. Paul's Parish, the writer was probably living there at the time the letter was written.

To Peter Timothy

Peter Timothy (c. 1725-1782), born in Holland, was the editor of The South Carolina Gazette when Gadsden wrote this letter for the paper. The son of Lewis and Elizabeth Timothy, he had come to Charles Town from Philadelphia with his parents in 1731, when they took over the newspaper in partnership with Benjamin Franklin. Succeeding his father at the age of 13 years, Peter Timothy became the official printer for the Province, and later was head of the postal system. With the approach of the Revolution, Timothy put the Gazette at the disposal of the Whigs, and took an active part in politics. He served as a member of the Commons House, secretary of the "Council of Safety," clerk of the General Assembly and in other capacities, eventually being arrested at the fall of Charles Town. Timothy was taken to St. Augustine with Gadsden and other patriots. Shortly after his release he was accidentally drowned. Hennig Cohen, The South Carolina Gazette 1732-1775 (Columbia: University of South Carolina Press, 1953), pp. 3-16; Douglas C. McMurtrie, A History of Printing in the United States, 2 vol. (New York: R. R. Bowker Co., 1936).

This essay grew out of the preceding and Philopatrios pieces. Here Gadsden brushes aside two additional opponents in the election controversy, William Miles of St. Paul's Parish, and William Simpson, chief justice of the Province (1762-1763), to contend with Henry Laurens. Gadsden notes that he and his old friend had come to a parting because of the "Iago-like" Miles and Simpson, and other confidants of Laurens, and that he had grown weary of Laurens' seemingly consistent enmity. Laurens revealed his feelings privately; when writing a friend he called Gadsden a "poor rash headlong gentleman . . . a ringleader in popular quarrels." Laurens, although maintaining the constitutional rights of the Assembly, thought that Gadsden's election from St. Paul's was illegal. (Wallace, The Life of Henry Laurens, p. 111). But one "By Stander" supported Gadsden, saying: "I look upon Mr. Gadsden to have arisen up with a spirit of love and zeal," and accused his enemies of "writing from private connexions, views and interests," while "Mr. Gadsden has writ for the public benefit, for the honour of the community, for the love of truth." SCG, March 26, April 30, 1763.

March 12, 1763 [1]

Mr. Timothy:

In my last, I declared I would relinquish the public dispute, to any body else that would please to take it up. I continue in that determination, as I neither think it in the least necessary, or am inclinable, to mention anything more merely relative to that subject.

I was then in hopes too, to have no farther occasion of appearing in print; but Mr. Simpsons and Col. Lauren's letters in Mr. Well's weekly gazette no. 222,[2] both dated 28 February, oblige me thereto, in order to remark on some extratordinary passages in each. I shall begin with a few observations on one or two in the *moderate* Mr. Simpson's (I intend nothing farther on his letter). His insinuations of scurrility and defamation against me are very strong. I have no inclination tho' to submit to his judgement in these respects, but shall with the greatest deference, to the public's; and, in order that whoever may see yours and Mr. Well's papers in their travels, may judge of this matter, if worth their notice. I must beg the favour of you to reprint *Mr. Simpson's* anonymous letter, with his name at the head, that it may be known *every where* who the author is. Facts I always thought, and think still, are stubborn things but a thousand assertions, without proofs, are not worth a farthing. I deny then, that there is the least title like scurrility in my last, nor shall there be any in this; and perhaps this caution may have been used not out of favour to *Mr. Simpson,* but to myself, from an opinion that dirt blunts the edge of every tool, and prevents its cutting. If he calls his own words repeated in mine and retorted on himself as his, by that name, I have no objection; but then he must recollect surely, that ought more properly to be called his scurrility, not mine. Upon the whole, any complaint of scurrility now-a-days, must appear so stale, that I am surprised a man of *Mr. Simpson's* discernment would run the risk of being laughed at perceiving such a thing. I do assure him, that it was possible for me to spy only a single unchaste expression, that had the least look that way, in either of his obliging favours, or *Col. Lauren's,* it should not be taken notice of, in that light, as affecting me; in short, I think this encroaching on the province of the reader, as seeming to respect his judgement and candor, for all such things are well known to be but mere outside dress and nothing else; truth indeed may make a suspicious appearance in such a spotted garb, but she will be truth still, and her admirers will soon find her out, tho' masquerading it in a dirty wrapper. I am sorry, in retorting

---

[1] *SCG,* March 12, 1763.

[2] Laurens' essays have disappeared, along with the *Weekly Gazette.* Gadsden included a lengthy extract of Simpson's letter to the *Weekly Gazette* as a postscript to this letter to Peter Timothy. Simpson accused him of courting popularity at the expense of the Crown's prerogative.

partiality upon Mr. *Simpson,* that he should think I meant to insinuate, that he had actually been so in any instance as a judge *upon* the bench. I never meant any such thing, nor will my words, unless greatly perverted (I think) bear any such interpretation. I declare, with great pleasure, that I never knew anything to his prejudice in that character. But, with regard to myself, I still say and think, it was very odd for a judge to insinuate so black a crime (which to me is only another name for the vilest knavery) against me without attempting to bring the least shadow of a proof. If gentlemen in that character, take such or any improper liberties, they cannot but expect to be particularly pointed at, and reminded of their inconsistency with the station they act or acted in, which is all I meant to say to him *as a judge,* by returning his own words and insinuations upon himself. As to his argument, relating to the public matter in dispute, if he has not there given sufficient room for my explanation (as he calls it) I must confess, I am at loss to know what can.

Here I would beg leave to take notice, that he ought to have returned to the assembly "the affidavit in writing," that he says the church-warden for *Prince William's* parish "made and signed," in relation to the writ he executed, and Mr. *Simpson* observed was wanting "as soon as the writ was delivered to him." As he acknowledges he did not do so, he must be thought so far deficient in his duty; the assembly had a right to that affidavit; he must therefore blame himself, and only himself, for not furthering them with that matter (which I never knew of before) as the cause of forgetting, that the gentlemen returned in that writ were perhaps greater favourites with him than Mr. Gadsden, which seems to have occasioned all his resentment: Such stuttering and wincing, upon so slight a touch, entirely owing to himself too, I am afraid I will be thought no very good symptom.

Now, to acquit myself of defamation, I beg leave to inform him, that the fact in Mr. *Mile's* letter, I heard of very soon after the committee sent for him, when, and never before or since, to the best of my recollection, did I ever see that gentleman. Before the committee, he appeared extremely cautious, answering with great circumspection, to such questions only as were asked him. In the time intervening, between my hearing of the fact to the publication of my first letter, I took all opportunities of enquiring into Mr. *Mile's* character; and after hearing, that he bore that of a very honest, steady, discreet, and cautious man, but also this circumstance too, that he very rarely came to town, I thought myself justified in throwing but the hint to Mr. *Simpson* that I did; had he not resented it so highly, nothing farther might have been said about it. However, this matter rests between him and Mr. *Miles,* whose character will not suffer me to think, he can have been so monstrously malicious, as to invent a story, without any possible advantages to himself, that carries the strong circumstance of matter and time at least; for, 'tis well known, there were writings talked of very strongly at that time, and such too, if we may judge (exclusive of the then reports of their content) from Col. Lauren's threat, now published, as at least "to make me *feel* were not quite Dull" *ex pede Hercules* [from a part one may infer the whole]. Had I taken no notice (especially after Mr. *Simpson's* insult) of this matter, known to so many, my silence might have been construed, by my good friends, into a consciousness of my being "such a one" indeed, as to be unworthy the notice of any parish. Feeling my own innocence, I therefore threw out a hint, to discover in print a public owner of those writings that have been endeavoured (if Mr. *Miles* says true) to be made use of secretly to my prejudice, in order to have an opportunity of vindicating myself, if necessary; my design has succeeded, by this discovery; I therefore take my leave of Mr. Simpson, and pass to Col. Lauren's Letter.[3]

Which would be very alarming indeed, did it contain anything, affecting my character, but his mere talk and say-so. Proofs are wanted, to support his assertions. If he has any, I call upon him to produce them. ['Til] he does, I hope the compassion of the public will join with mine in pitying him (which I most sincerely do) for having so egregiously exposed himself; for I beg leave to assure him, that all my feelings are on his account, in this matter. I thank God, I find myself therein so *totus teres atque rotandus* [highly polished], that I have not the least occasion for any on my own: not an atom of the dirt so plentifully thrown, but has slid off entirely from me; and I heartily wish, that none of it may rebound and indelibly stick on himself.

I now purpose to answer, with all the temper and candor I am master of, every tittle of his letter relative to myself, without any evasion; that is, such as he has condescended to bring any shadow of an argument in support of. In order to convince him, if possible, that I hold strictly to my own principle, that "a man can vindicate himself in a matter of consequence always will," tho', bye the bye,

---

[3] William Miles and Jacob Ladson were the Wardens of St. Paul's Parish in question. They testified before the House Committee on Elections that they had properly taken the Oath administered by Andrew Leitch, a magistrate and vestryman. But apparently Miles intimated something to the contrary afterward, either in a letter to the *Weekly Gazette* or privately to Laurens or Simpson: *SCG,* December 11, 1762.

the present appears not much in that light to me, yet it shall be answered; and it [,] my earnest zeal to serve the public (for I am conscious of no other *crime,* if that is one) has not rendered me too contemptible and beneath their notice, I must intreat their patience, in this first unwilling intrusion, forced upon me, concerning myself *alone.*

Mr. Lauren's letter contains eighteen paragraphs, of different lengths all which I purpose to remark upon in the order they stand, so far as they concern me, and no farther,

The 1st, contains something a little unintelligible about "my own concession" of obliquely aiming at him in my last letter.

The matter is this: A common friend to us both told me, that Col. *Laurens* had hinted to him, and another of our friends, his suspicions that I had aimed at him in my last printed letter, contrary to a former engagement. My reply was frankly this That the words "duped father," in my letter, Col. *Laurens* might very justly take to himself, if his conscience told him he was the author of those writings mentioned in Mr. Miles letter, if not, he had no right so to do.

These two friends, at my earnest request, last September was twelve month, enquired into an affair of the nearest concern to me, which Col. *Laurens* had made appear very black indeed against me, at the ferry. This kind enquiry of theirs, produced his acknowledgement from under his hand, that he had been wrong. I will say no more. I only give this hint here, to all those gentlemen who recollect the matter, so publicly spoken of at the time; and submit to them, whether that ought not to have made the Colonel a little more mindful of producing his proofs, when he thought of attacking me again, especially in so outrageous a manner. As it has not had that effect on him, it will, I am sure, at least leave *this* on those that hear him and know that affair (others may know it very easily) not to credit him without, in any thing against me, for "he has written with a spirit of wrath and uncharitableness, and with a most *unbounded* assurance, giving groundless assertions for facts."

After our friends had cleared up the affair just hinted at, they insisted that, if we could not be again at an amicable footing, we should at least, for the sake of our common friends, let all matters subside. This was agreed to, and is the engagement, Col. Laurens told our friends I had broke thro', by the slant in my letter; but I think not; and to make it evident, that *He,* not I, did so, for the satisfaction of all my friends, was almost the only reason that determined me to answer his letter at all.

Several months after *our engagement* separately to our friends, my two letters, signed *Philopatrios,* came out, in neither of which Col. Laurens is aimed at. Notwithstanding this, from the information of several friends many months since; from the writings that were said to be coming out, mentioned in Mr. *Mile's* letter, which this gentleman has now shown himself to be the author of; as well as from his own threat, that I shall "feel they are not quite Dull" when they come out; 'tis evidence, I say, from all these things, beyond doubt, that they contain personal strokes and reflections against me, and in an extraordinary manner too. But why was I struck at in those writings at all? Must not that he called a breach of his promise, made to our mutual friends? What he calls mine, is manifestly occasioned by his; of course his *must* have been first. My oblique aim, as he calls it, and as it is, was intended to shame the author, if possible into the printing of these concealed writings, whispered about in many companies several months together; if not cause. If he took my glance to himself, the only proper answer would by himself, by others; the effect is the same to me, and he is the have been (in my humble opinion) to have printed those writings forthwith, without saying a word; this would have been taking my hint effectually, showing some candor, and (let me tell him) prudence too, by giving me an opportunity to vindicate myself without farther exposing himself; this was what I aimed at. Is it not possible, to point out errors, and to set truth in a clear light, without striking at or ridiculing the publisher of any facts (when so doing it contrary to agreement) especially when such publisher promises to retract his errors when convinced? Can, or ought he to do so sooner? Has any trial been made to convince him? How does Col. *Laurens* know then, that he will not be convinced, and that he will not keep his word?

2d paragraph: To this paragraph I will forbear saying more, than that I will never publish any thing again but with my name at length. The letters signed Philopatrios I was known to be the author of, as soon as they were published, *equally* as well, here, as if my name had been subscribed. This Col. *Laurens* cannot be ignorant of.

3d. In this (as well as the 5th) paragraph, Col. *Lauren's* mentions his remarks only on Philopatrios' *first* letter. Has he made none then on the second, which is by far the most material? As to any round assertions scattered in this letter, relative to Philopatrios' materials, facts, visions, prophecies, *etc.,* I would just observe here, once for all, I will not enter into that subject by retail; when *all* the colonel's last years animadversions are published, it will be time enough then to talk on this matter, if he offers anything worth notice. 4th. What the fourth contains, relative to Mr. Simpson entirely, is already answered.

I believe Col. *Lauren's* did not communicate any of his writings or observations to Mr. Simpson, "in any manner whatsoever that *could authorise him* to put that question to Mr. Miles," or with any intention to throw me out at any election. I never said, thought, insinuated that he did; but still those writings, if Mr. Miles says true, has seemingly been made use of for that purpose; perhaps they were handed to Mr. *Simpson* by a third hand, for I cannot think that gentleman's curiosity would permit him to forbear peeping into so celebrated a performance, that the author declares "he had no objection to any gentleman's reading."

The 5th, 6th, and 7th paragraphs may be observed on together. Here I acknowledge, that my brother told me, about August last, that a worthy friend to the colonel and me, had hinted to him, that he believed he could procure me a sight of Col. *Lauren's* writings on Philopatrios. The next day, I asked that friend, whether Col. *Laurens* himself had made that offer? He wa[i]ved satisfying me; and when I pressed him to let me know, whether he had not, directly or indirectly, heard, that Col. *Laurens* suggested, that Mr. *Gadsden* might see these writings if he would? He then said, that he would not deny, but he had heard such a thing mentioned in company. I told him, that was enough, I guessed whence it came. I deny ever to have had any other notice whatever, of such an offer, to the best of my recollection. I then declared, to that friend and many others, that I would not see the performance 'till printed; that I longed to see it so, and would answer it, if I could, and was worth it. Indeed several hints, from friends, convinced me it contained something that would make me *feel,* and oblige me to take public notice of it. But how could I have answered it *before?* Answered what? A manuscript acknowledged to be "a little prolix"? And then seen *occasionally?* For Mr. *Laurens* does not pretend to say, that he desired that friend of mine he speaks of, to signify that I might take a copy; and if he had, I would not have been at the trouble or expence. In short, *timeo Danaes and dona ferentes* [I fear the Greeks even when they bring gifts]. I immediately told this friend, and numbers of others, that *ever-generous* offer appeared to me as a very artful trap, to catch me in a dilemma; and to furnish the best pretence that could be made, should I read it, for not printing it at all; which I was firmly persuaded was never intended, by most of the prompters at least, who then *too* only seemed to want to set the colonel and I a squabbling, and thereby divert the stream. Had I seen it, it might have indeed with some colour of excuse, have completed its intended tour *incog.* at my expence; and the flimsy pretences for not printing it (which Mr. Timothy's advertisement of the fourth of this month has now fully detected, and shewn to be only *specious* declarations and mere evasions) might have then imposed abroad, tho' not here, upon many; and my adversaries generosity, together with scraps of his *unanswerable* writings, been pip'd about

"Over the hills and far away."

I was aware of this, and therefore determined to secure an opportunity of making a reply; and such one too, that the public might understand what I replied to, by having an opportunity to compare both together.

Besides, was it not a long time, and publically said, that this manuscript was sent to Philadelphia to be printed there. I never heard, 'till since Col. *Lauren's* letter went to the press, that he had altered his mind, and declared to a gentleman, about three months since, that he had determined not to print it. Did it never voyage to Philadelphia or elsewhere at all?

I acknowledge it to be a fact, that Mr. *Simpson* saw Philopatrios' second letter in manuscript before its publication, and that I sent him a printed copy; and I dare say Col. Laurens is not unacquainted with part of the cause of this wonderful wonderment; and whenever he or Mr. *Simpson,* if either of them think it worth the public notice, will publish *all* that part, Mr. *Gadsden* will not be at the least difficulty to make it appear very reconcileable with his declaration, that he never was, is, or desires to be, a favourite of his, by publishing the remainder with notes, if necessary. Mr. *Gadsden* is under a promise. Mr. *Laurens* knows it no doubt, and can't do it with propriety; but he assures the public 'tis only like the mountain and mouse. However, Mr. *Gadsden* thinks this hint would have come better from Mr. *Simpson* as it does not, it confirms him in opinion, that Col. *Laurens* has, at least, to be as good a favourite with that gentleman as himself, otherwise he can't conceive how the colonel got this curious anecdote he seems so fond of. Mr. *Gadsden* is not conscious of having slandered any man in high or low station; and as to private whispering, he laughs at such an insinuation, and is sure all that know him will laugh at it too.

8th. Mr. *Gadsden* here acknowledges an instance of Mr. *Lauren's* candor, in rightly supposing he meant annalyzer, by the word analyst. He admits the correction, is obliged to him for it. However, he heard of it, as he did also of his being bound over for breaking the peace at that time, what Mr. Gadsden never was in his life. These are facts the Colonel must have forgotten surely; but as they are so, let him step up into his niche himself; his title is now indisputable; and whose fame the verses at the pedestal are intended to celebrate, no mortal will then be in the least doubt about. Other instances might be produced, of our Colonel's bad memory, but I have done with him, except one remark more.

The Colonel, at the bottom of the copy of verses, says, "I can assure Philopatrios, that *this* scrap was not prompted;" I will therefore believe him: But as he does not hint the same of the other scraps of this letter, I must beg leave to think *many* of them were; and, before I conclude, I will take the liberty to the Colonel again, that he is dup'd (he had no occasion to take this word amiss before, for it has often been the case of many a sensible man). These prompters, I say, have dup'd him, who, I am positive, love us both alike, that is, not at all; for, in fact, all our world knows, they care for nobody but themselves; and if Col. *Laurens* should praise nine of them, and happen at any time to drop a wry word of the tenth, the electrical grin will be immediately *refixed* against him: To demonstrate this, I don't know that I may turn apologist too one of these days, for the first of those ten, that may happen to make *another faux-pas* as all vulgar eyes look upon to be shameful; by doing this, I am sure, I shall then be reinstated into their good graces *as much as ever,* and have that all important, all significant cue on my side, to assist me to *out brazen truth, fact, eyes, ears, and common sense,* and upon the very same terms that the Colonel has, that is *just* as long as it suits their purpose, and *just* no longer. Consider this Colonel, and recollect *fas est ab hoste doceri* [It is permitted to learn from your enemy].

I now beg leave to conclude, with this repeated remark, to these diabolical prompters and suggesters, *delenda est Carthago* [Carthage must be destroyed], I find then at any rate. Their hellish machinations have hitherto proved abortive;

9th. Col. Lauren's animadversions on Philopatrios, in the exact state they were in when handed about last year, "I do really long to see in print," and expect "that my curiosity, shall be gratified;" and in order to remove the scruples of my new and dear friend Mr.

Wells, I will subscribe for half a dozen copies, which number I expect to have, let who will print them; but I must leave Col. *Laurens* to "agree upon the point of printing" himself; and in order that no "honest men may acquit the Colonel from gratifying my craving desires," let me explain to such, his pure contrast of my motives for printing Philopatrios, and shew them, that he can thence plead no reasonable excuse to come off.

10th, 11th, 12th, 13th, This contrast not only depends upon the comparison of several serious and direct expressions of mine, with a single and plainly ironical one, which is not quite fair by the bye; but also on a manifest twisting of the signification of the word purely, which diverts the Colonel *purely* for these four paragraphs throughout. This word has three meanings, and the dictionary (Johnson's) will tell him so. Its first and most natural is "in a pure manner"; its second, "innocently;" and the third "merely," the sense he takes it in. Now if he'll only be pleased to take it in either of the first two meanings, which the irony plainly requires, down will come at once all that he has built on that Capital word, and of course Mr. *Gadsden* recovered his memory, and fully reconciled to Philopatrios, without treating his country like an harlot. This mysterious word being now, I think, sufficiently unriddled, and farther flips only suggested, not produced, we may skip to the

14th paragraph. I was for many years a warm, sincere, and disinterested friend to Mr. *Laurens,* and defy him to produce one instance wherein my actions, in all that time, failed of my professions; or what friend or friends of his Iago-like, I ever exerted any artifice or strategem to separate from him. Mr. *Laurens* was I acknowledge, reciprocally my friend too. I thought him, I found him so, upon several occasions. His gross and public affronts, several years since, without making any concessions, convinced me he wanted candour at least; these occasioned the first breach between us. I am very sorry his behavior since, has not appeared to me in such a light, as to regain my good opinion; of no importance to him I dare say, and therefore beg to drop the subject, first desiring him to burn all my old papers, for fear of *more* mistakes. I assure him I have not one letter of his by me, that I know of, of an older date than June 1760.

15th. I am sorry that Col. *Laurens* causelessly attacked me, in his writings on Philopatrios, and gave room for those insinuations that have too evidently been made use of to prejudice me, but without effect, thank God. Had he not done so, neither he, Mr. Simpson, or I, could have had any altercations in this matter.

16th. This paragraph does not affect me, therefore choose to pass it over.

17th. I beg leave here to observe, that my state of retirement has lately been employed consistently with my duty, on a necessary public matter, which I have had the satisfaction to find has not proved altogether unaceptable, to such as I am sure Col. *Laurens* will allow to be good judges.

18th. I now come to the Colonel's last paragraph. And here I am ready to "submit to the judgment of the public," and to "Col. *Laurens*" himself for correction, "whose name with most propriety ought to grace the head of his own parody of verses, his or mine, and fill up the following blank. In the first rank of these did ———— stand." For, with regard to the mob or riot he alludes to, 'tis well known, what occasioned it was entirely over before Mr. Gadsden reached the Bay; the mob was then dispersing. Had he come soon enough, he might have been diverted, and instructed at the same time, by Col. *Lauren's* exhibitions in the *Broughtonian art;* but he was too late even for that entertainment; I trust in God they always will; and do assure them, that dullness, prolixity, conceit, calumny, or, in short, any thing else whatever, they, or any others, at their *good* pleasure, can only say of me, shall not discourage me, when I think the cause of truth materially concerned, from shewing what risques I am ready to run for her sake. Nor will I ever stand still, as an idle spectator, and see an honest worthy man, that I know deserves well of the public, ill-treated, by any set of knaves whatever, without lending him all the assistance in my power. I have more than once felt the exquisite pleasure, of doing so with some success; and I would as soon tell a famishing wretch that stared at me for food, be thou fed, without giving him anything to eat, as stand idly by upon such an occasion, and content myself with barely wishing a person well. I am   .   .   .

CHRISTOPHER GADSDEN.

P.S. My separate and particular compliments to *Drawearsir Stricture,* Esq.; and let him know, as the Indictment is now read, and acknowledged to be very full, that the court is impatient to have the witnesses called in to support it; amongst these, unless I should be so unfortunate, as to have my worthy friend and old [stiff?] stand-by goodman Fact, strongly against me, I hope I shall be in no danger of a happy, speedy and entire deliverence, never more to appear in court again upon this affair; but should my old friend knit his stern brows and depose against me, it must be all over with me then I confess and I shall be obliged to make one appearance more, only to confess judgement, and shew some signs of grace left.

To all whom it may concern, Know Ye, that William Simpson, Esq.; clerk of the council, is the author of the following Innocent letter, containing nothing like "scurillity," and as he will tell you, no doubt "no unjustifiable insinuations," first printed anonymously in Mr. Welle's gazette no. 210, and now reprinted at Mr. Gadsden's request, that the world may know to what moderate gentleman they are obliged, for that sensible, delicate, all-political First Stroke.

Extract of a letter to a gentleman
in Charleston:

Sir:

By observing the various complexions and characters of men, and analyzing the several errors to which they are liable, we shall find, that it is generally some mistaken opinion of right and wrong, that misleads and governs the bulk of mankind, and gives rise to all the irregular passions which disquiet their minds. Some false species of good borrowing delusive colours from the fair and genuine forms of virtue, having passed into the region of fancy, unexamined and undistinguished by the judgement, first raises admiration, then passion, which being succeeded by choice, gives birth to resolution and that issues in a wrong conduct.

I write not to justify or condemn a late public resolution, therefore think myself not the less fit to express the sense of an honest man, warm with the love of his country, and zealous for her interest.

A paper intitled, the South-Carolina gazette, from saturday January the 29th, to saturday February the 5th, 1763, came to my hands this day; but instead of being entertained with the weekly occurrences, which I have always understood to be the only end of that paper, I found myself engaged in reading a long and unintelligible controversy concerning a late unhappy dispute. If a further vindication of the proceedings in that matter was deemed necessary, I sincerely wish, for the honour and credit of the province, some impartial and judicious person had undertaken the talk; for a dull, unvaried, incoherent chime of inconclusive arguments, flags the attention, and produces that insipid langour, which is no friend to true persuasion, whatever it may to ductile credulity; besides, he who suffers himself to fall into an abandoned conceit of his own merit; or a mean passion for popularity, those fatal rocks that so many have split upon, can never be considered as a proper person to do justice to a cause wherein a whole community is immediately concerned.

I am heartily sorry for the unfortunate event that has happened; but we may rest satisfied, that our good and gracious sovereign, who disregards the person that complains, and attends only to the justice and merit of the complaint, will discountenance by every possible method, unconstitutional attempts either on the prerogative of the crown or liberty of the subject; but in my humble opinion, there is nothing so likely to promote the interest and preserve the tranquility of the province, or its dependance upon the mother country, as the maintaining with a strict and steady hand the necessary powers and just prerogatives of the crown, and the preferring an uniform and settled principle of government, to an occasional departure from it, for any temporary motive whatever; especially where such principle is established by law. For it is contained in the very idea of a law, that it is to be observed. Therefore he who is a party to any laws, or professes himself member of a society formed upon laws, in dispensing with them, denies laws to be what they are, or himself to be what he is supposed to profess himself to be.

I am, Sir & c.

St. Andrew's parish,

[*William Simpson*]

9th Feb. 1763.

To William Samuel Johnson and Charles Garth

William Samuel Johnson (1727-1819) of Stratford, Connecticut, statesman and lawyer, famed for effecting the compromise over representation in the Federal Convention, and first President of Columbia College, New York (1787-1800), attended the Stamp Act Congress for Connecticut where he was an important member of the committee to frame a remonstrance. He moderated the conservative opinions of the "Eastern gentlemen" with the more extreme beliefs of Gadsden and his fellow delegates. George C. Croce, Jr., William Samuel Johnson, A Maker of the Constitution (New York: Columbia University Press, 1937), pp. 57-58; Edmund S. and Helen M. Morgan, The Stamp Act Crisis, Prologue to Revolution (Chapel Hill: University of North Carolina Press, 1953), pp. 108-9.

Charles Garth, colonial agent for South Carolina, Maryland and Georgia, at various periods after June 5, 1762, was a member of Parliament from the Borough of Divizes (1765 to 1780), when he became Commissioner of Excise. Associated with South Carolina through his cousin, the former Governor Thomas Boone, and related to the Colletons through his grandmother Elizabeth, Garth closely followed and propagated provincial interests during the crises. He reflected English urban, rather than rural views on taxation, and urged repeal of the Stamp Act. Garth believed that ancient statutes prohibited the levy "for want of a representation," and differed from his Whig colleagues who emphasized the unconstitutionality of "internal taxation." He died in 1792. Joseph W. Barnwell, "Hon. Charles Garth, M.P. . ." SCHM, XXVI (April, 1925), 67-92; L.B. Namier, "Charles Garth and His Connexions;" "Charles Garth, Agent for South Carolina," English Historical Review, CCXIII (January, October, 1939), 443-70; 632-52.

Charleston So. Carolina [1]

Dec. 2, 1765

Dear Sir:

As I am persuaded it will give you pleasure to hear what our Assembly has done in the Common cause, in order to promote the important matters agreed upon at Congress, I will make no further Apology for giving you an account thereof.

As Mr. Lynch, Rutledge,[2] and myself were informed at N York that our Assembly were to meet the 28th October, we thought it absolutely necessary, that one of us should set off as speedily as possible after the breaking up of the Congress in order to catch our House before their adjourn[ment]. This fell to my lot and accordingly I left [New] York with the papers two days after in a very small schooner crowded with passengers, full of these hopes; but unfortunately through the over-timourousness of the Master, who stretched too far to the Eastward, I did not get here till the 13th last month, and in less than 48 hours after, had the pleasure of seeing my worthy Colleagues, Mr. Lynch and Mr. Rutledge, in a short passage by the way of Philadelphia. We found the Assembly (not expecting us so soon) had adjourned to the 25th of last month.

As soon as we arrived and could get copies of the minutes of the Congress made out we dispatched them as we were desired, to Georgia and No. Carolina.

The 26th a House was made, and the enclosed Report together with the minutes of the Congress, their declaration of opinions, and the engrossed addresses to the King, Lords, and Commons, laid before them. The declarations and the addresses were accordingly read that morning, and then the House adjourned to 4 Oclock, P.M., of the same day, when the whole was agreed to unanimously (excepting by one member) *totidem verbis* [in as many words], and the address ordered to be signed by the Speaker, and as a fine ship, the only one, then in Harbour, that had cleared out before the first of November, for any part of Great Britain, was ready and obliged

---

[1] Original not found. Copy in Robert W. Gibbes, *Documentary History of the American Revolution, 1764-1776* Columbia: Banner Steam-Power Press, 1853), p. 9. The Gibbes' version does not contain the Post Script appended to the copy sent to Johnson that appears in the Bancroft Transcripts, NYPL., and which is given here.

[2] Thomas Lynch (1727-1776), father of the Signer of the Declaration of Independence, accompanied Gadsden and John Rutledge to the Stamp Act Congress. Like Gadsden, Lynch opposed sending any remonstrance to Parliament denying its authority. He became a member of the First Continental Congress and served in the Second Congress until his death. *DAB,* XI, 523.

to sail the next morning, being a spring ship, the Comee [Committee] of Correspondence was immediately ordered to write a letter to the Agent, and enclose them which was done, and the vessel, *the Charming Charlotte,* Capt. Reeves, luckily had an opportunity of getting over the Bar the next morning with a very fine wind.

The next day the House did us the Honor to give us their thanks by the Speaker signifying their approbation of our whole conduct in the most ample and obliging manner. A Committee was afterwards appointed to draw up such particular resolutions on the present occasion as were thought necessary for the House to enter into, which they accordingly did and reported, and to which, after making a very few alterations, the House agreed, and ordered to be published—enclosed is one of these publications. As soon as this business was compleated the House adjourned till after Christmass (to the 7 Jan.) having first ordered the Committee of Correspondance to write more fully to the Agent upon these important matters by the packet, that will sail in about ten or twelve days.

The short letter that has been sent to the Agent you have herewith a copy of, as also of another wrote by Mr. Lynch, Mr. Rutledge and myself from New York the day after the Congress, and put into Capt. Davis's bag the morning I sailed.

Our people have behaved as firmly in the Common cause as any upon the Continent, without having done the least mischief, and I make little doubt of their continuing so to do, though we have a number of cunning, Jacobitical, Butean rascals to encounter with, that leave nothing untried to counterwork the firmness and loyalty of the true sons of liberty amongst us; these are such infernal fiends as none of the sister Colonies, north of us, have to dread, but with all their cunning (though that is generally accounted a more formidable enemy than mere force) I hope, and indeed do not doubt, but the wretched miscreants will find themselves disappointed, and their American posterities as well as ourselves, by our uniform spirit of firmness, made happy in the preservation of their and our just rights, and priviledges, whether they will or no; the friends of liberty here are all as sensible as our brethren to the Northward, that nothing will save us but acting together. The Province that endeavours to act separately will certainly gain nothing by it; she must fall with the rest, and not only so, but be deservedly branded besides with ever lasting infamy.

For my part, I have ever been of opinion that we should all endeavour to stand upon the broad common ground of those natural and inherent rights that we all feel, and know, as men, and as descendants of Englishmen we have a right to, and have always thought this bottom amply sufficient for our present, important purpose. I wish the Charters (we have as good a one as most) being different in different Colonies may not be the political trap, that will ensnare us at last by drawing different Colonies upon that account to act differently in this great common cause, and when ever that is the case all will be over with the whole. There ought to be no New England man, no New Yorker, *etc.* known on the Continent, but all of us Americans.

A *confirmation* of our essent'l Common rights as Englishmen, may be pleaded from Charters safely enough, but any further dependance on them may be fatal.

I am the more riveted into this opinion from all the Ministerial writers that I have seen: *fas est et ab hoste doceri* [it is all right to learn a lesson, even from an enemy], and from [none] more than that famous Author of the regulations lately made concerning the Colonies,[3] published the present year with great eclat, pages 17, 18— also page 22nd where he informs us of the reasons why the New Provinces are not yet permitted to have Assemblies, which are easily seen through.

'Tis pity, that every Assembly in each Province would not have a constant eye upon the attacks that may be made upon the essential parts of the British Constitution in any, and the agents of the whole ordered to assist upon such occasion, for any single Province being once deprived of a material right, 'tis presently made a precedent for the rest. The late attacks upon different parts of the Constitution in different places are very alarming, and has the appearance of design; in New York on one point, in our Province on another, in Jamaica on a third, in Maryland on several; and the striding encroachments of the Council almost everywhere *etc., etc.,* this by the by.

I still wish what Mr. Lynch and I were so earnest for, at the Congress, that we had stopped at the declarations and petitions to the King, as the House of Commons refused to receive the addresses of the Colonies, when the matter was pending in Parliament, as we neither hold our rights from them or the Lords, as his Majesty is, in the petition, desired to lay the matter before the Parliament. How-

---

[3] Gadsden refers to a pamphlet written by Thomas Whatley representing the views of Lord George Granville to whom he was Secretary. The piece is entitled *The Regulations Lately Made concerning the Colonies and the Taxes Imposed upon Them, considered* (London, 1765). It argued the Parliamentary right to tax on the grounds of "virtual representation." *See* Morgans, *op. cit.,* pp. 75-78.

ever, as the Congress thought otherwise, and union is most certainly all in all, the Memorial to the Lords and Petition to the Commons were supported by us here equally with as much zeal as if we had voted for them at the Congress, and God send the desired success, and establish harmony once more between us and our Mother Country.

But had we consented to the addition that was so strenuously proposed to be made to the first declaration of the opinion of the Congress, I am sure we should have been far, very far from having the thanks of our house. The attachment the Eastern gentlemen seemed to have had to it, I imputed to their Charters, but I must own, I was unable to account how any other gentlemen could be so particularly fond of it. I wish these Charters may not be the bane of us all at last, as it seems to be the common fetch of the P[arliamen]t and ministerial writers at present that the King could not grant the exemptions claimed under them.

I should be very glad to have the pleasure of hearing from you, & am yr. most hble. servt.

Christopher Gadsden

[P.S.] Pray my compliment to Mr. Rowland and Mr. Dyer.[4]

Mr. Tilghman [5] was so obliging as to spare me one of the three Virginia pamphlets he had at the Congress, which are as much applauded here, as with you; and of which a very large impression has been struck off here from my copy.[6] We are very hearty here.

The alloy is very insignificant with regard to the whole lump.

---

[4] David Rowland and Eliphalet Dyer were members of the Stamp Act Congress from Connecticut. Morgans, *op. cit.,* p. 103, 42n.

[5] Edward Tilghman of Maryland was a member of the committee which drew up the remonstrance. Christopher Johnston, "The Tilghman Family," *Maryland Historical Magazine,* I (September, 1906), 283.

[6] What pamphlets Gadsden alludes to is not known. However, Richard Bland's *An Inquiry into the Rights of the British Colonies . . . an Answer to . . . the author of that Pamphlet* (Williamsburg, 1766) parallels Gadsden's ideas. Bland disagreed with John Dickinson that Parliament had the right to tax but had never used the right to tax "internally." Bland contended that Parliament possessed no such power without colonial consent. Furthermore, he said Parliament was not the repository of English rights but that these rested in "the Law of Nature"; and the relationship between the colonies and the mother country was a "Compact." Another "Virginia" pamphlet was possibly Daniel Dulaney's *Considerations on the Propriety of Imposing Taxes . . .* (Annapolis, 1765). The Preface is dated "Virginia, Aug. 12, 1765." It was a response to several "ministerial writers" but chiefly Whatley. The third might have been Bland's *The Colonel Dismounted* (Williamsburg, 1764), which questioned the royal right to tax and therby interefere with "our Internal polity." *See* Clinton Rossiter, "Richard Bland: the Whig in America," *William and Mary Quarterly,* X (January, 1953), 33-79.

To William Samuel Johnson

Charlestown, S. C.,[1]

April 16, 1766

Dear Sir:

About three weeks since, I received your very obliging favor of the 10th January; about a fortnight before which by the means of my friend, Mr. Torrans,[2] I sent you, under his cover to his brother-in-law, Mr. Wm. Smith [3] of New York, copy of our Committee of Correspondence's letter of the 16th Dec. last, to our Agent Mr. Garth, together with a copy of all our public matters, that occurred here since my last, of the 2d Dec., which I hope you have received.

We were in hopes, the first instant, that we had very nearly cleared ourselves of the difficulties attending the Stamp Act, as our four assistant judges at the time, gave it as their unanimous opinion that our Courts ought to be opened and business carried on as usual,

---

[1] NYPL. An enclosure (not included) contains a transcript of the opinion of Chief Justice Skinner, and of Rawlins Lowndes' dissent on the use of Stamps which Gadsden describes in his letter. Bancroft published it in the *Historical Magazine*, V (September 1861) 260-62, probably because of Gadsden's remarks on slavery.

Several letters signed by Gadsden, together with the members of the Committee of Correspondence, were published in the *SCHM*, "The Correspondence of Charles Garth," Robert W. Barnwell, ed., XXVIII, 85-88, 226-30; XXIX, 42-43, 115-6, 213, 304-5; XXX, 27, 179-80, 181-2; XXXI, 59-62, 126-7, 132-4; XXXIII, 135-8, 262-4. The Stamp Act Crisis, and the struggle with the courts, are related in Edward McCrady, *The History of South Carolina under the Royal Government, 1719-1776*, (New York: Macmillan Co., 1899) pp. 560-85; for Gadsden's activities, Woody, *loc. cit.*, pp. 3-12.

[2] Torrans was a Charleston merchant who, in partnership with John Gregg of London and one Paug of the city, carried on the business of importing slaves and white immigrants. Sellers, *op. cit.*, pp. 114-7.

[3] William Smith (1728-1793), the historian and jurist, was at the time one of the leaders of the anti-Stamp-Tax Whigs of New York. His view, similar to Gadsden's, was that the tax was unconstitutional. Like Gadsden, he was one of the directors of the mob. He later became a Loyalist, however, and after visiting Charleston in 1780, wrote a pamphlet, *The Candid Retrospect or the American War Examined by Whig Principles: DAB*, XVII, 357-8; Carl Becker, *History of Political Parties in the Province of New York* (Madison: University of Wisconsin, 1909), pp. 38-39; Morgans, *op. cit.*, p. 184; William H. W. Sabine, *Historical Memoirs of William Smith* . . . (New York: np, 1956), pp. 29-36.

without stamps. In this they overruled the Chief Justice,[4] whose character and abilities (if he has either), you cannot be unacquainted with, who was of a different opinion. But the clerk of the Common Pleas, Mr. Dougal Cambell, refused to do his part, and make an entry they ordered; they appointed another to do it, and out of tenderness to him, did not commit him for his refractoriness, not being aware of such a refusal and, expecting he would think better of it the next day, or if he did not, that the Lieut. Gov.[5] upon their application, would suspend him, accordingly the next day finding Mr. Cambell obstinate, and they could not meet again as a Court till May, they waited upon the Lieut. Gov. to suspend him, when his Honor gave them the greatest reason to expect he would (as I have it from three of the Judges themselves) and only desired they would reduce their application to writing. This they did laying their complaint against their Clerk generally as a refusal to obey the orders of the Court without mentioning anything relative to the Stamp Act. In the meantime the clerk petitioned the Lt. Gov. upon which his Honor told the Judges that he thought himself obliged to lay the matter before the Council, consisting chiefly of Placemen and men of known arbitrary principles and very slender abilities; they advised his Honor against the suspension and what is very extraordinary these very gentlemen a few days afterwards, upon an application to his Honor for a special Court in behalf of a transient person, to recover a debt according to a peculiar Law of this Province, which was also laid before them advised his Honor to order the Chief Justice to hold such a court which his Honor did, and the Chief Justice has refused to do. Thus stands this interesting affair at present. The Assembly the middle of March had agreed among themselves for the conveniency of the country gentlemen, it being planting time to adjourn for six weeks, *de die in diem* by the Speaker or any seven town members according to a provision in our Election

---

[4] Charles Skinner was chief justice of South Carolina from 1762 until 1769 when he was replaced by William Wragg. McCrady, *Royal Government,* pp. 465-7 described him as an "Irish man of the lowest class" without legal but with mechanics' training. In 1767 Gadsden attacked Skinner from his position on the House Committee to investigate the state of the Courts, reporting him as wholly ignorant of the law.

[5] Lieutenant Governor William Bull (1710-1791) was born at Ashby Plantation, the second son of Governor William Bull. Educated in medicine at Leiden, captain and later Brigadier of Provincial Forces (1751-1759), Lieutenant Governor Bull enjoyed a distinguished public career as member and Speaker of the House, member of the Council, and as governor of the Province five times, the latter position invariably during difficult periods of history. Bull was also noteworthy for his interest in education. He was held in such high esteem by South Carolinians that, despite his loyalism in the Revolution, he was spared the confiscation of his estate. *DAB,* III, 252-3; "The Bull Family of South Carolina," *SCHM,* I (January, 1900), 84-85.

Law unless any thing very extraordinary should happen in the interim, in such case upon proper notice they would come down.

They are accordingly summoned to attend the 21st instant, a week sooner than the agreed adjournment upon the important matter when I make no doubt they will take every step becoming the representatives of a free people. Our Lt. Governor in his private character is a very agreeable polite man and very well beloved, but as a Governor is and always has been the weakest and most unsteady man I ever knew, so very obliging that he never obliged. The regard for him as a private gentleman has had too great weight with many in our house and occasioned great difficulties. In short 'tis a great and common misfortune, that weak and good natured men very often carry not only their own private attachments, but their particular and sensible compassions, if I may use the expression, to very unwarrantable lengths and are often driven thereby into the greatest inconsistencies being as it were tossed perpetually from one particular feeling or compassion to another, without any permanent principle to rest upon. This seems to have been the case with one or two of our counsellors, who are really honest, well meaning but very weak men in the matter just mentioned. Mr. Cambell's case appeared to them very hard and pitiable as a private man, who they were made to believe (though it was perverseness in him) liable to great penalties *etc.* upon his complying with the Judges order relative to the Stamp Act notwithstanding that order was founded on the Lt. Governor's certificate that no stamps were to be had. Out of a strong, tender, sensible, feeling for his case, they advised the Governor not to suspend him. A very few days after the same uneasy sensation upon finding that an honest, transient person was likely to lose his just debt through the knavery of a settler, obliges them to give an opinion that subverts the other.

Enclosed you have the Chief Justice's opinion and that of the judges, this last drawn up by my friend Mr. Lowndes, a gentleman who though without the happiness of hardly a common education, yet by his own application and close attention to public business has made himself deservedly conspicuous and respected. I told my friend, I differed from him in the principle he went upon, that is, I should have built chiefly on the constitutionalness of the Act and asserted it so, roundly; he, I know, thinks it as unconstitutional as I do, but imagined it more prudent and advantageous in our present circumstances not to touch upon that string. He and neither of his brethren are of the Law so that you must make all allowances.

71

The 9th instant a number just sufficient to make a House met together only to order the resolutions of the Congress and their several addresses to be printed. This was occasioned by some industrious insinuations and misrepresentations of those matters by a set of Jacobites we have in town; indeed the people in general were desirous of seeing them and as we know the vessels in which the papers went, have been long since arrived, and that the addresses must (or ought to) have been presented several months ago unless artfully suppressed, the House generally agreed thereto.

We are a very weak Province, a rich growing one, and of as much importance to Great Britain as any upon the continent; and [the] great part of our weakness (though at the same time 'tis part of our riches) consists in having such a number of slaves amongst us, and we find in our case according to the general perceptible workings of Providence where the crime most commonly though slowly, yet surely, draws a similar and suitable punishment that slavery begets slavery. Jamaica and our West India Islands demonstrate this observation which I hope will not be our case now, whatever might have been the consequences had the fatal attempts been delayed a few years longer, when we had drank deeper of the Circean draught and the measure of our iniquities were filled up. I am persuaded with God's blessing we shall not fail or disgrace our sister Colonies at this time. Many are the difficulties we have had to struggle with, and not the least of them are owing to a number of artful Jacobites in town who leave nothing untried to poison the minds of the people, but thank God the country in general are very hearty, where are few of these wretches. We are determined to be patient 'til we hear the final issue of this affair, that we may avail ourselves of every justification if pushed to extremities. But if we be, there are no lengths but many gentlemen and others who are to be depended on will go to maintain our liberties, and the North Carolina Association which we all admire here is what I believe, will be generally signed and supported. Our latest accounts to be depended on are from Liverpool of the 12th of February, when the fatal matter was not determined and the opinion of its issue various. In order that you may judge what a set of wretches we have amongst us in town, I will mention to you the following anecdote that happened not many nights since upon or soon after the arrival of the above Liverpool news. As a gentleman of reputation was going to a tavern upon a dark night he overheard in the street a very extraordinary expression, which induced him to stop and which he thought a sufficient excuse for his listening unperceived, to the discourse of two persons, who were then in close conversation, an elderly man and a young one as he took them to be: one of them said he hoped the Stamp Act would not be repealed, for it would be a fine opportunity for Charles and he would go any lengths; the other replied, He wished so too, but that as he was now in easy circumstances he should be afraid to venture unless there was a great probability. These are the wretches that have been principally the occasion of the *Apostacy of Georgia* and are laying every snare they possibly can for us, while our ports were shut, and no probability as they thought of their being opened. These were the folk, who were continually saying: We don't like the Stamp Act any more than you do, but why don't you get the Port open upon the same terms as they are in many places to the northward? When about three months were elapsed and a very great number of shipping were in harbor chiefly owned in Great Britain, and we were afraid that the number of sailors would force the stamps upon us, as had been done in Georgia, and plainly saw such a design working and with the assurance of Mr. Randolph [6] the Surveyor General for the Southern District, who providentially arrived at this critical juncture, a push was made to open our ports, that happily succeeded, then these contradictory wretches did everything in their power to prevent it. Thank God, we have to get over most of our present difficulties, and I believe have been of as much service to the common cause by that long detention of such a number of British owned shipping (which we kept as long as we dared) as long as any of our sister Colonies upon the continent.

For my part I have always been of opinion that these unconstitutional proceedings that have occasioned so much uneasiness were intended by the Jacobitical party that seem to have been too long and still to be uppermost, to throw the nation into confusion, in order to create a necessity for that slavish alteration which they wish for, and supposing it should happen, which God forbid, though to me it would not be surprising to hear it very shortly, then according to the old proverb, they that hide can find, so in this case he upon whose account this confusion is created, may be thought capable of early putting all to rights again, no doubt on such a resolution, the Cider [7] and Stamp Act, *etc.* would be immediately repealed with the most pretended abhorrence in order to acquire a necessary popularity and to gain time to fix himself in the saddle and then good (or rather bad) night to the English liberties on the other side

---

[6] Peter Randolph, Surveyer General of Customs for the Southern District, apparently gave permission for ships to sail without stamped paper, as he had done in his home colony of Virginia. John Richard Alden, *South in the Revolution,* (Baton Rouge: Louisiana State University Press, 1957), p. 76.

[7] The Cider Act of 1763, an unpopular English excise tax, passed under Grenville. Bernhard Knollenberg, *Origin of the American Revolution* (New York: The Free Press, 1960), pp. 35, 47.

of the great herring pond at least. The Cider Act immediately after so scandalous a Peace, seems to have been for a trial of the People's spirit, which instead of appearing in the Old English manner upon such an alarming occasion, evaporating altogether in talk and newspaper essays, the Ministry thought they might do any thing. God grant that our stand may be of service to the cause of liberty in England and effectually awake the starters and big talkers in their sleep there. But I have done and heartily beg your pardon for this tedious prate. Pray make my compliments to Messrs. Dyer and Rowland, and be assured that I am, with great sincerity Dr. Sir Your affectionate hble. Servt.

CHRISTOPHER GADSDEN

To Sylvanus

Charles Woodmason (Sylvanus; 1720-?) immigrated to South Carolina from England about 1752 and settled in the Pee Dee region as a planter, later becoming a storekeeper, also. He was active in the affairs of the Parish of Prince Frederick Winyaw in the area, and held several civil and military offices. About 1762 or 1763, he moved to Charles Town where he was appointed to other public offices. Woodmason was popular and successful in the city until he made application to become a stamp distributer in 1765, which request, although unheeded, brought him into immediate disfavor. Perhaps this sudden change in attitude prompted him to seek the position of itinerant minister in the upper part of St. Mark's Parish, some eighty miles from Charles Town. The next year he went to England, as there was no Anglican bishop in America, and he was there ordained as a minister and licensed to work in South Carolina's St. Mark's Parish. Returning from England, he began his clerical duties throughout the Piedmont area, among people whom he spoke of as "the Back Inhabitants." Woodmason had become familiar with the people and their customs while conducting a store on Black Mingo Creek in the Pee Dee area. As their spokesman, he attacked the Assembly, Gadsden particularly, for the Lowcountry's system of "virtual" representation of the Backcountry. Perhaps his excoriation was influenced by Gadsden's leadership for repeal of the Stamp Act at the time Woodmason applied for the position of stamp distributer. He called Gadsden "the Scriblerus of the Libertines," and grouped him with other low-

*country leaders "who bounce, and make such Noise about Liberty!
Liberty! Freedom! Property! Rights! Privileges [sic]! and what
not; And at the same time keep half their fellow Subjects in a State
of Slavery."*

*During Woodmason's career as a minister in South Carolina, he
was constantly at odds with the newly-organised Light Baptists who
were competing with his Anglican program of worship and belief.
In 1772 he went to Virginia and, from time to time, visited churches
in Pennsylvania and Maryland. Finally, in 1774, Woodmason returned to England where in 1776 he asked aid as a Loyalist refugee
from the Bishop of London. Presumably he died in England, although neither the date nor place has been ascertained. See Richard
J. Hooker, ed., The Carolina Backcountry on the Eve of the Revolution (Chapel Hill: University of North Carolina Press, 1953), pp.
xi-xxxv, 260-78.*

March 28, 1769 [1]

Mr. Crouch,

I wish your Correspondent Sylvanus had at least postponed his
political Problem or Query, inserted in your last Paper, 'till he had
seen whether the present Assembly would confirm the Church-
Warden's Return (that may be made for aught I know) of Members
for *a* Parish where it's [its] Back Inhabitants 'have been denied the
Liberty of voting,' because, in my humble Opinion, 'till such Confirmation from the House, the Query, so far from having any Dependence on, or connection with 'the Reasoning adopted by the two
last Assemblies of this Province,' is altogether premature, and impertinent, and has the appearance besides of coming from no friend
to those constitutional Liberties of the People, so well maintained
by those Assemblies he mentions, in *Union with* those All our Sister
Colonies on this Continent, especially where it seems to be insinuated that this Denial was *general* 'at the late Election,' including as
it may seem Every Parish extending to the Back Parts, not, as the
case really was, only at the election of a *single* Parish. What! because
the Church-Warden or Wardens of *one* Parish (or suppose more) in
the Province may have acted improperly, (which has been, and will
be, often the Case) is it *therefore* to be concluded the Assembly or
whole Body of Representatives will do so too. I do not know whom
Mr. Sylvanus may have conversed with since 'the late Election,'
I am sure I have not been in Company with one person in or out of

---

[1] Charles Crouch's *South Carolina Gazette and Country Journal*, March 28,
1769. Published in Hooker, *Carolina Backcountry on Eve of Revolution. . .,*
pp. 264-5.

the Assembly, but such as appeared concerned for what happened in *that Parish* Election, and made no Hesitation to declare, they looked upon it (if conducted as represented) to be illegal and void, to all Intents and Purposes.

It is to be hoped all such artful Insinuations and mischievous *Catches,* as well as every political Legerdemain whatever, to divide 'the Interior and Frontier Inhabitants from those in the Towns and upon the Sea Coasts, and *from one another,* in order to set us by the Ears together, to divert us from the Grand *Common* concern, at this momentous Crisis, not only of All the Inhabitants of the Province and their Posterity, but also of All British America, will be seen through before it is too late, and we are rivited in a Slavery beyond Redemption, and by far exceeding that of the Subjects of any absolute Monarch in Europe, who have but *one* Master to please, and he *at Home* with them, whereas we at this vast Distance shall have some Hundreds at least, if the late Measures are fixed upon us, and the Scriptures tell us no Man can serve Two Masters.[2]

YOURS & C. AMERICUS BRITANNUS

Charles-Town, April 1, 1769.

---

[2] Woodmason was still serving St. Mark's Parish when he wrote the letter signed "Sylvanus," to which Gadsden sent this reply, and also when he responded to Gadsden's letter shortly after this one was published. Woodmason asserted that the inhabitants of St. Paul's "were refus'd Polling" in his first letter, that "Inhabitants of other Parishes [were] also prevented from giving Suffrage."

Woodmason noticed that Gadsden had failed to protest and take the side of the St. Paul voters when the election had been "voted irregular." He explained why this took place:

> For they put a Note into the Gazettes, that the day of Election would be on such a day of the Month—Which the Back Inhabitants rely'd on Whereas the Writs mention'd a Prior day—So that when the People came down in a Body to vote—Lo! the Election was past and Gone, Ten days— And all the Satisfaction they could obtain was, to be told, that it was an Error of the Printers—To such mean Arts had they recourse!

From the time of the Townshend crisis of which Woodmason speaks here, Gadsden represented the urban parishes of St. Michael's and St. Philip's, where he had the strength and backing of the mechanics. As to "frontier" inhabitants, Woodmason claimed rightly that they held little representation because the parishes extended only to the Saluda River. Hooker, *op. cit.,* pp. 262-3. For further information on the problems of the Backcountry and Woodmason, *see* Richard Maxwell Brown, *The South Carolina Regulators* (Cambridge: Harvard University Press, 1963), pp. 182 *et passim.*

TO THE PLANTERS, MECHANICS, AND FREEHOLDERS OF THE PROVINCE OF SOUTH CAROLINA, NO WAYS CONCERNED IN THE IMPORTATION OF BRITISH MANUFACTURES

Resistance to the Townshend Acts of 1767 came very late to South Carolina. But in March 1769, under the prodding of Gadsden and his mechanics, Charles Town finally protested. By June, the mechanics and planters had agreed to the Articles of Association, the boycott of British goods. The Articles included ordinances against importing British manufactures and encouraged the production of American goods. On this last point, the merchants who drew up Articles of their own would not comply, thereby undermining the unity of opposition to Great Britain. But because of Gadsden's influence, the merchants finally relented although there still remained many stubborn, individual traders and transients. Among these, for instance, were the Scottish factors against whom Gadsden aimed this essay. See Sellers, op. cit., p. 206; Walsh, "Christopher Gadsden," loc. cit., 198-9.

June 22, 1769 [1]

Gentlemen,

Permit a fellow citizen, without farther apology, or the imputation of presumption, to offer you his sentiments, at this most *alarming* crisis, when we are visibly on the very brink of a steep precipice, and nothing but GOD's blessing on our own immediate Prudence, Union and Firmess, can prevent our being plunged headlong from it, into *irrecoverable* ruin and distress.

To flatter you, my friends, I never did at any time; at this, it would be little less than betraying you. Whatever then we may think of ourselves, we are as real Slaves as those we are permitted to command, and differ only in degree. For what is a slave, but one that is at the will of his master, and has no property of his own, but on the most precarious tenure. To this deplorable, this adbject situation, have we been reduced, by the oppressive and unconstitutional measures again revived, since the repeal of the Stamp-Act, and

---

[1] *SCG,* June 22, 1769.

particularly by several late acts of P[arliamen]t; one for rasing a revenue in America, the others for extending the jurisdiction of the admiralty. By the first, *our monies have been taken from us, without our* consent, by the last, in cases that come under those acts. We are deprived of our best inheritance, *a trial by* Jury *and the* Law Of The Land: when at the same time, one of these very acts takes especial care, to secure a continuance of these invaluable blessings, in like cases, to *our fellow subjects* residing in Great-Britain. What a melancholy, what a heart-burning distinction is here! And this is not all; for, if we have but eyes that see, and ears that hear, we can not but discover that the deepest scheme of Systematical Slavery is *preparing* for Us, to which the acts now complained of seem only to be *mere preludes*. Can we then hesitate one moment longer, to unite with our brother sufferers in the other colonies, in the Only Probable Means of averting so horid a train of perils as are staring us in the face: namely, that of coming into A General Resolution, *not to consume one farthing more of* British Manufactures *than we can possibly avoid?*

To suffer ourselves to listen to, or be amused with, any more idle tales, that *these acts will be* Repealed, upon a constitutional footing, if we are *quiet and easy,* can only serve to demonstrate, that our understandings are already sunk a degree lower, if possible, than the infamous situation those acts have already placed us in.

We have known, long since, that, 'tis the general opinion of most thinking men in this province, supported by that of all America, and of all our friends in Great-Britain besides, that Such a Conduct, *firmly, faithfully,* and *generally,* adhered to, must inevitably answer our expectations; regain our rights; and restore us again to the *honourable rank* of Freemen. Almost every one of you continually declaring his *assent* to this doctrine, as often as he hears it mentioned, there seems only to be wanted, to carry it into full and immediate execution, a General Form of Agreement,[2] enumerating, as nearly as may be, the articles we cannot at present do without. This at the foot hereof, you will see attempted. I wish sincerely, it had been undertaken by a better hand; but, having waited in vain, 'till there is not a moment longer to lose, I hope my friends, you will accept what I offer, in good part, such as it is; the substance of it having been mentioned to several gentlemen, it met in general their approbation.

The Importers of *European* goods will find themselves left out in *that form,* as well as in this address. I beg leave therefore, to assure *some* of them, whose love for the rights of all their fellow-subjects,

---

[2] *See* pp. 86 ff. for Articles of Association.

and firm attachment to the true interest of this province, I am fully persuaded of, that my leaving *them* out, upon this occasion, is owing solely to the manifest impropriety of doing otherwise; as they are only a part, and a *small part* too, of a body that, according to Lord H[illsborou]gh,[3] treated a proposal of this sort, last fall, with that Silent *contempt* his Lordship thought it deserved. Besides, we know very well, that the greatest number of these gentlemen are Strangers, many of them of a very few years standing in this province. And notwithstanding the numberless most obliging letters many of you must doubtless have received from one or other of them, courting your custom, and concluding with professions of the greatest *respect, regard,* and *esteem,* have They shewn, or attempted to shew, any thing, but an altogether *confined* regard to Themselves, and their own *private interest?* Have you had *real friends* enough amongst them to procure even One Meeting of the *Importers of European goods* to consult what they could and might do, to merit the continuance of your custom, by shewing a grateful inclination to assist and relieve you on this trying occasion; although almost every newspaper informs them, of the generous and exemplary sacrifices made, by great numbers of truly patriotic gentlemen, in the same business with them, to the Northward? So far from doing any thing like this, has not, on the contrary, every *difficulty* been Strained to the utmost, and your understandings been rather affronted, with numberless *weak* and *groundless reasons* that have been suggested, and *whispered* about, in order to frighten and deter you from acting as you ought on this occasion? Suppose you were to follow the *selfish* example these gentlemen have set you, might you soon, very soon, feelingly convince them, that You *may* do without *them,* but They *cannot* without *you?*

Now, can it be prudent, my friends, when our All is at stake, to leave it to the disposal of *such* a body, so composed, whose natural affection to the province is, too plainly, not to be depended on, and whose *private interest* is Glaringly against us? Must we not be infatuated, to the highest degree, to do so, and, in such case, deserve to be treated with More than *silent contempt* for men's *actions,* not their *professions,* on interesting occasions, are what, in our judgment of them, we ought to regard?

---

[3] Willis Hill (1718-1793), former president of the Board of Trade and Plantations, was appointed on January 20, 1768, Secretary of State for the colonies. He had instructed Governor Francis Bernard of Massachusetts to force the General Court to rescind resolutions against the Townshend Revenue Act, but the members refused, instead proposing non-importation, a proposal which was circulated throughout the colonies. In Charles Town, it was at first treated with "silent contempt," partly because of Hill's instructions to the lower Houses to ignore it, but more importantly because of the conservative merchants' reluctance. However, in time a boycott received the backing of the radicals. *DNB,* IX, 878-80; Greene, *op. cit.,* p. 374; Sellers, *op. cit.,* p. 204.

You are the Supporters of These gentlemen, the *consumers* of the articles They import, and upon YOU the taxes and burthens they are loaded with ultimately fall. Add to this, that it may be of no little moment to Lord H.......gh, or any future minister, as well as *these gentlemen* themselves, know assuredly, that whatever consequence he and they may think Them of, when You are but determined to set heartily about it, *both* cannot fail of being soon thoroughly convinced of their mistake, and that you know very well yourselves, what means to make use of, to recover your constitutional rights, without consulting *them* at all upon the occasion. Only let the freeholders and fixed settlers of the province Resolve *not to purchase,* and such a *wise* and *prudent* body of men will, *of their own accord* determine, I warrant you, as immediately, *not to import;* or if they do, what must be the consequence? And will not such a resolution be far more safe, easy and honourable, to you, than to listen to the appointment of any committee, or number of committees, however chose and formed, that may be proposed? And here we cannot be too cautious, lest a *mis-timed tenderness* for a few real friends, we have the justest reason to be assured we have among *these* gentlemen importers, may not outweigh, in one scale, our regard to posterity, and the distresses and tears of every American, in the other. *These* friends cannot, will not, I am persuaded, desire any risk should be run, or any less promising or effectual means be pursued, upon *their* accounts. We have no time now to try experiments. The most simple, speedy and probable means, such as will not produce quarrels, create much trouble that we all know will not be taken, or make only a *specious shew, without doing* (or perhaps, by many, intending) *any thing* are what alone ought to be adopted. If we would act like men of firmness, and real lovers of our country, the *private partial interest* of a few *Individuals* now existing, will not, by any means, be put in competition with the *lasting welfare* of All America, and All *their posterity.*

Give me leave, my friends, to remind you of the noble spirit you were actuated with at the time of the Stamp-Act, which then enabled this province to do as essential service to the common cause, as any, without exception, in America. The disgrace our neighbours in S[avanna]h were then brought into, by a partial use of the stamps in that *town,* served only to fire you the more, and to put you the more upon your guard. The same attempt here, by a set of the like interested, cunning, *systematical gentlemen,* tho' countenanced by some men of real worth (deceived, cajoled and intimidated by those masterly fawning dissemblers) had not the least influence upon your conduct. You *persevered* in the noble resolution you had taken, and by that means, with God's blessing, saved your country from thraldom and disgrace. But what is become of this spirit, my friends? Is it already, so soon tired with struggling for *your* Liberties, or, is it altogether evaporated, not one spark of it left! Like a mere Ignis fatuus, that suddenly and surprizingly (I hope not merely accidentally) started up at *that* time, and immediately after *vanished,* and that for ever? Are you now contented to let the same sett of crafty, dissembling, insinuating men, mere *timewatchers,* carry *their* point against you, when you can with infinetly more ease and safety, counterwork them now, than you could then? I hope not. Only be Rouzed from your sleep; dare to See the *truth,* to *Support* the truth, and the God of truth will make you FREE. I mean, not by any means, my friends, to endeavour to work you up to any act contrary to the strictest peace and good order, being well convinced, such act will do infinetly more mischief than good. Only let us join in, and keep close to, the resolution just proposed, and all we wish for is evidently before us.

I would only observe here, by the bye, that it seems amazing, and altogether unaccountable, that our mother country should take almost every means in her power, to drive her colonies to some desperate act; for what else can be the motive (besides oppressing them) of treating them with that contempt she upon all occasions affects to do? They are sneeringly told, they begin *now* to know themselves and her; and that *one* or *two* regiments at most, could march thro' the continent of America, from one end to the other. The *colonists,* by this, must certainly be taken for greater *cowards* than *East-India* Sepoys; or it never could be thought, were they disposed to be independent, that even thirty of the best regiments Great-Britain can boast of, would be able to march thro' *half* the province of North-America. She certainly forgets, that the people of the *New-England governments alone,* by their conquest of Cape-Breton, procured a peace for her in 1748, above *twenty years* ago, nor can she point out during the whole course of the last war, in what battle the *Americans* turned their backs; and particularly, it will not be denied, that, at the defeat of the rash, but brave, General Braddock, the *preservation* of great numbers of the King's regular troops, was *then* greatly owing to the *distinguished conduct* and *courage* of the *Americans,* on that melancholy occasion. Again She certainly does not consider that, by these oppressive and unconstitutional acts, she imprudently tries to *dissolve* the *principal* the *strongest* tie of our dependence. For in other respects, particularly those of a mercantile nature, are not several trading powers of Europe better customers to some of the colonies, for their productions than she is? For instance, what an insignificant part of our main staple, Rice, is consumed in Great-Britain? Not above five thousand barrels at most. And can she be so blind, or absurd, as to think, that if distress, dispair, and self-interest, should cooperate with any fair and safe opportunity, that in the course of some future war, may be given a better customer, who possibly may then have *more* than *two* regiments ready to land in America, that such dastardly wretches, as we are insinuated to be, may not only be afraid to refuse, but glad to jump at a change that we are sure, in such circumstances, cannot be for the worse? But to return,

You must expect, Gentlemen, to have some of the like difficulties and objections, to engage with now, as you had at the time of the *Stamp-Act. Men* of *arbitrary principles,* and wholly devoted to their *private self-interest,* are full as much awake *now,* as they were *then;* and were they not, the resolutions now proposed will, no doubt, effectually rouze them. But, for your comfort, the obstacles to encounter, are not *so great,* or *so many* now, as then, and you are better prepared by the experience of those times.

Though, I am persuaded, many of you must think, *every thing ought to be risked,* rather than lose the *two main rights* we are contending for, the distinguishing characteristicks of Englishmen; yet it may not be amiss to lay before you, a few of the flimsy pretences made by *some,* for not joining in the common cause; the bare mentioning whereof, will be exposing them sufficiently.

'Tis acknowledged we cannot, as yet, go so great lengths in this matter as our brethren in the *Northern* colonies. You will meet with men who are therefore, for our doing *nothing at all.* They will pitifully tell you, that the stand these provinces make is *sufficient;* and why should we trouble ourselves about it? What a contemptible opinion must such men, as these, have of the principles and understanding of the persons they broach such doctrines to? In a matter of the Utmost Consequence, we find we are not able to do *so much as we wish;* we must *not* therefore shew our goodwill and countenance to the common cause, by doing as much as we can? What sort of reasoning is this?

Others, with an affected zeal for the cause, will tell *homespun! homespun!* is the thing; if they could but get homespun, they would grudge no price for it. 'Tis plain, this is too often mere affectation because these men must know, that no considerable quantity of homespun is to be got, as yet, in the province. And when you talk to them about promoting a general scheme of oeconomy, and wearing our old clothes as long as they will last, buying from hand to mouth, and not a farthing more than can possibly be avoided, they will shake their heads, and tell you, in a common cant phrase, *Thats not the thing.*

Some will *very gravely* tell you, that if we join the other colonies in this matter, we shall *exasperate* the merchants of Great-Britain, and they will send us no ships next year and then, *what shall we do with our crops?* But the men who would impose such stuff for reasoning, are generally very cautious to whom they *whisper it*: well knowing, that we are largely indebted to those merchants, for negroes as well as other Articles; and they Will send their ships, for *their own* sakes, not ours. And besides, if we were clear of debt, to be the carriers, annually, of 130 or 140,000 barrels of rice, besides many other bulky articles; to have the commissions, *etc.,* on the gross sales thereof, and on all our indico, is so *tempting* a bait, that few know better the futility of this objection than the very men who raise it, it serving only to alarm persons totally unacquainted with the very first principles of trade.

I come now to the last, and what many say and think is the *greatest difficulty* of all we have to encounter, that is, to persuade our wives to give us their assistance, without which 'tis impossible to succeed. I allow of the impossibility of succeeding without their concurrence. But, for my part, so far from doubting that we shall have it, I could wish, as our political salvation, at this crisis, depends altogether upon the strictest oeconomy, that the women could, with propriety, have the principal management thereof; for 'tis well known, that none in the world are better oeconomists, make better wives or more tender mothers, than ours. Only let their husbands point out the necessity of such a conduct; convince them, that it is the only thing that can save them and their children, from distresses, slavery, and disgrace; their affections will soon be awakened, and co-operate with their reason.[4] When that is done, all that is necessary will be done; for I am persuaded, that they will be then as anxious and persevering in this matter, as any the most zealous of us can possibly wish; for where is that hard hearted mother or wife to be found, when properly warned, that every farthing she lays out, even *unavoidably* and *necessarily,* for herself and family, in *European goods,* tends only to encrease a power, that is, at that very time, distressing herself, her family, her dearest friends and relations, in the most essential and tender manner, and doing all it can to reduce them to the lowest infamy and disgrace. I say, where is that woman to be found (I am persuaded not in *Carolina*) who, when informed of this by her husband, that will not, so far from laying out at this

---

[4] This appeal to the Ladies of South Carolina was taken up again during the resistance to the Tea Act by the Reverend William Tennent, radical cohort of Gadsden in 1776. *See* Newton B. Jones, "Writings of the Reverend William Tennent, 1740-1777," *SCHM,* LXI (July, 1960), 129-45; (October, 1960), 189-209.

time any thing unnecessarily, be rather much grieved and distressed to find herself obliged, upon any occasion, to buy any the least article of British manufacture that her family cannot do without. I am very sure, our Women will not bear the thought that the ruin of their family may be laid at their door; they are not such absolute slaves to dress as hath been too often and too sneeringly represented; and I cannot but be persuaded, that *those of affluent and easy fortunes* throughout the province will, by their steady and good example, upon this important and trying occasion, manifest their sensibility of the distresses of their country, as well as how greatly they have been injured and misrepresented; and would they but postpone wearing their silks, or, at least refrain from *purchasing new,* 'till this heavy storm is overpast, it would certainly be a sacrifice worthy of them, save their country, and hand down their names to posterity with the greatest eclat.

Recollect, my friends, the many curious strategems you were continually surprized with, at the time of the Stamp-Act; the news from the West-Indies, from the Northward, etc., mostly coming by the flying, volunteer, *private-post,* at that time between this and S[avanna]h, all manifestly calculated to divert you from your intentions. Doubtless many pretty manoeuvres of this sort will be again played off. Regard none of them; never expect, or believe, these unconstitutional acts will be repealed, till you know, from certain and altogether *unsuspicious* authority, they are actually so. By this means, you will not be deceived as heretofore, by the artifices of any sett of *systematical Jacobites* whatever, whether in this town, S[avanna]h, or elsewhere. Dear *Charley*[5] is THEIR object; general confusion and uneasiness under oppressive, unconstitutional measures, can alone give Him any chance. This they all know, have long known, and visibly act accordingly. What becomes of *Old England,* or if reduced to be a *province of France,* they care not a farthing, provided their hopeful project succeeds. The Lord deliver us from the secret machinations of such wretches, and from any return of that detestable *Stuart* race! a race of pedants, pensioners and tyrants. But let me whisper these gents, without pretending to

---

[5] This is a reference to the Young Pretender, Charles Edward Stuart, and his Jacobite followers, the Scots, who failed to restore "the Chevalier," James Francis Edward Stuart, to the throne in 1716. "Bonny Prince Charlie" was still at large during this period, and the Scotch traders and factors came in for much abuse for their Jacobite views and their seeming adherence to absolutism which the radicals felt was merely an instrument by which they might engross "American" business. One Scotch mechanic was so upset by what he considered to be unfair opinions of Scotch traders that he protested loyalty of his fellow nationals to the American cause. *SCG,* July 4, 1774.

the gift of *second-sight,* that, however changed once more to the finest gentlemen in Europe, from being a great sot, and altogether lost and overlooked by all his friends (as some of us will remember was industriously given out a few years since) that Grand Favourite may be; and however their most sanguine expectations may be answered Elsewhere, which God forbid; yet even in that case, their pretty gentlemen would find it, with all his address, the most difficult thing he ever undertook, to get any the least footing on this side the water; so utterly are he and his family detested and abhorred, by at least 99 in 100 of all the *sons* of North-America. And the distresses which are now heaped upon them, greatly owing, as many imagine, to this general and *undisguised* spirit of the colonies, impossible to be unperceived by any of our *visitors of late years,* 'tis supposed, will not tend to encrease their esteen for him, or make his introduction amongst them the easier. It seems, we have lately, had a miniature of the Chevalier's charming open countenance most obligingly dropped amongst us. Did it, like the image of the great Goddess Diana of the Ephesians, fall down from Jupiter? Or how the Devil came it here? For what cause? *Not surely, that, we also may take and carefully keep such pretty little vauching vademecum copies of it, in order certainly and instantly to know, and engagingly fly to, the* Original, *upon occasion?* What Ideas must this naturally *leave* upon our minds at this time?

To conclude. We are now at a crisis wherein essential matters ought not be minced. I have therefore, my friends, though myself justified and obliged to speak, on this occasion, with that *freedom* the necessity of the times, and an anxiety, for the recovery and preservation of the common constitutional liberties of All the subjects of Great-Britain, to us Americans, prompt me to. When these foundation principles are well recovered, and once more firmly settled, every thing relative to the internal peace and welfare of the province, it is to be hoped, will follow of course; but till they are so, nothing can be expected of an honourable, durable or truly beneficial nature. For what is a *British subject,* or what are *our Assemblies,* while we are deprived of the rights we are contending for? And now, reader, well knowing by experience, and heartily despising the additional number of secret enemies a paper of this sort will necessarily expose me to, amongst the *purblind selfish,* the *cunning,* the *trimming,* and the *plausible;* and earnestly recommending to you, to consider what is *written,* not who *wrote* it, which is not of the least significancy.

Vive, Vale. Si quid novisti rectius istis Candidus imperti: si nil his utere mecum. [Live long, farewell. If you know something better than these precepts, pass it on, my good fellow. If not, join me in following these.] I am, GENTLEMEN Yours, & C.

PRO GREGE ET REGE

10 June 1769.

P.S. If the following Form Of Agreement is approved of, or some other to the same purpose, and generally entered into, I am told, a Plan of Association will be attempted to be set on foot, for the *planting* and *encouraging* Manufactures in this province, and for raising by subscription a fund for that purpose, wherein the easiness, practicability and utility of such an undertaking will be set forth at large.

FORM OF THE AGREEMENT

Whereas by an act of Parliament, imposing duties on sundry articles of commerce, with the express view of raising a revenue out of America, his Majesty's subjects residing there have their money taken from them unrepresented, consequently without their consent, contrary to one of the most fundamental principles of the English constitution, to which they have always thought themselves intitled. And Whereas by other acts, extending the jurisdiction of the admiralty, they find themselves, in cases that come under those acts, deprived of their best inheritance: trial by jury and the law of the land; at the same time this [inestimable?] blessing is secured by the very same statutes, in like cases, as our fellow subjects residing in Great-Britain, thereby making an invidious distinction, and affording one glaring and [woeful?] instance at least, of the partiality and mischief that attend legislation without representation. And Whereas all the humble petitions of such of the colonies as have had an opportunity to make them, for redress, have been rejected, and the prospect before us appears daily more and more gloomy and melancholy, We Therefore, the underwritten planters, mechanics, and freeholders of the province of South-Carolina, no ways concerned in the importation of British manufactures, being sensibly affected with the abject and distressful situation we are reduced to, by the operation of the aforesaid acts of parliament, and fully convinced of the necessity of exerting ourselves, without further delay, in a most firm, but peaceful manner, for obtaining relief, do, 'till, by the repeal of the said acts, we find ourselves restored to the honourable rank of freemen, and the enjoyment of those common essential, constitutional rights we are thereby deprived of, firmly and solemnly engage to, and with each other, as follows:

I. That we will give the preference to, and by all means in our power encourage, the use of North American Manufactures, when to be had; particularly of any make in this province, as Hats, Shoes, Stockings, and Leather Breeches, Saddles, Cordage, cut and dried and pigtail Tobacco, Bar Iron, *etc. etc.*

II. That we will be as sparing as possible, in the use of all *British* manufactures.

III. That we will, after the signing this agreement, use No Mourning of any sort, upon the death or at the funeral, of any of our friends and relations; nor, upon any account whatever, give away any scarves and gloves, upon such occsaions, or any thing else of *British* manufactures in lieu thereof.[6]

IV. That we will purchase only the following articles of British manufacture: For Our Plantations And Several Employments:

Negro Cloth, Blanketing and Osnabrugs, Plantation Tools, and Other Tools necessary for our several occupations, Canvas, Nails, Powder, Bar Lead, Shot, Oakum, Salt, Coal, Woolcards, and Card Wire.

For Winter Wear For Ourselves And Sons:

Coarse Cloth, not exceeding *Fifty Shillings* per yard currency, always giving the preference to Blue.

And For Our Summer Wear:

The cheapest Fustians, or articles of that sort . . . For stockings and Linens, when not to be had of *American* manufacture, we will not give more than *Thirty Shillings* a pair for the one, and *Twenty Shillings* a yard for the other.

V. That in the use of Such Articles as may be wanted for our Families, our Wives and Daughters and Younger Children, Furniture for our Houses, and Tables, that we cannot do without, and cannot get of American make, we will be as frugal as possible, recommending the strictest oeconomy.

---

[6] This refers to the practice at funerals of giving gloves; scarfs; and rings containing a miniature of the departed one, as a remembrance. These articles were presented to close friends and members of the family, but the ceremony was discarded on the eve of the Revolution as aristocratic and British. Generally, such items were imported, even though there were local artisans who manufactured them. Gadsden gained much "publicity" when he broke the tradition at the funeral of his wife Mary Hasell, in 1765. The abandonment of the custom marked the man who supported American rights thereafter.

VI. That in the use of Tea, Paper, Glass and Painters Colours, we will be particularly sparing, 'till the duties on these articles are taken off.

IN TESTIMONY *of our full assent to the foregoing agreement, we have hereunto set our hands, according to the dates placed against each of our names respectively.*

N.B. Gentlemen inclinable to promote this interesting matter in their several parishes, may have printed copies of this form of agreement, with sufficient room at the bottom and back thereof, for numbers of subscribers, at TIMOTHY's Printing Office.

William Henry Drayton

William Henry Drayton (1742-1779) was an advocate of British rights in 1769 during the resistance to the Townshend Revenue Act. His attack on the mechanics and his contest with Gadsden brought him unpopularity in Charles Town, and he departed for England where he was hailed as the Crown's champion. He was appointed by King George III as privy councillor for the Province of South Carolina, and on his way to America in 1772, Drayton received the appointment also as assistant judge. Aspiring to the chief justiceship, he was passed over for a native-born Englishman, and this together with the frustration he suffered at the hands of another British placeman over his scheme to lease Indian land, caused him to embrace the American cause. As one of the young "aggressive aristocrats," extremely wealthy, Drayton then took a prominent part in the Revolutionary movement, and urged Carolinians on the open road to rebellion. Drayton served on the Secret Committee, and was President of the Council of Safety, becoming a scourge of loyalism. In 1776, he was named Chief Justice of the Province under the new government. Drayton was elected to the Continental Congress in 1778 where he vigorously prosecuted the war, serving until his death in Philadelphia from typhus fever, September 3, 1779. William M. Dabney and Marion Dargon, William Henry Drayton and the American Revolution (Albuquerque: University of New Mexico, 1962), pp. 25-207.

Letters of Freeman [1]

Summary

1769

Gadsden attacked William Henry Drayton and William Wragg for claiming that the boycott, (the Articles of Association), against England to secure repeal of the Townshend Revenue Act was unconstitutional. He asserted that the boycott was "strictly justifiable" upon natural and constitutional principles, the British Ministry having forfeited that right to the people because of its misuse of power. Gadsden maintained that Americans, without recourse short of force, had united in the boycott to protect their natural rights, and that the Articles of Association should be successful because of the resulting unemployment in England, a state the Ministry could not ignore. He commented that the Association was the best method of bringing Parliament to the realization of its errors, among which he thought was the "impolitic" policy of laying duties on Britain's manufactures. Such parliamentary, tyrannical disputes, he said, disrupted and reduced imperial trade at a time when other nations were trying to build their commerce, and that these "oppressive measures tend . . . to bring on, rather than prevent," the independence of America." Independence for Americans, he thought, would be "the greatest misfortune that could befall them, excepting losing . . . their rights and liberties."

When William Wragg raised the point that a reduction by the merchants on the interest on loans would serve the people better than the extra-legal Association, Gadsden retorted that such a proposal had little to do with securing American rights. Furthermore, he said, legislation would have to follow the natural laws of trade; otherwise, economic injury would result.

To Alexander Gillon, who had been "published" by the Committee to enforce the boycott because it was "inimical to American Rights," Gadsden observed that his monetary losses were secondary to the general aim. He appealed for continental support of the boycott, saying that in "arbitrary governments, tyranny generally descends . . . from rank to rank, through the people, till almost the whole weight of it, at last, falls upon the honest farmer, mechanic, and day

---

[1] Drayton, *Letters of Freeman.* Gadsden is identified in the Preface to the book under the pseudonym "Member of the Assembly and Signer of the Resolutions" and the initials, "C.G." His three essays are on pages 16-22; 155-90; 211-26. These and the other essays, by Wragg, John Mackenzie, "a Mechanic," and Drayton, written in the form of letters to Editor Peter Timothy, were compiled from the issues of the *South Carolina Gazette*, September–December 1769 and republished by Drayton. Copies of *Freeman* are in the South Caroliniana Library and the Library of Congress.

DRAWING OF GADSDEN'S WHARF
By Vernon Bailey Howe, 1906

laborer. When this happens, it must make them poor, almost ir-
remediably poor indeed!"

Gadsden lastly appealed to the rich planters and merchants to
act with benevolence and give the example to the lesser man by
supporting the resolutions.

To John Swift

John Swift (1720-1802), merchant and City Councilman (1757-1767) of Philadelphia, known as the "Old Collector," was an outstanding socialite. Swift with some other gentlemen inaugurated the famous Philadelphia Assemblies, the first, traditionally, having been held at Swift's home. Thomas Willing Balch, "The Swift Family of Philadelphia," Penn. Mag. Hist. and Biog., XXX (1906), 129-58.

Charles Town So. Carolina [1]

6 September 1770

Dear Sir:

My Brother James Gadsden going by this Opportunity to Philadelphia and intending to return with my Son and Daughter (Mr. and Mrs. Rutledge) [2] whom he expects to meet there, I coul'd not deny myself the Pleasure of writing to you by him, and shall be much obliged to you to introduce him to Mrs. Lydia McCall's [3] family and to the rest of our Worthy Friends. His stay with you will be very short. He expects to be back again here in November. I wrote to Mrs. McCall by my Daughter who went by Way of Rhode Island.

I am Sir with sincerest Wishes for the Welfare of your Family. Yr. most obdt. Servt.

CHRIST GADSDEN.

---

[1] Dearborn Collection, Houghton Library, Harvard University. The letter is addressed: "To John Swift, Esq. % favour of Mr. James Gadsden."

[2] Elizabeth Gadsden (1729-1775) and Andrew Rutledge (1740-1772). They were married 26 September, 1767. He was a merchant in Charleston and brother to John and Edward Rutledge. Elizabeth later, after being widowed, married Thomas Ferguson, also a merchant, August 2, 1774. *SCHM*, XXXI, 12.

[3] Lydia Abbott McCall (d. 1795) is noted as a socially prominent lady in Gregory B. Keen's "The Descendants of Joren Kyn, the Founder of Upland," *Penn. Mag. Hist. and Biog.*, V (1881), 458-9.

To Samuel Adams

Samuel Adams (1722-1802) of Braintree, Massachusetts, perhaps America's first professional politician, was the leading colonial protagonist of independence; Gadsden has been called his Southern counterpart. As chairman of the Masschusetts Committee of Correspondence, Adams remained in close touch with Gadsden and other provincial radicals. An astute and tireless political organizer, Adams utilized the thoughts of such men as James Otis, Richard Bland, Patrick Henry, and Gadsden, to give cause and reason for revolution. John C. Miller, Samuel Adams: Pioneer in Propaganda (Boston: Little, Brown and Company, 1936). The Writings of Samuel Adams, Harry Alonzo Cushing, ed., 4 vol. (New York: G. P. Putnam's Sons, 1906), I, 108; III, 141-3; IV, 285.

Chas. Town So. Carolina [1]

23 May 1774

Dear Sir:

I received your obliging favor handing to me the Letter w[hi]ch your committee honour'd me with. I am pretty sure I answer'd the last Letter received from you and shou'd have continued writing but many affecting Circumstances in my little Family intervening those together with a large Wharf or rather, quay, the largest in America, which I undertook at first to relieve my Mind for the almost insupportable Loss of my eldest Son, a very promising youth of about sixteen years old, has so taken up my attention that unless when the Assembly was sitting I very seldom appear'd in publick.[2] It always gives me the highest pleasure to receive a Line from you. Your Perseverance and Firmness in the Cause of Liberty do Honour to America and I almost envy you for the particular Notice Mr. Wedderburn has been pleased to take of you in his defense of Hutchinson or more properly in his abuse of Dr. Franklyn.[3]

---

[1] Samuel Adams Papers, NYPL.

[2] Gadsden's son was Christopher (1750-1766).

[3] Alexander Wedderburn was Solicitor General of England. Wedderburn denounced Benjamin Franklin before the Privy Council for Franklin's part in the downfall of Governor Thomas Hutchinson of Massachusetts. Franklin had

You will see by the inclosed to your gentlemen of the committee how matters have been conducted here, numbers of the Trading part have separated themselves from the general Interest and neglected our publick Meetings excepting when an extraordinary point is wanted to be carryed. At our last Meeting about two Months since chiefly by these means it was agreed that no Tea *at all* shou'd be imported, contrary to the Opinion of the steady supporters of the Cause of Liberty here, who were for restraining that Matter only to Tea that *wou'd pay the Duty.* However these were glad to lay hold of any Thing to bring us to some general agreement and tho' they argued very strenuously against exposing themselves to unnecessary and impolitick Temptations, yet when that Measure was carryed, were amongst the first to sign it but were followed by very few in Trade, who were the principle promoters of it, under a pretense truly that that was doing Nothing, that the agreement ought to extend to Wine Coffee *etc.* The Design of these *overvirtuous* Gentry was easily seen through, yet vexed and chargren'd as we were at such treacherous Behaviour, we cou'd not help smiling at so sudden and extraordinary a Change.

You must not always judge of the Sentiments of the People of Carolina by their Public Meetings in Town [4] where (I don't know how it is with you, but so it is with us) all the Ministerial men in the Province almost to a man are collect'd, and are artful and strenuous in their Opposition. The Country Gentlemen are hearty and spirited but supine and I am sorry to say that few of them will give themselves the Trouble purposely to come down to attend the publick Meetings; however I am in hopes that this affair relating to your government will effectually rouse them. We are a weak Colony from the Number of Negroes we have amongst us, and therefore exposed to more formid[able?] ministerial Tricks than that *pretended* to be for you; however I think you may depend that when our assembly

---

somehow secured Hutchinson's correspondence with Thomas Whately, a former member of Parliament, who was secretary to George Grenville. The letters were inimical to American rights. Franklin sent the correspondence to Samuel Adams and other Massachusetts radicals, instructing them that it should be read in private and returned secretly. Adams, however, made political capital out of the letters, and revealed Franklin's role in the affair. Miller, *Samuel Adams,* pp. 278-81.

[4] After 1769, the chief organ of public opinion on revolutionary moves became the "Meeting of the Inhabitants," whose will was executed by a General Committee composed of "Planters, Merchants, and Mechanics." These meetings represented the town and lowcountry, but not the backcountry, although, when America was on the brink of war, some representation was accorded the west. The Provincial Congress developed out of this extra-legal body. *SCG's,* 1769-1776; *Extracts from the Journals of the Provincial Congress of South Carolina,* William Edwin Hemphill, and Wylma Anne Wates, eds. (Columbia: The South Carolina Archives Department, 1960), pp. xvi-xviii.

meets to do Business that every abhomine of our Mother-in-Law's Intentions toward you will be shewn, and if any Thing occurs that you think can be done by us for the Service of your Province at this interesting juncture, you may depend upon my at least taking the first favourable Opportunity that offers with propriety to move it, or procure it to be moved to the House.

I am Dr. Sir with great Sincerity
Yr. obliged hble. servt.

Christ Gadsden

Charles Town [1]

5th June 1774

Dear Sir:

I did myself the Honour to write to you and the Gentlemen of the Committee for your Town the 23 Ult since which (only two or three days ago) we first saw that diabolical Act of the British Parliament Respecting you which has rais'd our utmost resentment and Detestation and hope will produce the desired Effect of Rousing us from our Supinness.[2] We know the distress your town must be under and feel for and Sympathize with its Inhabitants Extremely, and at the same time, we will not doubt their Firmness. Inclos'd is Copy of a Letter wrote to the Committee of Philadelphia in answer to one Received from them a few days Since. We are at a Loss to know what General Plan will be adopted by the Northern Provinces; when we do, I am persuaded you may depend that we will join thereunto to the utmost of our Power and when once Entered heartily, you will I hope find us *as before* the Last to desert the Cause.[3] The Overhasty breaking through and forsaking the first Resolutions without previously consulting or so much as acquainting

---

[1] Samuel Adams Papers, NYPL.

[2] The Boston Port Bill, March 31, 1774.

[3] Much resentment was harbored by South Carolinans at the ending of the Association in 1770 by northern colonies even though the Parliament, while repealing the Townshend revenue measure, kept a tax on tea to maintain the principle of supremacy. New York was the first to "break" the Association, and other colonies followed rapidly. More conservative, Carolina elements utilized this rupture, reminding the radicals that the northerners would desert them if their interests so dictated, leaving Carolina alone. Gadsden's letter indicates that, contrary to Carl Becker's observation, (*op. cit.,* pp. 93-94), New York's apparent, unpatriotic selfishness was not displayed as a bad example by the radicals but instead was used by pro-British men to sow seeds of disunity. *See* Benjamin Woods Labaree, *The Boston Tea Party* (New York: Oxford University Press, 1964), pp. 46-50.

our Committee therewith disgusted many and has been the Principle and most successful handle made Use of by our Anti-American Jesuits here to deter us from Farther Engagements. Our town is filled with ministerial Gentlemen: some in Place and ten times that Number out of Place in expectation of Being soon provided for *according to their Merit,* therefore more formidable, who are pleased and tickled no doubt in their Heads with this Act and promise themselves much therefrom in reversion. For as King James the first in his Journey from Scotland to London said of a Baronet whose noble and delightful seat highly pleased him, that he would make a Bonny Rebel, so I am persuaded there are not a few Amongst us who are hopeful that this Act will Occasion many Bonny Rebels in America. Pray let us know as soon as Possible what is determin'd upon. We will not think so basely of you as to Imagine you will pay for One Ounce of the Tea; whatever of moment is done here you may depend on being Acquainted with. If matters are carried to Extremities, from which they cannot be far now, I hope every one of us will be ready at all Hazards to avert by every means in our Power the abject Slavery intended for us and our posterity; for my part I would rather see my own family reduced to the utmost Extremity and half cut to pieces than to submit to their damned Machinations. I observe your Owners of wharfes Quays *etc.,* are particularly levell'd at upon this Occasion; they are all it seems to be made dependant on the ministrey. I have been above Seven Years at hard Labour and the utmost Risk of my Constitution about one of the most extensive Quays in America during which Time no negroe in any of our swamps has been more exposed, at which thirty of the largest Ships that can come over our Bar can be Loading at the Same time and all afloat at low water with their whole loads in, and have exceeding good and Convenient Stores already expected thereon Sufficient to Maintain Sixteen thousand Tierce of Rice. In short in this affair all my Fortune is embarked and by God's Goodness my plan is very nearly completed yet, and notwithstanding this act against you is manifestly held up in terrorem and it has been for some time strongly insinuated ever since Lord Hailes call'd our assembly to Port Royal that if we are not *Quiet* we may expect the seat of Government will be removed thither;[4] still my Friends

---

[4] The Commons House of Assembly appropriated money in 1769 for the support of John Wilkes, the English political reformer, but the Council and Governor vetoed the bill. The House countered by denying that the Council was an upper house of legislature, asserting that it alone could issue money bills. As in the time of the Boone controversy, the South Carolina House sat but would not legislate until the Governor and Council conceded, virtually ending royal provincial government. On October 8, 1772, in order to decrease the influence of the town's radicals on the House, Governor Charles Greville Montagu temporarily removed the seat of government from Charlestown to

may be assured that I trust in God. No motives whatever will make me neglect or slacken in the common cause as I hope I would sooner see every inch of my Quay (my whole fortune) totally destroyed. Rather than be even Silent much more give up or persuade Others to give up one essential Point therein. Let the ministrey change our Ports of Entrey to what distance from Charlestown as often as the Devil shall put it in their heads; you cannot imagine what pleasure and Satisfaction it gives us here to find that at least eleven out of the twenty-nine Gentlemen who signed that Spirited Petition to the Parliament while the Horrid bill against Boston *was machinating,* are natives of this Colony; at home or abroad, in good Report or Ill report, it gives us the highest gratification to see that Carolina Hearts beat [in] unison to the Common cause and if you can but furnish us with a Receipt Effectually to cure supineness which is all our political disorder, for our Hearts are otherwise good as I wrote you before *ens* [*eris*] *mihi magnus Appollo* [You will be for me the great Apollo.] and then we'll make the Jesuitical mist of cunning vanish before us. I am not sorry to hear that Americans are looked upon in London with such Contempt. For my part, I wish it may increase while our mother *in law* behaves as she does; it will I hope keep our Gents more in their own country and be productive of many other Salutary Effects. Only 29 Americans to be found in London to sign their name in Opposition to so horrid an Act seems very strange indeed. We ought and hope will assist one another to the utmost and bear our private Sufferings with Fortitude, always presenting to our minds how many Generations, how many Millions depend with Regard to everything that is dear and valuable upon earth to human Beings upon our spirit and constancy at this alarming Hour. Our assembly setts this week and I am very hopeful that we shall meet with a proper spirit and convince you demonstratively that we Sympathize with you in deed whatever occurs then worth your notice I intend for the Subject of my next; in the interim I am Dr. Sir Your most Humbl. Obedt. Servt.

CHRIST GADSDEN

Port Royal, Beaufort, with no effect except to inflame the radicals further and give them an even more powerful voice. Jack P. Greene, "The Wilkes Fund Controversy in South Carolina," *Journal of Southern History,* XXIX (February, 1963), 3-52.

Charles Town 14th June 1774 [1]

Dear Sir:

I have just time enough to Acquaint you by this Opportunity that our Assembly was unexpectedly prorogued to the 2nd of August and to cover the Inclosed [below] by order of our Committee to the Gentlemen of yours, I wrote you very fully the 5th of this Instant and also on the 23rd of May when I did my self the Honour to write to your Committee; our Committee met last night and ordered a General meeting of the Inhabitants to be call'd the first Wednesday on July and such steps are taken to bring them together from all parts that I am hopefull we shall have a very full meeting. I am Sir your most Obdt. Hble. Servt.

CHRIST GADSDEN

ENCLOSURE

Gentlemen:

Our Committee met last night and ordered me to acquaint you that they are extremely sensible of the critical and distressing Situation to which the Liberties of the Americans are reduced by the late oppressive and unconstitutional act of Parliament, and most sincerely feel for and sympathize with the Inhibitants of your city. They are thoroughly sensible that you are suffering for your activity and Spirit in the Common Cause and as it were in terrorem to us all and are well convinced of the necesssity and Importance of a union amongst all the colonies on this unhappy occasion as well as the fatal mischiefs that must follow the want of it, and your committee may be assured Gentlemen that every thing that can be done by our Committee to promote a good understanding and harmony amongst the Colonies will be done and nothing in our power Omitted to avert the fatal Dangers impending over us all. The Committee have ordered a general meeting of the Inhabitants to be call'd the first Wednesday in July, being the earliest time they judged they could be convened, Considering the extent and other Circumstances of our Colony and have taken such steps therein as they are hopeful will Occasion a full meeting. In the meantime they wait with the utmost Impatience to hear what general Plan is adopted by the northern Governments in which they make no doubt ours will cooperate as far as the nature of our situation will admit.

---

[1] Samuel Adams Papers, NYPL. The letter is marked "copy."

On the Otherside you have the list of our Committee any fifteen of which are allowed to do Business, a Letter directed to the Committee of Correspondence in Charles town will be Sufficient.

I am Gentn. your most Obedt. & Hble. Servt.

Christ Gadsden Chairman
by order of the Committee [2]

Charleston

14 June 1774

To the Committee of Correspondence In Boston
[On the Other Side]

Rawlins Lowndes [P.]	John McQueen
Christopher Gadsden [M.]	William Cattle
William Gibbes [M.]	Thomas Bee [P.]
Mark Morris [Me.]	Benj. Huger [P.]
John Huger [P.]	Danl. Cannon [Me.]
Joshua Lockwood [Me.]	Charles Pinckney [P.]
Daniel Legare Senr. [P.]	John Logan [M.]
Joseph Verree [Me.]	John Parker [P.]
Oliver Cromwell [Me.]	Sampson Neyle
John E. Poyas [M.]	Jacob Motte [P.]
Alexander Gillon [M.]	John Colcock [L.]
Thomas Heyward [*Lawyer, P.*]	William Savage [P.]

---

[2] In July 1769, a Committee was elected at a Meeting of the Inhabitants of Charles Town under the Liberty Tree. The Committee was charged chiefly with the enforcement of non-importation. Representing the town, the Committee was composed of thirteen mechanics and thirteen merchants, with the same number of planters supposedly representing the country. This body became a powerful, though extra-legal, organ of revolution. By 1774, it had been enlarged to forty-five, the planter element outnumbering other classes, and became the Committee of Correspondence. To give the new body a broader representation for taking up the matter of resistance to the Tea Act, and sending delegates to a Continental Congress, a new election was called. At that moment, the Royal Government was practically inoperative, as the Assembly had not conducted business with the governors following the Wilkes Fund Dispute. Therefore, this Committee constituted the beginning of the Provincial Congress in South Carolina. For further purposes of identification: [M.] for merchant, [P.] for planter, [Me.] for mechanic, and [L.] for lawyer have been inserted beside the names of the members. (The "Inhabitants" did not originally make this distinction.) *SCG*, July 27, 1769; *Extracts Journals of Provincial Congress*, Hemphill, and Wates, pp. xvi-xviii. The advertisements in the *SCG* for 1774; *The Charleston Directory for 1782*, and Walsh, *Sons of Liberty* were also employed for identification.

James Parsons [*L.*]
Peter Timothy [*Me.*]
John Rutledge [*P., L.*]
William Moultrie [*P.*]
Miles Brewton [*M.*]

Benjamin Stone
James Skirving Jr.
Elias Horry [*P.*]
Thomas Lynch [*P.*]
Thomas Ferguson [*P.*]

Benj. Elliott [*P.*]
Charles Elliott [*P.*]
John Berwick [*Me.*]
Thomas Savage [*P.*]
Arthur Middleton [*P.*]
C. C. Pinckney [*P., L.*]

William Williamson [*P.*]
Roger Smith [*M.*]
Robert Ladson [*P.*]
Thomas Eveleigh [*M.*]
Edw. Rutledge [*P., L.*]

Chas. Town 28th June 1774 [1]

Dear Sir:

The Foregoing [*June 14*] and inclosed [*below*] are Copies. This comes by Capt. Dove to Salem, by whom Mr. Handcock, Mr. Revere and yourself will receive a Letter from Mr. Clarkson and myself, a letter sign'd jointly covering Bill of Lading for 194 whole and 21 half barrels of Rice, shipt by the Desire of several Gentlemen here to their Address for the distressed in your Town as that Letter mentions more particularly.

I have not Time to add, only to assure you that you may depend that We are thoroughly alarm'd here, and will be ready to do every Thing in our Power. We depend on your Firmness, and that you will not pay for an ounce of the damn'd Tea.

Our Committee met to Day, and in hopes of hearing again from you have adjourn'd to the Day before the General Meeting. I am well convinc'd you will not receive less than the Value of a thousand Barrels of Rice from us. I am happy in finding our principal People so thoroughly sensible of their Danger and that you are suffering for us all. I am Dr. Sir. Yr. most obed. hble. Servt.

CHRIST GADSDEN

---

[1] Adams Papers, NYPL.

To Boston Committee of Correspondence

[Enclosure]

Charlestown South Carolina

28 June 1774

Gentlemen

At the Desire of the Gentlemen whose names you'll see in an Advertisement in the inclosed paper who have been requested to receive the Donations offer'd in this Colony for the Benifit of such Poor persons in Boston whose unfortunate Circumstances occasion'd by the Operation of the Late Unconstitutional Act of the British Parliament may be thought to stand in need of immediate Assistance, we have the Honour to send you the inclosed Bill of Lading for 194 whole and 21 bbls. rice laden by us on board the Sloop *Mary,* John Dove, Master for Salem there to be delivered to your order and disposed of *in any manner* that you may judge most conducible to the above mention'd Intention of the Donors. Your steady generous and truly patriotic Conduct Gentlemen will not permit us to apologize for sending this to your address upon the Errand it comes. We beg leave to assure you that the people of this Colony sincerely Sympathize in the most feeling Manner with their Brethren at Boston and are well convinced that their Steadiness and Spirit in the Common Cause of America has brought upon them that oppressive ministerial Vengence the Effect of which they are now suffering. We are persuaded that the Contributions we have reason to think are now making in all parts of the Province will not fall short of a Thousand Barrels of Rice; what are now sent you are only those of a very few, not exceeding twenty Gentlemen. All our friends in the northern Colonies may we think rely that the People of this Province will join in every thing in their Power to promote the Common Cause. They long to hear the final Determinations of your Neighbouring Governments, with regard to non-Importation and non-exportation. As to the first the people here in general are inclin'd to, and at the Commencement of the new crop the first of November; if it is then found absolutely necessary, we make no doubt the Other will be attempted; in the meantime what Rice is

100

remaining of this Crop, (as when beat out it is perishable) will be shipt off, and then every Body will be upon the same Footing and start Fair together. A Congress seems to be much wish'd for here. The Determination of that wou'd have the greatest Weight. This goes under cover to Rich'd Darby Junr. Esq. of Salem at Salem and will be forwarded to you immediately. We hope shortly to have the Honour to write to you again and are Gentlemen

Your most hble. Servt.

CHRIST GADSDEN

[Secr.] Clarkson

To Thomas and William Bradford

Thomas (1745-1838) was the eldest son of William Bradford III of Philadelphia (1721-1791) who was called the "patriot printer of the revolution." Bradford began the Weekly Advertiser or Pennsylvania Journal in 1742, which was published nearly continuously during his lifetime and until two years after his death. William Bradford expanded his newspaper activities, becoming a leading publisher and bookseller at "The London Coffee House." He also issued, in 1757 and 1758, The American Magazine and Monthly Chronicle, and later, with his son, The American Magazine or Monthly Repository. An ardent patriot, William Bradford enlisted in the Continental Army during the war, while Thomas conducted the business. McMurtrie, History of Printing in U.S., II, 55-57; Arthur M. Schlesinger, Prelude to Independence: The Newspaper War on Britain (New York: Alfred A. Knopf, 1958) pp. 33, 54, 74, 176, 209, 285, 289-90.

Chas. Town [1]

28 March 1775

Gentlemen:

I received your favours of the 4th and 12th Instant.

The Box of Pamphlets by Wright came to hand Safe, but am afraid shall not be able to get many of Mr. Dickinson's efforts, as

---

[1] HSP. There is no addressee. The letter appears to have been written to the Philadelphia printers William and Thomas Bradford whose Charleston accounts were handled by Gadsden.

these take a small Run here on their first coming out and afterward are but very rarely enquired after; besides I live quite at one End of the Town, that I am much out of the way for a matter of that Sort. I imagin'd I should have been able to have got off 500 of the Proceedings of the Congress at our Provincial Meeting, but unluckily we then got into some long Disputes and Heats which tho' they all subsided, and we all parted good Friends at last, yet they took up so much Time that almost all our Country Members left Town immediately on the breaking up our Congress, and a little before that Time Mr. Wells had printed the first Extracts in a small Type and ordinary paper which had taken a much greater Run then I imagined; upon the whole I am glad you have sent the Congress and Jamaica Petitions which will be a means of getting off the remainder of one of your Boxes (say 500 of the Continental Proceedings). The other has never been open'd and I think you had better let me bring them back with me together with what may be unsold of Mr. Dickinson's Pamphlets.[2] I find our people in general content themselves with taking our public Proceedings as they find them in our News papers, in which they have been all reprinted. As to sending them to Georgia, that can't be done, as we have determin'd to have nothing farther to do with them, as they have not agreed to the American Association and besides, I don't think many of them would be got off. I Expect to see you by the return of More and Wright, when I shall bring with me the Money for what I have sold or may sell before I leave this place, which I am persuaded you'll find to be near about the Sum at which you charged the whole 1000 of the Continental proceedings, so that you will have the other 500 that I propose then to bring with me almost if not altogether clear to you.

We have the same accounts from England that you have, and to about the same time. Every Thing, thank God, seems to be in a fair Way. We are all very firm here and may be depended on.

You'll please to add the following Names to the Subscrption for your paper, and send it as you did at first to be left at Mr.

---

[2] The Bradfords printed all of Dickinson's works except *Letters from a Farmer in Pennsylvania* (Philadelphia: David Hall and William Sellers, 1768). Dickinson's latest effort, printed by the Bradfords was *Essay on the Constitutional Power of Great Britain over the Colonies . . . with the Resolves of the Committee for the Province of Pennsylvania and Their Instructions to Their Representatives* (Philadelphia, 1774). For mention and summary of other Dickinson pamphlets *see* C.J. Stille, *Life and Times of John Dickinson, Memoirs of the Historical Society of Pennsylvania,* XIII (Philadelphia, 1891), 66-198. Biographical sketches of William and Thomas Bradford, *see also DAB,* II, 552-3; 563-4.

Ramage's Tavern in Broad Street,[3] for whether it has been out of peek [pique] or what to Mr. Calvert,[4] the papers have not been sent to him so readily, as they used to be at Ramage's. I am Gentn, Yr. most hble Servt.

CHRIST GADSDEN

New subscribers [5]—Thos. Horry, Patrick Hinds, Wm. Sommersall, Thomas Corbett, Jacob Motte, Dr. David Oliphant, Wm. Parker,

---

[3] Ramage's Tavern was apparently a meeting place for the radicals. As part of a demonstration November 21, 1774, to celebrate deliverance from the Gunpowder Plot and the landing of William III, Peter Timothy reported that "a Magnificent Exhibition of EFFIGIES, designed to represent Lord North, Governor Hutchinson, the Pope, and the DEVIL, were placed on a rolling Stage, about Eight Feet high and fifteen Feet long, near Mr. Ramage's Tavern in Broad Street, being the most frequented Place in Town . . .' :" *SCG*, November 21, 1774.

[4] John Calvert, tavern keeper and clerk, was one of the original members of the Liberty Tree gatherings. Gibbes, *op. cit., 1764-1776*, pp. 7-11.

[5] Thomas Horry (1748-1802), planter of Santee, was a member of the Committee of Correspondence, but later in the rebellion was regarded as a Tory after having congratulated Clinton on his conquest of Charleston. "Garth Correspondence," *SCHM*, XXXIII (October, 1932), 264; "Correspondence of Hon. Arthur Middleton," XXVI (October, 1925), 208, XXVII (January, 1926), 5, 9. Patrick Hinds was a shoemaker of Charleston. *SCG*, January 21, 1773, Petitions, Accounts of Patrick Hinds, South Carolina Archives Department. William Sommersall was a merchant who supplied arms for the Congress. "Miscellaneous Papers of the General Committee, Secret Committee, and Provincial Congress, 1775," *SCHM*, IX (April, 1908), 70; "Death Notices from the South Carolina Gazette," *SCHM*, XXIV, (July, 1933), 150. Thomas Corbett was a merchant of Charleston of the partnership, Corbett and Mansell. *Charleston Directory for 1782*. Jacob Motte (Jr.) was elected Powder-receiver in 1759 and was a member of the Provincial Congress in 1775. A.S. Salley, Jr., "Col. Miles Brewton and Some of His Descendants," *SCHM*, II (April, 1901), 131; Hemphill and Wates, *Journals of Provincial Congress* p. 74. Dr. David Oliphant was a member of the Council of Safety and the Legislative Council in the Provincial Congress and after the war served in the South Carolina Senate. *Ibid.*, pp. 132, 154, 265; *Senate Journal, 1783; Committee Book of the Senate, 1782-1783*, S.C.A.D. William and John Parker were barrister-planters and members of the Provincial Congress, John representing St. James; William representing St. Thomas and St. Dennis. *Journals of Provincial Congress*, p. 4; McCrady, *S.C. in Revolution*, pp. 475, 486, 651; *SCG*, July 22, 1769. Dr. George Haig was a member of the first Provincial Congress from St. Paul's, a physician who had a plantation on the Stono River. *Journals of Provincial Congress*, p. 4; Cohen, *op. cit.*, p. 47; *SCG*, May 4, 1769; "Marriage and Death Notices from the City Gazette," *SCHM*, XXVII (July, 1926), 179. James Parsons, a lawyer, member of the Assembly, representing St. Bartholomew's Parish, 1760-1775, was elected Speaker of the House in 1776. Greene, *op. cit.*, p. 483; *Journals of Provincial Congress*, pp. 51, 132, 154, 266. James McCall was a merchant of Charleston. *SCG*, April 30, 1772; Cohen, *op. cit.*, p. 154. Peter, Philip, and Isaac Porcher. A brief genealogy and biographical information of the Porchers are in "Letter from Stephen Mazyck to Philip [Peter] Porcher," *SCHM*, XXXVIII (January, 1937), 11-12. Philip became a loyalist. Benjamin Mazyck (1715-1800) was a planter from St. James, Goose Creek. McCrady, *Royal Government*, p. 486; "Marriage and Death Notices from the City Gazette," XXVI (October, 1925), 232. Major Isaac Harleston became a

Dr. George Haig, James Parsons, James McCall, Thos. Farr Jr., Peter Porcher, Benja. Mazyck, Philip Porcher, Gideon Dupont, Isaac Harleston, John Parker, Isaac Porcher.

To the South Carolina Secret Committee

The Battles of Lexington, Concord, and Breed's Hill (April 19, April 19, and June 17, 1775, respectively) had nearly exhausted ammunitions of the Army. A desperate scramble to replenish arms took place, resulting in raids on the royal magazines. In South Carolina, raids were led by some of the Province's leaders, including members of the Secret Committee to which this letter was addressed. William Henry Drayton, pro-British in 1769, had become an avowed radical. Charles Cotesworth Pinckney (1746-1825), a youthful lieutenant of the First South Carolina Regiment, son of Colonel Charles (1722-1758) and Elizabeth (Eliza) Lucas Pinckney, was of an aristocratic plantation family. Charles Cotesworth Pinckney became the high Federalist of the X.Y.Z. affair, and vice presidential and presidential choice of the party early in the nineteenth century. Rising to the position of colonel under Gadsden by the time of the British attack on Sullivan's Island in 1776, Pinckney also took part in the abortive St. Augustine expedition, and suffered capture at the fall of Charles Town in 1780. This period was made even more difficult for him when his cousin Colonel Charles Pinckney, the 1776 President of the Provincial Congress, swore allegiance to the British, earning a heated denouncement from Gadsden in the Jacksonborough Assembly. Arthur Middleton (1742-1787), of the Middletons of St. Andrew's Parish, was a signer of the Declaration of Independence, and President of the Continental Congress. Mrs. St. Julien Ravenal, Charleston: the Place and the People (New York: Macmillan Company, 1912), pp. 146-8, 172, 183, 197, 225, 253, 266, 280-81; A.S. Salley, Jr., Delegates to the Continental

---

Continental Officer, serving throughout the war. He was from St. James, a member of the first Provincial Congress, and took part in the Battle of Fort Moultrie. McCrady, *Royal Government*, pp. 524-5; p. 143; "Notes and Queries," *SCHM*, I (April, 1900), 176. Thomas Farr, Jr., was a planter of St. Paul's Parish who, toward the end of the British occupation of Charleston, became a spy for the Americans, reporting British movements to General Nathanael Greene. "Revolutionary Letters," *SCHM*, XXXVIII (January, 1937), 7-10.

Congress from South Carolina, 1774-1789: Bulletins of the Historical Commission of South Carolina No. 9 (Columbia: S. C. Historical Commission, 1927), pp. 5-16. Robert W. Barnwell, "Correspondence of Hon. Arthur Middleton," SCHM, XXVII (Jan., 1926), 8-9.

Philadelphia July 1, 1775 [1]

Gentlemen:

By directions of the Continental Congress, we have sent the vessels by which this came, to procure from you a quantity of Gun-Powder for the use of the armies now actually in the Field for the Service of America. The frequent service and skermishes in the Neighborhood of Boston have so exhausted their Magazines that an immediate supply is absolutely necessary.

We entreat you to purchase all that can be bought in Town, and to dispatch this vessel with it for this place as soon as possible, together with as much as can be spared out of the Public Stock without danger to your own safety.

Should there be any damaged Powder on hand, please send it also, as it may be recovered here.

By one of the Resolutions enclosed to the General Committee you'll see that it is recommended to the Southern Colonies to secure all the Salt Petre that can be got as well from the stores as from private Persons, which, as you have no Powder Mills erected or Persons skillful in making gun-powder, we wou'd advise may be sent to be manufactured here. Should you be able to send more than four Thousand weight of Powder we wou'd wish the overplus may be sent by some other Opportunity.

In order to prevent Suspicion we have sent Bushels of Indian Corn in this Vessel which may be sold or Exchanged for Rice, in which the casks of Powder may be concealed so perhaps as to prevent suspicion shou'd she be unhappily unable to avoid being overtaken by a cruizer.

---

[1] The Charles Roberts Autograph Collection, Haverford College, Haverford, Pennsylvania. The original is addressed to the Secret Committee in South Carolina, William Henry Drayton, Arthur Middleton, C.C. Pinckney, and inscribed: "Application from our Members in Congress for Gun Powder, July 1, 1775." Charles Pinckney, as president of the Provincial Congress, had also appointed to this committee Edward Weyman, a cohort of Gadsden during the meetings under the Liberty tree. Weyman was a mechanic, a glass grinder and manufacturer of mirrors, and an upholsterer. He was one of the leaders of the mob who in 1775-1776 terrorized the otherwise-minded with tar and feathers. William Gibbes, father of the nineteenth-century historian, Robert W. Gibbes, was a merchant of the city who hid the stolen arms and powder at his wharf.

The utmost secrecy and dispatch are absolutely necessary.

As large quantities of powder will be wasted we strongly recomment that you continue to import all that you can, and think it probable that large Quantities, might be got from the government of the Havana as we can find no application there from any of these Colonies.

We are, Gentlemen
your most Obed. Servants

HENRY MIDDLETON
THOMAS LYNCH
CHRIST. GADSDEN
JOHN RUTLEDGE
EDWARD RUTLEDGE

To Dudley Saltonstall

Dudley Saltonstall (1738-1796) of New London, Connecticut, was a captain in the merchant fleet before the Revolution. He was placed in command of the Alfred, one of America's first Naval vessels, becoming commander in 1779 of a fleet to engage the enemy at Penobscot, Massachusetts. The attack proved a disaster, for which Saltonstall was blamed and dismissed from the service. The following letter is one of the earliest to issue from the Committee on Marine of the Continental Congress, of which Gadsden was a most enthusiastic member. G. W. Allen, Naval History of the American Revolution (New York: Russell and Russell, 1962), I, 28-29; 30-32.

Philadelphia, Nov. 27th, 1775 [1]

Sir,

The Congress is now preparing two Ships and two Brigantines to be fitted out as soon as possible to cruise against our common enemy. They have thought of you as a proper person to take the command of one of these Ships as Captain. If you enter into this service, which we take to be the service of your country, you will give us the earliest information and repair to Philadelphia as soon as your affairs will possibly admit and bring with you as many officers and seamen as you can procure at New London and between

---

[1] Franklin D. Roosevelt Collection, Hyde Park.

that place and Philadelphia. Those who may not be able to come with you, leave proper persons to encourage and conduct along after you.

If money should be necessary for the performance of this service you may draw on McEleazer Miller, Merchant in New York who has money in his hands for that purpose.

In a day of two after you receive this, you will receive by the Messers Mumford the Conditions and encouragement offered the Seamen.

We are Sir

Your humble servants [2]

STEP. HOPKINS

CHRISTOPHER GADSDEN

JOHN ADAMS

JOSEPH HEWES

SILAS DEANE

---

[2] On October 3, 1775, the Rhode Island delegates proposed that a naval force for the defense of the colonies be considered. Two days, later, a committee composed of John Adams, John Langdon of New Hampshire, and Silas Deane of Connecticut, was chosen to outfit vessels to intercept two Canada-bound British transports laden with munitions. Edward Rutledge "eleoquently" opposed and compared this resolution to an "infant taking a mad bull by his horns," saying it would ruin the character and corrupt the "morals of all our seaman." Gadsden and the Rutledges were at odds, as was evidenced by their argument over non-intercourse in the Provincial Congress and Edward's description of Gadsden's being "wrong-headed" and "violent." Gadsden's work—shown in this letter— to erect a navy, did nothing to endear him to the pair. On October 13, Gadsden was placed on a new committee to outfit a cruiser, and this may have been the beginning of the Committee on Marine which absorbed the naval preparations of a number of Congressional and state committees. Of the Committee, John Adams wrote that it contained "the true origin and foundation of the American Navy. . ." Its members were: Stephen Hopkins, governor of Rhode Island and delegate between 1774 and 1780, who secured the appointment of Eseck Hopkins, his brother, as Commander; Joseph Hewes, a North Carolina delegate, 1774-1777, who was returned in 1779 but died that year; and Silas Deane of Connecticut, who regarded Gadsden as among the most fiery delegates, even surpassing the New Englanders. Deane did yeoman service; yet later, unfortunately, a cloud of suspicion was cast over him for his activities in France, where he was gathering supplies to advance the American cause. John Adams, active radical in the Congress, always found Gadsden allied with his views: namely, in opposition to petition the Crown, (Dickinson's efforts in 1775), and positively to arm, confederate and unify the colonies, to seek foreign alliances, principally with France and Spain, and to declare independence beforehand unequivocally. Edmund C. Burnett, ed., *Letters of Members of the Continental Congress,* 8 vols. (Washington: Carnegie Institute of Washington, 1921-1936), I, 18, 30, 65, 108, 216-7, 246, 272-3, 300, 302, 350-52. For all of Gadsden's usefulness, Thomas Nelson, Jr., of Virginia considered him "disruptive" and was relieved to see his departure in February, 1776; *ibid.,* p. 339; Worthington C. Ford *et al.,* eds. *Journals of the Continental Congress,* (Washington: Government Printing Office, 1904-1906), I-V, 12, 21, 86, 106, 177, 191, 234, 262, 277, 293-4, 420, 428; Charles Francis Adams, ed. *The Works of John Adams* (Boston: Little Brown & Co., 1851), II, 503-6, III, pp. 11-13.

To Admiral Eseck Hopkins

Eseck Hopkins (1718-1802) of Providence, brother of Governor Stephen Hopkins, served in the Rhode Island General Assembly. He was a successful sea captain and carried on privateering ventures during the French and Indian War. Hopkins, in the fall of 1776, was appointed by the Continental Congress commander-in-chief of the newly formed American navy. Gadsden, as a member of the Committee on Marine, had vigorously pursued this project, eventually convincing his colleagues in Congress of his confidence "that we may get a Fleet of our own" to match Britain's. Gadsden's words had circulated among the delegates that "this would give great Spirit to this Continent, as well as little Spirit to the Ministry." Gadsden was one of the founders of the American navy. William Bell Clark, ed., Naval Documents of the American Revolution (Washington: Government Printing Office, 1964), I, pp. 628-9.

Philadelphia, 10th January, 1776 [1]

Dear Sir:

Inclosed is a Copy of an Order from the Committee [2] to Stone,[3] sent by the directions of Congress, on an application from Maryland, which it is necessary you shou'd have.

---

[1] Correspondence of Eseck Hopkins, Rhode Island Historical Society. The document is published in *The Correspondence of Eseck Hopkins: Commander-in-Chief of the United States Navy,* Alverda S. Beck, ed., introduction by William Davis Miller (Province: Rhode Island Historical Society, 1933), pp. 26-28. Another version is in *American Archives,* Peter Force (comp.), Fourth Series (Washington: Government Printing Office, 1843), IV, pp. 620-21. Other letters to Hopkins signed by Gadsden and the Marine Committee are in Beck, *Correspondence,* pp. 23-25, 28, and *The Letter Book of Eseck Hopkins . . . ; 1775-1777,* Alverda S. Beck, ed. (Providence: Rhode Island Historical Society, 1932), pp. 15-17.

In the introduction to the *Correspondence,* William Davis Miller mistakenly attributes to Gadsden a letter written to Hopkins dated January 13, 1776, concerning the Gadsden Naval flag, "Don't Tread on Me." The letter was signed by Timothy Matlack, assistant Secretary of the Congress: pp. 12-13, 30-31. The Gadsden flag was not the Stars and Stripes, but "a curious banner" made of yellow silk, bearing a lively representation of a rattlesnake and the motto, "Don't Tread on me." A flag of this description was presented by Christopher Gadsden to Congress on February 8, a few weeks after the banner of the colonies was unfurled at the mast-head of the flag-ship *Alfred.* Mrs. Reginald de Koven, *The*

108

I also take the Liberty to send you a List of the Field Officers and Captains of two Regiments of Foot, and three Companies of Artillery, all Provincials, station'd in Charles Town, So. Carolina, shou'd you go there, upon your arrival off the Bar, the pilot will inform you what officer is at Fort Johnson or any of the nearest Batteries to you, from whom you may depend on all the assistance they can give; they are, most of them, gentlemen of considerable fortunes with us, who have enter'd into the Service merely from Principle and to promote and give Credit to the Cause, they take it by Turns to be at the Fort, and the Zeal and activity of all of them are such that you can't happen amiss let who will be there. In Charles Town my particular Friends, Mr. Lowndes, Mr. Ferguson, Col. Powell, Mr. Benj[ami]n Elliott, Col. Pinckney, Mr. Drayton, Mr. Timothy, and the Rev. Mr. Tennent, a Countryman of yours will introduce you to many others, who will be glad to have an Opportunity of obliging you and promoting the service.[4]

I wrote yesterday to Mr. Ferguson, one of the Gentlemen just mention'd, by way of Georgia, by a Gentleman I can depend on who will destroy my letter shou'd he be taken. In this letter I have hinted to look out for you, and be ready to assist you at a Moment's Warning. The two large ships seen off Virginia, the 29th of last Month we are told were not bound there; however, you will know more certainly by the Time you get out of the Capes I make no doubt. I hope you will be able to effect that Service, but whether you may or not, sooner or later, I flatter myself we shall have your assistance at Carolina, where you may depend on an easy Conquest, or at least be able to know without Loss of Time, when off our

---

Life and Letters of John Paul Jones (New York: Charles Scribner's Sons, 1913), Vol. I, 90-92.

[2] The original naval committee of Congress in October 1775 was composed of Silas Deane, of Delaware; John Langdon, New Hampshire; and Christopher Gadsden, South Carolina. Stephen Hopkins proposed the formation of a navy; and it was decided that two ships would be purchased, the *Lexington* and the *Reprisal*. The original committee on October 30 was increased to seven. Added were John Adams, Stephen Hopkins, Joseph Hewes, and Richard Henry Lee. The *Alfred* and the *Columbus* were added, and on December 13, thirteen more ships joined the fleet. The committee was increased with a member from each colony or province.

[3] The "Inclosure" was from the Marine Committee to Captain William Stone. It ordered him to convoy vessels named by the Committee of Safety of Maryland after which he was to join Hopkins' fleet. Stone commanded the *Hornet* and *Wasp*. Also contained in the enclosure was a list of officers and captains of the First and Second South Carolina Regiments and the officers of artillery.

[4] Rawlins Lowndes, Charles Pinckney, Thomas Ferguson and George Gabriel Powell were members of the Provincial Legislative Council. William Henry Drayton was Gadsden's adversary as "Freeman" in 1769. Peter Timothy, printer of the *South Carolina Gazette*, was Clerk of the Assembly of 1776. Benjamin Elliott was a member of the Council of Safety. Hemphill and Wates, *Journals of Provincial Congress,* pp. 51, 132, 154, 265-6.

DRAWING OF GADSDEN'S PERSONAL FLAG

Bar the Strength of the Enemy, and shou'd it be too much for you prudently to encounter which I hardly think probable if soon attempted with the assistance to be depended on from us you may in such case Retreat with great Ease, Safety and Expedition.

Wishing you every success you can possibly wish yourself, I am Dr. Sir Yr. most hble. Servt.

CHRIST GADSDEN

P.S. Pray make my Compliments to Capt. Saltonstall and the Rest of your Captains, and shall be oblig'd to you if you go to Carolina to introduce them to any or all the Gentlemen I have mention'd who I am sure will be glad to shew them every Civility in their power. I hope Capt. Whipple is better.[5] One of the Maryland gentlemen, Mr. Alexander[6] a Delegate of the Colony, tells me there is a very good Ship of about 20 guns there easily fitted out which he is in hopes will join you with the *Hornet* and *Wasp,* and that he shou'd press it to be done. This I mention by the by.

Philad. 15th January 1776[1]

Sir:

I last Night received my Orders [to] go to So. Carolina and expect to set out a Thursday morng. [,] for one of our Pilot Boats [is] now at New Castle in which I shall take my Chance. Shou'd you come our Way if you think proper to let me know to morrow or next Day what Signals you will shew when off our Bar, you may depend on my keeping a good Look-Out for you, and to let no Body know the Signal but where it is necessary. I am Sr. yr. most hble. Servt.

CHRIST GADSDEN

Some one of the Fleet if to gather [together] or the Small Sloop if alone will higst a Striped flagg half up the flying Stay.[2]

---

[5] Captain Abraham Whipple of the *Columbus.* Beck, *Correspondence,* p. 37.

[6] Robert Alexander of Cecil County, Maryland, was a member of the Marine Committee replacing Samuel Chase. Alexander's correspondence seems to indicate that he was opposed to independence, and when William Howe's army landed in Cecil County, Alexander defected. Although later he wished to return to Maryland, he was prevented, and his estate was confiscated in 1780. Alexander became the Crown's agent for adjudicating the claims of Maryland loyalists. He died in London. "A Maryland Loyalist," *Maryland Historical Magazine,* I (December, 1906), 317-23.

[1] Rhode Island Historical Society. Published in Beck, *Correspondence,* p. 30. With the State in danger of attack, Gadsden was ordered to his command as Brigadier General. He returned to the Provincial Congress in February 1776, presented his flag and, upon proposing independence, threw the body into heated debate. Hemphill and Wates, *Journals of Provincial Congress,* p. 183.

[2] The "yellow silk flag," was the special standard of Hopkins as commander-in-chief of the navy. Possibly the flag Gadsden referred to was the Union Flag with thirteen stripes in the field, emblematic of the original colonies. American Archives, ser. IV, Vol. IV, 964. *See also* Hugh F. Rankin, "The Naval Flag of the American Revolution," *William and Mary Quarterly,* 3rd series, XI (July, 1954), 339-53.

To Major General Charles Lee

Charles Lee (1731-1782) was a professional soldier who was born in Chester, England. He first arrived in America to take part in the French and Indian War, later moving to Virginia to live in 1773. At the beginning of the American Revolution, his experience won him a commission as Major General, but Lee wanted the high command, and was thereafter embittered against General Washington. After having directed the building of fortifications of New York City in 1776, Lee was ordered to Charles Town which was attacked by the British on June 28, in the Battle of Fort Sullivan (later Fort Moultrie). Lee placed Christopher Gadsden in command of Fort Johnson, but the Fort was too far removed from the battle site for any participation. Lee received credit for successfully defending Charles Town, despite his having advised Colonel William Moultrie to abandon Fort Sullivan. Lee's brusque manner and harsh behavior brought criticism, and his subsequent career was stormy. Returning to the North, he continuously disregarded Washington's orders, and at one time was challenged to a duel by John Laurens of South Carolina. Lee was court-martialed and suspended from the service for one year, and in 1780 was dismissed. John Richard Alden, General Charles Lee, Traitor or Patriot? (Baton Rouge: Louisiana State University Press, 1951), pp. 119-35, 194-292; The Columbia Encyclopedia (3rd. edition; New York: Columbia University Press, 1963), p. 1192.

Fort Johnson, 12 June '76 [1]

Sir:

I have the Honour to send to your Excellency by Coll. Pinckney a return of Col. Huger's and my Regiment. Besides these [,] Capt. Stones Company of James Island Militia is also under my Command consisting of about sixty Men, thirty of which are kept constantly on the Patrol Duty watching the Enemy's Motions at the different Landings within Seven Miles of us; the other thirty are always in readiness to assist at the Western Battery. We have 43 Cannon

---

[1] Dearborn Collection. A version is printed in the *Lee Papers, NYHS Collections,* II, 66.

mounted at this Fort [and] the Battery and as Col. Huger's Men are all just rais'd and thirty six of my own Regiment, new recruits, none of which have been used to Cannon, they must be extremely awkward thereat. Many of our Cannon are very heavy and require a great Number of Men, and shou'd we have warm Work, and the Enemy attempt to Land we can have but a very small Body to oppose them without having many of the Cannon.[2]

Our Carpenters and Labourers have deserted us many Days since, which has put our Works entirely to a Stand [still] ; were it not for this, in a very few Days more I cou'd have the Curtain [3] of the Upper Battery compleated so that the Platforms might be ready to be laid the moment the plank arrived.

I beg leave to refer your Excellency to Col. Pinckney for any Thing relative to the Regiment. I shall be always ready with the greatest Pleasure to execute any of your Excellency's Commands. And am Yr. Excellys. most obed. hble. Servt.

CHRIST GADSDEN

P.S. One of the Enemy's Tenders, having been drove by the Gale almost in reach of our Cannon, the Enemy thought proper to abandon her, about half an Hour ago, and one of our Pilots has taken Possession of her, and is bringing her up. I am in hopes this Storm will do the Enemy's Business Evil.

'Tis now the 13th. The above is what I intended to have sent to Your Excellency yesterday but the Weather prevented me. The two large Ships of the Enemy that were at anchor off the Bar are drove from their anchors and not to be seen. A Sloop also of theirs we imagine must be drove ashore, as we see nothing of her.

[2] The officers whom Gadsden named as being under his command were of the First South Carolina Regiment of Foot, with a small detachment of Artillery. Second in command was Charles Cotesworth Pinckney of the Infantry, and under him, Lieutenant Colonel Issac Huger. *Wells' Register and Almanac,* pp. 93-94.

To Colonel William Moultrie

William Moultrie (1730-1805), a continental officer of the American Revolution, was born in Charles Town. He fought against the Indians in 1761, and was a member of the Colonial Assembly before the Revolutionary war. Colonel Moultrie was given the command of Fort Sullivan which was attacked by the British under Sir Peter Parker June 28, 1776. The fort, built of palmetto logs, withstood the British naval bombardment; and in a land skirmish, Colonel William Thompson's troops repulsed the British under Sir Henry Clinton. This was the first major victory for the Americans. The enemy sailed in late summer for New York, leaving South Carolina relatively free of attack for the next four years. Elsewhere during the year the military situation was bleak.

Historians regard Moultrie as the hero of the Battle of Sullivan's Island; and Gadsden acclaims him as such in the letter here. Moultrie possible saved Charles Town again in 1779, but he was captured when the city was surrendered to the British in 1780. Moultrie was promoted after the Battle of Fort Sullivan, and his fame brought him such popularity that he was twice elected governor of the state (1785-1787; 1792-1794). Robert Lee Meriwether's biography in DAB, XIII, 293-4; McCrady, South Carolina in the Revolution, pp. 128-62. See also Alden, Lee, pp. 119-35.

Fort Johnston, July 1, 1776 [1]

Dear Sir:

I most heartily congratulate the Colony on the drubbing you gave those fellows the other day, and only wish you had had powder enough, that it might have been complete. Enclosed I send you a copy of a letter [2] I sent General *Lee* this morning, containing the information I received from five honest fellows (*Americans*) that got away last night.

If they come up again, they are determined to come as close to the forts as possible, in order, I suppose, to command us more easily

---

[1] *American Archives,* VI, 1192. Original not found.
[2] Not found.

from their tops. Two of these men were on board the Commodore ['s ship, *The Bristol*] in the action. They say your first fire killed a man in the tops, upon which the Commodore ordered them all out of the tops, from whence they assured us there was not a gun fired. The *Sphinx* lost her bowsprit by running foul of the *Acteon,* and they were obliged either to cut away their bowsprit or the *Acteon's* mainmast. These men all belonged to the *Acteon,* and two of them were drafted on board the Commodore just before the action. I fired three cannon at the *Syren,* merely to please several of my officers, which fell far short, as I expected. We admired your behaviour, but could do no more. My compliments to all your corps; we drink their healths every day. If you will send this account to General *Armstrong* [3] I shall be obliged to you. Yours, sincerely,

CHRISTOPHER GADSDEN

P.S. As soon as the action began, the Commodore ordered to be put into a place of safety negro *Sampson,* a black pilot.

To Major General Charles Lee

Chas. Town Light House Island [1]

2d Aug. 1776

Sir:

In Consequence of your Excellency's Permission for a Detachment of my Regiment to come here after the Enemy [who is] supposed to be at this Post, I set off at sundown yesterday from Fort Johnson with a Detachment of 120 Rank and file of my Regiment and when we were near the Island were joined by Capt. Stone with 36 of his Company. We landed about 10 o'Clock last night, and as soon as we could Form (in less than five minutes) after leaving 35 Armed and about sixteen Boatmen to take care of the Boats, I immediately hasten'd along the Beach from one End of the Island

[3] Brigadier General John Armstrong (1758-1843) of Pennsylvania and Brigadier General Robert Howe of North Carolina were aides of General Lee. Alden, *Lee,* p. 115.

[1] Original in pencil in SCHS. A version is printed in the *Charles Lee Papers,* II, pp. 196-7.

to the other and when I thoroughly investigated that, marched up to the Light House, which we found totally deserted, and are now in possession of it. I intend to stay till tomorrow Evening and in the mean Time I wish we could decoy or provoke the Men-of-War's people to land; were they to land all they have and to leave their Ships at Anchor without a Man on board, I should not doubt with the Honest Fellows I have with me, with God's Blessing, to give your Excellency a very good account of them. We have no pen and Ink with us. Your Excellency may depend on every Thing being done in the Power of Yr. Obedt. hble. Servt.

CHRIST GADSDEN

P.S. The Ships are within a good Random of a Battery that might be erected on the Beach opposite them. I believe they intend to go as soon as they can.

To John Lewis Gervais

John Lewis Gervais (1741-1798) came to South Carolina from the Germanies, settling in Ninety Six. He became a wealthy and influential planter before moving to Charles Town. Gervais held seats in the Continental Congress, the Provincial Congress and on the Privy Council.

Sullivan's Island, 21 September 1776 [1]
Sir:

We are out of Rum, of which for the Work I am about [,] I am obliged to use a great deal; pray send a Hogsh'd for this Garrison as soon as possible by Capt. Nam [?] if you can. I am Sir

Yr. Hble. Servt.

CHRIST GADSDEN

---

[1] SCHS. The addressee, Colonel John Lewis Gervais, served as Commissary: *see* note of Colonel Robert to John Lewis Gervais, September 21, 1776, SCHS. Several notes to the Commissioners of the Navy were written by Gadsden concerning his work on the fortifications at Sullivan's Island. They have not been found, but are mentioned in the *Journal of the Commissioners of the Navy of South Carolina*, A. S. Salley, Jr., ed. (Columbia: South Carolina Historical Commission, 1912), pp. 29, 30, 44, 79, 82, 86, 99.

Sullivan. Island, 8th Octr. 1776 [1]

Sir:

We have not one Barrell of Pork left therefore desire you will send us down a Months Salt provisions as soon as possible for a Store. The Adjutant Mr. Hamilton [2] will tell you the reason of this. I shou'd also be glad you wou'd send me a Hogshead of Rum for the Regiment by first Opportunity. I am oblig'd to give a great deal of Rum to the Labourers *etc.* about the Bridge.

I am Sir

Yr. Most Hble. Servt.

CHRIST GADSDEN

To Governor John Rutledge

John Rutledge (1739-1800), statesman and jurist, was born in Charles Town and educated at the Middle Temple. A naturally gifted man, with considerable knowledge of the English Constitution, he ably represented the eighteenth-century ruling class of South Carolina. He was a delegate to the Federal Convention of 1787 and was one of the notable framers of the Constitution. Although Rutledge was an ally of Gadsden in disputes in Carolina and against the British empire in the 1760's, the two became rivals by 1775 because of Gadsden's emphasis on colonial unity in opposing Parliament. The political break came over the British boycott in 1774, when Rutledge secured an exemption of rice. Gadsden fought against this in the Continental Congress and carried the debate to the Provincial Congress. Henry Laurens, writing to his son John, said ". . . I humbly think he was wrong on both sides and his behavior underwent much censure; it seems to have confirmed a Serious Separation between him and the two Brothers [the Rutledges]." See Laurens Letter Book, January 18, 1775. SCHS.

Gadsden's desire for independence, his views of popular government, and his support of the disestablishment of the Anglican Church

---

[1] Library of Congress.

[2] Lieutenant John Hamilton of the First South Carolina Regiment. He was wounded at the Battle of Stono in 1779. He died in 1799. *SCHM,* V, 90-91; VI, 21, 22, 24; XXV, 153.

as embodied in the State Constitution of 1778, caused marked, bitter differences between him and Rutledge. Despite this, Gadsden in 1800 speaks of him as that "great and good" John Rutledge. There is no dependable biography of Rutledge. A brief essay by R. L. Meriwether appears in DAB, XIV, 259-60. For a general account of his life, see McCrady, Royal Government; and Rogers' Evolution of a Federalist, with references to his post-Revolutionary career, p. 168, passim.

Fort Moultrie, 14th Dec. 1776 [1]

May it please your Excellency:

At low water I went with Mr. Mitchell [2] over to the redoubt on Haddrell's Point; from the Stakes I shew'd your Excellency, where I mention'd I though't it best to make the Communication between this and Haddrell's, we went from hence at low water in a Boat about 160 or 170 yards; the rest of the way I walked up with him [Mitchell] and Mr. Baldwin quite up to the redoubt which is directly opposite. The Foundation is hard all the way. In no one place I was up near to the calf of my Legg. The Distance I must have walked your Excellency will see by the enclosed Sketch taken by Mr. Mitchell. Your Excellency will excuse me for mentioning that it is my humble opinion nothing can be more material than this communication (I mean a good one) not only to Charlestown, but to the Colony in general, and the sooner 'tis set about the better; there is not the least difficulty in doing it if hands and Materials are immediately furnished. Not only a retreat will be thereby gain'd from this Island if necessary and succours speedily threwn in when wanted, but the garrison itself will be made abundantly more comfortable and satisfied in many respects; in short with such a Communication this may be one of the strongest and most desirable ports in America; without it, it will be impossible for the regiment that keeps it to be without frequent Desertions and Dwindling every Day without hopes of Recruits. I hope your Excellency will excuse the earnestness with which I press this Matter as I think it of the utmost Consequence and your Excellency may Depend that I will give my utmost atten-

---

[1] Dearborn Collection. On the eve of the British attack on Fort Sullivan in the previous June, General Lee fretted over the lack of a retreat route for the troops if the enemy were to make a successful landing. Therefore, Lee had a crude "bridge" erected, which the complacent Colonel Moultrie was much amused at, confidently stating after the fight that he never had any intentions of permitting the British a landing. Gadsden agreed with Lee's sensible measure; in command of the position, Gadsden undertook to build a more solid structure. In 1784, however, Gillon ridiculed Gadsden's project as a costly blunder. Alden, *op. cit.*

[2] William Mitchell was a carpenter: *Charleston Directory, 1790.*

tion to it if ordered to be put in Execution. Mr. Cannon [3] and I have had some talk about the method I would favor, which would be to make a bridge about 25 feet wide at the Channel and in other places leave a number of openings about 14 feet wide for the water to flow underneath: no matter if the openings are numerous, as we can easily make them solid hereafter, when by experience we are acquainted with the effects of the Tides on the Bridge. The parallelograms on Pillars that we wish to be full 18 feet wide, those on each side the Channel to be sunk first and so sunk backwards to the land at the low water mark. I am Your Excellency's Most Obedt. Hble. Servt.

CHRISTOPHER GADSDEN

To Thomas Mumford

Thomas Mumford (1728-1799) was a merchant of Groton and New London, Connecticut. A revolutionary radical following the Sugar Act, he was active in procuring supplies for the Continental Congress. With other merchants of Groton, he owned the privateer Fanny, which met with some success cruising against the British. Mumford was a confidant of Silas Deane and Gadsden, and was employed by Deane as agent of the Committee on Marine in 1775. Mumford was elected to the General Assembly of Connecticut, and became Justice of the Peace for New London, 1775-1777. He died in Norwich, September 4. Oscar Zeichner, Connecticut's Years of Controversy, 1750-1778 (Chapel Hill: University of North Carolina Press, 1949), pp. 46, 203. Public Records of the State of Connecticut October 1776-April 1780, 2 vol. (Hartford, 1894-1895) I, 57, 293, 305. Penn. Mag. Hist. and Biog. LXX, 203, Burnett, Letters of Members Continental Congress, I, 229-30. Francis Caulkins, MSS, New London County Historical Society, New London, Conn.

---

[3] Daniel Cannon was a carpenter and house-wright, and a Commissioner of Fortifications. He was one of Gadsden's mechanic political-associates and one of the influential workmen of Charleston. Johnson, *Traditions*, p. 34; *South Carolina Gazette and General Advertiser*, May 20, 1783; Gibbes, *Documentary History*, p. 10.

Fort Moultrie on Sullivan's Island [1]

19 February 1777

Sir:

I was favour'd with yours of the 8th Ultimo a few Days ago forwarded to me by Capt. Chester from Winyaw. I am extremely glad to hear my Friend Col. Dyer [2] is well and returned to the Congress. Pray make my Compliments to him and to Deane when you see him and his Lady. I am much obliged to you for the Cheese which I make no Doubt is good; 'tis on the way to me but not yet come to hand. I envy the English Tyrants in nothing so much as their Cheese, their Porter and their New Castle Salmon. I can see no Reason why you Gentlemen in New England shou'd not cure your Salmon in the same manner. I am persuaded they wou'd find their [accounts?] in it, at least in what might be exported here, for where there wou'd be one purchaser for what you send in the Common Way, you wou'd have ten for that done up in the New Castle method and a much wider and better Sale.

Thank God we seem to be in a fine Way to drive the Tyrants from America. We had a report yesterday that your Troops under Heath had drove them from New York. God grant it may be true. My Friend Genl. Moultrie who commanded at this Post (which I have now the Honour to command at) last year, gave the British Fleet the best Drubbing they have had in America and in my Opinion had he had powder enough, he wou'd have either sunk them or oblig'd them to Strike. I then commanded at Fort Johnson on the other side the Harbour, just without gun shot. We fired only three Shot at them just to let hem see we were not asleep.

I have been employed these six months in making a Bridge from hence to the Main near three Quarters of a Mile over, and have very near completed it; when that is done this Harbour may be made, and I make no doubt will [be], almost as strong as Gibraltar. Vessels drop in here daily and trade begins to flourish again very much. We shall all soon fetch up our [torn] Way when once we drive the Tyrants clean out, which I make little doubt this years Business will affect, as we grow more and more united. Numbers of the Theorists join us Daily, as they begin to be convinced we are of the safest side, and the terrible consequences that wou'd attend our being defeated even to themselves alarm and rouse them much. If this Letter gets time enough for Capt. Chester, I have ordered a Barrel of Rice to be put

---

[1] Ford Collection, NYPL.

[2] Colonel Eliphalet Dyer was an associate of Gadsden at the Stamp Act Congress. Dyer represented Connecticut in the Continental Congress, 1774-1776, 1782-1783. Lynn Montross, *The Reluctant Rebels* (New York: Harper Bros., 1951), p. 426.

on board which beg your acceptance of. My Son [3] who is an officer in the first Regiment joins in Compliments to you. I am Sir Your most hble. Servant.

CHRIS GADSDEN

To Governor John Rutledge

Fort Moultrie 4th July 1777 [1]

Dear Sir:

I did myself the Honour to write a few Lines to your Excellency the other Day by my Worthy Friend Col. Daniel Horry.[2] I now beg leave to introduce his Brother in Law Col. Chas. Cotesworth Pinckney to your Excellency. He is Col. of the Regiment I lately commanded, the first of this State, station'd at Fort Moultrie under my immediate Command. He is a polite spirited, active and Worthy Officer, and tho' I am sure he has no Occasion for my assistance to be made known to your Excellency being so nearly connected with other Gentlemen much better able to do him that Service, yet my sincere regard for him made me unable to forbear contributing my Mite and at least shewing him my good Will on this Occasion.

I dare not rob the Publick any farther, by taking up any more of your Excellency's precious moments, excepting most sincerely to congratulate your Excellency on the return of this auspicious Day. I refer your Excellency to Col. Pinckney for every thing worthy your Notice here. and am with the greatest Esteem Yr. Excelly's most hble. Sevt.

CHRISTOPHER GADSDEN

---

[3] Thomas Gadsden, lieutenant in the First South Carolina Regiment, 1776, was apparently not in the battle at Fort Sullivan, as he is not listed under Gadsden's command in 1775. Under Robert Howe in 1778, he was promoted to captain, but on November 17, he was granted "leave unlimited," surely because of his father's altercation with Howe. "Order Book of John Faucheraud Grimke," *SCHM*, XIII (April, July, 1912), 91, 152-3.

[1] Library of Congress.

[2] Daniel Horry of St. James, Santee, was married to Harriott Pinckney, sister of C. C. Pinckney. Horry was a member of the First Provincial Congress, but took the Oath of Allegiance to the Crown during the occupation. His estate was amerced by the Jacksonborough Assembly. He died November 12, 1785, at his plantation. *SCHM*, VII, 105, XIX, 177, XXXIV, 199, XXXIX, 129.

To William Henry Drayton

Chas. Town 7 March 1778 [1]

Dear Sir:

I promised You when any Thing very Material occurred to acquaint you therewith. The Day before Yesterday we presented our Constitution to the president for ratification, which he rejected for the reasons you'll see in his Speech Inclosed.[2] This has thrown us into Great Confusion indeed; we are to meet this Morning to choose another president, and we still hope to pass it totidem Verbis in the Course of Next Week. No Material Alteration has been made to it since you left us. We had a Conference with the Council on some Amendments they sent up which the house disapproved of; however they were at last brought over. I Shall not detain you farther from the Speech excepting by remarking That the president has perverted our Sense (in my Opinion) of the Word "Accommodation" Strangely in our first (or the old) Constitution that Word being Embodied as it were with "unhappy Differences with. G. B." [,] "during the present Situation" and "an Event which tho' traduced and treated *as Rebels* we still Earnestly desire" plainly and incontestably shews that in that Temporary Constitution it refers to a *reconciliation* with G. B. and our becoming Subjects thereto again. Is this such an Accommodation as we are still to look forward to?[3]

See the Speech. You'll see many other Strange Things therein in my Opinion. God Bless You and be assured that I am with Sincerity Yrs.

C. G.

---

[1] South Carolina Miscellany.

[2] Drayton and Gadsden were members of the committee to draw up a new State constitution. A major crisis arose over the desire of Gadsden and the radicals for an unequivocal statement asserting independence. Rutledge, representing the conservatives who regarded the conflict as a civil war, looked forward to an accommodation with Great Britain, and he resigned the presidency in protest. Rutledge's speech is in McCrady, *S.C. in the Revolution,* pp. 238-9; for the history of the constitutional issues, *see* pp. 235-45.

[3] Constitution of 1776 is in *Federal and State Constitutions. . . . ,* Francis Newton Thorpe, comp. (Washington: Government Printing Office, 1909), VI, 3243.

To Benjamin Franklin

Benjamin Franklin (1706-1790), great American statesman, was in England when the furor over the Stamp Act arose. As trouble grew between the American Colonies and the British government, he came back to Philadelphia. Franklin first made Christopher Gadsden's acquaintance at the Continental Congress (1776). Gadsden, Franklin, Silas Deane, Richard Henry Lee, and John Jay, were appointed by the Congress as to a committee to protect the trade of the colonies.

Franklin was on the committee which drafted the Declaration of Independence and was one of the three diplomats in 1781 who negotiated peace with Britain, laying the groundwork for the treaty which followed. Near the end of his life, he took part in the Federal Constitutional Convention in 1787. Journals of the Continental Congress, II, 1775, p. 177.

Chas. Town So. Carolina [1]

14 May 1778

Dear Sir:

I take the Liberty to Introduce the bearer Mr. Thomas Waites [of South Carolina] to your Notice, a young Gentleman who was educated at Philadelphia and of best Connections here. His Business to France is on our Common Cause and if he arrives safe intends himself the Honour to wait on you at Paris. Shou'd he have occasion for your Countenance, I shall be extremely obliged to you to give it; your time must be so continually employed and we know always for our Good, that 'tis a Sin against America to trespass upon it in the least.

---

[1] Benjamin Franklin Papers, American Philosophical Society, Philadelphia. The letter is addressed: "To the honble Benja. Franklin Esq.; Ambassad. to the united States of America at Paris; in Favr. of Mr. Thomas Waites." Waites was a young attorney who later was active in the Republican party, and was considered by Jefferson for the Supreme Court. This letter of introduction seems to have been the earliest record of Waites. He was one of the founders of the Georgetown, South Carolina, Library Society. John Harold Wolfe, *Jeffersonian Democracy in South Carolina* (Chapel Hill: University of North Carolina Press, 1940), p. 196. *See also, SCHM,* XXV, 95.

By the last Accounts from Pennsylvania: We were just about open
ing the Campaign and our prospects very promising. I am Dr. Sir
w. great Sincerity & Esteem Yr. most obed. hble. Servt.

CHRISTOPHER GADSDEN

P.S. Should [Mr. Silas] Deane be with you, pray make my Compliments to him.

Daybook Entries, June-September 1778

*The following document appears to have been a page from a Day-
book, and was partly written in shorthand by Gadsden. It contains
brief notes regarding a number of things: his duel with Brigadier
General Robert Howe of North Carolina; the Continental money;
and damage wrought by the Charles Town fire of 1778.*

1778 [1]

June   Andrew Russell carpenter and Cabinet Maker apply'd to
me to appoint John Collum [,] Shoe Maker his Attorney
to William Trezevant. Mr. Lowndes [2] being from Town.

[late   [The following are entries in shorthand:]

  Aug.?]   Copy of a resolution of Congress respecting General Howe's
command here which he told Col. Elliott [3] the 26 August
78 that he did not receive until some days after the motion
in our assembly about his right to command here which
happened 20 August 77.

In Congress 15th April 77

Resolved that an allowance of 125 dollars per month be
made to Brigadier-General Howe to commence at the

---

[1] South Caroliniana Library. The sections of the Daybook in shorthand were
deciphered by Mr. Paul Napier of Arlington, Virginia. For the key and further
explanation *see* Walsh, "The Gadsen [*sic*] Diary Deciphered," pp. 17-23.

[2] Rawlins Lowndes, president of the Provincial Congress.

[3] Lieutenant Colonel Bernard Elliott of the Continental Corps of Artillery.
He died October 25, 1778.

time he was sent by Major-General Lee to command in South Carolina and Georgia the said allowance being considered as necessary to defray the expences of his table while he commands there and to continue as long as he shall be in such command and that the same allowance be made to any officer [of] equal rank who will hereafter succeed to the said command in that Department.

Extract from the minutes [of] Congress

William Churchill Houstoun [4]
Deputy Secretary

[end of shorthand]

N.B.

Sept. 18: Mr. Heyward [5] who return'd from Congress yesterday
1778　　says the Issues to the Time of his leaving Congress were 68,10000 [sic] Dollers Business Loan Office Certificates. Buildings in Chas Town Valued 6 May 1776 exclusive of Land Brick Foundations *etc.* say 1434 Dwelling Houses 2,502,52 Burnt the 15 January of 1778 of the above Buildings [Viz:] [6]

On the Bay	56	without stores etc.	£177 425
Broad Street	29		727 00
Elliott Street	51		89900
Bedon's Alley	15		28750
Church Street	17		24100
Tradd Street	34		73200
Union Street	32		20760
Chalmers Alley	9		9500
Unity Alley	8		3500
Queen Street	1		8000
	252		507,835

[4] William Churchill Houston (*c.* 1746-1788) of New Jersey was a delegate to the Continental Congress and to the Federal Convention of 1787. *Journals of the Continental Congress, 1777*, VII, 202, 269 70.

[5] Thomas Heyward is buried on his plantation. At "Old House" stands the monument erected to him by the State of South Carolina in the family burying ground. Salley, *Delegates,* pp. 16-29.

[6] Gadsden refers to the "Great Fire of 1778." For descriptions *see* Samuel G. Stoney, (ed.) "The Great Fire of 1778 Seen through Contempory Letters," *SCHM,* LXIV (January, 1963), 23-26.

To William Henry Drayton

Chas. Town 1st June 1778[1]

Dear Drayton:

I am much obliged to you for yours of 28th and 30th April and 4th May which came to hand last Week and as I had an Opportunity immediately to send them to Ferguson, they were accordingly. Powell[2] lives now in Christ Church parish in the Parsonage House. I had not a good [opportunity of] Conveyance to him till Day before Yesterday when I acquainted him with the good News. I find by Your Direction that you knew the House had dubbed me Vice President. This was done the *last Hour* of their Sitting by the plenitude of the Wanton power of a bare house. Parsons[3] was excused on account of his Ill health, and I saw plainly their Views, but cou'd not avoid accepting without throwing the State into Confusion. But this I did not do without letting them know I plainly perceiv'd their Motive—To get rid of me at the next meeting and to make me ineligible at next Election. We have no news here excepting that the Georgians have drawn us into an Expedition to the Southward. This is the 3d Summer we have against our judgment been lugged in in this manner; indeed this year, We have begun a little earlier, but still nothing like early enough, and I am afraid it will end like all the Rest. No Man more sanguine than myself for having Augustine; indeed we must have it, at any rate almost. I have long thought so, and more than ever now we are near upon a Treaty with Britain; otherwise it will be an eternal Thorn in our sides and every Year Worse and Worse, for from the Nature of our Estates in this Country being chiefly in Negroes, and those Negroes hired out by their Owners (which I have ever thought excessively impolitick) as labourers, Fisher-men, Carpenters, Brick Layers, *etc.* we must have; tis the Natural Consequence of such a State, a number of loose Idle people totally in

---

[1] South Carolina Miscellany.

[2] Colonel George Gabriel Powell was a member of the Provincial Congress and of the revolutionary Secret Committee with Drayton: McCrady, *S. C. in the Revolution,* p. 108.

[3] James Parsons was a moderate member of the Provincial Congress, *ibid.,* p. 30.

a Manner abandon'd as our very poor must be for want of Work, the Negroes eating them out of that and the prudent sober poor Man with or indeed without a Family in such Circumstances, will come here. These, and the Scum of all the States from Pennsylvania hitherward, all Deserters, Outlaws *etc.* will naturally flock to Augustine as an asylum and no doubt Britain will give them every Political Encouragement and what must be Georgia's and our Situation to be continually exposed to the Incursions of such desperate Rascals without Principle or property? Were I at Congress upon a Treaty, I would strive hard to have that Place Delivered up to the States, at least, that its Fortification be totally destroyed. Augustine wou'd be of more Consequence to the states, especially the [Senior] Ones and more easily given up than the Bahamas, which would be of more disservice than Use to us as it certainly would occasion great Jealousies and that with some shew of reason, to all the Foreign powers who have Islands in the West Indies; this we ought to avoid by every Means in our power. Indeed I have long been firmly persuaded that were the powers of Europe to agree to give us any of the best Islands in the West Indies, that it would not be the Interest of the States by any Means to accept them. The West Indies must depend principally, Nay almost altogether, on the States of America for their Lumber and provisions and what would we more? Augustine I say we must have if possible, but then the Plan should be concerted in the Summer, every Thing got ready by November and then March with 7 or 8 healthy Months before us; with such a plan well laid, I never thought the Difficulty very great. But our Summer Months are dreadful indeed. The sickness of the Troops is 10 Times more to be apprehended than the Opposition of the Enemy.

I read the Resolutions of the Committee of Congress with regard to Lord North's proposal with attention.[4] The Alternative left by Congress to the expected Negociators, I am extremely shagrined at, and am afraid will be productive of very ill Consequences. Suppose the British troops should be withdrawn which in my Opinion for many reasons they will and must be, and you suffer them to treat with you *before* they have acknowledged explicitly our Independence, will they, think you, do it afterwards? by no

---

[4] Lord North's Proposal was a reference to the Carlisle Commission which offered peace, a proposal based on the repeal of all objectionable legislation passed after 1763, and home rule for America. Some Congressmen rose to the bait, but the treaty with France arrived in time to dash British hopes. Gadsden thought the Commission dangerous, especially in view of the long quarrel over separation in South Carolina. Samuel F. Bemis, *Diplomacy of American Revolution,* pp. 67-68.

Means; they will leave that to hang over your heads, till a fairer Opportunity for them, and in the Mean time they will harrass you with their Navy or amuse you for the Present knowing that you must keep a considerable Body of Forces Always on Foot, and their Emissaries at the same Time will be poisoning the Minds of our people. My only hopes are that as the Congress came to that resolution *before* the Arrival of the Commissioners, that they will recollect themselves, and think better, begging their Honour's pardon, before they admit them to a Treaty. I have *no Favours* to ask of Congress, nor wish nor ever wished for any, but I cannot say but if a fair Opportunity should offer, I should be glad the Congress *collectively* were acquainted fully and candidly with my Affairs with Howe, as from what dropt from Heyward and Middleton in the House. Howe's letter [5] was laid before them at an unlucky Time for me and perhaps my Arch Enemy by some dextrous Movement took Care to time it so when they had just before thought themselves indelicately treated by 2 or 3 General Officers who seem'd to threaten them with a resignation. My Case was very different; I ever respected the Power of Congress and no man in America ever strove more (*and more successfully*) first to bring about a Congress in 1765 and then to support it *ever* afterwards than myself. My reason for resigning was as *you know* the Indelicate Treatment of a Thin House when I acquainted them or rather endeavoured to acquaint them that General Howe had no Appointment; no *fair* Sanction of Congress either midiately or immediately; all I wanted was to make him produce it if he had, which this State had a Right to see and so had I from the Nature of my Trust as next in Command. Had I seen any Authority of Congress I should have submitted, whatever my private Opinion might have been, out of respect to the Congress. Howe was at Georgia when Lee left it, had nothing to shew from under Lee's hand, to return here and take Command, but cunningly riggled into it as I always said. What happened afterwards when Genl. Moore was here was out of the Case. M[o]ore found him here *where* he had no Orders to be. As for my part I have *no Aim* but to be fairly represented to Congress, that I did not mean them any disrespect, and as I think I now have a fairer Opportunity from having some Friends among our Dele-

---

[5] The Gadsden-Howe Affair grew out of Gadsden's questioning of Brigadier General Robert Howe's right to Command in South Carolina, and the nearly disastrous expedition against St. Augustine. The incident was made a party weapon against Gadsden. *See* correspondence, July 4, September 9, August 15-16, 1778. The account of the duel was published in the *South Carolina and American General Gazette,* September 3, 1778; a satire by Major André was republished from a New York newspaper by Johnson, *Traditions,* pp. 205-6. For the abortive attempt by Howe on St. Augustine, *see* William Moultrie, *Memoirs of the American Revolution* (New York: D. Longworth, 1802), I, 203-40.

gates which was *not* the Case before. I should be glad, and obliged to you when a proper opportunity offers not to miss it, especially as you all know the real Merits of the Matter. Whatever may be thought of me, tis certainly a Scandal that our State should have suffered herself to be so long duped and degraded by such an *unexampled* instance. I never blamed Congress because they were never acquainted therewith. I have got the Crisis [6] as far as No. 5; when any more come out pray send them to me. *We have* had the 5th reprinted here from a Copy sent to me and made large Subscriptions to disperse it. Inclosed I send you a Copy of the Proceedings of the House and Committee relative to their proceedings on the late Presidents resigning his Commission, which I had copied out for you at the time but my Indisposition and several other Matters prevented my sending it sooner. I am Yrs. & c.

C. G.

P.S. Our last papers contain Nothing but what you sent us, so tis Needless to send them Pray shew this to some of my Old Friends particularly R.H. Lee if *with* you.

[Copy enclosed by Gadsden unavailable].

To General William Moultrie

Charleston, June 4th, 1778 [1]

Sir:

I received your favor, and immediately laid before the council, who desired me to give orders for fifty tents, 250 canteens and two doz. kettles, which are all we can spare. The pork you say you have already ordered. Inclosed is the order for the above articles which will be charged to Congress. I am & c.

CHRIST GADSDEN
[Order not Available].

---

[6] Gadsden referred to Thomas Paine's essays. *The Crisis No. 5* was entitled "To General Sir William Howe and to the Inhabitants of America," March 21, 1778, in *The Writings of Thomas Paine*, Moncure D. Conway, ed. (New York: G.P. Putnam's Sons, 1894-1896), I, 233-60.

[1] Moultrie, *Memoirs of the Revolution*, II, 216. Original not found. The letter concerns supplies for South Carolina troops under Moultrie's command before St. Augustine.

129

To Peter Timothy

Monday Evening 8th June 1778 [1]

Sir:

The President being much indisposed and likely to lose another of his Sons has requested me by letter to do the immediate Necessary public Business. None I think more so than to have 50 or 100 Copies of the proclamation immediately struck off from the Copy you have for the Country. This is necessary also in order to undeceive the Misled Inhabitants of Chas. Town and prevent farther Mischiefs as Nothing can be clearer than that there is not a *single* Tittle in the proclamation contrary to the Law it relates to, which I am persuaded will be seen by the Candid and dispassionate the Moment 'tis published. 'Tis Necessary also for the Vindication of the President and Council, that it should be immediately printed and dispersed;[2] their Characters, every Man of feeling must think are deeply concern'd and that being the case, shall the press be stopt and the only public Way of Vindicating public Characters shut up against the Contrary to common Equity and Expressly flying in the Face of an Article of that very Constitution which the people have sworn to support? I court no popularity am neither afraid nor ashamed to say *any where* that I advised this Measure; if wrong let the people impeach us; that is the Constitutional Method, unless restless flighty Men of which I am afraid we have too many amongst us want again to be running upon every Fancy to the Meetings of liberty Tree. Query whether this is not a Disease amongst us far more dangerous than any thing that can arise from the whole present Herd of contemptible exportable Tories. You have had a great Share I believe the greatest of the public Favours in the press Way, which would still have been continued to you. Was your press in the Situation it used to be; you well know,

---

[1] South Carolina Miscellany.

[2] On March 28, 1778, the Provincial Congress passed a stringent loyalty oath. It proved impossible to enforce, and during the absence of Rawlins Lowndes, Lieutenant Governor Gadsden urged the Council to issue a Proclamation staying the execution of the law. Peter Timothy was reluctant to publish the Proclamation, and Gadsden's former followers, the mechanics, rioted. June 15, 1778; *Charleston's Sons of Liberty,* pp. 83-87.

some kind of Business, cannot be delayed and therefore for the public sake must be sent where 'tis most likely to have the greatest Dispatch; if ever Business was of the Sort, the present most certainly is. I hope Mr. Boden [3] is now to be found and that you will not deny your press to the presidents proclamation. For my part I never wish'd for nor sought my present Situation nor was I put into it from favour to me but merely by the plenitude of the Wanton power of a Bare House. However as I am placed in it, I will do my Duty thereinto the best of my Judgement and will be intimidated neither by the Many nor few. I have administered the Oath to several this Morning and will to as many as call on me within the Time mentioned in the Proclamation; this I have publickly declared and wish it to be as publickly known as possible.

C. G.

To William Henry Drayton

Chas. Town 15th June 1778 [1]

Dear Drayton:

About the latter End of last or Beginning of this Month I wrote to you very fully in Answer to your Favours of 28th, 30th April and 4th of May per post. I then gave you every Thing I could pick up here worth your Notice. Nothing hath happened since except a Flurry in Town which your Congressional honours have been the Occasion of and of which the Authors and Abettors here seem to be most heartily asham'd. Your Resolution of 23rd April extending the Time of reception to the Tories [2] and which you inclosed to your humble Servant was no sooner seen, than the policy and propriety thereof instantaneously struck him, a Council being to meet that very Morning. I was happy to find his Excellency had it handed to him by your president. [I] immediately moved that we should do something here as nearly conformable as we could. This Motion I repeated Again and Again but for some Days was

[3] Nicholas Boden was Timothy's partner. Cohen, *op. cit.,* p. 244.
[1] South Carolina Miscellany.
[2] The resolution recommended mercy and pardon to the Tories who might join the rebels. *Journals of the Continental Congress,* X, 381-2.

delayed through a Variety of Accidents; on the 5th the enclosed proclamation was issued by advice of the Council, and none more pressing for it than myself. It was hardly got into the Sheriff's Hands before some Myrmidons Alarm'd the Town, Setting up a Proclamation against Law; we were going to ruin their Liberties and What not! The proclamation I believe was never read; a Deputation was sent to the President of Doctor Budd, Capt. Mouatt, Joshua Ward and some others.[3] His proclamation was returned to him in my presence which of itself is Insult enough but besides that the spokesman Mr. Ward told the President He thought the people were right and he would lose the last Drop of Blood to support them. This I thought so high an Insult that I immediately began with Ward, sarcastically applauded his Heroism and great Exertions for the publick Good. In return he told me I was a Madman, but first took Care to sneak out of my reach; however had he not, I should have done nothing more, as I was prepared, than what I did, laugh in his Face. The President did all that Man could do but to no purpose. A Meeting was call'd in the Evening, Doctor Budd put in the Chair, every press prohibited from printing the proclamation and the Magistrates detered from granting Certificates to the penitent. At this Crisis I Don Quixotte Secundus who never had acted the Magistrate before gave out publickly that I would give the Oath of Fidelity and Certificates to any applicants by the 10th and accordingly did so to many. I was in the Midst of the people where I found them chiefly a Mere Mob, with here and there some who ought not to have been, and I was sorry to see there and had reason to suspect *that Day* much *Negative* Impulse. I told them I advised the Measure, and that they should put a Halter about my Neck and hang me at once if they thought it wrong That they had a Constitutional Remedy; they might impeach the President and Council if they acted improperly and that they had better do that. But all to no purpose. In my Opinion, if they

---

[3] Dr. John Budd had gained the confidence of the mechanics. In the postwar years, he became an advocate of tax exemption for them. Joshua Ward was a lawyer and merchant who was active in founding an insurance company after the war. How Ward figures in the rioting against Gadsden is not known, but Henry Peronneau must have had radical democratic leanings. A lieutenant of Militia who underwent a court-martial, he emerged as a self-styled leader of the people in 1784. During that year Peronneau led a group of about two hundred tradesmen in a demonstration before the State House against an "aristocratic government." A general meleé ensued, during which rioters shattered windows in the building. Peronneau was arrested. *SCHM*, XXXIV, 78-79; IV, 209; II, 231, XXXIII, 2-5; XXI, 83; XVII, 8-9; III, 129; VIII, 21, 74; IX, 145. *Charleston Evening Gazette*, August 15, 1785; Nathanael Pendleton to Nathanael Greene, July 10, 1784; William Washington to Nathanael Greene July 8, 1784, Greene Papers, Clements Library, University of Michigan.

C·T·MORRIS

Let Blank leaves be inserted between every Leaf as far as page 75 & no farther — also thirty blank leaves at the Beginning ~~fifty~~

❁❁❁❁❁❁❁❁❁✺❁❁❁❁❁❁❁❁❁

J O U R N A L

OF the PROCEEDINGS of the

C O N G R E S S.

❁❁❁❁❁❁❁❁❁✺❁❁❁❁❁❁❁❁❁

Christ Gadsden

1774

were not set on the old Leven was at least not sorry for it, as it was echoed amongst the people, I am told, that had Mr. R. been president Nothing of this Sort would have happen'd. They Met again the 10th and after some Fuss between young Peronneau of the 2d Regiment and Doctor Budd, the latter was again placed in the Chair; when after a Variety of motions and amongst the rest to impeach President and Council, they at last came to the resolution penn'd at the Bottom of the printed proclamation and then broke up. That resolution I am told was penn'd by E[dward] R[utledge] and is printed in Wells' last paper *without the Proclamation.*[4] The one sent you is printed as you will see *since the 10th* as a Hand Bill and I question now whether it will be printed at all in the regular Gazettes, but from a different Motive, I am fully persuaded, than that through which it was prevented at first. That was Violence and party Manoevre. Now it will be hindered underhandedly by Shame if possible. I leave you to Judge of the Proclamation; for my part, I am extremely sorry for the Stop put to it, as it may be and I am afraid will be, of Great Disservice, in the Situation our Army is to the Southward where it would have been particularly Useful and not without its great Service elsewhere. But in Short every Thing done by Lowndes is to be withdrawn. I plainly see into Mischief. I am Dr. Drayton Yr. Most hble. Servant

C. G.

P.S. The principle Heroes of the Disturbance were young Peronneau of 2d Regiment, Hex[t] Prioleau, Doctor Budd, Capt. Mouatt and Josh[u]a Ward.[5]

---

[4] The notice of the meeting of June 10 of the inhabitants with their resolution is in John Wells' *South Carolina and American General Gazette,* June 11, 1778. Wells reported to Laurens that Lowndes, although always working in the interest of his country, had gained the political enmity of the Rutledges, (the *"Family Compact,"* as their opponents "stiled" them), because of his "attachment to Mr. Gadsden" and his acceptance of the president's chair vacated by John Rutledge. The Rutledges made use of Lowndes' unpopularity with the people. The "Violent Party" tabbed Lowndes a friend of the Tories, finding evidence to accuse him, in his caution to move against Britain on the eve of the Revolution. He was disliked, also, because of his strict investigations of the public accounts. Lowndes' "dealing out of the Public money with a very heavy hand has given much offence," said Wells. The "Civil and Military Departments" were complaining because of money matters, and he found the "Gentlemen of the Army" against him. John Wells Jr. to Henry Laurens, September 6, 1778, Kendall Collection, South Caroliniana Library.

[5] Hext Prioleau was a shipchandler and merchant who kept a store on Tradd Street near the Bay. *Gazette of the State of South Carolina,* July 8, 1778; "Records Kept by Colonel Isaac Hayne," *SCHM*, X, 228. Captain John Mouatt was attached to the South Carolina Continental Regiment and later became a prisoner of the British at St. Augustine: *ibid.,* XX, 261.

P.S. Poor Lowndes has lost two Sons [,] five Boys one after another; the only children he had by his last Wife.

Tis now the 16th. A Letter to the president was read yesterday in Council from Governor Hewston of Georgia, by which he seems to have the most Sanguine Expectations of success in his Expedition to Augustine. He says as to Men and provisions they have plenty, but for my part, the Season of the Year is what I ever dreaded most. God Grant they may be successful for in my opinion we shall never be quiet here till [we] have Augustine, but every Year will be worse and worse.

Perhaps you don't recollect the last Test Law. It no where prevents the Oath being administered *at any time,* nor doss it *oblige* the Delinquents to go off, but only lays them under certain Disabilities if they do not take the Oath of fidelity and Allegiance before a certain Time as that the Proclamation is not in one Tittle contrary to law and is only Similar to what has been done in England without blame, where a King upon an Application from the people, during the recess of parliament concerning any Law that they look upon as hurtful graciously tells them, that he will recommend their Application to his Parliament and "endeavour to obtain" (the very words of Lowndes) redress of Mitigation of the Law *etc.* A Mr. Brailsford and one Mr. Dee are in Gaol upon Information on Oath of setting on Foot a Club about the Time of passing our last test Act under an Oath of Secrecy the Chief Business of which seems to have been to delude our most useful Tradesmen and prevent their taking the Oath of Allegiance to your State telling them it was better to go off than go up the path with halters about their Necks.

Charlestown 4th July 1778 [1]

Dear Sir:

I have been long anxious to see Howe's letter to Congress [2] on my Affair, and am much oblig'd to you for finding it under cover of your favor of the 11th last Month, which came to hand the 27th. Never was Congress more imposed upon than by the plausible

---

[1] Laurens Letter Book, "Promiscuous Letters," 1778, SCHS. It is inscribed: "Copy of a Letter from General Gadsden to his Friend in Congress."
[2] Brigadier General Robert Howe's letter to Congress, dated Charleston, August 28, 1777, was published by Robert W. Gibbes in the *Historical Magazine,* IV (September, 1860), 265-6. Gadsden's letter to Drayton is a paragraph-by-paragraph rebuttal of Howe's. Gadsden hoped Drayton would publish it or, in some manner, make the facts to the Congress which had so unceremoniously accepted his resignation. However, for reasons unknown, Drayton withheld the letter, and Gadsden's case was never fully understood.

artifice and colouring therein contained. The only point in dispute between us, *by which authority he left Georgia to return here* is totally supress'd. General Lee certainly left him *there* then, if any where the command devolved upon him, and a written Order from General Lee to return here was necessary, and what I had a right to see, as next in Command, but I am well satisfied he had none such to produce. General Howe told me at Coll. Cattel's Table in presence of Lieut. Colonel Elliot of the Artillery Regiment Captain Scott and Pinckney of the first and I think Captain Ladsen that he had an Order;[3] I immediately reply'd that I only wish'd to see it to be satisfied, but finding this explain'd away to a *verbal* Order, I was desirous that Congress should be acquainted with my difficulties which in presence of the Gentlemen just named he promised to do and shew me his letter on the subject. I then was entirely satisfied to wait the Event; what greater experience has Howe had in the land Service than myself? My having been an Officer in the British Navy some time, gave me I think in *the most material* service here, that of the Garrison in a Harbour open to the Ocean, some advantages in Sea Attacks, what we are most exposed to, over him. I confess I have the vanity to think that my known steady, active, uniform, decisive conduct from the very first of our dispute with Great Briain, before, and at that thru first Congresses in America in 1765, 1774, and 1775 and ever since would have procured that usual small Boon of attention to a disinterested Officer of Rank and such a Character as to have given me an opportunity to explain myself upon such an occasion, and not have suffered me to undergo the mortification to find my Enemy's representation immediately and implicitly attended to, and the reasons for my conduct not worth a moments waiting for, or inquiring about. My New England friends particularly never found me so cool and indifferent to their concerns or taking all said or wrote about them for granted. The conduct of the then Carolina Delegates I confess was not much beyond my expectations. I intended no offence to Congress, have served in a Military Character as Colonel and General upwards of two years at my own expence for table and everything else, excepting barely a single Ration apiece for myself and Servants,

---

[3] The officers named are Lieutenant Colonel Barnard Elliott, Captain Charles Cotesworth Pinckney, Captain William Scott, and Lieutenant James Ladson, all of the First South Carolina Regiment. The altercation took place at Lieutenant Colonel William Cattel's plantation at Cattel's Bluff on the Ashley River. "Papers of the First Council of Safety of the Revolutionary Party," *SCHM,* I (January, 1900), 52, 53, 56; "Letters from Col. Lewis Morris to Anne Elliott," *SCHM,* XL (October, 1939), 122; "Order Book of John Faucheraud Grimke, August 1778 to May 1780," *SCHM,* XIII, (April, 1912), 90; *Wells' Register and Almanac,* pp. 93-94.

have not received nor ever intended to receive any Pay. Having these feelings, I thought I would not complain to Congress, as it might seem *at first* to proceed from an anxiety for Command and *afterwards* as fishing for a reinstation, than which, nothing was or is now further from me; these were perhaps proud feelings and deserved a severe mortification, and my expectations too unreasonable, be it so God Bless the Congress and prosper all their undertakings for the good of the United States. I must still beg your patience and leave to return Howe's letter with my remarks thereon, paragraph by paragraph. 'Tis really so very specious and artful that I cannot avoid it; with regard to myself, I am only solicitous about the propriety of my doubting his authority to command here *when he returned from Georgia* and of my laying the matter before the Assembly, especially when he had *forfeited his promise* of writing to Congress himself.

These remarks I now subjoin to this Introduction:

1 - 1 Remarks

1 - 1 Why General Gadsden adopted this Idea he has endeavoured to shew in the above introduction and following remarks and however strange it may seem to General Howe, he thinks he has there accounted for it.

2 - 2 "Where he [Howe] had station'd me," more than strange assertion—the enemy's fleet left us about 2nd or 3d August Vizt Colonel (now General) Moultrie being desirous to have his regiment reliev'd immediately, Colonel Roberts [4] was thought of for that purpose, but as soon as I was assured of Colonel Moultrie's intention, I particularly desir'd the then President Mr. Rutledge that my Regiment might be ordered to that Post. The President told me I would have been thought of at first, only he imagin'd I would rather remain at Fort Johnston after the improvements I had there made. My regiment accordingly relieved the 2nd at fort Moultrie the 9th Augt., 1776. General Lee and General Armstrong both here. In these circumstances how Congress could be told *"he stationed me there"* I can't conceive myself, unless General Howe

---

[4] Colonel Owen Roberts of the First South Carolina Regiment. He was killed at Stono Ferry, June 20, 1779. Francis B. Heitman, *Historical Register of Officers of the Continental Army* . . . (Washington: Rare Book Shop Publishing Co., Inc., 1914), p. 469.

(after Brigadier General Moore [5] left us who came here a very considerable time after he returned from Georgia) then issued a *cunning* Order altogether unnecessary excepting to give him a plausible pretence to figure a way with to Congress and get fixed here, for before General Lee left us, I had with his approbation undertaken the Bridge from Sullivan's to the Main, which he was anxious for, and had made a very considerable progress in it, before General Moore came here. Could general Howe then with any propriety order me from that Station? If not, why his Order to *station* me there? Was I not there already? But be this as it may, I never had any such Order sent to my Post, that I can recollect, and should have thought it very *strange* if I Had.

3 - 3 His answer indeed might have been *very short,* all I wanted to know was by what authority he returned here *from Georgia,* a very short answer would have satisfied me and no disputes ever happened had I not a right as the officer he took upon him to come here to command to see his Order for so doing? This was my pinning question that he evaded, and has purposely said not a syllable about it to Congress.

4 - 4 I understand always that he came here as a Volunteer from Virginia where I am much misinformed if he had those *"advantages"* he puffs away with, as having here, connections, blood relationship to first families, confidence of the army and public in general and what not. General Lee put him in Orders here the 12th June 1776 vizt in these words *"The Country Militia* to receive their Orders from Brigadier General Howe.["] At the time I went from Fort Johnston to fort Moultrie (about a week after the enemy's fleet left us) I believe it would have been very difficult for him or the Devil himself to have found ten of his Command in town—so much for that order the 7th August. General Lee order'd "a Detachment of 1 Capt. 3 Subs 4 Sergt and 70 Rank and file from the first battalion of South Carolina" the same number from the 2nd and 130 Rank and file from the 3d or Regt. of Rangers with the Common proportion of Officers to their number, and likewise 30 men from the Artillery with the Proportion of Officers Colonel Roberts shall determine to prepare "themselves immediately for a March. They are to *receive their instructions* from General Howe who will ap-

---

[5] Brigadier General James Moore of North Carolina was to assist in the defence of Charles Town with troops from his State, but he remained at Wilmington to observe the movements of some British ships. He arrived at Charles Town in November 1776, staying until February 5, 1777, when he was ordered to join General Washington. Moore died in April, at Wilmington while preparing for the march northward. *DAB,* XIII, 129.

point *two field Officers to take command of them."* The next day the 8th the Waggon Master is (order'd to) immediately report to General Howe what number of Public Waggons are in Town, and as soon as any others arrive to inform him of them. This is very little relative General Howe when put in orders on duty here by General Lee.

5 - 5 "And left me in the execution of it": How violently is Georgia *thrust* out here, where it presented itself so naturally, for there he was left *in the execution of Duty imposed* by General Lee and *there* the Command if any where, devolved on him as eldest officer, *not here,* he returned here without Orders. What I expressed myself dissatisfied with was not "this" as he would artfully hope Congress would think, no, with "this" I must have been satisfied, had it been the case here. viz. That he had been left here by General Lee, and the command by course of service devolved on him, but it being quite otherways and the Command *not devolving* on him here by course of Service, but he coming here of his own *sure motion* to take it, had not I a right to see some written order for his so doing? Might he not as well have taken an opportunity in the absence of superior officers to him to have gone back from Georgia to North Carolina or Virginia and been the light, Itinerant Brigadier General Knight Errant to General Lee's whole Department, and how North Carolina or Virginia would have relished that, needs no conjuration to tell.

6 - 6 The General is quite out in his pretended discovery of the source from whence I took my "notions" of a Brigadier General. I took them from the fountainhead of American Authority, that of Congress itself and particularly from their proper Order on their appointment of no less than six Brigadier Generals at one time, and amongst the rest General Howe himself the 1st March 1776. The words are these—"Resolved that Brigadier Armstrong be *directed to repair* to South Carolina, Brigadier Lewis and Howe to Virginia and Brigadier Moore to North Carolina and to take the command of the forces in those respective Colonies until they receive farther Orders from Congress or a Superior Officer." What cou'd be more prudent and necessary than such a Resolve as this? which had General Howe kept strictly to, there would not have been the least occasion for any dispute between him and me. Does not this order imply that a Brigadier ought on no account to leave his station without proper orders? And what confusion, Heart burnings and uneasiness too obvious to mention must naturally be the consequence if the lowest rank of General officers a brigadier,

the mere Colonel as it were of 3 or 4 Regiments is left ad libertum to go from one state to another. What is the most natural construction of the foregoing Resolve of Congress *applicable to the case* between General Howe and me? I think this. General Lee *his superior officer* in conformity to that Resolve, order'd him from the State of Virginia to accompany him to this, then invaded; here he properly was and could not leave that State but in consequence of the same Resolve of Congress, here again agreeably thereto, the same *superior* Officer orders him to another State, Georgia. Here again the same Resolve of Congress ought to have been his direction and as strictly observed, but was it so? By what order of either Congress or superior Officer did he leave that State? By none. So much for my "notions" of an American Brigadier General with regard to this matter between him and me.

7 - 7 This is a mere subterfuge, a piece of downright low cunning, Jockeying and sharping, and none but a Man determined at any rate to wedge himself into Command would stoop to it, the effect of low Ambition indeed. My thinking at first he must have had an order to come here from Georgia, its being everywhere said he was going away in five or six weeks; my delicacy upon that Account as he came to our assistance when under actual invasion; my then having a good opinion of him; my being at an out post on a laborious undertaking that required my residence there continually and several other reasons prevented my making any great stir about it at first, only thinking it to a particular friend or two, whose advice I could rely on. I was advised to be silent, as there was great reason to think he really was going. The Brigade appointed him by Brigadier Moore (of which presently) General Howe seems to catch at as his greatest Fort, but my answer to him here is *very short,* by whose or what order was he absent from Georgia when Brigadier Genl. Moore came here? He ought then to have been in that State. There he was left by General Lee and without a breach of the Resolve of Congress just mentioned could not have left here at all without some proper Orders. Will Congress countenance such Joyckeying? What is meant by "I had a Brigadier assigned by General Lee and General Moore which Brigadier was here when I became the Commander in Chief," I can't divine as Lee and Moore were never here together, and besides from their different rank could never issue a *joint* order as seems here to be *imply'd,* or perhaps this thick Mud is purposely thrown up to escape like a crab under it. They must be different Brigades, Lee's I have already noticed, as to that assigned by Moore 'tis nothing to the purpose, be it what it may for the reason just mentioned;

besides would he have screened himself behind this *after* appointment of a Brigadier exactly of the same standing with himself, and made from a Colonel of North Carolina too as well as himself, had he anything to shew from Major General Lee for his coming here? But this is a happy advantage of *connection,* old acquaintance from Children and *Blood Relationship.*

8 - 8 He promised me at Coll. Cattell's table to lay the matter before Congress and shew me his Letter. I thought this shew'd some Candour, was satisfied with it and told him so. But this I am now fully persuaded was done only to amuse and gain more time.

9 - 9 This deserves as gross a denial as can be given. I was very seldom in town, tho' my post in sight of my House, as all my friends and I believe the whole town knows, and where I was, my stay was always very short. Some little Time after the above Promise, I called on General Howe on what occasion I cannot recollect, did not stay I am persuaded ten minutes. I believe he then threw out something that seemed tending to this matter which I purposely avoided, resolving to keep him to his promise—and this I told him at the President's on the occasion he mentions.

10 - 10 W. Drayton's Motion was on the 20th of August 1777 "that a Committee be appointed and impowered to send for Persons, Papers and Records, and that they be directed to apply to Brig General Howe for Copies of the Commission and instruction *which authorized him to take* the Command of the South Carolina quota of troops in the Army of the United States and to report thereon." Is there any thing desired in this common Parliamentary Motion more than barely to know *by what authority* he commanded here? "To inquire into the *nature* of his Command and to send for *all* Persons and to call for *all* Records and Papers *requisite* thereto" is certainly not being so exact as might have been expected from a general so minutely attentive to every thing that passed first and last relative to this motion, he was really *we all know* upon very hard duty that day *at least,* and performed his part with admirable dexterity. A grand question it certainly was whether the American Military Command should be such a sacred Arcanum that any General, provided that he was on the list should, at his pleasure go out of one State into another, and upon his own *Ipse Dixit* Command the confidential Officers of that State he came into, without being obliged to shew the officer he supercedes his authority for so doing or being exposed to any Legislative enquiry that particular State might think proper to Order upon such an occasion; let me here

give you Copy of an Order issu'd by General Howe from Head Quarters the 9th of August eleven days before the motion in the Assembly presently after the Interview he mentions with me at the late Presidents where I gave him *notice* that such a motion would be made; 'tis in my opinion altogether unprecedented, and not very delicate with regard to this State and quite unnecessary as we were under no apprehensions of any Enemy at that Season— That "all Continental Officers of the Army who are Members of the General Assembly may consider themselves as exempt from Military duty whenever they choose or shall be required to attend the Hon'ble House of Assembly."

11-11   I believe every method was taken in and out of the House *from the date of the above order to misrepresent* the natural and necessary intention of the step proposed and intended to be moved in the Assembly, and to prepossess the minds of many of the Members against it, and I am sorry to say with too much success. Our Assembly consists of upwards of 200 Members of which 89 were present, many of the Members who voted against the Motion declared they had been mistaken, the tendency of the motion had been represented them in the most terrible colours. They were very sorry for it very soon afterwards. The misfortune was that members having [had] served but very little in Assemblies, and little used to the forms of Parliament. The right as the General seems to represent *even* to Congress that the Committee were authorized to send for *all* his Papers, and that thereby we might be involved in a dispute with Congress—to suggest that Congress can possibly take amiss an enquiry of the Legislature of any State whether any Man, General or not General pretending to be sent by them, mediately or immediately, is really what he pretends to be, and no counterfeit, is in my opinion one of the highest insults that can be offered to Congress and would if true justly tend to make the good People of the United States very jealous of their power indeed. The motion was for a Committee of Enquiry. The oldest members in the House could not produce an instance where a committee of that sort had ever been before denied. The gentlemen against the motion the Military, and the boasted connections of the General were remarkably and unusually exact in having on that occasion the strictest attention paid to the then *newly made* Rules of the House (which have been since reprobated) ; a remarkable instance happened in Mr. Lowndes, our present President who seconded the motion with a very few words indeed, merely of explanation of the intention of the motion; he spoke once afterwards in support of it, reserving himself to answer my objections, and upon getting up to speak again tho' he declared he had reserved himself for that purpose, and at first *only* to second the motion, yet he was not permitted to give his sentiments. This uncommon strictness had this happy effect that it opened the Eyes of many and occasioned them to consider *what* could be the cause of so extraordinary a struggle, which though too late to be of service at that time; yet there is very little doubt I believe that such an enquiry upon a like occasion will ever be rejected again, *be* the Military Industry what it may, more than it was then, can hardly be.

12 -12 To call this proceeding *extraordinary* may not be amiss but who occasioned it? General Howe who did not comply with his promise to lay the matter that you rise to it before Congress in time and would give no proper satisfaction otherways. But to say this matter is not proper to be agitated by an Assembly, is to say that the Representatives of a State have no right to enquire into a thing of the utmost moment to them and that may affect their very existence. That an officer shall leave one State (where perhaps they might want to get rid of them [him]) and of his own *mere motion* go into another State and supersede the natural officer of that State without producing proper credentials for so doing, may be of the most pernicious consequence. In a Brigadier, I think I have shewn 'tis expressly contrary to a declared Resolve of Congress. An instance of that sort cannot be too soon or too *effectually* remonstrated against, not only by the officer he supercedes, who perhaps may not be always so immediately attended to as the urgency of the case may require, but backed by the weight of the legislature of the State, it will not fail to be attended to with all possible dispatch, for if a precedent be admitted at one time, that may be followed at another, and in times of actual or expected invasion the Military power of the State may be taken from the Man the People had the highest confidence in and transferred to a stranger or one they knew little of, and perhaps too, one that neither Congress or a Prudent superior Officer properly authorized would by any means have approved of, and before Congress can be acquainted there with the intended remedy to so weak a state as ours particularly at so alarming a distance from them, may come too late, the mischief, and that perhaps the greatest may be done, the State betrayed.

13 - 13 No man has shewn himself more dextrous in the Political intriguing way than General Howe, and the late occasion mainfested it glaringly; his *advantages* were certainly made *the most* of that day. For my part I wish for nothing to speak for my Actions. By actions I form my judgement of all Men, and particularly of those in a Public Character; pretty letters and pretty Speeches, Connec-

tions, Blood Relationships *etc.,* give no man any solid recommenda
tion to me; however the General seems to be of quite a different
opinion, and I know they have been of service in preference to me
in more instances than one in the Military way, tho' I had my unsolicited Commission as Colonel of a Regiment, inferior to none in
America, when he was *asking* for one in North Carolina. My Commission was owing to unknown Connections, always the best in my
Judgement. However, if he is pleased with his boasted Connections,
I am entirely so with my *no connections but the public,* and thus
let this digression end.

14 - 14 "Come to me." Would it not be naturally inferred from this
Expression that I waited on the General at his House with my commission? I delivered it to him just as the Assembly adjourned, as we
were all going down stairs in presence, I may say, of all the Members.
As I never solicited any honours from my Country men either directly
or indirectly, so I was always determnied never to retain any, one
moment longer than it appeared to be their wish I should, *the not
hearing me upon a Point of duty* and what appeared to me of the
greatest concern to the State (for not suffering a thing to be committed is certainly not hearing) made me think it not safe or *for their
good* to hold so important a Commission any longer. Had the matter
been committed, reported on, properly and fully debated let the
determination been as it might, I should have acquiesced with pleasure
and never thought of resigning my Commission. As it was, I had no
longer reason to expect from the sample just given, their support, in
any future exertions for their service, and therefore I thought it
high time to resign; this was my *only* reason; no slight was ever
intended to Congress; however 'tis done now. I think still I could
not as a man of feeling that has shewn himself upon all occasions
void of all selfish and interested views, act otherwise. I have never repented it since, nor have the most distant wish it was undone. All
I wished for from Congress was the treatment I would have given to
a good subaltern or Sergeant who upon a similar sudden occasion
had done the like, that is, indulged his feelings so far as to have
given him an opportunity to telling what hurt him; but I was unlucky; it seems my Commission was laid before Congress when not
well pleased upon some occasion with an application from some of
their Generals. By Howe's Letter (which was all taken for Gospel)
my behaviour was made to appear not very satisfactory and my
Resignation immediately received without further ceremony. If it
had not been *necessarily* laid before Congress by the greatest and
most inveterate Enemy I have in the world, I might than have thought
the *Contretemps* owing to my ill luck only, and that Howe's immediate promotion was not set on foot by, and made part of a grati-

143

fication to an individual for his outing me. However I have no favours to ask. My principle motive in this is to lay open the artifices by which Congress have been imposed upon in this instance and thereby do a good turn to some better and more useful Officer falling into such circumstances, and prevent his being shuffled out in *like* manner. I serv'd this State and Congress as mentioned in the Introduction more than two Years, inferior to none in Zeal and attention to my duty and I believe improved the Posts alloted to me as much as any, and what upon this occasion may be pardonable tis well known here that though Colonel Moultrie defended his Post with the greatest gallantry when attacked by Sir Peter Parker's fleet, yet had it not heen for my particular attention to that Post from the moment of my arrival from Philadelphia while I had the command here, there would not have been a *defensible* Post there by the 28th June 1776 to *have defended*.

I have now done, my friend, and I dare say you think 'tis time. I scorn to treat Howe as he has me, determining to send him a copy of this, suppressing nothing but to whom 'tis sent. You have my full liberty to make what use you please of it, either in Congress or out, but by all means shew it to Heyward, Matthew's and Hudson and my old particular friends in Congress. I am determin'd to put Copies of both Howes Letter and this into the hands of numbers of our friends here. I am Dr. Sir. Your most hble. Servt.

CHRIST GADSDEN

To Benjamin Franklin

Charles Town So. Carolina [1]

15 July 1778

Gentleman:

I cannot deny myself the Pleasure of endeavouring to introduce the Bearer Commodore Gillon [2] to your Notice. He hath been always very active in promoting the American Cause and been of great Service to it in several respects as well generally, as particularly to this State and our assembly during its last Sitting appointed him Commodore of our Navy and in that Character he is sent to Europe to build or purchase three Frigates for this State. We have the highest Confidence in him as we are convinced, he cannot have engaged in this service, but from the purest Motives to serve the State and the Cause in general. Your Notice of him I am sure will be taken kindly by our State and particularly by Gentln. Yr. most obed. hble. Servt.

CHRIST GADSDEN

P.S. For News I refer you to the Commodore. Few men in this State are better inform'd, with regard to what is stirring in the Continent in General, as to what particularly relates to this State.

---

[1] Franklin Papers, American Philosophical Library.

[2] Alexander Gillon, going to France, was to borrow money and purchase three frigates for the new South Carolina Navy, of which he had been commissioned commander. Although one frigate, the *South Carolina,* was fitted out and performed service in the Bahamas, the enterprise ended in failure, indebtedness, and vexation for the State in the post-war years. D.E. Huger Smith, "The Luxembourg Claims," *SCHM,* X (April, 1909), 92-115; "Letters from Commodore Alexander Gillon in 1778 and 1779," *ibid.,* X, 3-9; 76-82; 131-5. The Luxembourg claims were also one of the sources of irritation between Gadsden and Gillon in 1784; *see* "To the Public, May 6, 1784."

This letter to Franklin availed Gillon nothing. Franklin, writing to Gillon, complained:

"I can have no hand in encouraging this particular loan" [of 1,800,000 livres by French subscription] . . . , "And I cannot but observe that the agents from our different States running all over Europe begging to borrow money at high interest has given such an idea of our poverty and distress as has exceedingly hurt the general credit, and made a loan for the United States almost impracticable." John Bigelow, ed., *The Works of Benjamin Franklin* (New York: Houghton, Mifflin & Co., 1904), VIII, 110-11.

To William Henry Drayton

Charles Town 15th August 1778 [1]

Dear Sir:

I am indebted for yours of 6th and 14th July. All your friends I assure you are concern'd that any Difficulties should happen so as to occasion a hesitation to Sign the Confederation. We cannot see the least Force in the Objections. A Confederacy ought most certainly to have been signed long since. What must the French think; have they not made an Alliance with 13 States but how can that be While no Confederation is made between themselves and if even upon Arrival of their Ambassadour, every State must be separately pleased, and throw so many Difficulties in the Way? What! Because one State has orders not to Sign, and another State has not received Instructions to Sign? Shall we who had positive orders to agree to the Determination of Congress, withdraw our Consent and make the Breach still Wider, and do all in our power to make Maryland more obstinate? Had our Confederation been signed, there would be no Room for any political powers or parties, Allies or not Allies, to interfere for their own purposes this is no new Thing (I am sure you know) in Europe. Witness Holland, Germany, Switzerland *etc.;* let us prevent all such Maneuveres as soon as possible. No thing will do it so speedily or effectually as a ratify'd Confederation. There is abundantly less risk in Trusting to a future Congress some 10 or 20 Years hence for correcting what may be amiss, than to let this matter lay any longer open. I Dread ten thousand Times more the restless Ambition of a few Individuals in each State to overset our Matters and enthral us, than I do any Thing of that Sort from any of the States themselves.[2]

---

[1] South Carolina Miscellany. A printed version: Edward I. Renick, "Letters of Christopher Gadsden," *American Historical Review,* III (October, 1897), 83-85.

[2] The South Carolina delegation signed the Articles of Confederation July 9, 1778, but not before Drayton himself had raised serious objections in his address to the South Carolina Assembly, January 1777. Drayton's suggestions were adopted by the State, but they were soundly voted down in the Congress. H. Niles, *Principles and Acts of the Revolution* (Baltimore: 1822), pp. 98-115; Journals of the Continental Congress, XI, 652-6. Regarding Maryland and the other states' reluctance to sign the articles, *see* Merill Jensen, *The Articles of Confederation* (Madison: University of Wisconsin, 1948), pp. 151 *et passim.*

Your Expences must be great at Philadelphia, immediately upon the British troops leaving it; this is an extraordinary Event; and I think we ought not to suffer you to be out of pocket and I hope we shall not.

I am sorry my Friend Lee seem'd so indifferent with regard to my Affair with Howe. I shall trouble you no farther on that Subject; only hope the Carolina Delegates will at least disabuse the Congress publickly, and not let them continue to think that my resignation was intended as an Insult to them, than which Nothing was farther from me, for I never thought them to blame. Had they sent Howe to take the Command of me, as we were of equal rank and he of another State, and had no greater Opportunities in the Military Way than myself, I should certainly have felt very sensibly the Stroke, concluded it proceeded from their Distrust of me, as not being of equal Industry, Capacity, or Integrity with him. I then should most certainly have sent *them* my Commission and eas'd their Fears at the same time lamenting the low State I stood in their Opinion. But as I always thought and think still, they knew Nothing of the Matter, but thought Lee had given him Orders to come here, and found that my Country would not hear me through the party Intrigues of a thin House. I therefore threw up my Commission here, and out of Delicacy to the Congress did not send it to them myself. All I expected was the common Compliment to an Officer, that I thought they did not wish (and I am sure has no reason) to get rid of, that of giving him an Opportunity before they accepted his Commission to tell what hurt him. Howe had had an exact Copy of my Letter of the 4th July to you and Numbers in Town have seen it, many of his Friends. I say the Congress never was so grossly imposed upon and if they do not resent such impositions, they deserve to be so again and again. Qui Vult decipi decipiatur [who wishes destruction will be destroyed]. I wish you were able to read the Copy I sent you. I was resolved to send my Observations by the return of same Express that brought yours concerning Howe's Extract. I wish'd for a little longer Time to furbish it up. From what dropt from Heyward my Apprehensions were first grounded, of the Congress looking upon my resignation as an intended Insult to them. I Therefore make no Doubt he will do the Justice to set the Matter to rights, and in order that he may be the better enabled to do, I shall be obliged to you, to give him, with my Compliments the inclosed Copy of my Letter on that Subject to you, which is fairly and exactly made out and also let him, see, what farther is mention'd in this Letter relative to that Subject.

Your last News tastes Moreish. We long for another Express. Nothing here worth notice only that we had almost a Hurricane last

Monday. My Bridge received very little Damage Indeed. I am Dr. Sr. Yr. & C.

C. G.

To Thomas Heyward

Thomas Heyward (1746-1809) was one of South Carolina's Signers of the Declaration of Independence. He was a wealthy planter, a soldier and jurist. While he was serving in the Continental Congress, Gadsden's resignation of his commission was accepted. Heyward was wounded at the battle of Port Royal in 1779, captured when Charles Town was surrendered to the British, and was imprisoned during the occupation. He returned to serve his State in the House. Heyward is also noteworthy for having founded the South Carolina Agricultural Society in 1785, being its first president. Salley, Delegates to Continental Congress, pp. 16-26.

Chas. Town 16th August 1778 [1]

Dear Sir:

As I never saw Gen. Howe's letter to Congress till 27th June last when I Receiv'd it under cover from Mr. Drayton. That, and what dropt from you in the House confirmed me in Opinion, that my Resignation, or the Manner of it appeared to Congress as an Insult upon them, than which Nothing ever was, or is now farther from me. I wish I had seen that most extraordinary Letter Sooner. I should not have rested a Moment till I had sent a proper Answer to it. Never was Congress more grossly abus'd than in his representation of the Case between him and me. I have no Favours to ask nor would accept of any Thing in the power of Congress to give. But the Imputation of an Intention to offend Congress is such a Sin Against America that I never deserved nor would choose to lay one Moment under. Had Congress sent Howe to take Command here, considering his Situation and mine, of equal Degree, and equal Experience, with this Advantage on my Side that I had the Confidence of the people and by their Means the Command, I should certainly then have perceived that Congress entertain a low opinion of me, as not fit

---

[1] South Carolina Miscellany.

148

for the Appointment and in that Case in a Decent Manner should then have sent *them* my Commission inclosed in a Letter. But as I was always convinced and am still that Congress knew nothing of the Matter but thought that he was order'd by Lee here, or that he was left here by Lee and that the Command in Course of Service naturally devolved on him neither of which was the Case, and found that by a Cabal and Intrigue and a Train Laid [*i.e.* a deceit] (unthought of by *me* and quite unexpected, having come from my Command from the Island but the Evening before to attend that and *only that* Motion which I had given long previous notice of)—the House would not hear me. I chose Rather thinking it more decent to Congress to throw up my Commission *here* and thereby to shew immediately from whence I felt the Stroke, and where I thought myself not afforded that Support, I had a right to expect: Supposing a Man of those Connections, Blood relationship, Advantages *etc., etc.,* that he puffs up and at the Same Time a Stranger to a Country in General to come, or Rather pretend as in his Case with me to come, to supersede the Officer in post recommended by the people. Is there one in Ten of such officers without such advantages whose representations would have that Chance of being attended to? Is it not therefore necessary that the legislature of that State should know of the Matter and back such representation? For my part instead of meeting with such Opposition (occasioned by as Artful Misrepresentations and I am sure there cannot be more so, as in his detail to Congress.) I thought I merited the Thanks of the House for my Watchfulness and those of the Military for endeavouring to get rid of an Interloper. I beg pardon for giving you this Trouble. I thought Yesterday in my letter to Drayton on this matter which I desired him to shew you, and give you a Copy of my letter to him of 4th July which I sent for you, only to have refer'd you to them. But as you was present at Congress when Howe's Letter was read,[2] I thought I would trouble you with a Line on the Occasion, which I wish in the Hurry I am in you may be able to read. I am Dr. Sir Yr. & c.

C. G.

N.B. My letter of 4th July Howe
has a Copy of sent by me.

---

[2] Howe's letter to Congress is published by R. W. Gibbes, *Historical Magazine,* IV (1860), 265-6. It is answered by Gadsden to Drayton, July 4, 1778.

To William Henry Drayton

Chas. Town 9th September 1778 [1]

Dear Sir:

Yours of the 25th July I have Received and am sorry you had not shewn my Letter of the 4th [July] to my Friends particularly to Mathewes, Heyward and Hudson,[2] especially as from Accounts I have heard in Town which are no ways contradictory to your Letter, Mr. Laurens must have seen it. Whatever, Mr. Lee or any other may have [heard?] you strangely Mistake me if you think I have any Interest to support either for myself or any Friend. I have declared over and over again that I wish for Nothing, nor will accept any thing from Congress. The Matter between General Howe and me is a public one which I thought my Duty to act in as I have done. My only Wish with regard to Myself is to wipe off any impressions Congress might have had, of my intending any Insult or resentment against them in the Manner of my resignation which I had reason to think was the Case.

A few Nights since there was a great riot begun by the English and French Sailors and I believe set on by the Tories in Town. The Militia were under Arms, several lives were lost as you will see by Timothy's paper which I make no doubt he sends you by this Opportunity.[3]

---

[1] South Carolina Miscellany. Published version: Gibbes, *Historical Magazine,* IV, 266-7.

[2] John Mathews was a delegate to the Continental Congress, 1778-1782, and in 1782 was elected governor of South Carolina. Richard Hutson was a fellow delegate who became the first intendant of incorporated Charleston. *DAB,* XII, 404-5; IX, 443-4; Salley, *Delegates,* pp. 30-31.

[3] In the *Gazette of the State of South Carolina,* September 16, 1778, there was published a proclamation condemning this altercation between American sailors and "sailors of Foreign nations." Lowndes used this to call upon all citizens and the magistrates to suppress "tumultuous" meetings in general, and indecent and illiberal national reflections against his Most Christian Majesty, Louis XVI. The riot between the French of the ship *Comte de Narbonne* and the Americans took place September 6. John Wells, Jr., writing to Laurens, maintained that enemies within were the troublemakers. There were several "villains" inciting the riot with "new" muskets among the Americans. Along with the general disorders, a ship-to-shore engagement took place between the Americans and the French. The French raked them with grape, while the Americans returned the fire from Burns' wharf, where cannon had been mounted. Several persons were killed and wounded. John Wells, Jr., to Henry Laurens September 6, 1778, Kendall Collection, South Caroliniana Library.

Since my last [,] Howe and I have had an Ecclaircisment en Militaire which much against my Opinion has been printed. As the Cause of it is not particularly Noticed, it may not be improper to Mention it. On the 17th of Last Month in the Evening I Received by the Generals Aid De Camp a long expostulatory Letter dated two Days before with a Demand of Satisfaction at the Close, Unless I made him reparation for the Expressions I had made Use of relative to him in my Letter of the 4th of July to you. I wrote him for Answer the next Morning: that I was ready to give him any Satisfaction he thought proper where when and how he pleased, That I thought he was the Aggressor in having wrote such an unnecessary Detail of that Matter, in it omitting my principal Objection and especially for not letting me, whom it so nearly concern'd have a Copy of it and that he had no Body to Blame but himself, That I never saw his Detail which had immediate effect for *10 Months* after the Date of it. Three Letters from him and two from me past before the Matter came to a point. In his he gave me such assurance that "he did not mean in any thing he said to reflect upon or injure me" and "as to Breach of promise I accused him of he declared he really understood me as he had set forth, so that if there was a Fault his Understanding and not his Integrity was to blame" and had "he imagined I wished to see his Letter he should most Chearfully have sent it to me," That "he had not least Wish to conceal it from me." My Friends Coll. Elliott and Coll. Horry who were the only persons that had the least Hint of this affair from me seem'd to think this a great Concession and required some Notice or Apology on my Side and our Friend Coll. Pinckney who was the General's Second appeared to be of the Same Opinion. But I looking upon it only as *private* and *personal* to me, whereas the Expressions of mine he particularly referred to (see Paragraph 7—7 of my Letter to You) related to the Manner of a *Public* Act. His getting, as it seem'd to me, into Command here, and as I did not see how it was possible with any kind of propriety or adherence to truth to abstract the private Matter from the public, I Determined to make no Concession but to meet him in any Manner he pleased. Accordingly on the 30th we met and were placed at the Distance of eight very small paces. As the General Demanded Satisfaction of me and I had already taken mine by Exposing his Letter with my Observations thereon I was Determined to receive his Fire, which I accordingly did; after some pause, fired my pistol broad off, and called him to fire again which he declined as in the papers. The Matter being thus over I then thought the Apology or rather Notice my Friends seem'd to think due on his Concessions would come in with propriety, I therefore then told him that tho' I might perhaps Mention the Matter *again,* yet [he] might be assured that I should never *in Future* make Use of any harsh Expressions concerning him.

I got a Cold the Evening of the riot; have had a Fever almost ever since and am now so poorly that I must Conclude. Dr. Sir Yr. most & c.

C. G.

To William Henry Drayton and John Neufville

Chas. Town [1]

22 Sept. 1778

Dear Sirs:

In my last of the 9th by Mr. Demar I sent you an Account of my Affair with Howe since which have Received yours of the 13th last Month. Mr. Heyward who left Congress the 23rd is also returned. I am sorry to find by him that you had never shewn him my Letter of the 4th July. Mr. Mathews and Hutson have both leave to Return I am told; when they come away I see how it will be; at best I find if it had been to be noticed, they wou'd just then been acquainted with it while my Enemy had time to digest his sneering Criticisms as he pleased. However I am glad to find on Account of the State that there is such a Harmony between you, and King Charles' Rule is thought no bad one by many Politicians, to overlook Friends and pay the greatest Attention to Enemies. With Regard to Genl. Howe and me, *every Tittle* that regarded merely myself and What in that Respect I was in any Ways anxious about was that my Friends wou'd take an Opportunity to exculp[ate] me from any Intention to Offend Congress by the Manner of my Resignation; as to all the Rest it is entirely publick Matter and concerning which I have declared my mind over and over and have not seen the least Reason to Alter my Opinion one Tittle [,] many to confirm it. The Many declarations of Genl. Howe that he never intended me any Offence or Injury in his Representation to Congress made my Friends Colo. Elliott, Horry and Colo. Pinckney [2] think that some Notice was due from me therefore [on] Account of the many harsh Expressions

---

[1] South Carolina Miscellany. John Neufville (1727-1804) was a member of the South Carolina Privy Council in 1779. He was a prominent merchant who had been an active rebel from the beginning of the Revolution. McCrady, *S. C. in Revolution,* p. 282; *SCHM,* VIII, 103; III, 84; XXVII, 169.

[2] Charles Cotesworth Pinckney acted as Howe's second; Bernard Elliott was Gadsden's. *South Carolina and American General Gazette,* September 3, 1778; Johnson, *Traditions,* p. 205.

I had made use of in mine of the 4th July which has been generally seen here. Therefore when the matter was over between him and me (I thought it highly improper before on Many Accounts) I then told him that *for the future* I shou'd avoid Names whenever I might have Occasion again to mention that Matter; in all other Respects as I said before my Opinions are entirely the same.

Your Letter of the 13th I gave to Mr. Ferguson [3] who shewed it to many Members and particularly to those you desired; they seem to think the [Secretary] appointed to the Deputation sufficient and to give a particular Secretary to a separate Member wou'd appear indelicate to the rest of our Members. For my own part not being in the house I can be of little use, but I perfectly remember that [what] the Secretary granted was on Account of the particular Accounts you promised to send for extensive Information. I made the Motion —That Secretary ought not to be employed but especially with Regard to our State and if the other Members do not use the secretary for the publick and distribute informations. I cannot think they will or can take it amiss that [it be] you who should make use of him. I thought Col. Laurens was President when my Affairs happened. I am therefore sorry I mentioned that Circumstance, which and which alone I shall be obliged to you to expunge out of my Letter of the 4th July; no Person knows me better than he does and he can't mention an Instance of any Publick Matter (or I believe indeed private either) that ever I undertook, I did not go through with; therefore he above all others must think I must have had some extraordinary Reasons for my Acting so suddenly in the matter [as] I did, and had he or any one of our Members only moved the Congress to give me an Opportunity to give my Reasons before my Commission was accepted it was all I wanted for. I had no Intention of taking it back. Tho' there is no love lost between him and I, yet I wou'd have done it for him. To go out upon any Question unless I really did not understand it, or that it related merely to myself, I ever looked upon as cowardly, and I never did and never will I hope in my life. [4]

Last Night we heard of the Surrender of Rhode Island with the Garrison Prisoners of War which we hope to be true. I am & c.

C. G.

---

[3] Thomas Ferguson, Gadsden's son-in-law, was a member of the House of Representatives, and in January 1779 he was elected to the Privy Council. McCrady, *S. C. in the Revolution*, p. 282.

[4] The Howe affair seems to have increased the enmity between Gadsden and Laurens. Disagreement between them had begun at the time of the Cherokee War controversy. In a letter of August 5, 1778, to Drayton, Laurens complained that Gadsden had tried to injure him for not representing fully his case in the Congress. Laurens defended himself, claiming that because of a number of resignations, Congress was in a dark mood; and when Gadsden's resignation was offered, the members shouted, "Accept it, Accept it." Edmund Burnett, *Letters of Members of Continental Congress*, II, 361.

P.S. Besides having a Stranger introduced to Command us without proper Authority, can any thing be farther if possible more humiliating unless it be to bind Georgia about our Necks in the Manner it is; *incidentally* upon a sudden Motion for Table Money to the Gen. which was the Primary Object, this is done in a Motion made (I am told) by a No. Carolina Member the 15th April 1777 upon a supposition that Lee had left Howe to command here and Georgia.

I saw this Motion while the late Matter was agitating between Howe and me, never before; it was never entered in Orders but seems to have been kept hitherto a profound secret.

To Thomas Bee

Thomas Bee (1730-1812). Despite jeopardy to his extensive property interests, Bee joined in the popular cause on the eve of the Revolution. He was elected a member of the Secret Committee and later Speaker of the House of Representatives, afterwards becoming lieutenant governor. In the postwar period, he became an object of wrath of the democratic forces in 1784 for what was termed his aristocratic leanings in the House. In 1790, he was appointed by President Washington to a district judeship. SCHM, XXVII, 3; see, Gazette of the State of South Carolina, April 29, 1784.

5th October 1778 [1]

Dear Sir:

The Honorable House thinking proper after having had his Excellency the Presidents message relative to his proclamation of the 5th June and the outrageous treatment it met with from a part of the people of Chas. Town [2] a month before then to postpone the matter to the next House in parliamentary language *ad Graeca Calendas;* considering the part I acted in earnestly advising that step in which I am conscious of having done nothing improper, I submit it to the House how they think I must feel under such at

---

[1] South Carolina Miscellany. Published version in Edward I. Renick "Letters of Christopher Gadsden," *American Historical Review,* III (October, 1897), 86-87.

[2] *See* letter to William Drayton, June 15, 1778.

least negative censure, especially after the deliberately gross treatment the Executive received from a Body of men mentioned in no part of our Constitution as I can rcollect, who called themselves the Flint Club.

The contemptible, suspicious, and useless situation with regard to the publick I find myself reduced to upon this occasion lays me under the necessity of entreating you to request the Honorable House for the public sake as well as my own, to deliver me from it by accepting my resignation as V. President,[3] perhaps. It may not be proper for me to let my feelings carry me farther. [I] am therefore resigned to stop here if Sir you think my particular reasons following are too free, improper from me, or will give offence to the House, which I should be sorry to be thought capable of intending; but if you judge not and the House will bear with the remonstrance of an old and faithful Servant, I shall then be obliged to you to lay before them.

I was the first man that moved in Council for our compliance with that recommendation of Congress which is the Subject of the President's proclamation of the 5th June and never consented to any publick Act more heartily and with clearer judgment as the best Measure this State could pursue at that very critical period exclusive of that respect for Congress which the true Interest of America and even the Existence of its free States always did and still requires to be shewn. A copy of this Proclamation his Excellency laid before the House with an account of the outrageous treatment it met with more than a month since in full as mild terms as it deserves.

The advice just mentioned to the President I avow to have given, am accountable for it to the State, and knew so at the time. Tis either impeachable or not, if the first I ask no favour but heartily wish to be tryed as the Constitution has appointed, being not conscious of any guilt and have a right to a fair trial. If the last, the future peace and safety of the State, good order, and good policy require that the Executive should be supported. *Principiis obsta* has been ever looked upon as an excellent maxim, for unchecked insolence very rarely decreases of itself and this I am persuaded the President and Privy Council will soon amply experience. The very existence of the State during the present War upon a sudden Emergency in the recess of the House (and none of us can tell how soon such emergency may happen), may oblige the Privy Council to advise the President to act really very opposite to some of our most favourite Laws. This advice indeed they must

---

[3] *See* letter to Drayton, October 14, 1778.

give at their own risk, and rightly so and tho' it would be as great political Cowardice not to give one's back upon an enemy in the Field of inferior Force—yet must not Men be blessed with an exalted virtue indeed and a superlative degree of firmness to run such risks when they have any reason to apprehend they will not be supported? If a proclamation of the President in consequence of a recommendation of Congress and the advice of the Privy Council is to be counteracted and defeated by a managed misinformed part of the Town dextrously practiced on (imperceptably I am fully persuaded to themselves) by the bellowing tools of a few ill-intending, restless, disappointed, self-important men behind the scenes (as I verily believe was the case the 5th June); if the magistrates are to be intimidated; if the presages are to be stopt at their nod and all this to pass without proper notice, the Privy Council will soon be of little use and must rapidly dwindle into that insignificancy, discredit and contempt which an artful and indefatigable Cabal earnestly wish to see them in and will miss no other sly opportunity to bring about. The next step to making that necessary and useful part of the Constitution contemptible will be of course to expunge them altogether when it is found (as in the nature of things must happen speedily if not timely prevented) that none but dastardly Trimmers, ambitious Caballers, interested Jobbers will serve in a Department rendered so low, suspicious, and despicable.

As V. President the Devolving of any part of the Executive on me being altogether contingent and the election of a new Assembly being so very near, the chance is very little indeed that my resignation now can be of any moment to the public. Did I think it of consequence no feelings ever so disagreeable, no indelicate treatment whatever would make me entertain the least thought of resigning. But when I consider too of what essential and lasting importance a Privy Council chosen as ours is must be to a free State, from the nature of their duty how obnoxious they are to selfish and ambitious men who wish to take advantage of the publick: how grossly the present Council has been treated: How cheap that alone must make them: convinced too that it is the duty of every man called upon by his country to fill a publick station to hand it down unsullied as far as in him lies to his successor; these considerations all put together call on me particularly to shew a feeling (as well as the publick sake as from a regard to my own character) by desiring to quit in the manner I do a station in which much insult has been experienced, more may be expected and little probability thro' want of *undelayed* support and countenance of being any use.

I am sure your Honour must be persuaded from the many peculiar and remarkable circumstances which attended my appointment that nothing could have induced me to accept it but the apprehension that an excellent Constitution which no individual took more pains about than myself might otherwise want some Formal Officer thought necessary in putting it in motion. I hardly know of any material fault in it but the great disproportion of members in a few Parishes with respect to others, a matter which tho' generally seen and admitted, having got a footing from necessity could not from want of proper data at its framing be then better regulated and which the Constitution in its 15th Clause has provided shall be set to rights at a future period, in the interim trusting to the virtue common prudence and true policy of such parts as glaringly have the greatest superiority both with regard to situation and number of representatives that no inconveniences or disturbances would arise on their part by their ungenerously and unwise assuming too much on their present advantages.

I have had without asking or soliciting any man's vote directly or indirectly the Honour to serve my country for many years in various stations, always totally devoted to that particular post occasionally allotted to me; never quitting it while the least hopes remained of having that necessary support the station required:— zealous and attentive in all to the honour of the public and their nearest concerns: unbiased either by friend or foe: intimidated by none: constantly attending to my duty while a member of the Assembly: making no promises but always keeping myself disengaged upon every question for any officer whatever wanted to any Department of the State, or concerning any other matter of moment till it came before the House and then voted according to *my own* best judgment for the good of the whole: always thinking it cowardly to leave the House on a division upon any question whatever, unless it merely concerned myself or I really did not understand the terms it was put in; seldom upon making a motion have I previously secured even a second; but more than that I always looked upon as caballing, warping Men's judgments and a kind of Treason against or at best pitifully and dirtily crimping for the State and if I now towards the close of a long, disinterested and laborious service ask any favour, either of individuals or the publick in General, let it be, to be looked upon only as a citizen detesting licentiousness and totally devoted to the cause of equal *constitutional* liberty, religious and civil to all, Governors and governed, and having not a desire (and who never had) for himself or family in these respects that he does not from the bottom of his soul wish for every Honest Man in the State and indeed in all the world.

157

Believe me Sir the exquisite feelings arising from a consciousness of having acted in this steady uniform manner in publick life has made me more than ample amends for every neglect, every disagreeable circumstance it has occasioned through selfish ambitious arbitrary or designing men whose private views have been occasionally thwarted thereby. I have served with pleasure under the President, am a witness to his indefatigable attention to the publick interest not only in his present, but in several other important stations, on very trying occasions, have long and well known his honest sensible Heart and fixed attachment to the publick good, feel extremely for his delicate situation and most earnestly wish for my Country's sake that he had the support he so much merits from every good and honest man in the State and *to which as a private citizen* I am hopeful of contributing my mite. In a publick station, as times go, I can afford him none. Give me leave to conclude with declaring that had I not thus shewn my public resentment in the strongest manner I am able against the proceedings justly represented by his Excellency the President, in his message of the 3d September, I should have ever thought myself accountable for all the riots and mobs throughout the State that may happen in consequence of that which happened in Chas Town the 5th June and as having abetted the artful opposers and disturbers of our peace by negatively, at least, assisting them in their indirect underhand practicings of the weakest part of the Constitution, the present allowed disproportion of members, in order to throw all into confusion and when an Opportunity serves get the whole new modeled more to their gout; and as sacrificing the duty I owe as officer to the whole state to the idle tickling of a momentary popularity with a too assuming small part. I am Sr. wth. great respect Yr. Honour's most obed. servt.

C. G.

To William Henry Drayton

Chas. Town 14 October 1778 [1]

Dear Sir:

I am obliged to you for the paper sent me by last Express. I find you are indefatigable. God prosper you. We are obliged to you for it. Johnson is driven off the American Stage I find, but pondering revenge.[2] However I hope his Sting is taken out. The House met according to Adjournment, very few Members indeed. The President made a very proper and spirited representation of the Behaviour of the Mob in Chas. Town the 5th June which Mob was ostensibly on Account of his Proclamation but really (as I am verily persuaded,) artfully atirred up and set a going by a Cabal. The House after having it before them a Month, through the influence of the Town Members put it off to the next House. In the Mean Time the President and Privy Council is to put up with the Insult—in as much afraid Mr. Lowndes would have resign'd which would have put the State into great Confusion, and would have given the party, who were hopeful that Officers would not have been found to set the new Constitution a going the utmost pleasure. The resignation of the Council would have done the same. As for my part as V. President and a new Election so near at hand, I thought my resignation could be of little Moment to the State and at the same Time thinking it would be of some good Consequence that some part of the Executive should shew a Feeling upon so monstrous an Insult as they received, I thought myself in a Manner peculiarly called upon to do it from my Station and accordingly wrote the within Letter to the Speaker which was laid before the House, who, I expected would have accepted my resignation immediately. However I was Mistaken for they did me the Honour unanimously to send 2 Members to desire I would continue. This I could not refuse; therefore still remain in Statu Quo, and I am

---

[1] South Carolina Miscellany.

[2] Governor George Johnstone of West Florida was one of the Carlisle Commissioners. Without consulting the others, he proposed a plan of reconciliation to Robert Morris, who reported it to Congress. Congress rejected the plan and resolved to forbid any of its members to negotiate with Johnstone. He was obliged to withdraw from the Commission, and returned to England. Burnett, *Letters,* II, 192; also *DNB,* X, 964.

not without reason to think my Letter has done some good, that may appear in Future. Williams and Hopton arrived a few Days ago in their Flag.[3] I am glad of any Thing to rouse us if possible from our Lethargy, but the Conversation with Johnson I look upon as a Matter of Course, and highly probable that had Mr. Williams been a N. Carolinian or Georgian just the same would have been said to him with regard to either of those States. If any Thing is intended, I rather think Johnson wishes to brew it up after his arrival in England, than that any Danger may be apprehended this Winter from Clinton. Our Masters the Assembly, Legislative and Executive, examin'd Hopton and Williams themselves and discharged them. The Council had examined them last the Evening before: but the People of the Town seeming so engaged, it was thought absolutely necessary to refer him to the House, even for our own sakes, for had we discharged him, and we could not have done otherwise, I make no doubt St. Michaels Bell would have set a ringing in a few Minutes afterwards. We are going to fortify in all haste and make no doubt shall persist, till we half finish'd some Works and do as after heretofore, then? I am Dr. Sr. &c.

C.G.

P.S. The Express is Waiting

To Thomas Bee

Charles Town Feb. 4, 1779[1]

Dear Sir:

As tomorrow is appointed for the Election of a Governor and Lt. Governor, when there is a sufficient Number present for that purpose, I would be much obliged to the Hon'ble House to permit me to resign my vice Presidentship that I may qualify and have an Opportunity to give my Vote on that important Occasion. I am Dr. Sr. Yr. Most hble. Servt.

CHRIS GADSDEN

---

[3] John Hopton and Robert Williams described a British scheme to invade South Carolina through Charles Town or Beaufort, with a fleet and an army of 10,000. Allegedly this information was given by Governor Johnstone before his departure. Hopton and Williams approached Richard Beresford who informed Laurens, and he sent the pair to the South Carolina legislature for questioning. Their story was dismissed as highly imaginative and as a maneuver for personal advantage. Burnett, *Letters, II*, pp. 422-3.
[1] South Carolina Miscellany.

To Samuel Adams

Charles Town 4th April 1779 [1]

Dear Sir:

I am much obliged to you for your Favor of Col. Ternant.[2] He seems to be an active, sensible and spirited officer entirely devoted to his Duty. He was in Town only a week or two after his Arrival when he seemed very poorly. He has been here once since for a few Days, sent up by Genl. Lincoln [3] on Business. I had the pleasure of seeing him at my House each Time and think myself happy to have been introduced to him.

I am the same Man my Friend with the same Principles I set out with at first, an American *at large,* anxiously wishing for the Happiness and confirmed Independency of the Whole, not having, indeed scorning a Thought in Favor of *any one* State to the prejudice of the rest. With the greatest Concern and Astonishment we view the Congress, as appears to us, divided into Cabals and Parties, where will, where must this End?

Our State particularly attentive to the Interest and feelings of America, was the first, tho' at the extreme End, and one of the weakest as well internally as externally, to listen to the Call of our Northern Brethren in their Distresses. No sooner this circular letter arrived here, but S. Carolina immediately roused in Unison with them. Massachusetts sounded the Trumpet, but to Carolina is it owing that it was attended to; she immediately in 1765 flew to the appointed Rendezvous and had it not been for her I believe

---

[1] Samuel Adams Papers, NYPL.

[2] Lieutenant Colonel Jean Baptiste Ternant of France was inspector of the Continental Army. He served with Pulaski's Legion and later commanded Charles Armand's Partisans. In March, he had been sent by Governor Rutledge to secure aid of the Spanish of Havanna against Georgia. This mission was a failure. McCrady, *S.C. in the Revolution,* p. 434.

[3] Georgia, under the defence of Robert Howe, was lost to the British, a devastating defeat from which Howe's reputation never recovered. The defeat augured ill for South Carolina which was now in desperate circumstances and seemingly without assistance from Congress. These are the reasons for Gadsden's plea. Finally, Major General Benjamin Lincoln of Massachusetts was given command of the Southern Department, in September 1778. Christopher Ward, *The War of the Revolution* 2 vols. (New York: Macmillan Co., 1952), II, 679-81.

you are well convinced no Congress wou'd have then happen'd, and Boston wou'd, if not been entirely ruin'd, continued much longer in her Distresses. In every stage of her Misfortunes we were all alive, felt at every Pore for her. Now the Tables are turn'd, and we in far greater Distress than New England ever was, from our internal Weakness and other Circumstances, and the Scantiness of our Resources.[4] But who feels for us? We seem to be entirely deserted, even the Continental Troops of our Neighbours are retained with the grand army and denied us. Where are our Frigates? From these Carolina has a right to claim assistance as from her great Distance from Congress. The unhealthiness of her Climate in the country in July, August, and September, and the Difficulty of providing for, and marching Troops over so vast a Tract, Land assistance is attended with many and great Difficulties. But this being the Case, it ought to occasion a greater Spur to help us by Water, where there is every Inducement in our Favour of a private as well as publick Nature, and our Sea Coast and Charles Town are remarkably healthy at all times. The Enemy's Force is very Trifling by Sea hardly worth naming. Georgia and this State, just to the northward of the Gulft at all Times a most excellent situation for Cruises, but more especially now, when the Enemy are in possession of Georgia, and in order to debauch and distress us, are importing immense quantity of Goods. France and Spain must give such employment to the Enemy's Cruises that 'tis impossible they can spare many here, and what they do send can't exceed Frigates; the shoalness of our water will not safely admit larger. Had we kept our Frigates five or six together, we shoul'd have pick'd up the Enemy's small Cruisers fast, or obliged them to cruise in Fleets, which woul'd have augment'd their Expences amazingly. But alas! for private purposes individuals have been indulged with single Cruisers. In short no prodigal ever squander'd his Inheritance more stupidly away than we have our Frigates to make Fortunes with which the United States have lost as it were in deba[u]chment. I am amazed we did not reflect sufficiently on what preserved our first Fleet under Hopkins. In the first plan was not that Fleet composed of all merchant Vessels not such as suited best, but such as coul'd be got? But even such a Fleet, in the Height of the Enemy's Power, and in the greatest plenty of their Cruisers, coul'd and did cruise for near three Months in the most dangerous Cruising ground, land on Providence, dismantle that place of her Cannon, and return safe at last, and wou'd have done so accompan'd with the *Glasion* one of the Enemy's Cruising Ships, had not our Friend Hopkins been too eager. What was all this owing to? Was it not to their Orders wrote in the strongest

Terms, (for I was on that Committee which fitted them out) not upon any account to separate? The like Orders now wou'd do wonders, only send four, five, or six Frigates at most, under an *honest Man,* with the strictest Orders not to separate, indeed swear him and his Captains that they will not designedly; give him from Augustine to Halifax to cruise in as he sees best, the good Effects of it wou'd be seen in Trade and everything else. At this time in no place such a Fleet cou'd be employed to better purpose than on our Coast and if you can't give us effectual Assistance by Land and you will make no attempt by Water, what advantage have we by the Confederacy? And what must we think here, but that we are intended to be sacrificed to make a better Bargain for the other States? Such Taunts as these my Friend I *particularly* frequently receive who have been always a strong advocate for the New England States and especially so, as a Friend in need is a Friend indeed, in the Day of their Distress and Calamity. Now I am *seriously* told, *did we not tell you so.* When their Turn was served we might go might go to the Devil. They are the only People can serve us by the Multitude of their Privateers, and this the best and safest (from the Power of the Enemy) cruising ground in America and yet so far from helping us with their private Ships that 'tis they who are the most strenuous in preventing the Continental ships (notwithstanding they have in a manner monopolized them on their Coasts, and never been without many of them) from being station'd here in this Day of our Trial for our assistance. We who never had but one of those Frigates and her coming here owing to mere Chance.

I dare say you can't remember when a Tiptoe Gentleman used to be tripping about the Congress, indefatigable in insinuating distrusts of the New England States (and whom I am sorry to see again upon a late list of your members) I say upon those Occasions when no Stone was left unturned and then with too much success to make us look upon the New England States with a kind of Horror, as artful and designing Men altogether pursuing selfish purpose. How often I stood up in their Defence, and only wish we wou'd imitate instead of abusing them, and thank'd God We had such a systematical Body of Men as an Assylum that honest Men might resort to in the Time of their last Distress, supposing them driven out of their own States. So far from being under any Apprehensions that I bless'd God there was such a People in America. That for my Part I never look'd upon any Danger from them but where I apprehended the most Danger to America I told Congress was from whence she was little aware. That was from the extreme back parts of Virginia, North and South Carolina, Georgia and Florida where

163

were a numerous Sett of Bandetti of no Property or principles whatever and ready to be made the Tools of power for the sake of plunder whenever they cou'd do it with impunity. That from hence the General Danger was most likely to arise and I remember when I sat down, a gentleman of Pennsylvania who was next to me, said, you are right Mr. Gadsden, and you might have added the Back Parts of this State too. I wish my Apprehensions are not coming about, without the most speedy Vigorous and effectual Steps are taken to punish it. Cataline's Gang was not more atrocious than such as are daily deluded over to the Enemy from our back parts, and if this State should Fall, which God forbid, the mortification will soon spread through North Carolina and Virginia and where it will End God knows and whether if the Southern States shou'd thus fall and under the prepossession that New England wants to leave them in the Lurch, what may be the Consequence even to them at a not very future Day is not very difficult to grasp.

As to myself, I thank God I hope I have as few feelings on my own Account as any Man in America, tho' I believe not many Men in it, have a better and more improvable Estate and don't own a Straw out of this State. But I feel greatly for my Friends for America in general. The Taunts of my Friends with regard to my Credulity, that we shou'd not be so neglected I confess is not a little mortifying.

I have now my Friend let my pen run and wrote you a long letter in the Openness of my Heart. You make what use you please of it. I am still the same foolish Politician that stand together on my own Bottom have no selfish Views either of a State or individually to Pursue and scorn to condescend to be of any Cabal. Must not such an odd Fellow often recieve sly and sharp Thrusts? I have rec'd many. But am with great regard. Yr. most affect. hble. Servt.

CHRISTOPHER GADSDEN

P.S. After I had wrote the foregoing I heard some guns fired and I went out to hear what for, and find that our two State Briggs were after a Cruiser only of six days just return'd with four Prizes taken off of Georgia, two from Antigua with 220 Hogsheads Rum and 30 Hogsheads Molasses on board besides other Articles one from our good Friends of Providence just running into Georgia, the other a retaken Brigg from Boston that had been bound in here. This shews what cruising ground is hereabouts; if we had plenty of Cruisers, our Ports wou'd be always open, but now we are obliged to keep them shut, for seven out of eight which lately sail'd have been taken, by the merest little dirty Vessels that ever appear'd before a Harbour

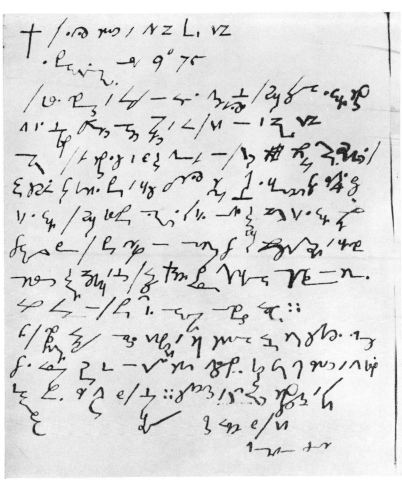

PAGE OF GADSDEN'S SHORTHAND

protected by a single Frigate or at most two. This is the reason we can't help our Friends with Provisions.

Chas. Town 6th July 1779 [1]

Dear Sir:

In the Overflowings of an anxious Heart on Account of the Situation of Public Affairs, I let my pen run away with me the 4th of April last and then wrote you a long Letter so scribbl'd that I question whether you were able to make out what I wou'd be at. Tho' I have rec'd no answer not yet the friendly Letter you mention'd in yours by Col. Ternant that you intended to write me, I cannot forbear troubling you with a few Lines by him on his return. Pray let me hear from you, it will always give me great pleasure, and make my compliments to our worthy Friend Mr. John Adams who I hear is on his passage back to you; let me know as far as you can how our public matters stand. As to Charles Town we have had a narrow, very narrow, escape indeed,[2] more from the treacherous Whispers and Insinuations of *internal* Enemies than from what our external and open Foes were able to do against us here. They are still hovering about us, at present at Port Royal Island, about 60 miles from hence, and not exceeding two thousand in number at most, protected by only three men of war of any consequence. Were our Frigates but ordered here, they would not only rid us of the Enemy entirely, but do the general Cause immense Service, but why do I say *our* Frigates, when by the Whole proceedings of the Congress, we begin to think, they imagine We have no right or pretentions to any share in them; a few Frigates four or five wou'd now (it indeed always wou'd) do us more service than as many Thousand Troops, their Business wou'd soon be done, I am

---

[1] Papers of Samuel Adams, NYPL.

[2] Prevost's Raid. General Augustine Prevost, to counter a move by General Lincoln against Augusta, crossed into South Carolina at Purrysburg. Opposed only by the retreating Moultrie, Prevost went to Charles Town, crossing the Ashley River and throwing the city and many of its leaders into a panic. Rutledge and some of the Council asked for terms, to guarantee the neutrality of the State until the end of the war when its fate would be determined by the victors. William Johnson, in his *Life and Correspondence of Nathanael Greene* (Charleston: A.E. Miller, 1822), pp. 271-2, implies that Gadsden may have saved the State from such a humiliation. With Thomas Ferguson, Gadsden vehemently opposed surrender. Gadsden's friend, John Edwards, a merchant, is said by Author Johnson to have wept at the proposal. But Gadsden went to the troops in the defences of the city and called forth an oath that if the capitulation were to come about, advocates of it would atone with their lives. However, the long haggling, together with the menace of Lincoln's rapid return, made Prevost uneasy, and the decision of Moultrie to fight caused Prevost to retreat. Moultrie, *Memoirs*, I, 434; McCrady, *S.C. in the Revolution*, pp. 352-3.

confident, if they came, and they might return to the Northward, again very speedily, as to any other assistance of that Sort from elsewhere it seems to be a *Vox et Praeterea Nihil* [merely promises]. The Enemy are within a few days March of the Town and if not sooner, when the sickly Months are over I make no Doubt they will be at us again, if you do not make use of the most probable Means to deliver us that is by Frigates. They expect reinforcements 'tis said but when, or from wherever uncertain.

As no one can give you a better Detail of the Occurrences here worth your Notice than Col. Ternant give me leave to refer you altogether to him on that Score.

We are much disgusted here at the Congress recommending us to arm our Slaves, it was received with great resentment, as a very dangerous and impolitic Step.[3] I am Dr. Sir Yr. most hble. Servt.

CHRIST GADSDEN

---

[3] In view of the imminence of invasion, the State requested further military assistance from the Congress. Congress replied that it could not satisfy the State. Instead, at the prodding of the South Carolina delegates, Colonel John Laurens and Isaac Huger, Congress suggested that able-bodied slaves be armed. It offered to pay the master for the term of the slave's enlistment, guaranteeing that, at the end of the war, each would be freed and granted the sum of $50. The measure was defeated in Council and the House of Representatives, where it was said to have been "received with horror by the planters, who figured to themselves terrible consequences." Benjamin Quarles, *The Negro in the American Revolution* (Chapel Hill: University of North Carolina Press, 1961), pp. 63-64; *Journals of the Continental Congress*, XIII, 386-88.

Proposals for the Surrender of Charles Town, May 8, 1780

Its situation hopeless, hemmed in Charles Town peninsula by the superior forces of General Sir Henry Clinton and the British fleet under Vice Admiral Mariott Arbuthnot, the American army commanded by Major General Benjamin Lincoln was forced to surrender, May 12, 1780. Gadsden, who had insisted that Charles Town be defended, and who would not permit Lincoln to retreat to escape the trap, must in part, at least, bear responsibility for the debacle. His proposal for terms of capitulation was not acceptable to Clinton. Ramsay, Revolution of South Carolina, I, 327; Ward, War of the Revolution, II, 702-3.

Proposals [1] from the Lt. Governor and the Council of the State of South Carolina unanimously agreed to at about three o'clock P.M. on the 8th Day of May 1780 and sent to the Honorable Major Genl. Lincoln to be inserted in the Capitulation he is about to make with His Excellency Sir Henry Clinton Knight of the Bath *etc.,* and the Honorable Adm. Arbuthnot. [2]

1. That The Citizens shall be protected in their Persons and Properties.

---

[1] Emmet Collection, NYPL.

[2] A letter, supposedly composed by Gadsden but never sent upon the advice of the Council, to General Lincoln, follows: "50 minutes after 9, May 9, 1780; To Gen. Lincoln:

Sir:

By favor of Colonel Simmons, at forty minutes past 2, P.M., of yesterday, I was informed of your determination to send proposals of terms of capitulation to the enemy, and that what I had to propose for the citizens, was to be sent to you before four O'clock. Antecedent to this information, I did not even know, except from common report, that General Clinton had sent in a flag very early in the morning, in consequence of which a council of sixty officers was called, including all the field officers of the militia. Strange that I, the supreme magistrate of the State, in town, and, *at the head* of those gentlemen, in their civil capacities, should not have been consulted at all on so momentous a matter; and much more strange still, when the consultation was so general. As I was acquainted that you were determined to send proposals, I had no time to lose; I therefore called a council as expeditiously as possible, and made up the article sent you in the best manner I could. What reason may have induced you to make proposals, and what they are, I know not; but my duty to my country obliges me to tell you, that I had a right to be consulted on this occasion, and as I was not, I do solemnly protest against such treatment, and send you this to let you know I do so. I should have rested much much better last night, had I certainly known that the enemy had deferred their answer until this morning. I am. . . . Johnson, *Traditions*, pp. 260-61.

167

2. That a Twelve-Months Time be allowed all such as do not chose to continue under the British government to dispose of their Effects real and personal in the State without any molestation whatever or to remove such part thereof as they choose as well as themselves and Families and that during that Time They or any of them may have it as their option to reside occasionally in Town or Country.

3. That the same protection to their personal property and the same Time for removal of their Effects be given to the Subjects of France and Spain as are required for the Citizens in the proceding articles

By the desire of Council

CHRIST GADSDEN
Lt. Gov.

To Major General Benjamin Lincoln

Benjamin Lincoln (1733-1810), of Hingham, Massachusetts, distinguished himself as a militia officer in the early part of the Revolutionary war. He was made a major general in the Continental Army, February 19, 1777, after which he contributed greatly to the victory at Saratoga where he was wounded. Upon recovery, he was dispatched to command the Southern Department. Captured and paroled after the surrender at Charles Town, he returned to his home. Later, Lincoln participated in the defeat of the British at Yorktown, where Washington accorded him the honor of accepting Cornwallis' sword from Brigadier General Charles O'Hara—a just turn of fortune.

In the following briefs, Gadsden indicated the sad finality of matters. However, toward the evening of the day when Charles Town was surrendered, Captain Johann von Ewald of Clinton's Hessian forces heard the shouts of American officers rising from the town: "Long live Congress!" For this they were obliged to give up their swords for fear of provoking tumult. The Hessian commented, "We are liked about as well as a Prussian officer in Dresden after the Seven Years War" — a spirit prevailing among the more untractable rebels which led to their imprisonment and exile from the State. Ward, War of the Revolution, II, 695-703. Berhard A. Uhlendorf, The Siege of Charleston (Ann Arbor: University of Michigan, 1938), pp. 6-7, 87.

Thursday Morning 11th May, 1780 [1]

Dear Sir:

The State of the Army is altogether with you. With regard to the Militia I am sorry to acquaint you that our situation is such, that in my Opinion, and that of all the Council no Time should be lost in renewing the Negotiations with Sir Henry Clinton. Perhaps a Flagg *simply* requesting a Conference on the Subject of Articles without propounding any, might be the most eligible method of recommending that Business. I am Dr. Sir Yr. most Hble. Servt.

CHRIST GADSDEN

12 May 1780[1]

Dear Sir:

I have received yours of this Morning; have just now laid it before the Council. We are all of us entirely at a loss how we are to act on this Occasion. What may be expected from us and what Custom and propriety require I shall be much obliged to you to let me know [in care of] the Bearer. Dr. Sr. Yr. most hble. Servt.

CHRIST GADSDEN

To General George Washington

George Washington (1732-1799). Gadsden met General Washington during the early sessions of the Continental Congress. His letter to the commander-in-chief shows a respectful familiarity. Here and in the letter of May 13, 1787, Gadsden related his experiences as a prisoner at St. Augustine where he, with other soldiers and civilians, was sent. Allegedly, all had violated their paroles by fomenting a "Spirit of Rebellion" among the conquered people of Charleston. The prisoners, after a year of confinement, were exchanged and permitted to sail for Philadelphia. There they were reunited with their families, who had also been summarily banished from Charleston. Mabel L. Webber, ed. "Josiah Smith's Diary, 1780-1781," SCHM, XXXIV (January, 1933), 31, 39; (April, 1933), 67-84; (July, 1933), 138-48; (October, 1933), 194-210.

---

[1] Houghton Library, Harvard University.
[1] Emmett Collection, NYPL.

Philadelphia 10 August 1781 [1]

Dear Sir:

The Bearer Mr. John Loveday [2] informs me that he hath had the Honour to be Recommended to an Office in your Excellency's Family by some of your Friends here. I cannot in justice deny him my Testimony of his Character.

He has been Messenger of the Privy Council of our State four or five years during which Time he has always behaved with the greatest diligence, Attention, and Secrecy and is, your Excellency may be assured a strictly honest Man. He was taken by the Enemy a few Days before Chas. Town capitulated, trusted with some important Messages from Mr. Rutledge, was immediately closely confin'd, and when We were shipt off to Augustine sent with us. He is a sober, prudent discrete man, very firm and steady to the Cause.

Sixty One of us with our Servants arriv'd in two small Vessels from Augustine, part about ten or twelve and the Remainder about five or six Days since, thanks to Heaven all in good Health and Spirits. We were in Augustine from the 15th Sept. to the 17th last Month, forty two Weeks of which I was confin'd in the Castle and none of My Friends permitted to see me, because wou'd not give another Parole. I told them I had kept the first as a Gentleman, defy'd (and do still defy) them to prove the Contrary and was determined never to take a second which wou'd imply a Breach of the first. Their Treatment of me when taken up the 27th of August last, was much more severe and pointed [than] against any of my Friends, which appears to me more owing to the Station I was in, than as Mr. Gadsden, (tho I believe no Favourite as such), and my not being mention'd in the Capitulation gave them an Opportunity to affect treating me with Rigour and Contempt. I thought it a Duty I owed to the General Cause to Refuse to the last giving a Second Parole, that I might be as a Standing protest against such outrageous Tyranical Conduct.

When in the Castle the Officers were order'd frequently not to convene with me; however many, of them often did, and all of them behaved with Decency. I never had the least Insult offer'd me there. Once indeed there was an Order against lighting a Candle In Consequence of which went without for two or three Nights, but the Pitifullness of this they were soon asham'd of themselves.

---

[1] HSP. The letter is printed in the *History of Castile de San Marcos and Fort Matanzas,* Albert C. Manucy, ed. (Washington, R. R. Bowker Co., 1955), pp. 28-29.

[2] John Loveday died in 1804 in Charleston, *SCHM,* XXVII, 226.

Mr. Ferguson and I are waiting for our Families expected in a few Days; as soon as we see them a little fix'd, we shall set off for our State as will most of the Carolina Gentleman here, and hope to be gone by the Middle of next Month as farthest. I beg your Excellency's and the Publick's pardon for the taking up so much of your precious Time and am with the greatest Esteem. Yr. Excellency's Most Obedt. & Hble Servt.

CHRIST GADSDEN

To Thomas McKean, President of Congress

Thomas McKean (1734-1817) was born in Chester, Pennsylvania, and practiced law in New Castle, Delaware. He was present at the Stamp Act Congress, representing Delaware. There he was numbered among the radical foes of Parliamentary taxation. McKean served in the Continental Congress throughout the Revolution, becoming president on July 10, 1781. After the war, he resided in Pennsylvania and was present at the State Convention for ratifying the Constitution. An active Republican, he was elected governor of Pennsylvania in 1799, holding office until 1808. He died in Philadelphia. Howard M. Jenkins, ed. Pennsylvania: Colonial and Federal, 3 vols. (Philadelphia: 1903), II, 159-86.

Philadelphia August 25, 1781 [1]

Sir:

From the perfect confidence we always reposed in the Honourable Congress, we judged it unnecessary, during our long and painful Captivity, to call their attention to our case. We are happy in finding that our confidence was not misplaced. We acknowledge with gratitude their early and unremitted attention to the object of our exchange, and embrace this opportunity of congratulating Congress, on the brilliant success which has hitherto crowned their vigourous and decided exertions, for the recovery of our State out of the Hands of the Enemy. We will not at present trespass on the time of that

---

[1] Papers of the Continental Congress, Record Group 11, National Archives. The letter is inscribed: "Aug. 27, referred to Mr. Sherman, Mr. Matthews, Mr. Randolph."

Honourable Body, by a particular recital of our sufferings. We glory in having had the honour of suffering in such a Cause; but at the same time think, that a regard to the rights of humanity and civilized society demands, that we should hold up to public view the conduct of that perfidious, that faithless Nation; a Nation, which during the whole course of the American War, but more, especially since the reduction of Charlestown, has been trampling on all laws human and divine. We have therefore appointed a Committee for that purpose. We will only so far anticipate the business of that Committee, as may be necessary to ground the following application. Although Congress must be in possession of the fact, that a number of us were apprehended and sent to St. Augustine, in direct and open violation of a solemn Capitulation, they probably may not be acquainted with all the circumstances attending that iniquitous and despotic procedure. They may not have been informed that it was done in the most sudden and instantaneous manner, so as to leave us no opportunity of making any provision for our support in a distant Country. The major part of us soon after our arrival at St. Augustine, received information that our Estates were sequestered, and the few who had their estates secured by the Capitulation, found it extremely difficult to derive any means of subsistence from them, as every difficulty was thrown in the way by the British, by extravagent freights and otherwise; and the scanty supplies which were sent, were repeatedly intercepted (we are willing to hope through mistake) by American Privateers. Those of our fellow-citizens who have arrived here from Charlestown, were taken up in the same sudden and unexpected manner, were equally affected by the sequestrations, and were indeed positively prohibited the bringing any money with them. From the above circumstances, we beg leave to inform Congress, that the Finances of all are in a state greatly exhausted and that many are reduced to the greatest straits. We therefore feel ourselves constrained, as well by the principles of humanity, as of duty, to solicit in the most earnest manner, all the aid in the power of Congress, in behalf of our fellow-citizens and fellow-sufferers, most of whom are impatient to return, and lend their assistance, to chastise a merciless and perfidious Enemy and to rescue their Country from their Tyrannical domination. We have been informed that General Green is urgent for the establishment of civil government in the State, and we perfectly concur with him in opinion, that it would be productive of the most beneficial and salutary effects. As we constitute a great part of the Executive, we are extremely anxious to contribute our share towards that desirable event; but have been advised by a gentleman of the Faculty from our State, who is perfectly acquainted with our climate, not to commence our Journey before the middle of September, so that we may arrive there about the middle of October. He is of opinion that our early arrival might greatly endanger our health, deprived of which we should prove an incumbrance instead of rendering the wished for Service. We beg leave therefore to inform Congress that having fixed the 15th of next month for our departure from this City, our utmost exertions shall be employed not to exceed that day; and we have to request of Congress that they will afford us such assistance, in the prosecution of our Journey, as they shall judge consistent with the public service.[2]

We have the honour to be, Sir, with every sentiment of esteem and respect for the Honourable Congress, Their most obed. Servts.

CHRIST GADSDEN,
Lt. Gov. of State of S. Carolina
of the Privy Council

THO. FERGUSON
RICH. HUTSON
B. CATTELL
DAVID RAMSAY

To Morton Wilkinson

Morton Wilkinson (c. 1745-1790) was a planter of St. Paul's Parish. A soldier in the Revolution, he was an ensign of the Colleton County Regiment of Foot in 1775, rising to the rank of colonel by the end of the war. He was a prisoner at St. Augustine. Wilkinson was a member of the South Carolina Privy Council, was elected to the House of the Jacksonborough Legislature in 1781, and to the Senate the following year, representing his parish. McCrady, S. C. in the Revolution, pp. 557, 572. SCHM, II, 6; XVIII, 187, XXXIV, 204. Biographical Directory of Senate of S. C., p. 333.

At the time this letter was written, Gadsden had recently been transferred to Philadelphia following his release from the prison in St. Augustine. Gadsden returned to South Carolina in early November of 1781.

---

[2] The Committee of Congress reported favorably on the petition and resolved to pay the petitioners "each two hundred and sixty-six dollars, and two thirds of a dollar in specie to be charged to the State of South Carolina. The Board of War was to furnish them with a wagon and team." *Journals of the Continental Congress,* XXI, 914.

Philadelphia, Sept, [1781] 1782 [1]

To Morton Wilkinson, Esq.:

You have my ardent and sincere wishes for your safe and speedy junction with our common friends. Our cause is good; the cause of humanity itself, and as it would be blasphemy in the highest degree, to think a Good Being would create human nature to make it unhappy, and countenance its being deprived of those natural rights without which our existence would not be tolerable; our cause may, therefore, be justly called the cause of God also. These were my sentiments at the time of the Stamp Act, the beginning of our dispute; they have continued to be so ever since, and with the Blessing of God, I am ready and willing to undergo any thing Heaven may still think proper to call me to suffer in support of it. We are tried, but I firmly trust not given over, and that God will once more restore us to our country and our rights, and that soon, when we shall have reason to look up to Him, and be convinced that his correction has been necessary, kind and proper, such as no father in quandam circumstances could avoid giving to his children, unless he had totally [left] them up to their own wild and perverse imaginations, and abandoned us altogether. That we may pursue every prudent, reasonable, humble and truly political step, devoid of passions and vindictive resolutions is my warmest wish. Revenge is below a brave man; vengence belongeth to the Almighty; He has claimed it expressly as His right, wisely foreseeing the shocking havoc man would make with such a weapon left to his descretion. However, a just retaliation, upon an abandoned and cruel enemy, may be sometime absolutely necessary and unavoidable, but when that necessity should glaringly appear, be used sparingly and with propriety, that is, as near as possibile on the offenders themselves.

This even humanity may require; might show steadiness and firmness, and would meet the approbation of all the candid part of mankind. Instead of bayoneting poor soldiers for the cruelty of their officers, when we have them at our mercy—when the unexampled cruel treatment of our friends in their power absolutely require a return, and when they have unjustly tortured or taken away the lives of any of them, a retaliation in such cases, in my humble opinion, would be much better taken of the officers; I would save them in the field, and immediately hang a few heads of them on the lines, in presence of

---

[1] Original not found; printed in Gibbes, *Documentary History*, pp. 221-3. Gibbes mistakenly dated the Letter 1782 and placed Gadsden in Philadelphia. However, Gadsden did *not* write the letter from Philadelphia in 1782; he was in South Carolina. He addressed a letter to General Greene from High Hills of Santee, November 4, 1781, having just arrived there and there is no evidence that he departed South Carolina afterwards.

the soliders taken with them, declaring publicly the reasons why it was done, and afterwards, if the enemy's lines were near, offer them the bodies of such officers to honor with what funeral they thought proper. The higher the rank of the officer that fell into our hands, the nearer should we come to punish the cause of the cruelties our friends had suffered, and in my opinion show the greater spirit and propriety in taking such a method, and the sooner prevent the repetition of the barbarities. Even Lord Cornwallis himself, if Fame says true, has been guilty of numberless cruelties, in cold blood, and if he fell into our hands, it would be the highest justice to make him suffer in an exemplary manner for them.

You will let our friends know our situation, and that though perhaps they cannot without great inconvenience detain all the prisoners they take, and are, perhaps, obliged, from peculiar circumstances, to parole [missing] must have been the case heretofore, yet such miscreants as have acted in high stations, have done us great mischief by the example of their defection, and otherwise are continually playing us tricks, and by no means are to be trusted, we hope they will for our sakes, keep such perfidious wretches at such a distance from Charlestown, and parolled if they think proper, at least, where they can do no more mischief. This, common fellow-feeling for our friends absolutely requires; indeed, a contrary conduct will encourage these worst of enemies, and make them contrive to throw themselves artfully in the way to be captured that they may carry on their cool, sly, detestable, villany with more security. I beg pardon, my dear friend, for troubling you with this long scrawl. My love to all our friends; tell them I hope to be with them soon, and to set out from hence as soon as possible after my family arrives— the beginning of next month at farthest; particularly make my compliments to Gen. [Francis] Marion. I am much obliged to him for his friendship at my plantation on Black River; entreat he will continue it. If you cannot see him, contrive, if you can, to let him know it. If any thing from thence, by his means or through any of my other friends, can be transmitted to my family here, it would be of great service to them, and what they will stand in need of. I am dear sir, your most affectionate humble servant.

CHRISTOPHER GADSDEN

P.S. Poor Knapp [2] should not be forgot. His firmness and integrity under the severe trials we have been witness to, entitle him to particular attention.

---

[2] Possibly John Knapp, a lieutenant and, later, captain in the First South Carolina Regiment who was mentioned in the *South Carolina Weekly Gazette*, December 25, 1784, as having died after a long illness. *SCHM*, XIX, 136: V, 152.

To the Delegates of the State of South Carolina

Delegates, to whom the following letter was addressed as "the most constitutional representatives of the State of South Carolina," were: John Mathews (1778-1782), Thomas Bee (1780-1782), Nicholas Eveleigh (1781-1782), Francis Kinloch (1780-1781), Arthur Middleton (1781-1783) Isaac Motte (1780-1782).

Philadelphia, September 17, 1781 [1]

Gentlemen:

As the most constitutional representatives of the State of South Carolina in this part of America, we esteem it a duty incumbent on us to address you on the Subject of the late execution of Col. Isaac Hayne,[2] a citizen of that State. We not only find our humanity shocked at the tragic procedure, and our indignation excited at the flagrant violation of the law of Nations therein committed; but when we contemplate the nature, apparent design and probable consequences of this unwarrantable system of policy adopted by the British, we are filled with the most alarming apprehensions. For if, whenever any of our citizens, through duress, or British artifice and chicane are seduced from their allegiance, a return thereto is punished with death; the natural consequence will be, that they will, when in those circumstances, either withdraw with their effects from the Continent, or being driven to dispair will become our determined Enemies. In either case, we shall be effectually deprived of their future assistance, and we do not hesitate to affirm, that notwithstanding the present flattering aspect of our affairs, the Independence of these States may still become a doubtful event. We are more im-

---

[1] Papers of the Continental Congress, Ms, item 19, vol. III, N.A. *See also,* Salley, *Delegates to the Continental Congress,* pp. 32-33.

[2] Colonel Isaac Hayne was a militia parolee after the fall of Charles Town, who was forced to take the Oath of Allegiance to the King or be imprisoned. Because his wife was dying and his children were ill with smallpox, he consented on the condition that he would not have to bear arms. Hayne received an informal promise to that effect from British General James Patterson, but considered himself released from the loyalty oath when he was later called upon to fight against his own countrymen. Hayne rejoined the American forces, was captured and hanged by the British for treason. *See* Ramsay, *Hist. Revolution of S.C.,* II, 277-84; 508-26, for more on his trial and execution.

mediately alarmed with regard to our own State, as there the evil already exists. It is notorious that the great majority of the inhabitants have from different causes taken British Protection. Now if the doors of return should be shut, we shall be totally deprived of the assistance of that large class of our citizens, and all the operations for the recovery of our State must be carried on almost entirely by Continental Troops. Whether the Army will be equal to this, and all other purposes of the War, Congress are the most competent judges. From the above considerations, we think it of the utmost consequence that an immediate and effectual stop should be put to this newly adopted system of British Policy. As ample and instantaneous retaliation appears to us to be the most probable method of effecting that desirable purpose, and as Lord Rawdon [3] who was the principal Actor in the Bloody Tragedy, and of course the most proper subject, has lately fallen into the hands of our Allies, the French, we do most earnestly request that you will exert your utmost influence with Congress that they would endeavour to obtain him for the purpose of retaliation. If Congress should think it necessary to have a more full and minute information on the subject, before they proceed to retaliation, we beg leave to observe, that it may be delayed until a full investigation can be had; but in the meantime, as he is so proper a subject, we most ardently wish that he may be secured. We have the honour to be Gentlemen, your most obedt. servants.

CHRIST GADSDEN, Deputy Governor of ⎱ THO FERGUSON
   State So. Car., ⎰ RICHD. HUTSON
   Of the Privy Council. ⎰ DAVID RAMSAY
      ⎰ B. CATTELL [4]

---

[3] Lord Francis Hastings-Rawdon, lieutenant colonel, was placed in command of British Troops by Cornwallis after his departure. Rawdon was captured on a voyage to England in 1781, when the vessel on which he was a passenger fell to the French. *DNB*, XXV, 117.

[4] David Ramsay (1749-1815), physician and historian, was active in the Revolution, serving the state then and after the war in the House and Senate. Richard Hutson (1749-1815) was a planter and a jurist who was elected lieutenant governor in 1782 by the Jacksonborough legislature. He was the first Intendant of incorporated Charleston (1783). *DAB*, IX, 443-444.

To Major General Nathanael Greene

Nathanael Greene (1724-1786), fought with General Washington in the Battles of Long Island, Trenton, and Monmouth, after which he became the efficient quartermaster-general of the Continental Army, resigning that post on August 3, 1780, to rejoin Washington. After the defeat of General Horatio Gates at Camden, Washington gave the command of the southern forces to Greene. General Greene proved a tenacious military leader, and was able to handle the often independent-minded South Carolina partisans. He was, with them, responsible for the reconquest of the State. Theodore Thayer, Nathanael Greene: Strategist of the American Revolution (New York, Twayne Publishers, 1960).

High Hills of Santee 4th Nov. 81 [1]

Dear Sir:

The bearer John Simple who drove our Baggage Waggon was promised that he shou'd be discharged, as soon as we arrived here. As he wished to return to his Family and has applyed to us for his Discharge; we have therefore this day given it to him, and beg leave to recommend him to you for a pass. The Man has behaved very well in his station and is very anxious to get to Philada. I am d. Sir in the Sincerest Esteem your most obedt.

CHRIS GADSDEN

We long to hear the Particulars of the late glorious Victory.[2]

P.S. All the Gentlemen with me give their respects to you.

---

[1] HSP.

[2] Gadsden refers to the engagement at Eutaw Springs, September 8, 1781. Both Greene and his adversary Colonel Alexander Stewart claimed victory, Stewart especially, because Greene was forced to retire from the field to his encampment, "High Hills of Santee." But Stewart had been so badly mauled that he was obliged to retreat to Charles Town, leaving the State virtually in the hands of the Americans. Thayer, *Greene*, pp. 375-80; Waring, *The Fighting Elder: Andrew Pickens*, pp. 95-102.

To Governor John Mathews

*John Mathews (1744-1802) of St. George, Dorchester, began his
service to South Carolina as an ensign in the Cherokee War. Afterwards, he studied law at the Middle Temple in London, returning to
practice in his native Province in 1776. He espoused the American
cause early. Mathews was elected Speaker of the General Assembly
in 1776 and served in the House of Representatives in 1778. When
Gadsden had refused the governorship of South Carolina, Mathews,
who was of a conservative turn in politics, was elected to the office.
His incumbency witnessed the British evacuation of Charles Town.
As the following letter shows, the evacuation was not brought about
without difficult negotiations concerning trade with England, and the
confiscation of Negroes. DAB, XII, 404-5.*

October 16, 1782 [1]

[Copy to F. Marion]

May it please your Excellency—as your Excellency has taken
the whole matter of the late agreement with the British on
yourself [2] and that by the Executive authority and executive

---

[1] Marion Correspondence, NYPL. This is a copy received by Marion. The
N.B. was apparently not affixed to the original letter to Mathews. Gibbes,
Documentary History, pp. 234-8, contains a version from the now-lost Peter
Horry manuscripts. Gibbes' copy includes the "N.B."

[2] The British merchants who had come to Charles Town during the occupation had flooded the city with unsalable goods. Upon the British evacuation, the
merchants were allowed to conclude their affairs. They secured an agreement
with Governor Mathews whereby they were permitted to sell their goods without molestation and without laws to confiscate their propery. The courts were
opened to them for the collection of unpaid debts. Knowing that his decision
on these matters would be unpopular and possibly regarded as unconstitutional,
Mathews hedged with the condition "if it is in the power of the Executive" [to
prevent confiscatory legislation]. He was party to the arrangement only because
he hoped that the British would return slaves seized during the war; and therefore, extracted this promise as a part of the agreement. The text of the Mathews'
agreement with the merchants is in Ramsay, *Revolution of S.C.*, II, 371-78.
Alexander R. Stoesen in "The British Occupation of Charleston, 1780-1782,"
SCHM, LXII (April, 1962), 81-82, claims that the Carolinians did not live
up to the agreement. The British, clearly, reneged and left Charles Town with
an estimated 5,333 Negroes in their possession. Ramsay declared the number
to be as high as 25,000. Wallace, *Short History*, pp. 330-31; Ramsay, *op. cit.*,
II, 384. *See also* Samuel Carnes to Rolleston, October 12, 1780, South Caroliniana Library; *House Journal*, 1783, fol. 238-9.

etc., mentioned in the 4th article, your excellency alone is to be understood,[3] I was in doubt with myself (and took a day or two to consider further of it) whether there would be occasion to trouble your Excellency with the tittle I mentioned but as I still unhappily differ from your Excellency in opinion and am persuaded if, from nothing else, from the want of precision lest in the expression of that Article the state at large will be led to think the privy council are made a part thereto, and of course myself a member thereof, as I dislike the agreement. Very cogent reasons oblige me to send your Excellency my formal disapprobation thereof nearly in the words. I immediately drew a rough sketch on seeing it, which I then shew'd to those gentlemen of the counsel [which] I mentioned to your Excellency and I should have sent it to your Excellency had not the counsel been summoned so soon. The doctrine broached at the last counsel, which I never heard or suspected before, that the privy counsel [is] in *no case* part of the Executive is in my opinion very alarming. It tends to make them insignificant and the next step is when an opportunity offers to expunge that body altogether from the constitution and prepare the way to reduce this Government to a kind of Principality. I have frequently in the assembly taken notice how great an eye sore the privy counsel seemed to be to some gentlemen amongst us and what indirect strokes were often aimed at them; that the Governor is the sole ostensible Executive of the State is readily granted; further that in all acts wherein he is not particularly restrained by law, he may be said to be absolutely so, but in such laws, wherein it is expressly directed that he shall not act, but by the advice and consent of the privy counsel, there they are certainly part of the Executive. For I have ever learned that what is so essentially necessary to a thing, that, that thing cannot exist without it, must belong to it and participate of its nature, so that in the last case, whenever the law requests that when a Governor is inclinable to do a certain Executive act, that Executive act shall not be done but by the advise and consent of the Privy Council; if it be done without such advise and consent, it is illegal; therefore they are a certainly a sine quibus non, to make the governor act legal *in such instances* and consequently in such cases are a necessary part of the Executive, and the individual members thereof may be said to be parties thereof. What confusion this can occasion or how by this omission there can be ten Governors in our State instead of one—notwithstanding what a learned or any number of learned lawyers whatever may say, I can not conceive. Besides in case of the

---

[3] Gadsden referred to the fourth article of the Agreement which pledged for the Chief Executive's office that "its whole power and influence, both in its public and private capacity, shall at all times be exerted for that purpose," *i.e.,* to prevent confiscatory acts, Ramsay, *op. cit.,* II, 371-8.

death of a Governor, during the recess of the assembly will not the Lieutenant Governor immediately succeed [and] in case of his death too, one of the privy council. Does not this shew they belong to the Executive, their participation of the Executive is but sometimes in particular cases and that only internally or privately (as a privy counsel) without any external authority whatever; this belongs solely to the Governor or Commander in Chief. This or something like it, I take to be the intention of the words in the 11th article of the Constitution *"in manner herein mentioned"* placed immediately after, to modify and restrain the words "that the Executive authority be vested in the Governor and Commander in Chief"; otherwise these words must be altogether nugatory and put for no purpose whatever. I will now beg leave to trouble your Excellency with the letter already mentioned.

"May it please your Exxcellency I have seen the agreement with the British dated the 10th, and I find by its 4th Clause, that as a particle of the Executive tho' unconsulted I seem to be made a party therein, to promote its acceptance with the public that occasions my troubling your Excellency by Letter as my conscience and duty oblige me to declare, that I disapprove almost every article; indeed I am not able to see any pressing occasion we had for any further meeting with the enemies Commissioners after the last, convened at their request, broke up which I was not sorry for, as we have so greatly the advantage of them in point of British property to lay our hands on when we please. This they well knowing, no doubt occasioned so much anxiety on their side for a further meeting. The agreement itself appears to me extremely injurious to the public and [I] fear it will involve us in endless consequences. British lawsuits no doubt our courts will be filled with but these are trifles to what might be mentioned. The exception in the first article, is not only in my humble opinion imprudent and impolitic with regard to ourselves, but when taken with the 2nd has unfriendly (if not inimical) aspect towards our sister states. Its 8th article is in the last degree humiliating. The great and tenderest care seems to be taken of the British Interest. Honor and even delicacy throughout the agreement, while our rights and what is essential to our honour and interests are totally omitted, or not mentioned with that unequivocal plainess and precision and that decisive firmness we had room to expect. The whole agreement causes such manifest appearance of timidity and over cautious fear of offending the British, that instead of hastening it has a natural tendency, when considered with the situation of the State for the last campaign, to retard their departure to the last moment they possibly can in hopes that (as only exterior advantages on their side oblige them to think of an evacuation) some external good luck may turn up

181

in the interior to bring about a recall of their Orders. The plentiful markets and great trade they have already had with our people during the whole summer, the prospect of still greater when the crop comes in together with no small advantages they may promise to themselves if they can but stay to dabble through their emmisaries at our ensuing election, must of themselves be strong allurements to a watchful enemy, not to hurry away sooner than is absolutely unavoidable. And must not their inducements be still stronger when they consider what is too glaring to escape them, the lax situation of our government for want of courts, notwithstanding the parade of an assembly sitting at Jacksonborough, the preference too currently given them of all kinds of necessaries for their specie and goods, rather than to our own army which has been more than once in want, even of our common staple rice and beef for several days together and (I wish I may not soon experience more alarming wants than any they have hitherto felt, if something more vigorous than in terrorem threats is not speedily and resolutely fallen upon) is no small addition to their other advantages. Above all are not the enemy sure that our army cannot compel them to go away or restrain them from making incursions almost any where for many miles, except just about the spot they occupy. There must be great incitement for them to stay if possible, at least they must encourage them to revisit us upon any favorable turn when the Gents accepted in the first article will be of more service to them than ever, as having experience they can put a confidence in them and of the most dreadful consequence to us, by having such powerful arguments to induce others to join them, and exert themselves to the utmost, to do us as much mischief as they possibly can, finding they will thereby recommend themselves the more to the British and stand the better chance to insure them protection upon a pinch. In my humble opinion, better *the whole value of these* fellows should be lost altogether, than that the public should countenance so dreadful a mischief. The agreement too seems so particularly careful of the great negro owners, that I wish the country at large may not think their honor and safety sacrificed to that particular species of property! The inhabitants near the sea are principally concerned in negroes; has their conduct during this campaign been so particularly meritorious? Their interest has indisputably occasioned more danger to the State than their fellow citizens, with less of that kind of property. Has that prompted them, as it ought to have done to exert themselves the more in its defence? Have they not, excepting a very few, been the most backward in the State during these critical Times to turn out? Not only so, Have they contented themselves with being merely negative? From whence have the enemy been all the summer so plentifully supplied and continue still to be so, but chiefly from them? I could trouble your

Excellency with much more on the subject—but I forbear, as I am afraid it will be too warmly agitated by and by. My duty to the State and regard to my own reputation, not desiring to be looked upon as a party to promote what I disapprove of, has extorted this letter from me which I hope will not give your Excellency any offence, which is far from my intention, for believe me, Sir; no man more sincerely wishes that your administration in these very difficult times may prove not only serviceable to the public but also more honorable to yourself and meet with general applause than I do. I had some thoughts of reserving my opinion on this measure in my own breast, until the assembly sat, but upon further consideration it appeared uncandid to your Excellency and looked too much like cunning which I abhor.["] I am with great respect Yr. Excellency's & c. & c.

C. G. (Copy)

N.B. The former part of this letter does not enter into the merits, whether the Governor had a right to exercise that particular act of agreement with the British *solely* of himself. But only takes up Mr. Rutledge's assertion in the Govs. fav[our]that the privy Council were a part of the Executive in no case whatever.

To Major General Francis Marion

Francis Marion (c. 1732-1795) of Pond Bluff, Santee, fought in the Cherokee campaigns of 1759-1761, and was a member of the First Provincial Congress. But he is most famous as the nearly legendary figure who led the partisans during the American Revolution, disrupting British lines of communication, preventing total conquest of the State, particularly in the dark days after the first Battle of Camden. Marion was elected as a member of the Senate at Jacksonborough while his men encamped at different places between the Cooper and Santee Rivers, guarding against any revival of British arms and making the enemy's retention of Charles Town militarily impossible. With Gadsden, Marion courageously opposed the punishment of the Tories. Robert D. Bass, Swamp Fox: The Life and Campaigns of General Francis Marion (New York: Henry Holt and Co., 1959).

(Near the Governor's Quarters)[1]

October 21, 1782

Dear Sir:

Your favour of the 18th I received yesterday by Mr. Ferguson on his return from Accabe, his commission about the Negros being at an end. The British it seems makes a pretence that it was because Maj. Rudolph[2] had taken a small party near their lines and unless Gen. Greene returned them they would not send a negro out, but this is a mere pretence; they had not the least right to make such a demand on the General. I should be extremely happy to have it in my power to oblige you and serve Col. Horry whose perseverance, firmness and merit must be evident to every body. Should the agreement be received, which I think there is little probability of, you may be assured that nothing in my power shall be wanting to serve him, Col. Horry[3] and as Col. Moncrief[4] has the negros [Moncrief]who is one of the principal opposers of the agreement being complied with, I will use my endeavors with the Governor if he can do it with propriety

---

[1] Bancroft Transcripts, NYPL. "Near the governor's quarters" refers to the Jacksonborough seat of government.

[2] Major John Rudolph of Colonel Harry Lee's command under Greene. Rudolph captured three British soldiers in a raid. On the pretense that the prisoners would have to be returned, sixty-three slaves claimed by Carolinians were withheld by General Alexander Leslie, last commandant of occupied Charles Town. McCrady, *S.C. in the Revolution,* pp. 613-4, 620, 660; Ramsay, *Revolution of S.C.,* II, 379-84.

[3] Colonel Peter Horry (d. February 28, 1815, aged 68), planter and soldier, was born in South Carolina. His grandfather was a refugee who settled in the "French Santee" after the revocation of the Edict of Nantes. In 1775, Peter Horry was a captain in the Second South Carolina Regiment, joining Marion's partisans after the fall of Charles Town, becoming the Swamp Fox's most trusted lieutenant. After the war, Horry turned over to the erstwhile historian Mason Locke Weems his papers and a "Memoir" of the campaigns. The Memoir became the basis of Weems' *Life of Francis Marion* (Philadelphia: Matthew Carey, 1809). Horry must not have recovered his Memoir from Weems, for it is now lost. A first edition of Weems' work has marginal notes by Horry correcting Weems. Robert Wilson Gibbes, in the *Documentary History,* published Horry manuscripts, among which were Gadsden letters; but these valuable manuscripts are unavailable, and are not found in the Gibbes Collection at the S.C.A.D. A Journal by Horry in the South Caroliniana Library contains a few lines relating to his "salad days" with Marion, but chiefly it consists of daily notations concerning his plantation near Columbia, South Carolina. Horry died in Columbia and was buried in the Trinity Episcopal Churchyard. See *Peter Horry's Journal,* 8 books, 1792-1814, and the annotated copy of Weems' *Life of Marion. See also* "List of Graves Trinity Episcopal Churchyard." W.P.A. typescript (1940), South Caroliniana Library; *DAB,* VI, 284; Heitman, *Historical Register,* p. 301; A. S. Salley (ed.) "Order Book of Colonel Peter Horry," XXXV (April, July, 1934), 49-57; 112-7.

[4] Colonel James Moncrief (1744-1793) of the British forces was an engineer and ordinance officer who employed slaves in his work. He carried away about 800 upon the evacuation of Charles Town. McCrady, *S.C. in the Revolution,* p. 661; *DNB,* XIII, 617-8.

to make a particular demand for them. The measure was certainly amazingly to the advantage of the British nation, and if their troops here had not as little spirit with regard to them, as our people manifestly shew with regard to the State (by that damned communication with the Town, which has now overrun all Banks), they would gladly have complied with the agreement to a tittle, but private interest on their side has overset it. Leslie has been very anxious about it for months past, and seen the advantages we had over him and made several overtures before it was brought to a point. For my part my friend I was always for keeping coolly the ground the assembly left us, pointing out to the enemy the glaring superiority we had and at the same time hinting that if they wantonly distressed us, the assembly however willing of themselves would certainly make use of the means in their power to do the State justice. This as often as I had opportunity in private conversation with the Governor I constantly gave as my opinions. However his Excellency thought otherwise and without consulting the privy counsel at all made the agreement himself; as soon as I saw it, I was very sorry for it, looking upon it as weak in itself, unnecessary, impolitic, humiliating and big with bad consequences to the state, and finding by the penning of the 4th article, that the privy counsel seemed to be made parties thereto; tho' never consulted upon that ground, I took the liberty to write to his Excellency, expressed my disapprobation of it in the warmest terms, and pointed out many of its defects. This I mention to you as a friend. We are all indebted to you my dear Sir; and I shall always be happy to have it in my power to discharge part of my public debt to you by rendering you any agreeable service. They still talk of the Enemy's evacuating soon. I cannot but hear of the motions tending thereto as well as others, but seeing no reasons from *within ourselves* to oblige them to go away and but too many for their staying, I am still—and shall not think they intend absolutely to go until I hear they are over the bar; all their manoeuvering seems to be attended with a mixture of as much delay as possible, as if they still waited further orders, and were determined not to go a moment before they could not possibly avoid it. I am Dr. Sir Yr. Most obdt. Servt.

CHRIS GADSDEN

P.S. Pray remember me to Col. Horry and all enquiring friends with you.

(Near the Governor's Quarters)[1]

Oct. 29, 1782

Dear Sir:

Hearing my friend Ferguson was unwell I made an elopement to see him and just returned last night, a little before your express called on me, much fatigued which prevented my answering your favor by him of the 24th. I am obliged to you for the paper you sent and I think it would be of general information to have it printed, but Dunlap is so unwell that he has left off printing and besides his paper is so small and types so large that I am persuaded not a fourth part would be contained in one of his *Gazettes* at a time; this would make it far less useful and entertaining, than if it came out all together. Should unexpectedly any opportunity offer of giving it to the public I will not slip it. The more I consider the late intended agreement the more disgraceful (and that *unnecessarily* so altogether in my opinion) it appears to the State. On the privy counsels not being consulted and yet seeming to be made a party thereto, I immediately wrote a letter to his Excellency to disavow my approbation of it, but previous to my sending it, receiving a summons to counsel, I kept it back till that should be over, expecting the matter might be opened there, but finding we were called on a different business, and no probability of it being then touched upon, as I saw, I took hold of something that seemed to tend that way and purposely brought in, indirectly in my argument on what was before us, pleading as an excuse that a particle of the Executive by the inaccurate wording of the 4th Article, I was brought in as kind of party to an agreement, which I almost totally disliked upon which Mr. E. R. to my astonishment said that the privy counsel were *in no case whatever* any part of the Executive which he said was also the opinion of another distinguished lawyer he named and the Governor himself said that old Col. Pinckney (who is conveniently dead) had told him the same. This I think as well as some other circumstances leave great room to think that tho' the natural council appointed by the State were not consulted on that most important occasion, yet that certain lawyers at least, if not others were. This novel and dangerous doctrine is so contrary to the spirit of our Constitution and plain letter of many of our laws so soundly and positively asserted, and tho' Lowndes's Lieut during his administration, and J. Rutledge a great part of his, I had never heard a tittle of or had the

---

[1] Bancroft Transcripts, NYPL; a printed version is in Gibbes, *Documentary History*, pp. 240-3. The Bancroft transcript contains the Post Script which is not included in the Gibbes printing, and there are a few minor differences in wording, punctuation and spelling, between the two versions. Bancroft's is printed here.

least suspicion of any such tenet could be advanced till the morning I heard it declared in the strongest terms in counsel and a little before by that Gentn. openly in the Governor's Porch. This induced me when I went home to add a note by way of preference to the letter I had prepared to send to his Excells. Copy of which I now enclose to you; the proceeding on the cause of it will serve by way there of explanation thereto.

We have been wanting my dear Sir; more troops for the Genl. all this campaign, but in my opinion we have wanted still more an efficacious civil power and if the enemy leave Charles Town (which still is a doubt with me notwithstanding I can't help saying appearances as well as others their advantages over the country at this moment are so amazingly beyond any thing ever had) I say in case of an evacuation and the sword has a little rest which as we must lose no time to join shoulder to shoulder to check the capaciousness, tyranny and insolence of too many of our lawyers, or this state will never be at peace or in a respectable situation again, and the citizens thereof upon an equal footing with regard to the possession of their property which in my opinion for many years past the poor and middling people have only held rather from courtesy, owing principally to that cause rather than right. Nothing but the infinite number of our laws and what is quoted as authority in our courts (which a tolerable room without exageration would not hold) together with the perplexity and confusion gave these gentlemen their importance or indeed any importance at all. These may be reduced I am persuaded to an octovo vol.; at most very few of them will ever help we may be sure. But the business is of such necessity that it must be done, as soon as possible or we shall be undone, for otherwise their insolence as lawyers will be soon equal to what the famous Roman Catholic Bishop Becket said to a gentleman he was not well pleased with; he told him very haughtily that he hoped to see the day, when no Jack gentleman would dare to stand with his hat on before the lowest priest. Without great care this or something like it will be soon the case with regard to the Lawyers here. I never thought there was much riddle and finesse necessary in good government, that honest men of good plain common understanding that would take pains to judge and always judge for themselves, not suffering their understanding to be in any mans keeping, were fully equal to the purpose, but how is the case? The people may appoint whom they think proper (as in privy counsel) these may be consulted occasionally to pick the guilding off of ginger bread or some such trifling matter, but in an affair of the utmost consequence to the safety honor and interest of the State, it cannot be expected they are fit judges—(tho' perhaps a matter not even depending on any difficult principal of Law), No, without the lawyers have the principal hand in it, or indeed the whole cooking of it, all is undone. I wish this may not have been nearly the case, my friend, on a late occasion, which I think almost as disgraceful to the State as were the agreement itself. The public is extremely obliged to you, for your vigilance with regard to the Gents. sending provisions to Town. I believe I can't be reckoned a severe man in my politics, but I assume I have done all in my power for many months to no purpose to get means used to have some of them tried by the Sedition Law, if convicted perhaps my bowels might yearn over a poor necessitious man as to endeavor to procure his pardon, but if a rich fellow, if I had ten thousand notes they should all go for a halter for him, and nothing else. Owing to these rascals the too great encouragement and continuance the army have given over, since the beginning of the campaign to that villianous destinctive trade with the Town and so [to] that impolitic infatuation from Christmas last of propagating the enemy's [humors] about an evacuation, were brought to the present dilemma which is if the enemy actually go, they even then leave us with the highest contempt and may return but should any external advantage to them, make Sir Guy [Carleton] revoke his orders—what becomes of us all then? in the shocking corrupted state the people are now in? Tis heads or tails with us and the stake I am afraid no less than the whole state. Sir Guy is looked upon as an excellent officer, having the good of his nation disinterestedly at heart, no doubt so wary a commander must have men here whom he can depend on to give him the minutest information of our situation in all respects[.] Pardon me my Dear Sir; for troubling you with so long a letter when your time is so important to the public; and believe me to be with sincere esteem. Your obdt. Servt,

CHRISTOPHER GADSDEN

P.S. I send to the Governor every day for my rations of beef. This moment my boy has returned without any—bringing a note that there are none and that the army is dissatisfied about them. I wish these dissatisfactions may not increase daily more and more and bring on some dangerous crisis. The whole proceeds from the damn'd Town trade where they live in clover. The same note mentions that the Augustine Fleet is arrived 31st. I heard last night that Mr. Crouch [2] died at Hort's the night-before. I suppose you have a copy of the late agreement, if not let me know and I will send you one.

---

[2] This could not be Charles Crouch who was the publisher of the *South Carolina Gazette and Country Journal* and one-time apprentice to Peter Timothy, for Cohen dates Crouch's death in 1775; *The South Carolina Gazette, 1732-1775*, pp. 5n, 6, 13n, 23, 6n. The Bancroft transcript is in error in naming Crouch. Instead of Crouch, the person to whom Gadsden refers is Benjamin Franklin Dunlap, publisher of the *Jacksonborough Gazette* and the *Parker's*

Nov. 3, 1782 [1]

Dear Sir:

Your favor of yesterday came to hand this morning. I from the first saw, that a certain set of gentlemen wished to frame, what is called our Constitution (for a proper constitution we have not) with as high a tincture of aristocracy as possible and in spite of the endeavors of a few and the highest intentions of many (dupes) it has too great a tendency that way. There are two kinds of aristocracy[,] one open and acknowledged; the other secret, by far the most dangerous. Of this last several vigorous buds were inoculated into our constitution, which have throve astonishingly by the artifice of designing, interested ambitious men, who intended nothing but their own end, or those of their party or profession at the time. No instance showed this more plainly than the choice of governor. We are not apparently confined but from the infinite number and confusion of our laws, our choice is secretly restrained to a gentleman of that order, as the most probable to answer our purpose, so that the lawyers may be said to be *the aristocratical number,* from whence in all probability in the present state of our laws, will be always chosen and this they too well know and plume themselves therein accordingly, and if honest men do not join firmly and steadily as soon as opportunity offers, to cure *radically,* this already shocking and continuously growing evil, our posterity will, as I have often said in the Assembly years ago, be more abjectly at the feet of the lawyers, than ever our forefathers were at those of the Priesthood. [I] should not be surprised, if our lawyers should, no long time hence in order to outdo His Holiness insist that their *wished for* Chancellor the Pope of the Law pageantry should have perhaps his - - - kissed. Their haughtiness is now intolerable. They seem to think themselves the optimates on all occasions, are gaped on like heathen idols and allowing to the above cause, would it not exceed the compass of a letter, I could point out many of the aristocratical shoots in our constitution slily thrust in and after all many of those very gents when the matter was over, by way of sneer christined our mongrel state a republic which it is as much like as I am like a fine race horse. For it is essential to a Republic to have its laws plain and simple, as far as possible and known to every member of the least attention; by this means the Romans could take their principal officers frequently

---

Ferry Gazette. William Hart, at whose home Dunlap died, was the executor of the Dunlap will. *South Carolina Gazette and General Advertiser,* September 9, 1783; *see also* Brigham, *op. cit.,* II, 1051-1052.

[1] Bancroft Transcripts, NYPL.. Copy also in *SCHM,* XLI, 50-52. Several of the letters printed in the *Magazine,* however, are not Gadsden's. Only those printed here are his. No place is named, but apparently as in the preceding, and following, "Near the governor's quarters."

from the plough; till our laws are so reduced and plain that from any of our General Assemblies [we may find] at least 2/3ds of the members, with the assistance of a privy Council, equal to that important office, we shall never be a happy people. The God of Heaven grant us to see such times, for the happiness of a government depends in a very great measure on the numbers therein capable of every department (and particularly the principal) and this depends again on the plainness and simplicity and general knowledge of the laws. Is it not a shame, that any gentleman should not know the law of his country? But is not every Gentleman in this State subject to this imputation? For who can know our laws or the 50th part of them? This is as true as dreadful my friend and the root I have long thought of all our evils clear, but this effectually (for to do it by halves will answer no purpose) and then nothing but our perverseness and baseness can prevent our being once more a happy and respectable people, as much so the full as any State on the continent. This not done we must still grow more and more contemptible and unhappy till we deteriorate to nothing and end in a stink. I never thought either Col. Harriott and Tucker ought to have had the important trusts, they have so long held. They never had my votes, nor had I opportunity to offer them. When I see the Governor, which I expect will be soon I shall hint to him, what abuses are made, but I assure you I am little attended to, not hardly any of the Council seem to be but E[dward] R[utledge]. I will postpone giving you my opinion about the 5% act.[2] As I differ from you from the necessity of the case in several respects relative thereto. Your express waiting for this I conclude. Dr. Sr. with great Esteem your humble servt.

CHRIST GADSDEN

Nov. 5, 1782 [1]

Dear Sir:

I should in my last have given you my opinion of the 5 per ct. law, but was afraid of detaining your express too long. In this my friend I differ from you but only from the necessity of the case.

---

[2] Harriott and Tucker had been permitted to trade with the enemy in occupied Charles Town.

On the recommendation of Congress, South Carolina passed an act February 26, 1782, permitting the national body to levy a 5% ad valorem duty on imports. The congressional measure failed to gain the unanimous consent of the states, therefore, South Carolina repealed its enabling act, March 13, 1783. Frank Zarnow, "Tariff Policies in South Carolina, 1775-1789," *SCHM*, LVI (January, 1955), 31-44.

[1] Bancroft Transcripts, NYPL. A badly hacked version is printed in *SCHM*, XLI, 52-53.

The Congress as the representative of the United States must have a general and certain fund (besides our continual, annual, common quotas, equal to what each state can bear) for important and many of them secret occasions; this was foreseen from the first, but how to be done with the most efficacy and least offence. The questions after numberless considerations and turnings of the matter every way— That of a Tax of foreign imports was fixed on, as the most equitable, practicable and eligible upon the whole because almost, if not altogether, every individual in the United States consumes more or less of the imports of that trade and consequently must pay accordingly and not a dite more; this concurs with your opinion, that the consumers, but 'tis a burden arising *voluntarily* from an indulgence in *foreign* articles, nine tenths in general I believe (even these times) superfluities and luxuries. So far I think this tax may be said to have more than one view, and this latent, not impolitic from a young rising Power. If any other method more agreeable to all parties could be devised that would certainly do the above business and pay off the great load of continental debt, we are in arrears to the Widows, Orphans and army *etc.* so as not continually to depend on the humors and caprice of the Assembly of perhaps one particular state I make no doubt it would be adopted with readiness by Congress and the discoverer receive the thanks of a grateful public, equality and certainty are the grand and necessary objects aimed at and I confess though I have turned the subject in my thoughts, I cannot think of a Tax that can be devised, that will answer both so effectually and the tax being wholly on foreign articles, he that is most luxurious and extravagant will pay most tax. Whether the Collectors are appointed by Congress immediately or through financeers by their authority amounts to the same at last. It would certainly be more satisfactory to each State to appoint them themselves. The disagreeableness of this must have struck Congress without doubt and occasioned great debates and I—[*sic*] In their fixing it in the manner they have rather than the other was to prevent disputes and jealousies and in any failing to have a person in their own power and of their own choice, that they are supposed to know, to call immediately to account. The tediousness of referring to Assemblies, who often may be adjourned, when these applications are most pressing, wanted to be made, is as shocking as well known; if a No Cos [Northern Company's] man is sent here as a Tax Collector, [or?] one of our citizens devilish rascally constitution indeed [!] if we send him away honest to get corrupted in the very short time of his appointment. The Congress as a body I take to be as honest and respectable as any in the world and mean as well (though no doubt have had in-

191

dividuals at times rascals among them). 'Tis our safety, as well as principal interest to support their honor and dignity as much as possible, and give them no room to think we have not the greatest confidence in them; their task is very difficult, extremely so these times. I am astonished to have weathered it so long and carried us through so many Scyllas and Charybdas; the greater danger from them will arise in my opinion from their sitting too long in one place, to give opportunity to selfish or ambitious individuals of their body to clan and intrigue with men of the same stamp without, from whence as from an undercurrent many dangerous consequences may arise especially to individual states that the Congress as a body never intended, I think one to our State, that by the mere goodness of Providence, we have escaped, was deeply laid against us and when in our deepest distress *only* this may I wish and design to try in the next house to have our delegates directed to bring about a removal from Philadelphia for this reason; they have been too long there, self interested, the citizens by cajoling with particular members in some instances have thrown their villainous means, and indirect, dangerous growing influence in my opinion in Congress themselves. I have now given you my thoughts, on this fruitful important subject as well as the time would permit freely my friend and without disguise as I think all honest men who mean to do any good, should to one another especially these times. I have no wish but for the public and that the meanest honest man may enjoy every social right and comfort under a good government that I wish for myself. God forbid that any mistake of mine, should be adopted to the prejudice of the public, that that be several in the best manner is all my wish by whom is of no consequence to the whole. One of the best ways to come at truth, the only thing a man of virtue wants to convince and govern him seems to me is for a number of friends to throw out their thoughts without reserve to one another, upon proper occasions, such as this by letter or in free conversation.

I am told and hope 'tis true all the guards hereabouts within these few days have been ordered to be very strict. I wish it may continue. Had it begun at first, as above a twelvemonth ago I over and over pressed Mr. Rutledge to get it done, we should long since have been *respectable* in Charlestown; but better late than never; and we must hope for the best. Major Forseigh,[2] who lodges in this house, and was at the lines yesterday, tells me some officers that he saw declared to him they did not expect to go before Christmas. I believe they wish to load some of their transports with our new rice, and long for our planters beating out their crops, which our

---

[2] Major Robert Forsyth of Virginia. He was Deputy Commissary-General. McCrady, *S. C. in the Revolution,* p. 233; Heitman, *Historical Register,* p. 233.

Governor, in private conversation a few days ago, told me he had forbid. I wish he may hold in the mind until they are tried out; but I have my doubts of those great ones; you are not obliged to me, but the paper for easing you of the trouble. I am Sir, your most hble Servt.

CHRISTR GADSDEN

17th Nov., 1782 [1]

[Dear Sir:]

. . . I am happy to find that my opinion of the 5 percent Act has any weight with you; the scruple you mention still sticking by you depends on the gen'l principle the law was framed upon the necessity and expected certainty of the funds for what reliance could they have on it if they found merely the caprice of a single Assembly might overset it? This fund, honestly and prudently managed, (when our independence is fix'd) must bring in an amazing sum; and I am in hopes will then soon be sufficient to rid the individual states altogether of one of the two heavy burdens they must be left under: that is the Continental arrears; and then each State will have only its own private department to struggle with. This will be a great easement; and I confess I know not from whence it can be expected, if this Bill should fall to the ground. I am really anxious to have it pass all the States, that we may avail ourselves of as large a proportion of foreign

---

[1] This appears in the Bancroft transcripts. A version also was published in *SCHM*, XLI, 55-60. The letter concerns the work of the Jacksonborough Assembly, January 1782, during which Gadsden was chosen governor by a close vote. His refusal to accept the office was based on the grounds of infirmities and old age. His moving rejectance speech is reported by Ramsay, *History of Revolution of S. C.*, II, 349-50; *History of S. C.*, II, 463: "I have served you in a variety of stations for thirty years, and I would now cheerfully make one of a forlorn hope in an assult on the lines of Charlestown if it was probable that with the certain loss of my life you would be reinstated in the possession of your capital. What I can do for my country I am willing to do. My sentiments of the American cause, from the stamp act downwards, have never changed. I am still of opinion that it is the cause of liberty and of human nature. If my acceptance of the office of governor would serve my country, though my administration would be attended with the loss of personal credit and reputation, I would cheerfully undertake it. The present times require vigor and activity of the prime of life; but I feel the increasing infirmities of age to such a degree that I am conscious I cannot serve you to advantage. I therefore beg for your sakes, and for the sake of the public, that you would indulge me with the liberty of declining the arduous trust."
Arthur Middleton briefly described the scene of the election:
"Jany. 30. Our Election for Govr. came on yesterday when Genl. Gadsden was chosen by a majority of two (I think). His declining the office, and his manner of doing it, is the most illustrious action of his Life. I am glad the compl[iment] was paid him, but more so he did not accept it." Barnwell, "Correspondence of Hon. Arthur Middleton . . . ," *SCHM*, XXVI, 193-4.

trade as possible without room for offence; for our allies, if done after a peace, may take it amiss, which now they cannot have the least pretense to, our necessities being so visible. I perfectly agree with you, we can not be too watchful and jealous of men in power, and cannot look too narrowly into all their actions, and suffer nothing extraordinary to pass unnoticed without the plainest and most indisputable mark of necessity for its cause. With regard to the Confiscation Acts [2]—it has haunted me, not only ever since, but (if I may say so) long before its existence, from the first appearance of the favourable turn Providence gave to our affairs; even whilst I was in Augustine Castle, before I was permitted to see or join my friends in that town which happened about twelve days previous to our leaving it, upon the news of the general exchange. At and from that time, I say, to this hour, I have met with [continual?] rebukes from my friends, and not a few gross affronts for doing everything in my power to restrain and to mitigate their rage and impetuosity; even before I left Augustine, I was sneeringly told the confinement in Augustine Castle had wonderously turn'd me; and from thence till I join'd the Governor in October last year, where another dreadful rock, I did not dream of, started up and terrified me extremely, the fatal communication with Charlestown; these two dangerous rocks have unitedly [taken] possession [of] and distressed my imagination ever since. I was instantly struck with forebodings that they would demolish us at least; a vindictive spirit on the one hand would increase and spread the resentment of citizens one against another, and a trading spirit introduc'd into an army, no matter from what pretence it might take its rise, would make it to their interest to corrupt the people, to prolong the war, and end, probably in the destruction of

---

[2] The Jacksonborough legislature confiscated the real and personal property of "known" Loyalists, *i.e.,* those who joined the British armed forces, who had failed to surrender to the Americans after the prescribed date February 20, 1779; those who in a public address congratulated General Clinton and Admiral Arbuthnot upon their conquest of Charles Town; those who had congratulated Cornwallis on the victory at Camden; those who held commissions of the King; and those whose activities manifested their attachment to the British cause generally. Many of the above were to be banished from the State. A second act provided for an amercement of 12% of the real and personal property of those who had taken the protection of the British during the occupation of Charles Town. It was this last which particularly "haunted" Gadsden, for he felt that the innocent civilians were at the mercy of the conquerors and that in order to feed themselves and their families were obliged to take protection. Cooper, *Statutes,* IV, 516.

Gadsden further remarked, as reported by "Cassius" (Aedanus Burke), that the Confiscation Act was "like an *auto de fe,* a sort of proceeding used in Portugal against heretics, where they were dressed in frocks painted over with figures of fiends and devils, to excite a horror against them in the multitude." Cassius, *An Address to the Freemen of South Carolina* (Philadelphia: Robert Bell, 1783), p. 18. Sound policy, Gadsden thought, required men to forgive their neighbors who, from a variety of circumstances, became "tories." Ramsay, *History of Revolution,* II, 350.

the State: for Trade is the greatest band that ever existed; if there is anything deserves the name of the Great Whore of Babylon, it is certainly her ladyship. From my arrival I have had continual quarrels on these two subjects. I was soon told by the violent confiscation men it t'was very probable that my open declaring for such mild proceedings would very probably get me left out of the house: and, when unexpectedly elected, the greatest affront and the most cowardly stab in the dark was levelled at me by a set of dirty tools, set on by an artful cabal, thinking to intimidate me, as party rage could invent. However, I despised the low attempt and continued to opposed the Confiscation Bill with all my might; and with the greatest anxiety I fought it through, inch by inch, as unjust, impolitic, cruel, premature, oppressing numbers of innocent for one man supposed to be guilty, formerly signing a paper, when visibly under the power and restraint of a known cruel, oppressive and tyrannical enemy;[3] and I insisted, over and over again besides that the Bill was manifestly calculated to defeat and to destroy the very intentions of those who were its most sanguine favorers, with regard to any emolument they expected the public to derive therefrom; and that it was like a man exhausting himself and beating about him with the greatest fury and rage, thoughtless and regardless what friends he must unavoidably hurt, or of the numberless advantages he thereby gave his enemy over him. I prest it again and again, *only to defer* it till we got possession of Charlestown, which was not so near, in my opinion, as they imagined; and that doubtless this very measure would tend manifestly to prolong, if not prevent, that desirable event; and reminded them of the proverb not to sell the bear-skin before they had catched the bear; but all to no purpose; and when the Bill came to the last definitive passing I then told the House, holding up both my hands, that before I would give my vote for such a Bill I would suffer them to [be] cut off. When I saw this wretched Bill would unavoidably pass, in order to put the best face on it abroad and make it of some little use at home amidst so many dreadful mischiefs it was big with, as well as to disappoint some land jobbers who were very eager for it to gratify their voracious appetities this

---

[3] By this time, Gadsden had somewhat changed his views on the punishment of the so-called Tories. In December 1781, the Horry brothers, Thomas and Elias, who had signed the complimentary addresses to the conquerors of Charles Town and Camden, surrendered to Gadsden. Thomas Horry, once a member of the Committee of Correspondence with Gadsden, offered his hand. Gadsden told him that he did not shake hands with rascals. When Elias inquired what would be done with them, Gadsden retorted, "Done to you? why hang'd to be sure." The pair ran off, but was apprehended later. In this letter from Edward Rutledge, Gervais was credited with the remarks but, later, Rutledge noted that Rutledge was mistaken and that Gadsden was responsible. *SCHM*, XXVI, 208; XXVII, 8, 9.

way, as if they and their families were alone to live in the land, I mov'd and procur'd that part of the introduction relating to Cornwallis' Orders, *etc.,* should be inserted. I also penned and brought in the 20th Clause as it stands, which met with general approbation, indeed was oppos'd only by (if he is not damnably belied) the greatest land jobber in the State. The 28th Article is likewise owing to me. I had also leave, and penned, and brought in a Clause that the next heir, if not below a son, brother or nephew, that had behaved uniformly and unexceptionably in the interest of the State, should succeed to his relation to forfeiter: but this I lost, not without reason to think I was jockeyed by a lawyer, to whom I shewed it before I presented it, who pretended to be a friend to it, and, I think acted otherwise by mistake or design: but tis now a law and we must patiently wait till the next Assembly to endeavor to have its severities at least mitigated where there is room; and I am sure, if I am on the floor, it shall not want my utmost endeavors to bring it about; and happy shall I be if they are attended with any success;[4] for I have long thought it would be difficult to pick out anyone on the Confiscation List, that was not a saint to anyone of those damned provisions Supplies [provisioners of supplies] for some time past to Charlestown; if the former was the open murderer of a man or two, have not these rascals been the secret murders of hundreds by the consequence of their rascally conduct? Not so much by gun and bayonet (tho' many that way) as by lingering diseases, and destroying their constitutions; and those, perhaps, as fine men as any in our State. I have told my friends if I die now I lay my death to the charge of those wretches, as much as if they had shot me. I am sure the loss of as good a Constitution as most men were ever bless'd with lays at their door; and that of our Continental friends and who debauched perhaps too many of them. I purposely picked out one of the worst wretches on the list to make my comparison from. What then think you must be my abhorence of these life traders when I compare them with many others? and what still when with a poor man who to preserve ease and comfort to a numerous family and visibly in the hands of a shocking enemy, has signed only a Cou[r]tier address to obtain it? I have not words to express how shocked I am at the baseness of men; and when I make the above comparisons I almost abhor my own species. Private men are thrown frequently into passions and extravagences, which if not timely opposed, infect like the plague the mass of the people, and these, too often secretly stirred up by artful, ambitious, men, to serve their own

---

4 The legislature in 1783 eased the punishments of the Confiscation Acts against the "tories," a move influenced by the constant criticism of such men as Gadsden, Burke, Marion, and at the request of the Continental Congress. Cooper, *Statutes,* IV, 553, 624, 639-66, 687, 699-721; McCrady, *S.C. in Revolution,* p. 588.

detestable selfish purposes, best served by throwing all into confusion; but the representatives of a State, when met on a public duty, are supposed to be without passion, or if in any degree worthy the great trust they are in, they ought at least to possess themselves sufficiently to oppose with firmness the rash impetuosity of the people, and correct it as much as possible. On the contrary, how many do we see for a momentary dirty popularity, give way to and amour [humour] every whim and violent caprice, no matter where they lead to. No punishment of a citizen should go further than the public safety will warrant. For my part I think it sufficient that such as are suspected as dangerous, should be restrained from electing or being elected, or not put into any office of trust till the war is over, and afterwards referred to the then Assembly to judge if their intermediate conduct entitles them *on petition* to be restored to the favor of their countrymen. Besides this, they should be fined a certain number of soliders in proportion to their estates and misdemeanours, to serve during the war, as should with moderation be judged. This would appear to all the world reasonable and equitable; and I confess is the utmost I ever wished or ever now wish to see (excepting with murderers who are out of the case); many who have erred merely through weakness and timidity and not suspected of any malevolence against the government, I would let off on the last terms only as much lenity as possible, consistent with safety should always be shewn from one citizen to another. This I have always been led to think not only as the most humane but the truest and soundest policy. In short, he that forgets and forgives most, such times as these, in my opinion, is the best citizen. From the bottom of my heart I pity the poor culprits. It may, without incurring censure be observed that though the law is extremely severe in the 24th Section with regard to any person assisting to conceal any of their effects, *etc.*, yet 'tis not so with their persons. Again, though as severe in the 16th respecting shipping them off when found, yet vessels will be so scarce (occasioned in a great measure by the impolicy of the act) that it will be impossible to put that part into execution for a considerable time; and, besides, 'tis an ill wind blows no good. The infinite numbers of much greater offenders, the provision suppliers to Charlestown, must I think feel some compassion to these unfortunate men, or they will be more hardened and abandoned even than over the Scribes and Pharisees with the woman taken in adultery. Upon the whole we shall certainly lose many citizens who may be made good on the one side and nobody gain anything thereby in my opinion but the lawyers who will palm immense sums on this melancholy occasion, and thereby make themselves still more formidable. I have already heard, and I believe from good authority of 100 guineas fee from one defaulter, intended to be offered which is nothing to what others will be tempted to offer; so that these poor men will be squeez'd and glean'd every way; rather than go they will give anything; and, perhaps, when they have given their all, or almost all obliged to go at last without a thing in their pockets: for what is given to lawyers is thrown into the bottomless pit, not to be got back. I am not without great suspicion that the law was made, and the people's passions fomented, with this design not a little in view. I know two lawyers who were extremely severe in this Act, to whom more had been forgiven and overlook'd by the public people than almost to all the culprits in the Act put together. It put me in mind of the Two Servants in Scripture, one of whom owed his lord an immense sum, which was freely on his petition, forgiven him, who went out and instantly distressed to the utmost of his power, his fellow servant, who only owed him a trifle. [With greatest esteem, yr. humble servt.]

[CH. GADSDEN]

To Gervais and Owen

John Lewis Gervais and John Owen (d. 1815) were merchants and attorneys of Charles Town who handled Henry Laurens' affairs while he was in Europe. The merchants held land in common in Ninety-Six where Gervais formerly lived. Both were active in the politics of the Revolution, Owen being imprisoned by the British in St. Augustine during the occupation. He returned home in time to sit in the Jacksonborough Assembly. The letter from Gadsden typifies the plight of South Carolinians at the end of the war. Starr, "Letters of John Lewis Gervais to Henry Laurens," SCHM, LXVI, 15; "Josiah Smith's Diary," XXXIII, 283; XXIV, 81, 200. Charles Wills, Book E, 1807-1818, pp. 526-7; Charleston District Letters of Administration, Book A, p. 451, S.C.A.D.

[Charleston,[1] August 20, 1783]

Dear Sir:

The Enemy have left both Mr. Laurens' and my dams in a bad Situation; when Mr. Laurens joined me (as my Dam is within my

---

[1] Gervais and Owen Letters to John De Neufville, 1783-1789, Library of Congress. This letter is a copy; at the heading is an annotation: "Copy of General Gadsden's Letter dated the 20th August 1783." No place is named in the copy.

Land), he promised to secure me to the Southward, so that even only a fence might be sufficient within: this a few days after the evacuation.[2] I acquainted Mr. Owen therewith and often Since. He repeatedly assured me the hands should go about it this time and that [the fence] and the Dam shall remain as it was. 'Tis not in my power to delay any longer, and I expect my hands from my plantation in a few days to set about my Dam as soon as they come. Whether Mr. Laurens does his Dam before, or after mine, it will not cost him either a moments longer Time, or be one hours more work to him, and [it] would save me full 2/3ds of my Work on that Inner Dam (which is *all mine and done totally at my Expense*) that has served for Numbers of years past as a *common* boundry to us both, and is a *necessary* one to him. I say it will save me full 2/3 of my work, as it will dry my mud which is very soft within, and in several other respects by keeping the tide from me facilitate my Business much; at no additional expense to Mr. Laurens. I shall be much obliged to you to know, whether Mr. Laurens intends repairing his Dams or not, and when they are to be gone about; it will be very unreasonable if he does, to join me a second time, without easing me at no additional cost to himself on a work *as necessary,* when done, to him as myself

I am Sir

---

[2] Laurens was a member of the commission to negotiate peace with England.

[3] Gervais and Owen refused the requests because of the number of workmen required who could not be spared without losing a promising crop of rice. This answer is attached to Gadsden's copied letter.

To the Public
May 6, 1784

Turmoil and suspicion marked the years immediately following the Revolution. Commoners were fearful that the benefits of independence would be enjoyed only by the aristocracy who had dominated the province and state. Their belief was based on Governor Mathews' agreement with the British merchants, and the Confiscation Act's repeal. These issues, combined with the uncertainty of post-war trade, had caused rioting by July 1783, which continued intermittently for more than a year.

Leading the anti-aristocratic democrats were such men as Henry Peronneau; William Hornby, a brewer ("Democratic Gentle Touch"); Captain William Thompson, an inn-keeper who filled the Charleston newspapers with essays calling for "social equality," or caused the streets of the city to be glutted with Tory-hounding and property-destroying mobs.

Alexander Gillon, who had invested heavily in confiscated town acreage, seized upon the prevailing discontent and factionalism, to become the darling of these democrats. Gadsden quickly discerned that Gillon was the principal mover behind those he labeled the "bellowing tools" who were threatening the peace and stability of republican institutions. Gadsden exposed and condemned Gillon for personal motives in playing upon the spirit of the mob and helping to create disorder. Simultaneously, Gadsden tried to convince the restless populace that it was necessary to have order with liberty. Walsh, Sons of Liberty, pp. 111 passim. John Richard Alden, The South in the Revolution, pp. 327-8. Thomas Waring to Andrew Pickens, July 22, 1784, Waring Papers, SCHS. Nathaniel Pendleton to Nathanael Greene, July 10, July 17, 1784, Greene Papers, Clements Library. Commissioners of Confiscation, Sale Book, SCHS.

It must distress [1] and alarm every good Citizen to see the many insults on Government so frequently happening, not only from the Press but at the corner of almost every street. Where can this end?

[1] *Gazette of the State of South Carolina*, May 6, 1784. The essays of Gillon and his followers are in the *Gazette of the State of South Carolina*, April 22, 29, May 13, July 15, 26, 29, 1784. I.M.K.'s essay, *ibid.*, April 29, 1784.

Is it possible such public outrage can come from anything like friends? Are we henceforward to look upon ourselves under an orderly established Government, or a set of *self-created* upstart bullying consors? No man that is not willfully blind, but must have seen from whence sprung the shameful Riot of last year; which it is well known has greatly injured the Trade and Credit of this Country, and particularly hurt many of our most deserving Citizens: nor does it require any extraordinary penetration to discover that I.M.K.'s account of whipping a Mr. [William] Rees, is published by *our censors,* as a prelude to some farther intended Town Manoevre, this frolick no doubt, took its rise in the country in order not to be behind hand with our last year's renowned exploit, and the Champions of the town are again probably to strike some notable stroke for the admiration of their Country Party, thus we may have this blessed business continued by action and re-action, *ad infinitum,* if not entirely prevented. Amazing reverence and respect, notwithstanding all this, is pretended for the Assembly: but is this possible, when private judgement is set up against the laws of the land? This Mr. Rees I know not, and am very little acquainted with any one of the thirteen persons so insolently ordered away the other day, but this is worthy of most mature consideration, that if one man, can pick out a Mr. Rees, against law, another, and a third, and so on, may pick out a Mr. Any-body and every body; and then, what must become of Law, Order, and Government? It is a maxim with most wise States, that it is better ten bad men escape, than one innocent man should be punished. States act, or ought to act, without passion. But do we find individuals do so? Would they not reflect, if they did, how many widows, orphans, and other honest public creditors they are whipping, at the same time they are flogging one poor mortal, that has incurred, and perhaps deserved their resentment? This is, and has certainly been the case, nay more, they at the same time, may be said, by these rash, lawless proceedings, to be in a manner whipping every honest man in this State, from the richest rice, tobacco, wheat Planter, *etc.,* throughout the State, down to the lowest sober housekeeper: for what must become of any or all of us, if our trade fail? Have we any other way to support ourselves, or maintain our families? What foreigners will trade with such mad-men, not only regardless of, but even insulting *their own* Legislatures? Prudent strangers, will certainly be on their guard, and avoid us. Who then will be principally whipp'd, or receive the "juice of the hickory," as I.M.K. phrases it? I say yourselves, the few individuals thus illegally punished, will see themselves amply revenged, and the Farmer and Planter of all denominations, will have no body to thank at the end of the season, but these Rioters, if they get little or nothing for their year's labour.

Heaven has blessed us with one of the most valuable States in America for trade, not only from its excellent situation, its many various staples and productions, but also from its climate, our ports being open the whole year, when many of our Sister States often lose a fourth part of their annual foreign trade, by being shut up by the ice. Besides our metropolis is as healthy a spot, I believe as almost any in the world; with all these advantages, and many more that might be enumerated, if we acted but a tolerable prudent part there is hardly a doubt but in three or four years at farthest, all our *public* creditors might be paid every farthing, and the State in as high, or higher credit than ever. Are we then to risk all these great and plain prospects? For what? A narrow pitiful, unmanly gratification of revenge on a few individuals at our feet! Shabby politics indeed! Is not this biting our nose to spite our face? It is very lamentable that civil wars, the worst of wars, are far from being a new thing in History, almost all nations have had them, and what has been generally done by a wise people when they were over? What is to be wished we had done, made an example if necessary, *after a fair and candid trial,* of three or four of the most notorious Delinquents of rank; of the highest authority; and universally known, whose weight and influence must have been of the most pernicious consequences, and then passed a general Amnesty; this would have done honour to the State, soon and effectually restored peace and harmony to it, on the most solid basis, but to counter-act the law of the land is shocking and insufferable. And where will this capricious *Retail Tyranny end;* 'tis continually started up here or there, and carried on merely as the gnawing worms of malice or resentment may bite individuals. As to weighing punishments in equal proportion to offences in civil commotions where such numbers have been concerned, 'tis what never was, and never can be the case; and none but the shallowest chimerical novices in matters of policy, can suppose it to be practicable. A respectable and fatherly Government will commiserate all its subjects, overlook all it can, consistent with the *safety* of the State, punish with reluctance, and when obliged to punish, do it with spirit and propriety, always shewing itself ready to protect the poorest citizen, and not afraid of the highest.

Captain T[hompson]'s affair has been productive of the consequences I apprehended.[2] I am sorry it happened, but still I cannot

---

[2] Captain William Thompson, a tavern keeper, and John Rutledge engaged in a heated argument concerning Rutledge's having declined an invitation to dine with the Society of the Sons of St. Patrick. On Rutledge's request, the House of Representatives investigated Thompson for having insulted a member of the body. Thompson was taken into custody and released only after posting a peace bond for his future good behavior. He then accused his tormentors of "aristo-

see how the Assembly could have acted otherwise; they were I think unanimous in their determination; and is it not strange when several of Capt. T........'s friends were on the floor, that none of them should object to any part of it? If Assemblies have not *individual* as well as *collective* privileges *while the House is sitting,* adieu to public business and freedom of debate; it would probably be filled with a few or none but insolent bullies, fine persons indeed to carry on the affairs of State, if Capt. T. .... had suppressed his resentment for any supported affront, till the House broke up? As to the Banishment Bill, I never heard it so much as whispered till a few days ago, and am persuaded it would never have been countenanced by the House had any such thing been proposed: and can any man in his senses think the assembly accountable for what any single member *may have talked of?*

When this Anti-Britannic Society's Rules [3] (partly published in your last paper) make their compleat *substantial* appearance (no doubt with the names of all their *immaculate* members to give the greater light) the public may then perhaps see the propriety of their *energetically significant appellation.* In the interim, I hope I shall be pardoned, when I declare that at first sight it put me in mind of the Fable of the Frog and the Ox; the young Frog's *swelling importance* was just as *energetically significant,* in my humble opinion, as the most ridiculous pompositious jargon. Carolina, that has not twenty of her natives at sea, immediately to set up an *Anti-Britannic Marine Society.* Laughable indeed! If intended to raise a Navy, That is expressly contrary to the Confederation, and I confess the very thought of such a thing gives me the gripes, before we recover from the endless expences and embarassments of the wretched bargain made for us only in the *bare hire* of one single frigate.[4] This of itself is a heavy burden and has involved us in almost inextricable difficulties, but the reversionary legacy introduced to us piping hot from the Frigate, just before here departure, notwithstanding many seem so fond of the new thing, I am afraid will (if It has not already) prove, a far worse concern than even the Frigate itself, *a mere Pandora's*

---

cratic" and illegal procedure in having arrested him, and further stirred the anti-Tory element to condemn the government. *Gazette of the State of South Carolina,* April 22, 1784. Journals of the House of Representatives, March 20, 1784, fol. 329-33, S.C.A.D.

[3] The Marine Anti-Britannic Society was the radical anti-Tory club of which Gillon was president. Its activities were also directed toward the exclusion of British merchants, and reprisals against the post-war maritime policy of Britain which forbade American trade with the West Indies. *South Carolina Gazette and General Advertiser,* December 16, 1783. The rules of the Society were printed in the *Gazette of the State of South Carolina,* April 22, 29, May 6, 13, 20, 1784.

[4] Gadsden referred to the Luxembourg claims.

box, notwithstanding Its *fine promising cover.* For Heaven's sake let us get back again into statu quo before we think of such wild projects. But perhaps the Society's fine title, may have led me into mistakes, and when something beyond the Forms is published, I may find nothing more held out than a charitable institution, to provide a fund to encourage parents, (who can't do better for them) to send their children to sea. If this be the real intention, why make a party, a national affair of it, and thereby counter-act themselves. The interfering with politics, will [swerve] many worthy men from assisting to promote, an otherwise laudable design: and for such a purpose would not a *Marine Society,* be title enough? Does not the unnecessary addition look of itself *suspicious,* but how must our suspicions *be further increased* when we have to reason to think the *energetic title,* is to continue only "until circumstances point out the the propriety of an alteration:" I believe so, and if the Puppet Leaders succeed in bringing about those circumstances that are probably in their view, to point out the propriety of the alteration, we shall be in a fine pickle indeed! I wish an artful Cataline is not at the bottom of all this. I am told that Mr. *Official* Secretary [5] has declared that, like another Pompey, at a stamp of his foot, he could start up 500 men: for what? To bring about *the circumstances wanted to make an aberation?* What modesty and influence this, for a man of yesterday! Anti-National Club we ought to [avoid?] to prevent jealousy; and not let the Powers of the World at large, which we wish to deal with, think we are giving undue preferences. The consequence will be, we shall be filled with intriguing emissaries from all parts, *trained to imposition,* anl carrying on the views of their different States, under *infinite disguises.* We may have an anti-Gallic Club, carrying on a Spanish interest; and [an] anti-Spanish Club, a German interest; and an anti-Britannic Club, a Dutch interest, and so on; but let us have nothing to do with all this, expecially as private persons, or private Societies; let us be obliging to all our national Customers, forward the business of all of them as much as possible, but give an undue preference to none. This is what the peace, the prosperity, and safety of this State requires; and every industrious individual throughout our country would soon reap the benefit of such conduct. Let us leave national concerns to our Legislature, it belongs to them, and *them only.* If any important matters seem to be overlooked or neglected by the House, let us address, remonstrate, *respectfully for our own sakes* as well as their's. The parliamentary way of doing business is calculated very wisely, in order to give the people an

---

[5] James Fallon, of Georgia, a little known person who became Secretary of the M.A.B.S., and a confederate of Gillon. *Gazette of the State of South Carolina,* April 22, 29, May 6, 13, 20, 1784; U.B. Phillips, "The South Carolina Federalists," *American Historical Review,* XIV (July 1909), 529-43.

opportunity before a matter is concluded, to present application if they judge proper. If you think you are overlooked, or the national business neglected, mark the men, and above all your caballers, forestalling your votes. The public business is heavy, and he that does it faithfully must hurt his private fortune. The worthy man offices seeks; the designing man cabals for them to give himself importance, to carry on his own designs, and when he has got them, neglects the duty expected, and abuses your confidence. I say mark all such men in your Legislature, as you think neglect their duty; and in the next election, withdraw your votes from them; this is right, this is proper, *but while matters are pending, and before they are finally concluded upon,* instead of remonstrating with decency, against what you disapprove, to fly immediately to outrage and effigy making, *is abusing yourselves;* and can the world think such conduct proceeds from a love of Order and Government? I am sure not.

It is time now to beg pardon for this long intrusion on the patience of the public; nothing but the consequences to be dreaded from the licentious spirit so artfully and industriously stirred up by a few restless men, has occasioned this my feeble attempt in opposition; as I thought it my duty to offer my mite on the occasion. The men at the bottom, *whether of yesterday or the day before,* who, under public pretences, are thus for dark, ambitious, or (not unlikely) speculating purposes, which they dare not own, disturbing the peace of the public, and causing the government to be bullied, 'tis to be hoped will one day be fully discovered. Providence has miraculously given us everything we wished for, a happy issue to our struggles for our liberties; happy if by our own folly and imprudence we do not make them otherwise. On this event, my countrymen, give me leave most sincerely to congratulate you. I have ever shewn myself without disguise an open Republican; 'tis the kind of Government I ever wished for this State; and I wish our *overcareful reformers and self created censors,* may have that cordial regard to it they pretend.

I am sure their conduct shews nothing but what is a disgrace to Republicanism, and what men of Aristocratical principles cannot be sorry to see. Such mobbing doing has generally stopt there or thereabout at first, and not long after settled on a Monarchy. Any government is indeed better than a licentious one. If we are to have masters, let everybody know who they are, that we may act accordingly. But if one club of men may issue *official Mandates,* why not another, and an hundred. I like a King as little as the author of the Chronicles can do, of any name whatever; nor do I like a Stadtholder a bit better: God forbid we should ever have to do with either. I have been with you, my countrymen, from the first, and shared with you in all your distresses and dangers, have never been afraid to oppose some of you, and that with no little danger to myself on certain occasions, when I thought you wrong, and none of you have ever suggested that I ever flinched from you in person or pocket, or was wanting in true affection to you. I am now ready with the blessing of God to resign my latest breath, and spend the last drop of my blood in defense of the Laws and support of the Government *agreed upon* in our country: and nothing would shew my friends, the disinterested, honourable and generous principles we have acted upon better than every man's (whatever station his country may have put him in during the war) falling cheerfully into the ranks again; returning to his business with attention and diligence; and sacrificing all his resentments and private feelings, to the good of the State. This, I think, is *true genuine Republicanism,* and he is the happiest and best citizen, who can now forget and forgive the most. Sorry I am to see any worthy man tarnish his former conduct by contrary behaviour, and seeming to expect that, for doing *no more than his duty,* he has a right to be idle (indeed worse than idle) the remainder of his days, and is to be found anywhere sooner than in his rank, usual place of business, or shop.

A STEADY and OPEN REPUBLICAN

To the Public
July 17, 1784

This essay answers one by the brewer William Hornby ("Democratic Gentle-Touch"), who attacked Gadsden for desiring to lead an undemocratic few who would dominate the state. But Gadsden contends that "Democratic Gentle-Touch" was a puppet for whom Gillon moved the strings and made the motions.

Qui vult decipi, decipiatur [Whoever wishes to be deceived, let him be deceived.]

Shall I not strip the *Gilding* off a *Knave?*
Unplac'd, unpension'd, no Man's Heir or Slave?
I will or perish in the *gen'rous* Cause:
Hear this and *tremble!* you who 'scape the Laws.

If we do not suffer ourselves [1] to be miserably duped or bullied by a few sly *mischief making* nicknamers, national Emissaries, and other indefatigable sons of *Cunning,* who wish to set us by the ears for *their own* purposes; this state will, in all probability, very *rapidly* arrive at every improvement, as well in matters of Government as of property, convenience, and every other desirable attainment, that any *industrious,* reasonable man can wish for. We have the seeds of them naturally sown amongst us, and our soil excellent. Let us only permit that natural forbearance, good humour and harmony we were famous for, to keep down rank and poisonous weeds from checking their growth; and there cannot be the *least* doubt but *common* interest, joined with the *revival* of our old *friendly* habits, will soon give all the cultivation necessary to bring them to the *fullest* maturity. When men have lived long together, in a happy agreeable neighborhood, and taken pleasure by mutual act of attention, kindness and good will to promote the welfare of each other; should a sudden shiness and distrust arise between them, and for want of timely explanation, come to open variance, owing to the *insinuating designing* artifices of some *plausible* go-between; lately returned amongst them, *well acquainted* with their different connections, turns and inclinations; in order to carry on, with more case and less risk of detection, some deep, dirty, interested purposes, *antecedently* planned. Let his low tricks and detestable views be once found out, and our old friends *again* reconciled; how must they look upon the vile cause of their coolness and separation forever afterwards? And shall less contempt be shewn to a *wholesale dealer* [Gillon] this way; the principle ring leader of our late public disturbances? who, not content with using every means in his power to perpetuate and widen our late unhappy occasions of difference; which the peace, good order, prosperity and safety of the State require to be forgotten as soon as possible, *is farther,* with *restless* industry, *feeling* all pulses, prying peeping about; and *ransacking* into every hole and corner, to find out and stir up some *new* pretences of uneasiness and discontent. [As] Such, without any breach of charity, must appear the writer, or rather supervisor of a paper published in this Gazette of the 13 May, as a pretended answer to my address to the public on account of the late riots, printed in that of the 6th, to any candid observing reader: for he manifestly, not only leaves no stone unturned to *prevent* our old private piques and animosities from subsiding, but strives with *all* his might, by adding *fresh* fuel to the fire, to raise the flame to a *still* greater height; and every low artifice, that dirty self interest, deception and duplicity can invent, are employed for this end. A very recent moving appeal to the public,

---

[1] *Gazette of the State of South Carolina,* July 17, 1784; May 13, 1784.

besides last night's riot, and a paper then first seen and directed to the Republican Whigs, from the secret Committee of Correspondence, for the Whig Club of 600, with the *Circular Letter* they are instructed to publish, manifest glaringly that the mobbing and bullying business in town, is far from being over.[2] It was, perhaps, prudent to keep all hush for a few weeks, to take breath and look about. Since, therefore, nocturnal scouts are again making excursions, it may not be a amiss, by a few remarks (which if everything had remained quiet would Never *have seen* the light,) on the paper just mentioned, to *open* the eyes of the public to the *insidious* designs of the promoter of these mischiefs, in my opinion, *much deeper* laid than many are aware of; and to show besides, the contempt this *man of importance* must have for the understanding and spirit of his fellow citizens in general, to dare to come before them in the *impudent* garb of *malicious* falsehood, and the most scandalous *wilful* misrepresentation of Facts, as well of a *public as private nature,* that it is possible to conceive. I pitch on this piece above all other publications of the sort, because the master himself has stepped forth and shewn himself *clearly* to any man not wilfully blind; and I wish it was in the hands of *every* good considerate citizen in this state, to serve as an *antidote* against such *detestable* disturbers of the public peace and *mischievous wou'd-bes,* in future. His insinuation of my being concerned in "Aristocratical designs of ruling by a few," I laugh at, and trust *every* man in America, that knows anything of me, will do *so* too; the active, steady, uniform, open, unequivocal, (and if I may upon this occasion be permitted to add) *disinterested* part I have always taken in every matter of moment, from my first entering into public business, now near thirty years since, to this hour, and particularly in the *present* House of Assembly, I flatter myself *must* be looked upon as opposite to any thing tending towards Aristocracy, as light is to darkness. Notwithstanding the *endearing* appellation "my Country," placed so *engagingly* at the entrance, and Mr. "Gentletouch" [Hornby] posted *in the rear of all,* as a *tribe,* vigilant, knowing officer, to make any diversion to prevent the great *layer* out of this work [Gillon], from being exposed to vulgar eyes, *'tis impossible* not to distinguish the masterly *directing* hand pervading *the whole;* so many striking marks, so many smart airs, so many je ne sais quoi's, and *above all,* so many anxious bowel yearnings in *his paternal character* of natural tenderness, for the preservation of a favorite child,

---

[2] In July, 1784, bands of anti-Britannics nightly roamed the streets ferreting out and punishing Tories. Disorders became even more serious when such former officers in the Revolutionary militia as Colonel Horry led counterattacks against Gillon's followers, to end what was quickly becoming a reign of terror; *see,* for example, *Gazette of the State of South Carolina,* July 1, 8, 29, 1784; *South Carolina Gazette and Public Adevtriser,* July 10, 1784.

popping upon us at every passage, and almost at every turn together with a violent *winching* fit towards the close, where, as if *actually* on command *in another character,* he *bounces* upon us *"on his own credit,"* with all the sneering effrontery of overbearing insolence and self importance; I say, all these [strong resemblances], with many more (some of a *negative* nature) that cannot escape an attentive reader, put it *past* doubt who is the *great* planner, at least of the *most essential* parts of that performance. This *important* man condescends to let us know, *with the gravity of a professor,* by way of introduction, that his reflections on the enormities of *private* slander, on false patriotism and Claudius, (*kindly warning* us, that "patriotism has been the pretense of traitors and malcontents in all ages") "on true patriotism," on "the submission of a free people to government," and how long it will last," *etc., etc.,* drew from him his remarks on my paper. After all this *grimace,* and a quotation of a few of the first lines of my address to the public, where I lament the *many* insults on government, that had lately happened, *all at once,* quite regardless of his *grave* reflections but that *instant finished,* he *immediately* subjoins, "I would ask this gentleman and the *other nabobs,* and *their creatures,* did they, at the time of the Stamp Act, *stickle* so for government?" Permit me here, my dear reader, quite *gratitide-struck lost* and *overwhelmed* with so much *unexpected* kindness, (before I touch upon the question ask'd) not to lose a moment to introduce this *most worthy* personage to your acquaintance, as his honor Mr. Dupe-Master General [Gillon], "an appellation *energetically significant"* of those peculiar excellent talents, which, *beyond all gain saying,* he so eminently possesses, that has so long exercised *"to the wonderful* emolument of the good people of this state; and on all *future* occasions, there is not the least doubt of his honor's readiness at all times, to call forth all *"his own credit"* and powers, *again, and again* to their service, whenever a proper occasion offers for any farther public *dupeworthy* trust. Now to the question. It may be asserted with the *greatness* truth, that no kingly ruled *province* in America had less of mobbing in it, *antecedent* to the Stamp Act, *than this.* Though we had many disputes of great consequence with all our last British governor, yet *not the least sympton* of mobbing appeared: *not even* when, to *try* their tempers and *bring them* to improper compliances, the assembly were the *most haughtily* and *provokingly* ordered to sit at Port-Royal, and that too at the *most unhealthy* season of the year—but every member, almost to a man, made it a point to go, and not the least disturbance to government was attempted, and at a time too when 'tis *well known* those assemblies were *well beloved* by the people. All these disputes were settled, *where only* such like business ought to be, *in the legislature*: and *continued* to be so till *necessity alone,* (the only colour of excuse for the *least* appearance like mobbing) when every thing dear to us as men, to our families, to our posterity, was looked upon to be at stake, occasioned that mobbing and bullying affair his honor alludes; but *half the state* could have informed his honor, that I was at the northward on *public* business when they *both* happened; however, a mistake of this sort is *easily pardoned* to one who was not In, or a citizen Of this country in 1765; and in 1775, when the other happened, I think I saw his honor at Philadelphia. But, thank God, these times are (or ought to be) over; the glorious ends aimed at are accomplished: *equal* (if not our own faults) to the *highest* expectations of the warmest and steadiest patriots. Your *keen* speculators indeed, and the *dexterous* mob managers may wish to keep the trade *still* going; and *no* wonder, to them and their friends *in the secret,* it cannot turn out an extremely *lucrative* kind of monopoly; but how *ruinous* must it be to the *public* in general? Heats and jealousies, the natural consequences of the times, were *subsiding fast,* had not this writer and his dupes established a *lasting* fund for keeping them up. The candid part of the citizens that unavoidably remained within the enemy's lines till the evacuation, *did not expect,* as they were *in the power* of the British at the *very time* of the general election for this assembly, that they should have been permitted to vote: their being restrained at *particular* elections since, is what may have touched their feelings.

'Tis well known the writer of this paper did all in his power, in time, *before* any writ was issued, at the *first* sitting of the house to remedy this *expected* uneasiness, so that his *Nabobship* must have almost *rivalled* our Dupe Master General himself in *duplicity,* had he been concerned in that stroke of Nabob policy, so maliciously insinuated— but is there a member that *expects* the present assembly will meet again? and will not all disqualifications cease at the next general election? Why then are we *wantonly* asked this mischievous and *insidious* question, *"is our present legislature the free choice of the people?"*

What good end can all that *out-of-time* condolence, all that wheedling and cajoling "of the honest quiet citizens taken in town, and forced from circumstances, to take British protection" answer? Why all that fulsome, pitiful, *"lick-spittle"* declamation, founded in falsehood and the most *"rascally"* misrepresentation, (as will be shewn presently) in behalf of the Scape Goat he talks of, and in order *spitefully* to stab in the dark, some supposed friend of mine? Whoever is at a loss to account for this humouring, this blowing hot and cold, this all things to all men, let him only have patience a very few months, and all his wonderment will cease. He will then, or I am much mistaken, see that *"rascally caitiffs"* cunning time-watching Proteus's, *forward officious* Sempronius's have not forgot to play their parts *as dexter-*

210

ously, to the mortification and deception of honest, faithful, well meaning citizens, as any did or could do "who took shelter under Governor Matthews's proclamation." Human nature in this is, alas! *too stationary,* the crafty *still* too often outwit the simple and innocent; but thanks to an over-ruling Providence the cunning seldom fail, with rope enough, to out-cunning themselves at last and when their *short swing* is over, their memory is detested forever. We are asked another curious question: "Do not the fears and jealousies of the good people of this state, at this day, spring from the *like* sources and when under the *former* government?" Though I am persuaded there is scarcely an honest man of common sense, in the state, will think this question *wants or deserves* any answer, yet let me be forgiven for not passing it by unnoticed; The former source of "opposition, was an attempt to tax us all together unrepresented, against which the United States repeatedly petitioned for redress *to no purpose.*" Instead of *relief* were they not insulted? What is the *present* case? Supposing from unfavourable appearances, want of time to make immediately an exact discrimination, from a variety of pressing business of the utmost consequence, crowding upon the legislature *all at once,* and from a thousand other circumstances the natural consequence of the times, several worthy citizens have been debarred of their votes; are not the restrictions of the law itself, though made under *all* these untoward circumstances, and even in the *very din* of arms, and when piques and resentments were *at the highest,* Only temporary? and do they not *actually expire* next general election? Again, the banished, amerced, *etc.,* by the confiscation law, (which 'tis to be wished had never been passed) have *almost all* of them petitioned the legislature, and have not all their petitions *not only* been received but committed, and attend to without a *single* exception that I know of? In consequence of this attention *becoming* a legislature, have not *numbers* of petition[er]s been relieved in whole or in part? Can this be compared to the *unnatural, unfeeling* treatment the *repeated* petitions of the United States *met* with? Could we, or indeed all America *together,* have prevented one single member of the British parliament, however *obnoxious,* from being elected *again and again* in every succeeding parliament? Is that the case with us now? This writer says, "He *knows* the generality of the citizens despise the generality of the members of this assembly."

Well then, will not the *generality* of electors, at the next election, have it in their power to turn them *all* out and put in others? And if they also behave amiss, to send them too about their business two years after? What would his honor have more? Can there be then any occasion for mobs or riots in *such* a situation? I wish the *next* election may shew that he and his dupes *know* their own minds, and are then *satisfied* to see that the Jacksonborough restrictive regulations are no more, and that they may not endeavour to intimidate many of the very men they are now pretending to pity, from voting at all, if they are not previously assured that they will vote as they want them, in order to pack an assembly to their mind, as they seem to be aiming at. After such long *trying* civil commotions, could it be expected, from the slightest acquaintance with human nature, that *every thing* would be settled again in a *moment?* The candid, the humane, the benevolent, the generous, rejoice to see the progress already made towards that *general* harmony we were formerly so famous for, and every good citizen longs to see again firmly established. During the struggle some distinction might be necessary, that of Whig and Tory as good perhaps as any; but now the keeping these cant words afloat, can answer no end but to keep alive old piques and resentments, make many families unhappy and spoil good neighbourhood; and (in this,) give *dexterous* knaves and *national* emissaries, an *excellent* opportunity of combining together, and playing into each other's hands and set one against another, to their no small advantage indeed and sport; but to the ruin of the community in general, and verifying the coarse proverb, while two dogs are fighting for a bone, a third comes and runs away with it; for believe me my friends, these *knowing* hands care no more for either side, then the sly dog did about the two others that were fighting, and only want, like him, to make the most of our quarrels. The sooner, therefore, these noisy mischief making names Whig and Tory are consigned to oblivion, the better, and if the strange sound Nabob, that like an ill-boding Comet, has lately been *forced* into our Hemisphere, and make its appearance on our Horizon with such a *wonderous* blazing tail, would as *suddenly* disappear and keep their company it would be better still. Never did any people want for union more than we do at this moment, and every true lover of the state, and of his family, will do his utmost to promote it. If this writer knows any "mal-practices peculation and corruption in any public officers," let him do the public *open* justice, and not insult the public understanding, and would the delicacy of every man of feeling, by stabbing in the dark, the honor and character of gentlemen *in the gross,* by such mysterious whisperings, and "rascally" insinuations, left as it were on purpose, *in terrorem* to (reputation) brokers, party tools, and election jobbers to make *the most of,* and apply *occasionally* to any officer of spirit and honor, that seize and opposes their *deep* nefarious designs. The wit about the word *"upstart" must* be entirely lost to any attentive reader; however, it shews how *hardly* pressed his honor must be to catch at such straws. That word *where* it stands, has clearly *nothing* to do with birth or family, but *merely* relates to "Censors," and any man, be his genealogy what it may, his father's

212

or mother's able to be reckoned up by him or not, whether they be rich or poor, is a self created upstart Censor, whenever he exercises that office without right.

His honor sneeringly asks, "what idea they affix to the words good citizens?" I'll tell him what idea I have of them, from a translation (in a note Mr. Pope's works) of an *unexceptionable* author and lover of mankind, of *more* than two thousand years standing,

> Whose honors with increase of ages grow,
> As streams roll down, enlarging as they flow

> —POPE

"The citizen (says Plato, in his 5th book of laws), who does no injury to any one, without question *merits our esteem*. He who, not content with being *barely* just himself, opposes the course of injustice, by *prosecuting* it before the Magistrate, merits our esteem vastly more. The first discharges the duty of a *single* citizen; but, the other does the office of a *body*. But he whose zeal stops not here, but proceeds TO Assist The Magistrates In Punishing, is the most valuable blessing of society. This is the most Perfect Citizen to whom we should adjudge the prize of virtue." Now which of these three degrees of good citizenship has his honor's conduct exemplified *since his return* amongst us? Has it done no injury to any one? Has it been visible in opposing *the course* of injustice before the magistrates? Or, has it shewn itself *in assisting* the magistrate in punishing, as the magistrate can *only* punish according to law? Or has it been glaringly in direct opposition to *all* three? We are asked, "Is it not injurious to any state that imports more value than they export? When this is the case must not the balance always be unfavourable?" I answer, in proportionable degree, as the citizens of the state may be the importers, it must be detrimental to *such* citizens, who are and ought to be but few, in comparison of the *whole* state; but in our situation at present, and as it is likely to be for some time, I deny the supposition altogether; indeed, I think 'tis quite the reverse, for let foreigners import as much as they will, the more the better (unless perhaps of a few articles that may be thought *pernicious,* which may be restrained by particular acts). Certainly the more goods at market the cheaper we may get such articles as we want, and besides, the more importers the more purchasers we shall have for our own produce, and thereby reap another greater advantage, by getting abundantly more for our years labour than we otherwise should. I grant it may not *suit* private schemers, who wish to grasp *all* they can to themselves.

In my last I had said, "what foreigners will trade with such mad men, not only regardless of, but even insulting their own legislature *etc.,*" To which is replied, "foreigners are not, nor will not be disturbed, and it is plain they know it, as appears by the vast quantity of foreign goods in the city, and still coming in with every tide." The *plain* reason here given by this great favourer and *stickler* for mobs, may be alledged as a much plainer, that many foreigners did not know of those mobs, or at least, were hopeful that they would *soon* subside, as they knew we had had time to cool and reflect upon the many ill-consequences of *unavoidably* attending them. However, this *we know* for certain, that several were actually discouraged, who had heard of our last year's riots, the number of which, the longer we countenance such disorderly doings, must increase, till at length we may be looked upon, in the eye of foreigners, as incurable, and the character of a mob government, not more disgraceful than distressing, indelibly fixed upon us. But this is not the only place where his honor seems to think *a little mobbing,* now and then, a useful expedient, and may prevent over-importations, "causing a balance of trade against us, and gradually sinking us into extreme poverty, when we can not import at all." For my part, in our situation, I look on all this as a mere chimera, and that this Bug-bear of a balance of trade, should it happen, will be, generally speaking, against the over-importing merchants, and them only, who alone will be accountable for the consequences. But here it may not be *unpleasant* to remark, by the bye, that if this writer is serious here, which I much question, is he not coming into my opinion, and as it were unawares confessing, that mobbing and riot have a *natural* tendency to cramp and narrow trade? And this very probably may have been the design of the promoter of our mobs, like a juggling sharper, to cramp and narrow our trade as much as possible, to himself and friends. Attend, my good reader, to the following quotation from my paper, strangely mangled, interlarded, and most villainously tacked together—"But to counteract the law of the land," says this immaculate writer, (meaning me) "is shocking and insufferable, as it endeavors to counteract our *Aristocratical* designs of ruling by a few. But not so formerly, when our Open Republican and his colleagues were very active in pulling down Kingly rule, to set up *their own domination.* But opposition to a few tyrants," he says "is capricious, retail tyranny," *etc.* "a gnawing worm of malice and resentment, to bite individuals." If I thought a writer, capable of penning such *gross* falsehood and perversion, *could feel,* I should certainly pity him, but supposing it impossible, I leave him entirely to the reader; who is intreated to turn to his paper and mine, and when he has compared them together, he will scarcely be able to forbear concluding that the man, *desirous* to *palm* such *barefaced* imposition on the public, *must* be capable of *any other infamous* attempt *whatever,* that *may suit* his ambitious or interested designs. Another quotation cannot be passed by unnoticed; 'tis much mangled, curtailed and transposed, but with *abundantly more* art and slyness than the preceeding, as the reader will see by my real words and his quotation, placed in opposite columns, and the parts *practiced upon,* distinguished by a different character.

My words are "tis to be wished we had made an example, *if necessary after a fair and candid trial,* of three or four of the most notorious delinquents, [Tories] of rank, of the highest authority, and universally known, whose weight and influence *must* have been of the most pernicious consequences, and then *passed a general amnesty."*

His quotation runs thus, The steady and Open Republican says, "that we should have made examples of three or four of the most notorious delinquents, of rank, of the highest authority, and universally known, whose weight and influence have been of the m o s t pernicious consequences *after a fair and candid trial."*

Let me now first ask this honest quoter why are my words "if necessary," left out, are they not *essential?* That it was not my meaning to make an example of any, unless *necessary,* appears plainly, not only from *these* words, as well as from my *whole* conduct, but also from another passage in my paper, a few lines below them, which is thus expressed, "a respectable and fatherly government will commiserate all its subjects, overlook *all it can,* consistent with the safety of the state, *punish with reluctance,* and when obliged to punish do it with spirit and propriety; always shewing itself ready to protect the poorest citizen, and not afraid of the highest." Again the critical reader will observe not a little management in leaving out my word, *"must,"* however that will pass by, but why are my words "after a fair and candid trial" shoved from their own place in the beginning of the clause, and placed *at the end of all?* Was this *manouvre* in order to *leave out, with a better grace, these words,"* and then pass a general amnesty," which ought to have occupied that very spot, *to shew the end intended,* that if it should prove necessary, and the state be *obliged* to punish, or make a few examples, then an amnesty passing *immediately thereafter,* would tend to satisfy and quiet the minds of the citizens, that here would be *no more examples* but that every thing was over and done with. This writer says that "in consequence of such advice" (that is what he made me to say)

Gen. W.[3] was pitched upon to be the Scape-Goat," that is at any rate, necessary or not necessary, as he had no relations or friends, but what *his money* made for him:" What a sly and *deep* insinuation! This envenomed arrow! Is it thrown against particular members, or the *whole* body of the legislature. Gen. W. had his own time *to prepare* himself, before his trial, had *the most* patient and candid attention paid to him, *during* that trial, of *any* person in the confiscation list, and the house have *decided* upon his case in *the most favourable* manner. Why then *any more* said about him? I wish everybody acquiesced *so perfectly* in this decision of the house as I do, and have ever done in *all* their decisions? Our Dupe Master General must certainly have some [mysterious?] reasons for the tete a tete he had with the General a very few days *after this, up the path*: that may come to light, by and by. That, and *all* this more than ordinary [striving?] must appear Very Extraordinary, the more so, as last night's Virtuous address sets him down as a "catiff." Has our *Sempronious* found him refractors and is afraid he will not answer *his purpose* next election? But, to return, if where offenders are numerous and it be *necessary* to make examples or Scape Goats (if this writer will have it so) which *must* be taken somewhere, where will you take them? From the *lowest* or *middle* ranks? Would that answer the end, *so probably* and *surely* from the *highest*? besides would it not shew, a wretched, timid, indecisive, see-saw, spirit in any government to do so, and be a great encouragement to your high restless *sparks,* to begin new commotions, thinking the state is *afraid* of them?—In short, if in consequence of *such* advice as my *genuine* words import, if necessary, three or four, "after a fair and candid trial," were to have been made Scape Goats of, and then an end put to our unhappy civil dissensions by a general amnesty. In consequence of *whose* advice *by dozens unnesessarily* pitched upon, and *without* trial? To answer what end? Had not their several cases *already* been determined upon by the legislature of the land, and what was thought necessary, with regard to each of them, ordered and fixed? I say, after such *solemn* determinations, what can be designed by such sly insinuations, but to *insult and affront,* in the most open, and grossest manner the whole state, in the persons of its representatives? Notwithstanding the "no other" (or only) "view" which the

---

[3] Brigadier General Andrew Williamson was the so-called "Arnold of Carolina." Early in the Revolution, he had been active on the American side, performing valuable service. But his role after the fall of Charles Town was open to suspicion and contemporaries thought him a traitor. However, Annie King Gregorie, in her article in *DAB,* XXX, 296-7, intimates that he may have been an American spy. Williamson had given information to Colonel John Laurens concerning enemy movements out of occupied Charles Town, while he was ostensibly in the service of the British. And General Greene intervened to save him from the proscriptions of the Confiscation Act, the object of controversy in this part of the essay.

great man himself tells us that the Marine Anti-Britannic Society have in their "undertaking" yet I confess many facts and dates (besides last night's) *so notoriously* contradict this assertation that I cannot help being of opinion that this "only view" is *only a mere specious* pretence, *preconcerted* by him and his *peculiars* In The Secret to be *held up* in order *to dupe* the uncautious undesigning man withal, when the *real end plainly* appears to be *to raise* a sworn Political Phalanx to be ready at his beck on *all favorite* mob or electioneering occasions, and I am sure if the public are to judge of what may happen *hereafter* by the *precious foretaste* they have *already* had from this *pretended gracious* fountain of benevolence, it must much dread that all its *future* tender mercies will be *bitter* cruelties indeed. *Our great leader,* in his *usual* manner, has made me say of the Carolina frigate, that she "had a wretched bargain made for her, and from which more evils sprung than from Pandora's box; and then, by way of comment, asks me, "what better *success* had the Prosper and other state vessels, *etc.,*" If the reader will be at the trouble of comparing my words with this *twisted* epitome, he will find *no stress at all,* laid by me on the success, but merely as my words shew "on the *wretched* bargain made (not "for her" but) *for us, only* in the *bare hire* of one single frigate; and the *reversionary legacy or new thing* introduced to us piping hot from her, "which *reversionary legacy or new thing*" I was afraid would prove *a far worse concern* than even the frigate itself, *a mere* Pandora's box." The intent of this *twist* is so *easily* seen through, that it would be insulting the readers understanding to *point* it out.

When the public at large, (as not unlikely one day they may) come to be fully acquainted with the *exact* and *genuine* history of the *bare hire* (I say now only of 3/4ths) of this frigate, and the most *enormous* sum it has amounted to; the situation *she was in* when hired, to be got to sea *at our risk and expence*: to be manned, maintained, and fitted out in all her cruises, and to be returned to Port L'Orient, in France, at the expiration of three years, *wholly* at our expence also: how unsuitable she was to our bar; and how it could possibly be thought, that the *bare* hire of 3/4ths of a single frigate, *so situated* as she *was,* could be an object of any moment to this state: besides many *other* circumstances and curious observations, that will naturaly arise from the very *articles* of the *wretched* bargain itself, *where* the interest of the state seems, *almost throughout,* to have given way to a disposition *to douceur and oblige.* I say, when all these things come to be *fully* known, it will make the citizens of this state, I am persuaded, stare, and not a little wonder, how the accounts relative to her, should pass the assembly *so readily,* especially too, when, added to what has been just now mentioned, the Commander of her had been so frequently, so freely, and so publicly talked of;

his *unexpected* return too, with several officers of great importance, to the ship, just *immediately before* she put to sea, must, *with what followed,* appear *not a little* mysterious. In consequence of this manoeuvre, by the bye, a very worthy man, long-known and esteemed among us, whether he was pitched upon to be the *Scape Goat* or not, cannot be proved, but that he became so by it, is not now, I believe, much doubted. It is impossible for any officer, so *circumstanced* as this gentleman [Gillon] was, to have met with more candour, more generosity and more dispatch, in such complicated public matters as his accounts related to, especially when many of the members of this very house (which he tells us, "he knows the generality of the citizens despite the generality of the members,") *well knew,* that so far from being *obliged* to purchase or hire such a ship, so situated, his orders must have been put to the *capstan,* and stretched every *strand* to the utmost, to draw out the interpretation he gave them. However, as we were all *happy* in meeting one another, in the *first* assembly *after* the evacuation, and unwilling to make *any* man *otherwise,* whom we did not suspect was an enemy to our cause: as it was not *impossible* he might have *conceived* his instructions in that light, and ABOVE ALL, as the Honor of the country was at stake, viewing the matter as relative to foreigners, to have it *speedily* settled: *this* weighed much with many of the very gentlemen, (so Be-Nabob'd by him, or *under* his auspices) to throw *no impediment* in the way of its quick and favourable settlement. These, 'tis well known to many of my friends, were my *private* sentiments, and induced me to endeavour, as much as any gentleman in the house, to bring this *most disagreeable* affair to a close as soon as possible. Had the house been *disposed* to have attended to unfavorable reports, with regard to his honour's conduct in this business, from first to last, when *respectable* names might have been mentioned, what a field for suggestion would have been opened, of a different cast from those blind hints, dark surmises, sly insinuations, with which this writer has filled his *dirty* performance, in order, if possible, to blast or *at least,* to tarnish the honor and reputation of some as good and firm friends to this country, as any it has. This *ungrateful* man experienced nothing but moderation, kindness, and every degree of tenderness and delicacy from the assembly itself, from that very assembly which he treats with such contempt. What kind of *bowels* too must *he* have, so *directly after* to use or cause to be used many of his fellow-citizens in the *cruel* manner he has? Does it not exactly resemble the conduct of the servant, who, after having been forgiven *ten thousand talents* by his compassionate Lord, *immediately* on leaving his presence, took by the throat and cast into prison his fellow servant, who owed him only *an hundred pence*? Again, *what danger* has this *assuming* great man *ever* shared with us? I believe not a *single* one. Was he here in 1776, at General Clinton's and Sir

Peter Parker's attack? Why was he not? He was in America, and that attack 'tis well known was *no sudden* affair. Several more very curious questions of this sort, and from as early periods as our Liberty-tree transactions might be asked.[4] As to his appointment, very few in the state or indeed upon the continent in *several* respects could be *more desirable.* What *uncommon* opportunities had he as a *knowing* merchant; *the years* he was in Europe in an honorable public character from this state, to know and see *long before* the gentlemen in trade here could, how our affairs were *likely* to turn out, and govern himself accordingly? What openings had he to *settle* plans, form correspondences, *etc.,* before he got the frigate out to sea. Were we half as dextrous at insinuations as he has shewn himself, might it not be said, supported by *much stronger* appearances than any he has suggested, that *this* engagement for *only* three-fourths of a *hired* frigate, *situated* as she was; so *difficult* to be got to sea; the time *when* it was done; with many *other* odd *misterious* concommitant circumstances were all *mere* manoeuvring *contrivances* to create delays to stay in Europe *as long* as with any *tolerable* grace his honor *could,* for *other* purposes than the *interest* of our state required? And when he got to sea *at last,* the scale having *visibly* turned in favor of America, and was almost daily turning more and more, were not his expectations sanguine with regard to prize money! And did he not actually take several very *valuable* ones without the least danger, or more trouble than perhaps firing a single gun to bring them to? Though this we have heard him *publicly* call his *hard earned* prize money! What officer *here* had any chance like this of *hard or soft* earned prize money, or indeed *any* chance *at all* but that of continual fatigues, distresses and dangers, without any *particular* prospect but that of his pay, *still* not got? Has any officer in this state *like* this gentleman been able (if inclined) to be *continually* buying up confiscated estates by the dozen as it were? Would not this open another large field for many *strange* questions? but "I really am ashamed to insult the public understanding by a recapitulation of the male-practices," that this very man by *his own method* of accusation, with *far less* circumstantial appearances, has with *so much* effrontry in this

---

[4] This is apparently a reference to Gillon's troubles with the General Committee, on the enforcement of the boycott against the Townshend Act. In 1770, Gillon wanted to sell imported wine, but the Committee forced him to store it. *SCG,* Feb. 1, 1770. *See* letters in *Freeman II.* In 1774, however, Gillon served on the Committee of Correspondence with the mechanics' leaders. Walsh, *Charleston's Sons of Liberty,* p. 64, 9n. At the time of the first British attack on Charles Town, Gillon was procuring munitions for the Continental Congress. He had secured a contract to purchase supplies in Europe amounting to $250,000 at 5% commission over a three-year period, but was called upon by the State to fit out the South Carolina Navy, and consequently refused Congress' proposition. *DAB,* VII, 296; *Journals of the Continental Congress,* IX, 944-9.

paper *insinuated* with regard to óthers, and therefore *not unjustly* to be suspected of dabbing not very *cleanly* himself. To return, at the *very last* of this war the enemy were not near so rigid and severe to their naval prisoners of any rank as they were in the beginning; so that, had his honor been taken he would not in all probability have experienced any thing like the distresses numbers did at the first of the struggle. But this *lucky* gentleman was not taken *at all,* so could not have set *any* ill usage from the enemy to irritate him, and on his return, had he not received every indulgence from the state he could *possibly* expect? What kind of disposition then must this man have, so wantonly to occasion such distresses and *severe* animadversions on the conduct of others, which he *can have,* but from mere *tinctured* hearsay? I hope the reader will excuse my so long attention to this point, and pardon *the manner* I have treated it in; it was to shew that his honor ought to have been one of the [leading] men in the state, on *numberless* accounts, to [take] such *extraordinary* airs upon him, and to make so *very free* with others by wholesale.

We are told that "the commander of the Carolina" was *"on his own credit obliged* to *purchase* and fit out the ship, as foreigners had not so favourable thoughts of our *Nabobs,* as they had of themselves, so would not trust them." I have already shewn he was not *obliged* to purchase, and of consequence not to fit out the ship; that he did it "on his own credit" (if any part was done so) might be owing very probably to the *cautious* foreigner on *seeing* his credentials, mistrusting, and with *reason,* that the state might throw the matter on his honor for *stretching* his orders so unacountably. But it is well known, his honor was bent on the hire of this ship at any rate, and as our attorney, being of course obliged to sign the articles of agreement, this matter might not be *unwillingly* pressed upon him, to have an opportunity to *figure* away here as prettily as with the laughable *swaggering* ribband in Europe: with what *grace* could his honor *have refused* being acountable? Would *any* gentleman in the state with the *like* commission as his honor *have refused* so to be, if desired? What *extraordinary* risk did he run? Was he not on a *fine* scheme, with a sanguine prospect of prizes of which he would have a large share as commander and *besides,* the public fourth part in his own hands as a counter security to *indemnify* himself withal? The words "on his own credit" are too *general,* that they seem intended to *puff* him, throughout the state, as a mighty great man; as if he had "purchased" the *whole* of the frigate, and paid for her *every* farthing himself; but how can that be? Though we were unlucky in part of our indigo sent to Europe, yet *some did* arrive at his disposal. Besides we know a gentleman, who had not the least prospect of advantage in any shape, only as a native of the state then in Europe, *did* stake his own credit and fortune to a very large amount in this matter, also *happy* in an opportunity to *assist* the state, and that too without parade or noise, and we well know *he had* a fortune at stake. Add to this, could not the *late* gallant young colonel [John] Laurens have told us; and would he not have told us, amongst several other things, that he had assisted, *very considerably too,* in fitting out this frigate? How was it *possible then,* that it could be done "on his own credit?" in the general unlimited manner *boasted* of? But after all, does not the 11th article of the agreement itself say, that "Sieur G......, hath pledged the public faith of the state, and has *engaged* and *mortgaged* generally all its property, possessions and revenues, *as well as his own,* both present and future in solido," for the compliance of this bargain? If *all* the estates in this country were to be mortgaged, must not *his own* be so too? therefore what occasion was there for the *unnecessary* mention of it at all? it must have been inserted for *form's* sake as our attorney, or more probably for an *occasional* puff. But we are told that the Reason why this great man "was obliged to purchase and fit out the ship on his own credit" was, "foreigners had not so favourable thoughts of our *Nabobs* as they have of themselves, so would not trust them." The most candid reader, I believe, must be at a loss to apply the word "Nabobs" to any persons short of the *whole* state. For was it less than the *whole* state, by their representatives that set the business of purchasing the three frigates (of which the *hired* Caroline was an *unnatural,* forced, succour, they never dreamed of) a going? Had any *private* persons, *Nabobs or not Nabobs, any thing* to do with it? Is it not then *clearly* the *whole* state, and *nothing* less, that can be *sneered* at by the word "Nabobs"? We *often* deserve not a few rubs, I confess, on our great credulity and impetuosity at times. But this our Dupe-Master General's *sneering* exultation over us is *rather* too much; however I hope it will have *this* good effect, to make assemblies *abundantly* more circumspect in future, and not suffer themselves to be so instantaneously ballooned into expensive, romantic projects as they have been, by artful, specious job seekers, who *generally* choose to give us the *preference* of their ingenious experiments.

How the bridge, that joined Sullivan's island with the main,[5] came to be lugged in here, without rhyme or reason, I cannot conceive. What likeness between that and the frigate, excepting *a little merely in their exit,* by the British? But the "success" of the frigate, as I said just now, was *scarce* thought of by me; the *wretchedness* of the bargain in itself, the *reversionary* legacy, the *new* thing introduced amongst us, and the *worse* than Pandora's box, *in consequence* of that

---

[5] Gillon intimated that Gadsden had profited from building the military bridge from Sullivan's Island to the mainland; *see* letter to John Rutledge, December 14, 1776.

new thing, were the matters *I dwelt upon, relative* to the frigate. Now, in the name of wonder, what *reversionary* legacy is to be expected? What *Pandora's* box? What *mob establishment* does, or can a *single* man in the state *apprehend from,* or *about* the bridge? The *universal* anxiety, and wishes for *such* a bridge, and the opinion of Gen. Lee, that the fort on Sullivan's island *might be called* a slaughter-house *without* it, would have been *as well* known to this *prudent* bird of passage, this *exquisite* discerner of the times, as it was to numbers of others, had he been here at the time; and why he was not, has been already asked? The bridge is left to others to judge, "what more use, or less expence than the Carolina frigate, it was of,"—I *only* beg leave to observe, that the undertaker [Gadsden] of that bridge, made *no bargain at all* about it, so could not make *a wretched* one. He only acquainted the Governor and General Lee as was his duty as an officer, in an important matter that seemed to be much wanted, and he thought himself competent to, that he had a *sufficient number of hands and materials found him,* he was persuaded he could build such a bridge as was wished for; his offer was readily and cheerfully accepted; hands and materials were *accordingly found him,* and the bridge was built, *as he thought, to general* satisfaction, for which *he never charged* the public *a copper,* or would accept of *any gratuity whatever,* for his attention and direction of that business; neither *did* he finger, or *would* finger one farthing, *directly or indirectly,* paid for it, more than for the wages of some negroes of his own that were employed about it, at the *common* rates allowed to every body else. However, the public know the utmost of the expense of the bridge, and 'tis done with entirely, and nothing farther apprehended. It was certainly of *some* service at the time, in giving employ to numbers, and the money it cost, Was all spent Amongst *ourselves.* Has that been the case, or anything *like* the case, with regard to the frigate? On the contrary, where is *the Apollo* that can tell us when we can see *the end* of the frigate business, and the embarrassments attending it, all owing to a manifest *stretch* of power in *our sweet bargainmaker.* I am obliged to the gentleman for indulging me with an explanation, why "a party, a national affair" was made, with regard to the title of his *favorite* society. But I must beg pardon for *still* thinking, that whatever orders the "Court of London," or any other Court, may make with regard to the "carrying" or any other "trade" that in short, everything *national* should be left to our legislature and them only.

The interference of clubs and private societies, in such matters, instead of being of any public use, *only* serves, if attended to, to embarrass the assembly, and split the members into parties. If one club meddles, may not another, and a third, and so on, with *equal* right and propriety? It is not impossible too, they may *differ* from each other in many material points; what is to be done then? *Which* club to be followed?

If any society "wish to express their sense" on any public matter of moment, if it was drawn up in a sensible *respectable* address, well supported with proper arguments, and presented to the legislature when sitting, so highly constitutional and useful a step might not seldom be of great service, as I have frequently known such addresses *much wished for* by the members of the house on difficult points, especially when, as they often do, come *suddenly* before them; this would greatly tend to *harmonize* and *improve* public confidence *within* and *without* doors, and be the best means to prevent misunderstandings and jealousies, and bring about *many* desirable points of the greatest consequence that are much wished for. One was carried in the present house by the most decisive majority, that I know, for thirty years past, was in vain attempted in every assembly, I mean the *ad valorum tax;* this is a manifest *public* testimony, that a *generous* spirit now *prevails,* not wishing to take advantages of each other, but only desiring that every citzen may bear his part of the public burden, according to his strength, more or less and *no further.*

Our method of balloting at election is, not *only* the most peaceable, but in *every* respect the most *safe* and eligible: I wish our Mob-favourers are not *manoevouring* to overset it; for whcrc is thc *difference to the public* of my standing up, (and at the risk of a broken head) *openly* naming whom I vote for, or *suffering* any *election-jobber* or *jobbing-society,* whatever to *thrust* a vote into the *box*? All things of this sort, we ought to be extremely jealous of, such *indirect* doings can never be founded on *true* republican principles and *real* public good, but *must* be built on *what* are opposite thereto as light is to darkness. Let us then with *all possible* diligence and watchfullness, *shake off* that *epidemical* laziness and neglect we are too remarkable for, respecting our elections, acting as if we thought it a matter of indifference whether we voted or not. To our *remissness* is this *momentous* matter, numbers of the evils we have endured are to be charged. An Anecdote of *more* than thirty years standing, is well known, that a very wealthy Church Warden, long since dead, to rouse his Parishioners from this dangerous lethargy, told them, if they *omitted* coming to vote, he would *reserve* his own vote to the *last* moment, and then put it in for the *most disagreeable* man to the *whole* Parish, he could *think* of: the hint he gave being *totally* disregarded, though a gentleman highly esteemed among them, he therefore voted as he said, and the member elected by his *single* vote, was returned and served; who afterwards humorously declared in the house, that he had been *unanimously* elected. Entirely owing to this *raging* mischief, stupid party tools have been often riggled into the house, that, if the *tenth* part of the electors had voted, would not have stood the *least* chance, whose business *there,* has *often* been, with the most observant eye, to watch their *Leader,* and be up or down, according to his nod; and on *pressing* occasions, to *slip* out, or from bench to bench, to jog or start the *careless* to attend and mind where their head man was *sitting,* that they might not *blunder* when the question was put, for want of *seeing* him *in time.*

Let us vote with care, uninfluenced and peaceably, avoiding *all innovations* that have the *least* tendency to sap our *old* mode of doing it; that by the *most mortifyng* disappointment, All busy party *tools, disturbers* of the peace, with *"six hundred"* or six thousand at their heels, dangerous innovators and *officious* time-servers, may be Convinced, at the close of the poll, that their pretty manoeuvers were *no* recommendation to men who had the good of the community *at heart,* wished to be *well* governed, and *resolved* to be *so,* by every *prudent constitutional* step in their power. An assembly *thus* chosen, will do *every thing* they *can* for their constituents; but blunder as they *may,* they will hardly blunder *so much* as any club or society that might be pitched on. It requires no great conjuration to see a wrong step *when taken,* and assemblies, as well as indivduals, must be expected to make mistakes sometimes; but, because assemblies legally chosen by the people, may and do commit errors, shall we therefore suffer them to be despised and *virtually* discharged, by substituting *private* clubs in their room, *not voted for at all?* Can we think these clubs will commit *less* mistakes? We ought to remember, that we *disgrace ourselves* whenever we treat our assemblies with contempt, or *proclaim* any mistakes they *may* have made; the *least* said upon such occasions, and the *sooner* they are put to rights the better; and a respectful address to the legislature, to get the matters *reconsidered,* is by much the *best* and speediest, as well as the *most probable* way of accomplishing what we wish for.[6]

---

[6] This essay must also be regarded as an attempt by Gadsden to defeat Gillon in the next election for "Intendant" (Mayor) of Charleston. In September, running against Richard Hutson, Gillon was soundly thrashed, 387-127. His defeat set back his career politically, but apparently brought peace to the city for the first time in years. Gillon retired to his plantation on the Congaree. In 1788, he entered the Congressional race but lost again. However, in 1793, he was elected to Congress. *South Carolina Gazette and General Advertiser,* September 14, 1784; Rogers, *Evolution of a Federalist,* pp. 162-6; Charles Gregg Singer, *South Carolina in the Confederation* (Philadelphia: University of Pennsylvania Press, 1941), pp. 27-29.

The followers of Gillon, the so-called "democratical party," were defeated in the Assembly election in 1784, if one may judge from the following: In a letter of John Lloyd to T.B. Smith, Lloyd related that "the malecontented party have by several publications endeavoured to influence the elections throughout the State to make a choice of men to represent them in the general assembly, from

The more any people *respect* the laws of the land, the *happier* they *must be* amongst themselves, and the more respectable abroad. This is a very *old* maxim.

I have made an observation or two, *en passant,* on a most *extra-ordinary* paper that has just made its appearance, calculated *most glaringly,* under *gilded* appearances, for the *worst* of purposes: several *very good* recommendations are *certainly* in it, but if there can be any genuine true whigs, *duped* into a countenance of that publication, as it stands, I am sorry to say, they could not, in my humble opinion, besides *disgracing* themselves, have taken a method *more* effectual, if not to prevent, *at least* to retard the accomplishment of *even* the good things *wished for,* in a desirable manner. This paper which it is *almost impossible* to use as harsh terms, with regard to it, as it deserves, I shall leave to the animadversion of others, after making a few observations on *one plausible* proposal, "the earnest recommendation that no man be chosen, who shall not (under his proper signature) bind himself to vote *as his constituents shall direct,* and act, not as heretofore, but consonant to the instructions they shall give him." [7] This proposal, however *specious,* has a great *tendency* in our circumstances, *not only* at times, of hindering and embarassing public business, but, very probably, prove a dangerous *Jesuitical* imperium in imperio, and serve to put the legislature into *leading strings,* and make them as a body contemptible, and their members as *individuals* obsequious to the great man of the club; for the members of three fourths of the parishes and districts, at a distance, would *frequently* be at a loss to act, on account of *inadequate* instructions, which must often happen, unless the *instructors* can be supposed to be conjurors. What must be done then, when, very likely it will be *impossible* their constituents can be *convened* in time to collect their *general* sense? To obviate this difficuty, there will be a necessity for a *secret* (or some)

---

the lower class. The gentlemen of property, to preserve their necessary consequence in the community and in order to prevent anarchy and confusion, have almost unanimously exerted themselves in opposition to them, and it is with particular pleasure I inform you they have pretty generally carried their point, especially in this city, so that we shall have exceedingly good representation, and by that means support the honor and credit of the country." Lloyd to Smith, December 7, 1784, Charleston Library Society; also quoted in U.B. Phillips, "The South Carolina Federalists," Pt. 1, *AHR,* XIV (April, 1909), 537.

Gadsden probably refers to a publication, no longer available, called *The Circular Letter.* It was published by Gillon and his followers, who maintained constantly that the South Carolina legislators misrepresented their constituents. This quote can not be found in Philodemus' (Thomas Tudor Tucker) pamphlet, *Some Conciliatory Hints* (Charleston, 1784), although Tucker supports the idea of instructing delegates. He denies that he had any reference to the *Circular Letter.* The source of the evils of tumult and aristocratic rule. he maintained, was the Constitution, which he described as a mere act of the legislature not resting on the consent of the governed. He wanted a new constitution based on a convention, pp. 2-21.

committee, *near at hand,* the chairman, or *grand* director of which, will, even *if not* of the assembly, have *more* influence than *half* the members of the house; but should he *be a member,* and dextrous *at intrigue,* "with *his* committee, *all* under an oath of secrecy," the mischief will *still* be worse. Again, can all the electors in a parish be supposed to come into such a proposal? Those that do not, the member instructed will be no member to them; of course, in that case, they are *virtually* deprived of the efficacy of their election vote. Will they be *satisfied* with this? *can* this step then tend to *harmonize* the state. In circumstances so various, and so suddenly changing, as in our state, and many of those changes of the greatest moment, it is *impossible* for any set of men *at a distance* from the legislature, to foresee or guard against; therefore, it hath been *always* thought better, upon the whole, to leave the members *untrammled,* to act by their own best judgments, upon any point of importance, after it has undergone *a thorough* discussion in the house. Parochial business, indeed, may be *absolutely* directed, and with propriety, because the parish *must* be conceived competent in its own concerns, and what are *merely* such, the representative is *obliged,* in my mind, implicitly to comply with, be his own opinion what it may. Instructions *too,* on general matters, *not absolute,* may doubtless be of very *great* use, on *particular* occasions, and give great *confidence* to members, to know with *certainty,* the mind of the *majority* of their constituents; but, to be pinned down *absolutely,* will, as I *have seen* instances, serve not *only,* at times, to make your members appear very *ridiculous,* but, in consequence, to resolve never to *serve again.* Will this be the means of getting the most capable and best men? Are such, that will serve, in plenty? and will many such *"offer themselves as candidates?"* Parishioners, that do their duty as citizens *ought* to do, will not *fail* to give their votes at elections; and they must be *sad* judges indeed, if they cannot find *a few* honest proper men that they *can trust;* to serve them *only* two years; but if any representatives wantonly counteract the *plain* sense of their parish, choose them no more, which is much better *upon the whole* than *sitting* them with absolute instructions; these like quack remedies are often worse than the disease. *Every* member of the legislature is under *two* obligations; *one* to his parish, whose instructions with regard to matters *merely* parochial are *implictly* to be obeyed; the other to the state at *large;* to discharge this, he is charged to attend to the *general combined* interest of *all* the state *put* together, as it were upon *an average.* Now is it *probable,* that this *can* be done in the *best* manner, as it ought to be, with absolute instructions, in the situation we are in in this state, and the many uncertainties we are encumbered with, arising from indolence, negligence, and a variety of other causes that I wish may not be incurable? I shall mention *only one* instance, and then *leave* this point to *others* to discuss with more accuracy. Is it *easy* to know when the *real* majority of a parish *have given* their instructions? Suppose this difficulty superable, is it more easy to bring them *together* to give them instructions? Must it not then greatly *distress* a good member, when he is *uncertain,* whether his instructions (the sense and *propriety* whereof he may be in *no* doubt about) come from the majority of the parish? But if he can satisfy his mind on neither of these points, how must he be still perplexed?

No man in the state has opposed, in the *proper* place, *every* appearance of *Aristocracy,* with more steadfastness and decision than myself. This the members, as well as the journals of the *present* assembly will testify, and so I flatter myself will *every* gentleman I have had the honor of serving with in all *former* assemblies; I don't know that I have deviated a *tittle* from the *well-known* political *govermental* principles I set out with, on our grand struggle, in compliance, (or in any other respect,) to any man, set of men, or family *in or out* of the state *whatever.* At the same time, I have always, with equal warmth and decison, shewn my *detestation* against any appearance of licentiousness; and I ever looked upon (however disagreeable any public measure adopted might be, and *how much soever* I opposed it *in* the house) the *not acquiescing peaceably without doors* in *what* the *majority* had *agreed* upon and *fairly* carried *within,* as one of the *strongest* symptoms of a tendency to that *shocking* political malady as can *possibly* shew itself. The *long* fixed maxim to myself, has *more than once* brought me *between* two fires; and perhaps it is owing to this, that my *Nabobship* has been so *furiously* attacked in *several* papers since my last address, all which, excepting that which I have *here remarked upon,* published in this Gazette, the 13th May last, (which I looked upon as our Dupe-Master General's or wrote under his inspection, it containing some such things, as his honor, *long before this,* was bound by every tie of duty, respect and gratitude to this state, to have *openly* contradicted, if he had not abetted them,) I say excepting this, *all the rest* I passed over in silence, as coming *only* from tools or dupes; and should have done the same with that too, (for no personal abuse or insinuation *whatever* would have *drawn* me into print *again*) had not those *alarming* disturbances, that *alone* occasioned my *last,* begun to be *revived.* It then struck me that there was *no end,* to be *see-sawing* about tools; that the *only* way *effectually* to check these riots was to *search* out the principal, The First Cause, which that paper gives *a plainer clue* to than any *other* thing or paper *whatever* that I have seen. This and this *alone,* induced me to drudge about a work almost as offensive as *raking* into a common jakes.

227

I by no means desire to serve in the assembly again, ardently longing to retire from *all* public Business. But I hope my fellow-citizens of all denominations *throughout* the state, will do me the justice to think that it is *impossible* for greater and more permanent, peace and happiness to be wished for, than is *cordially* wished for them, by their most affectionate,

A STEADY AND OPEN REPUBLICAN.

Charleston July 10, 1784.

P.S. I have *designedly* avoided saying any thing *further* about Capt. T_____'s affair, *what* is said in my last being amply *sufficient;* the arguments *there* used, if not *unanswerable,* are altogether *unanswered* by this writer, and even what *new* things are *brought* by him on this occasion, are, Every Article, *on British bottoms;* therefore, as a *zealous* Anti-Britannic, he himself, upon reflection, cannot but think *inadmissable,* at least till "The *Court of London* take off the *restraint* on the Carrying-Trade."

To the Public in General and to Commodore Gillon, in Particular

August [5], 1784

Alexander Gillon (1741-1794) was finally provoked by this essay and launched a highly personal attack on Gadsden in the Gazette of the State of South Carolina, September 9, 1784. Gillon resorted to mud-slinging tactics against the "Steady and Open Republican." He reviewed Gadsden's career and picked out every controversial moment, especially his disagreements with Laurens and the "abuse" of Howe. Gadsden, he said, was the real "tumulter." "Was it not you who was foremost in the riot of 1765 before L_____'s house?" Gillon asked, referring to the Stamp Act raid. Further he asked, was it not Gadsden who used his position in the legislature to secure a Tobacco Inspection Act by which Gadsden gained a monopoly over the shipments of the product? Gadsden, Gillon claimed, wanted the return of the British merchants and the Tories, for they were the only people who would trade at the wharf of "the friendless former

REFERENCES

A	Old Church Street	z	Centurion Street
B	Broad do	a	Chambers Alley
C	Mazicks do	b	Beresford do
D	State House	c	Union Street
E	Johnston do	d	Amen do
F	New Barracks	e	Unity Alley
G	Beef Market	f	Elliots Street
H	Church do	g	Longitude Lane
I	St. Philips Church	h	Stalls Alley
K	Gadsden Alley	i	Linches Lane
L	Armoury	k	Lambulls Street
M	Tradd do	l	Smiths Lane
N	Queen do	m	Bottle Alley
O	King do	n	Prices do
P	Union (Continued) do	o	Clifford Street
Q	Presbiterian Meeting	p	Allen do
R	Exchange	q	Orange do
S	St. Michael Church and Church Yard	r	George do
T	Bedons Alley	s	Squirrel do
U	Beresford do	t	Anson do
W	Bay do	u	Short do
X	Friend do	v	West do
Y	Archdale do	w	Boundary do

MIDDLESEX

1 Virginia .... Street
2 Pitts .... do.
3 Wilkes .... do.
4 Massachusets .... do.
5 Wharfe .... do.
6 Corsican .... Walk
7 Pit .... Street
8 Long Wharf and watering Place
9 Hand in Hand corner

A Plan of Charles Town

Copied with a Pen from an Old Dilapidated Plot without a Date.

J. Lodge Sculpt
No 45 Shoe Lane
LONDON.

PLAT OF "MIDDLESEX,"
GADSDEN'S PROPERTY AT CHARLES TOWN

mob-manager," whom he described as being eaten with jealously at the loss of his political allies, the mechanics. See D. E. Huger Smith, "Commodore Alexander Gillon and the Frigate South Carolina," SCHM, IX (October, 1908), 189-219; "The Luxemburg Claims," ibid., X (April, 1909), 92-115; and Berkely Grimball, "Commodore Gillon of South Carolina, 1741-1794," unpublished Master's Thesis, History Department, Duke University, 1951.

My Dear Sir,[1]

I Thank you for your kind favor in this Gazette, No. 2214, the many engaging public notices therein, are on a *double* account particularly agreeable: as *coming* from your honor, *all* my fellow citizens must be convinced they are *sincere and cordial;* and *to me,* so well timed, both in manner and kind, and so *delicately contrived,* that is the Only thing I could have wished for from you. I am *sure* it *must* do me honor *beyond* any thing else you *could have obliged* me with. I am glad your honor is so *delighted* with my last performance. Your comparison of it *"to a Bag of Feathers ript open in a gale,"* is pretty and ingenius. Your honor, I am persuaded, will be still *more pleased,* when you come to find (what perhaps has *escaped* you) that the bag I took the feather from was *your own* bag. My *contrivance* too, for the entertainment and clearer view of our friends, to *prevent* any feather coming out, *but in turn,* just as *uppermost* in *your* bag, *when adverted to,* must, I am sure, afford your honor an additional agreement; as I think it can not be displeasing to your honor to follow the *same* method with your present *"bag,"* I shall accordingly take notice of the feathers *exactly* as they rise. I think it may be fairly gathered from your honor's *own* acknowledgment, in your first clause, that I am no "Bush fighter, nor one that projects under covers; I wish to appear *equally* favorable in your honor's eyes, when I assure your honor, that all honest "discount" will be deemed good payment: *mere* compliments, your honor sees, I have cast up into *one sum,* and passed the amount *already* to your credit.

Unwilling to give Mrs. Timothy [2] the *least* uneasiness, I pressed her not to conceal my name from any person that thought himself *hurt* by either of my publications. Have you, sir, and your party, been as candid and as delicate? No sir; "taking to the Bush" and "projecting under covers," seem to be your *"principles."* You are pleased to say "the world has one thing to learn, that at the very time I had

---

[1] *Gazette of the State of South Carolina,* August [5], 1784.
[2] Ann Donavan Timothy was the widow of Peter Timothy who had drowned in 1782. She published the *Gazette* in partnership with E. Walsh after the death of her husband. Cohen, *The South Carolina Gazette,* pp. 246-7.

been busy in meditating, preparing and digesting my envenomed falshoods against you for the press, I possessed the treacherous duplicity of calling myself your friend." The last private interview I had with you, sir, was on the remarkable 28th of April; what I *then* said, you cannot have forgotten, I am sure, supposing you had never attended to the *numberless* hints of the same kind, that I had given you for *months* before; and you are too discerning not to have perceived my *coolness* to you ever since. The next week my paper of 6th May appeared, which contained nothing that you had *a right* to stomach, *yet* how was the writer of that paper handled by you, *I say by you or your tools;* and was a "general notoriety" wanting to discover the author of that paper? More than two months *after* this, my second address (which had not appeared but for the last disturbances) was published. *There indeed,* on the *public* account, not on *my own,* (for my own feelings, however strong, I wish to submit always to the good of the state, on the *largest* scale,) I endeavoured to delineate in some degree, your honor's *duplicity*: from that, "discount" honestly all you can. I do not mention this as an apology for my *"principles,"* for the *moment* I am convinced a man is attempting anything *dangerous* against the public welfare, that *moment* I am his opposer with *all* my might, be he *antecedently* ever so near and dear to me. Alas! sir, I have assisted to support you *too long,* not being willing to believe, notwithstanding *strong* appearances, you could have acted the part there is too much reason to think you have and are acting. Your "pity," sir, you know I do not want, and your "forbearance," most *valorous heroic,* I laugh at.

I must acknowledge there are some high *figurative* expressions, and beautiful *rhetorical flourishes* in my last paper, such as "rascally, Lickspittle," etc. but the reader, I hope, will find that I have *honestly* acknowledged from whence I *borrowed* them; some *faint* imitations, indeed, of your *exquisite* pattern, I may have attempted in the same paper, but alas! my genius is no way *equal* to the task; I must therefore yield the palm, and confess I stand *no chance* with your honor in the art of embellishing. How *inimitable* is the clause I am now upon, your honor seems here to have *outdone* your usual *out doings,* and to shine in character *altogether en professeur.*

The *"Land-Office"* never came into my head till I read your honor's favor; however, I am glad to find my publication came out *so opportunely.* The more generally it is dispersed, the better I shall like it, and still better if the *elegant* piece, to which it is a reply, your first "Bag of Feathers," I mean was *equally* dispersed. What pity that *master piece* is out of print; cannot we have a second edition, exactly printed as the first? I am persuaded it will sell.

My *last* paper, and your honor's *first* clause of this letter, I believe, will be sufficient to acquit me from *secret slander,* with those that do not know me; with those that *do* I am under no pain about the charge. I have said freely, sir some time past, that I thought your honor had at least a finger in the pye, with regard to the late famous manœuvers, and town proscriptions: and notwithstanding your *express* contempt of "mobs, riots, and tumults," I have believed for months past, what I did not last year, that there is reason to suspect you held the wire, and danced the puppets of the frolics at that time; but, sir, we all know that you are so *exquisite a discerner of the times,* that in the twinkling of an eye you instinctively perceive when you must "take the bush."

I am now arrived at your 6th "feather:" *what course* this and the following feathers take in the "gale," I beg the reader will *accurately* mark. His honor says "the only passages in your piece, which shall at this time fall under my notice are,

1st. Your charge of my having been the author or abettor of a performance under the signiature of a Democratic Gentle Touch.

2nd. Your charge of my having been the revisor of most of the pieces lately published.

3rd. Your charge of my having been at the head of a party you profess so vehemently to dislike."

With regard to the first charge, your honor has proved nothing to the contrary; you talk of one evidence which you have been Ashamed to name: I shall not put you to the *blush* by doing it for you, and shewing your honor *presently,* I am still of the *same* opinion I was about this matter.

Where do you find the second charge? Point out the place, give us, Commodore, its bearings and distance, otherwise this *honest* quotation, or whatever else you may call it, will only serve to trace out the close connexion and resemblance between you and the respectable author or authors of the paper I said you were the line-drawer or abettor of. This finesse, sir, to get to the *windward* of me, will not do. No sir, I will not be jostled from my point. The paper mentioned in the first charge, which was printed in this gazette in the 13th May last, No. 2202. This Paper, I said *in my last,* gave a *plainer clue* to discover The First Cause of our riots, than any Other thing or paper whatever that I have seen. This, sir, is *the paper* I *pin* you to, and though what I *now* say, may not amount to *legal* proof, (being told *for your honor's comfort,* in a note of a late "Virtuous" address, that our laws "are like cobwebs, they catch small flies, but let wasps and hornets break through,") yet, sir, I shall mention some circumstances presently, taken from Mr. Gentle Touch's paper, which, *no more* than *due* weight, given to them when added to what has happened in Charleston *only,* since *your* return amongst us, will incline, I believe, the most *candid* observer of these matters, to *more than* suspect, that your honor *abetted* that paper, and was *no stranger* to some of its contents *before* publication.

With regard to the last charge, I am a professed disapprover of all political parties in our circumstances, and long to see *no* parties at all amongst us, but every citizen *striving* to make each other as happy as he can; which, were it not for a *very few* men, *besides your honor,* I believe, would not have been *very far* from the case, at this hour; however, I hope it will not be *long* before it is so. I have a strong objection, also, to any political meddling, anti-national club of any sort, be their *professions* what they may; but, when added to this, a spirit of tyrannical severity and implacability, is *glaringly* manifest in their *very rules,* (the case of your favourite society) what *mischief* may not some members, under the influence of *such* rules, and especially when bound *besides* by an oath of *secrecy,* not attempt? What *cruel* injuries have not several quiet citizens, under the protection of our laws, *repeatedly* received from *some* lawless members of your society? Having thus glanced through what *you call* my three charges, let me now take up your remaining clauses, *chiefly* in reference to the first charge. You say, sir, "you have proof indubitable and unequivocal, in your possession, of the reality of the person and name, of the author of that piece, being possessed of documents the most authenticate, that the performance signed Democratic Gentle Touch, was not of your privacy or inspection." If you have *such clear* proofs, and to the *point,* you shew *little* regard, sir, to *your own honor* not to produce them. But were there not *more than one* person concerned in that paper? I have, sir, the *highest* reason to think there were more than one, two, or three. But supposing (*and only supposing*) that your honor was not concerned in that paper, does it not contain such manifest *falsities* and *dishonorable* insinuations, of a public nature with regard to A High Trust you were Honored with by the state, that by all the ties of honor and gratitude, you ought to have *publicly* contradicted *long since,* circumstanced particularly as you are and were? For it is now *more* than eleven weeks since that publication, and these falsities not contradicted by you. Instead of any thing *like it,* are you not skreening and favouring this acquaintance, who *dared* to treat the public in such an impudent manner? He holds your honor up, indeed, as a man of amazing importance, as if you were the guiding genius of this country. Will any generous mind have suffered himself to be plumed off *one single moment,* at the expence and disgrace of a *kind, benevolent* public to him? Would he not have *spurned* at, and exposed the *flattering fawner* instantly, or at least have contradicted so insidious an attempt upon his honor? What I allude to, is, towards the close of Mr. Gentle Touch's piece, where my first paper is quoted *not a little* cunningly and perverly thus, "This immaculate writer adverts to the Carolina frigate, which, he says, had a wretched bargain made *for her,* and from which more evils sprung than from Pandora's box;" and presently after adds, *"the commander of the Carolina frigate was, on his own credit, obliged to purchase and fit out the ship, as foreigners had not so honorable thoughts of our nabobs, as they have of themselves, so would not trust them."* The paper this is in was published the *very next week* after my first address. Is that not of itself an odd circumstance? Did we hear any thing *before* of the Carolina frigate? Is it not strange then that almost immediately after my mentioning "the *wretched* bargain made *for us,* in the bare hire of one single frigate," this clause should pop out in answer to that assertation, Full of falsehoods and scandalous reflections on the state. I cannot help observing here, that this passage from Mr. Gentle Touch, has a striking resemblance of his honor's letter I am now remarking on, and would lead one to think was wrote in just such another *frantic* fit of dispair. The above clause I *particularly* noticed in my last, to which I beg leave to refer my reader: I shall just observe here,

That no ship was *"purchased* at all."

That one (or three-fourths of one) ship was *hired.*

That his honor was not "obliged" either to "purchase["] or hire the ship.

That he did not do it *"on his own* credit."

That foreigners *did trust* the state for her as appears, not only from the articles themselves, but from the application of foreigners to the state for payment.

That his honor's name being inserted in the articles, was *of course,* as our attorney or agent.

That his honor's estate being particularly inserted in his general mortgage, of all our estates, for compliance with the articles of agreement, was, if not a mere form, a mere puff; for it was *necessarily* included with the rest, if it had not been mentioned at all.

That an intercepted letter of his honor's, *long since* published in the British prints, shews plainly, that his honor was *bent on,* and would not be *disuaded* from having that frigate; and No Wonder, for she put him into an excellent *preferable* situation to any officer here, had our state been *irrevocably* lost. She was certainly a fine frigate, and his honor's expectations were very sanguine indeed, with regard to prizes, whereof his own share, and the state's fourth part, which he had the sole direction of, would have given him a very good chance of more than indemnifying himself for what *he might have lost by this state*: but what chance at all had any that took an active part here, had such a dismal event happened?

Lastly, that the whole state are sneeringly and insolently called *"Nabobs,"* by this writer, *his honor's acquaintance,* and by the manner of expression, *very contemptible* Nabobs.

Now, sir, from whom do all these falshoods and insolent abuses come? Does it plainly, *beyond all contradiction,* appear that they come from a zealous advocate for, and member of the Anti-Britannic Society? Was not your honor the *founder* of that society? Was you not their *President* at or about that very time? How could you, when you knew numbers of good citizens were extremely uneasy at the ungovernable, riotous behavior of many members of that society, and zealous some of them were the writers of such papers, suffer so stagnant an insult on the whole state, under your note, and so many falshoods of the public nature, that you *must know* were falshoods, to pass *altogether unnoticed?* Was you not bound in a double respect, above any man in the state, to have contradicted such false assertions? First, as our late Commodore and Commander of the Carolina, who was best acquainted with every thing relative to that ship? Must it not have been *expected* from you in common gratitude, to have been ready upon such an occasion, to vindicate the honor of the state? For, was it possible for any man to have been more delicately treated in every respect, than you have been by the state? Again, as founder or President of your favourite society, ought you not in common prudence to have endeavoured to check and discountenance such behaviour in one of its members, as *publicly* as possible, to take off or lessen the prejudices against that society, sir, to be *paramount* to every thing *but* "Your Little Majesty?" You have shewn yourself, sir, at least, a *silent* abettor of this Mr. Gentle Touch, and he seems a, *furious stickler* for your honor, in his *admirable* vindication of you, published two or three days since, where he calls you "a gentleman of his acquaintance." I think he might have better stiled himself Your Confident, or private secretary,[3] (trim, tram): for unless he was *that,* or something like it, how came he (if the *only* writer of that piece) to jump so readily into so many curious circumstances about the frigate? Upon the whole, let others judge as they may, for

---

[3] Dr. James Fallon, *Gazette of the State of South Carolina,* April 22, 1784.

my part I think it no breach of charity, from these appearances, and many more that I could name, had I time, and it would not make this paper too bulky, to conclude that Mr. Gentle Touch's paper was not printed without your honor's privacy, and that you did *at least abet it;* and therefore, as it seems to be the production of a partnership, whose firm I know not, *respect* for your honor *obliges* me to think you must be the *head* of the house, and therefore entitled to the principal credit of it.

In the affair his honor alludes to, (near twelve months since)[4] I carried no arms *on purpose,* as I was hopeful to be instrumental in assisting the magistrates [5] to *undeceive* some *misled* citizens, that were expected to (but did not) make a disturbance, *without* arms than *with.* How *hard pressed* his honor must be, to take notice that I had a pillow as well as my cloak, carried to the guard room upon that occasion; he says, *more than once,* but his honor is mistaken, however, he is welcome to make the most of it, he may make it *twenty times* if he pleases. Would he catch at this trifle had he anything *more important* to say? Your honor is welcome to raise as many *masked* batteries, and throw as many random shot as your please against my "Bag of Feathers." No threats levelled at my friends and relations, or any other sort of threats, or dangers, or fears of giving offence, has, I thank God, ever swerved me hitherto in the least, from the *straitest* path I could find out for the *general* interest of the community At Large. Let me but *do* my duty, it is all I wish for, the rest *does not belong* to me. But here I can not help observing, that your honor has great advantages in *this* and another respect, over nineteen in twenty of the citizens of this state; for I believe your *relations* are as *few* in this country as it is possible for any man to have, that has any at all:— and besides has not your honor two rights of citizenship, (so that you can *"take to the bush"* when you please) one in Europe, one in this state? And supposing your honor should prefer the *former,* and only continue here as a *Bird of Passage,* until you have made up your mouth, (as the phrase is); is it not natural to think you would wish to return, with some *trading preference* in favour of your friends; and especially when we know your honor is a *double* Anti: not only Anti-Britannic, but as much *Anti-Gallic?* But would this suit *this* state? No, sir! From the moment we give any undue *national* preferences in trade, from that moment we may date the commencement of our ruin. For *national* preferences will cause national jealousies,

---

[4] Gillon accused Gadsden of carrying arms during riots occurring in the town between July 8 and 10, 1783. Apparently on Tuesday evening, the 8th, Thomas Barron, a British subject, insulted a Whig "Citizen." This set off a general fray. *South Carolina Gazette and General Advertiser,* July 12, 1783.

[5] Governor Benjamin Guerard had issued a Proclamation asking the assistance of citizens to aid the Peace Officers in maintaining order. *Ibid.*

nothing sooner, and in case of any resentments against us in consequence, *can* your *other* fellow citizens protect us? Have they not *often* employment enough at home to protect themselves? Lord Rawdon, during the times of the British [the Occupation], was *indefatigable* to come Country Over many honest worthy men amongst our citizens, who, or their ancestors, came from Ireland; and too many good men were *duped* by him or his emissaries, much to their disadvantage, which they have heartily repented since. I wish no more *takes-in* of this sort may be *as indefatigably attempting,* with *another* set of very worthy, industrious, peaceable men, and as good citizens as any the state has. The way to guard against such designs, is to look upon ourselves as true citizens of the world, ready to extract, like the bee, what is sweet and good, wherever we can find it, in order to encrease our common stock of human happiness, to the utmost pitch in our power, so as to invite, worthy, industrious, well inclined men from all nations, to come and settle amongst us, and partake of our fare, and let us give them a hearty welcome when they do come, and accomodate them all we can; but Never let us suffer ourselves, on *any account,* to be embarrassed with any country whatever. Idle and laughable to the last degree it certainly is, to suffer ourselves to be so duped, by *early* or *local* prejudices, however artfully humoured, and played off upon us, so as to induce us to enthrall ourselves with any *particular* nation, because forsooth, ourselves, our fathers, our mothers, or grand mothers happened to have been born there; *I say happened,* for is not my friends, every thing of this sort a *mere hap?* A true citizen of the world is a noble character; such Providence has put it into our power *now* to be if we do not play our cards very foolishly, and suffer ourselves to be *legerdemained* out of our country and honors, by plausible *national* sharpers, or *dwindle* into cautious sordid, selfish Negatives, when it is necessary to give an effectual, open, *clinching,* opposition, to the *deep* laid schemes of such sort of gents. The great trading nations *particularly,* we may be assured will not be *idle;* they will have their *dexterous, well trained* emissaries amongst us, that know their errand; these will endeavour to secure us as many positives as they can to favour them, by delusive arguments and other artful management; and your outward *appearance* gentlemen of *any consequence,* they will endeavour to compound with, by applying to their *feelings;* and douceuring them a thousand *pretty* ways into *negatives.* My friends cannot forget how often (so long since as under Liberty Tree) I endeavoured to imprint on them, to attend to the two grand distinctions in our (or indeed in every country), the landed and the trading interest:—That the First, without which the other would not and cannot exist, ought always to have the right hand; that trade, in short, (with its appendages) was only the handmaid to *her mistress,* agriculture; that the mistress would certainly do much better *with* the maid than *without her;* but still she may and *can* wait upon herself, and do *without her,* but the maid is Nothing At All *without* her mistress; every country therefore, must depend principally upon the farmers and planters, who are its most *natural* support upon all emergencies. That merchants *as* merchants were mere *Birds of Passage,* that being the *best* place to them, where they can make their quantum up *soonest;* when that is done it was *quite* a chance whether they *continued* in the country they made their fortunes in; but, that the landed man *was fixed* to his plantation or farm. You must remember, my friends, what offence this gave at that time; (and have I not *often* risked offending, rather than see you deceived or imposed on?) But did you not find my words true, excepting some characters, who gloriously exerted themselves to their honor, and who I am persuaded, will not tarnish their reputations, by acting inconsistently now. Whence came those shameful perversions of honest traffic; those sudden and artful depredations; those pernicious speculations, *etc., etc.* I mention this now to put the state on their guard, *lest the maid became the mistress;* the consequence must be nothing but disgrace, disorder, and rapid ruin to the state. Let us encourage all open, honest and profitable trade, and assist and accomodate the well meaning generous merchant all we can; it is our interest so to do; but we cannot take too much care to prevent *national* preferences being Smuggled in amongst us. The principal policy of this country in future, must be to watch the course of our trade, for it will Make Or Break Us, according as it is managed.

Your honor may in future advance *what you please,* and set all your myrmidons in *full cry* upon me, unless your assertions are *material,* To The Point, *well established,* and your quotations *fair,* without *twisting.* I shall leave you entirely to your reader, who cannot be *too cautious* of trifling any thing to confidence and *mere say so;* and I entreat your honor, always to recollect, that my signiature was and is, not "The" but "*A Steady and Open Republican;*" this *slipt* your honor in your *first* notice to the public.

My dear sir, tell your *acquaintance,* that figured away so blunderingly for you in last Thursday's paper, that *I was not* one of the committee, (but if I was, I do not see what that is to the *main point*) on your accounts, *as the journals of the assembly will shew,* and that you know I declined being so, and more than once whispered you, that had I been at your elbow, I should have done all in my power to have dissuaded you from the frigate bargain. Long before, and when your accounts were passing, and for months after, I took your honor to be a quite a different man from what I am very sorry to say, I think myself *obliged* to look on you at present (though I never did *like* the circumstance of leaving your command as you did). But sir, were your accounts *now* in passing, I should still endeavour to bring so disagreeable a business to a close as speedily as possible, for the public's sake alone. This was my principal motive *before, subordinate* to this, as the war was in a manner over, and I had *then* no mistrust of your honor's ungrateful behaviour to the public, and had every inclination to serve you, I never threw one impediment in the way, and avoided being on the committee, or prying at all into your accounts, as I was not. I do not recollect I looked over one account until immediately after the house adjourned, when your papers relative to your agreement with the Prince of Luxemburg, about the frigate, were laid before the committee ordered on that matter, of which I was a member; but that committee, from an extraordinary circumstance, was obliged to break up, (not through your fault) without making any report, so that matter lies over for future canvassing; and in my humble opinion, not a *moments time* should be lost to finish Entirely that unlucky affair; and I think it would not be unworthy of the *first* attention of the assembly, whenever it sits, for I confess, I am apprehensive of some *very disagreeable* consequences that may attend its laying over much longer. Pray, your honor, whisper your *acquaintance,* who is trying to make *mischief* with the motto of my *last* paper from Pope. *Your honor knows,* I have jocularly praised you for your judgment in tool choosing, but you never, in my opinion, *blundered* so much in your life, as in this *mere Knight of the Post,* this *Marplot.* I love a little fun sometimes, I confess, as well as the rest of my friends, and if I could have discerned *the least gilding* on him, I should perhaps immediately given chase and been at him; but a *sheer* . . . . without *any gilding at all,* cannot possibly afford the least sport; but, as perhaps, you may make *something* of him by and by, and I know nobody *more capable* of doing it than yourself, therefore heartily congratulate you on the *acquisition* of this *vartuous, disinterested,* Anti-Britannic Whig supporter.

I am, sans ceremonie,
A Steady and Open Republican, or

CHRISTROPHER GADSDEN

Charleston, July 31, 1784.

To Samuel Adams

Charleston 18th August, 1784 [1]

Dear Sir:

Several Months since I received a Favour from you, but nothing occurring worthy your Notice occasion'd my so long Silence.

Our State is getting to Rights very fast, a few Men who have hardly faced the least Danger amongst us during the Times of our Struggle, some perhaps that have almost done a few Months Militia Duty, and others that have had their Hen Roosts robb'd have been setting themselves up against the Laws and Determinations of our Assembly and occasion'd some Riots last and this Year, but I am in hopes 'tis all, or nearly, over, as 'tis our common Interest to support government and not let a few designing men set us by the Ears for their own purposes, which begins to be generally perceived to be the Intentions of our Disturbers, and the Citizens as generally determind'd to disapprove them. My youngest Son [Philip] who has behaved in every respect during the struggle, as I cou'd wish him to do, having never perfectly recover'd from the fatigues of those Times, finds himself obliged to make a Voyage to the Northward for his Health, and to return about the Middle of November. He sails this Morning for Rhode Island. He intends seeing Boston while away, and I have laid my Commands on him to wait on you with this. I beg leave to refer you to him for News. Pray my compliments to all Friends that think me worth inquiring after. I am Dr. Sir. wth. great Esteem Yr. Affect. Hble. Servt.

CHRIST GADSDEN

---

[1] Samuel Adams Papers, NYPL. It is addressed "To Hbl. Samuel Adams, % Mr. Philip Gadsden, Boston."

To James Duane

James Duane (1733-1797) was an outstanding colonial lawyer of New York and a conservative revolutionary who had supported Joseph Galloway in the Continental Congress. Duane survived attacks against both his patriotism during the war and his later desire for moderation in handling the Tories. Duane was elected Mayor of New York in 1784, and afterwards held the position of district judge. Duane aided in the founding of the University of the State of New York. Edward P. Alexander, A Revolutionary Conservative: James Duane of New York (New York: Columbia University Press, 1938).

Charleston 18th August, 1784 [1]

Dear Sir:

My youngest Son whom I have laid my commands on, to wait on you with this sails in a few Hours to Rhode Island to pass the Fall for the recovery of his Health and to return here about the Middle of November. He has in every Shape answered my utmost wishes, during our late Struggle, which thank God I have an opportunity to congratulate you, is so happily over, equal to our most sanguine Expectations. We are getting to rights here very fast, and shou'd have been so long ago, had it not been for the Selfish artful Views of a Few, making Dupes of some restless Men to carry their own purposes. Those that have suffer'd least; been exposed to the fewest Temptations; served perhaps a few Months in the Militia, and have undergone only one severe loss that of having their roosts robbed, are principally the Men that give us now the most Disturbance. The Numberless Artifices that were made use of by a few Men for Selfish and National purposes to inflame seem'd very alarming for some Time, but now their Intentions being generally seen through, and men aware of their Impositions, they are rather laughed at then dreaded!

I refer you to my Son for News. Pray my compliments to all enquiring Friends particularly to Mr. Jay [2] if with you. I am Dr. Sir With Sincere Regard & Esteem Yr. Most Hble. Servt.

CHRIST GADSDEN

---

[1] James Duane Papers, New York Historical Society. *DAB*, V, 465-6.
[2] John Jay (1745-1829), the New York statesman, diplomat, and chief justice.

To ----------------------------

My Dear Sir:

Your kind favour to our Worthy friend Mr. [Thomas] Ferguson,[2] arrived when he was no more with us. His Friends were long anxious about him, and used every means to prevail on him to detach himself from his Business, and try the Benefits of the Northern Air. This he too intended, but wishing to see his crop set, and flattering himself he was not too ill as his Friends imagin'd, he delayed alas too long. For Generosity, Hospitality, public Spirit and the most sincere and feeling attention to his Friends and Connections he has left few behind him here to equal him in those respects and indeed I don't know a man will be more miss'd on many accounts as well publicly and privately.

Mrs. Ferguson and Mrs. Gadsden join me in our best Respects to you.

Pray our Compliments to Major North. Mrs. Ferguson is much obliged to him for the Salmon sent her. I am Dear Sir, with the highest Esteem Your Most Obed. & hble. servt.

CHRIS GADSDEN

To General George Washington

Charleston 13th May 1787 [1]

Dear Sir:

I cannot let my worthy Friend Genl. Pinckney leave us in order to join You on so important a Business to America without embracing

---

[1] HSP. The addressee of this letter is unknown.
[2] *See* letter to W.H. Drayton, September 22, 1778.
[1] Washington Papers, Library of Congress. Charles Cotesworth Pinckney was journeying to Philadelphia to join the Constitutional Convention.

the Opportunity of paying you my Respects. I hope Heaven will favor the joint Endeavors of the Convention and make their Establishment effectually useful. We are all sure of your utmost Exertions to that Purpose. That Congress ought to be well supported and rendered respectable has ever been the Opinion of the firmest Friends to the Revolution and tis to be hop'd the unreasonable (I am afraid too often insidious) Jealousies of her abusing the Powers entrust'd to her are by this time subsided.

I am now altogether retired from public Business and return'd to the Care of my private Concerns, not only because their deranged Situation makes it necessary but also to set what little Example I can to promote an industrious Turn amongst our Choice Spirits, the best means, in my Opinion, to banish old animosities and to restore Harmony and good Neighborhood amongst them.

Our Assembly the last Setting past a law to prohibit the Importation of Slaves for three years,[2] and by a very large Majority rejected a proposal of making any more paper Currency.[3] These are no bad Symptoms of our coming to our Senses, and working to pay our Debts and keep up Public Credit. God Grant some farther Tendencies that Way may be thought of and carried at their next meeting to the Satisfaction of their Constituents.

That all the World Dear General admire and respect your Character can be no flattery to tell you so, nor that all the United States love and esteem you, and permit one the Honor my Dear Sir to assure that not an Individual in any one State of the thirteen does so more sincerely than your affectionate & most Obedt. hble. Servt.

CHRIST GADSDEN

---

[2] An earlier proposal to prohibit the importation of slaves was defeated by back-country representatives whose economy was beginning to expand. They considered non-importation a low-country maneuver to retain property, and hence re-gain political power. The success in prohibiting importation in 1787 came chiefly as a result of the unfavorable balance of trade for the State. But on the whole, non-importation was unpopular and difficult to enforce. For example, David Ramsay lost an election because of his anti-slavery views in 1788 and, soon afterwards, the slave trade was reopened. Singer, *S.C. in Confederation,* pp. 22, 24-35; Rogers, *Evolution of a Federalist,* pp. 34n, 136, 166; John Hope Franklin, *From Slavery to Freedom* (New York: Alfred A. Knopf, 1961), p. 139.

[3] In 1785, the South Carolina legislature issued £100,000 in paper currency backed by lands or plate, to be repaid at 7% interest within five years. The measure represented a compromise between the "hard" money and the "cheap" money proponents. Governor Moultrie had originally asked for £400,000, while Governor John Mathews had proposed only £83,000 in the Assembly. Ramsay said at the passage of the law that "there was a general understanding among the members of the legislature that no further sum should be emitted in any emergency," and it was this gentlemen's agreement to which Gadsden referred. Ramsay, *Hist. South Carolina,* II, 184-5; Singer, *S.C. in the Confederation,* pp. 17, 120.

To John Adams

John Adams (1735-1826), statesman, diplomat, second President of the United States, and Gadsden were warm friends and political allies during the Continental Congress. They worked together as members of the Committee on Marine and were of the same temperament for independence and the founding of a naval force. Gadsden supported Adams for the presidency, particularly in the election of 1800. This letter offers insights into Gadsden's thinking while he helped frame the Constitution of 1778, and it shows his changing ideas on the nature of the chief executive's post during the time of the Federal Convention at Philadelphia. Butterfield, Dairy and Autobiography of John Adams, II, 176-7, III, 316-7, 330, 350.

Charleston So. Carolina [1]

24 July 1787

My worthy Friend:

I am much obliged to you for your kind Remembrance of me, and the very acceptable present you sent me, by Mr. [William] Gibbes. Your Defence of our Constitution, which I read with the greatest Attention and as much pleasure, and am glad to hear by a Friend of mine at the Convention that 'tis much read there; he sent me a Copy printed at Philadelphia, but yours came to hand a few Days before. In another State I hope we shall be happy under a simple Government directed by infinite Wisdom and Goodness, but in the present, while struggling with such various and contradictory possessions, Nothing less than the most artful playing them one against another, wholesale and retail (if I may use the Expression) can insure us any tolerable lasting Peace and Security, either publicly or privately. "All Nature's Differences keeps all Nature's peace" according to your Well-chosen Motto, is as true a proposition as any in Euclid. I must own I was once fond of a simple Constitution of Government as much as perhaps as Mr. Turgot, but have been some Time convinced, however pleasing and entertaining it appear'd in Idea, that it was *there* only and cou'd not, as Mankind are adduced

---

[1] "The Papers of John Adams," Massachusetts Historical Society; microfilm in the Library of Congress.

243

to practice.[2] The three distinct checks you mention in Legislature, seems to be indespensably necessary with *one* Executive. I think we are so far happy in having all these at certain periods eligible by the People, but annual Elections are rather too frequent in my Opinion. Some of our Governors have not a Negative, this State's particularly, which I am sorry for, tho' at the early Time of framing our Constitution, or rather extraordinary governmental Law Inter arma, I confess I was then against it, but shou'd there be a Convention to revise it, or rather make a real Constitution, I wish our governors may be allowed a Negative. Unhappily, rather from inattention and Inexperience than Design, Our assemblies at Times have interfer'd too much in the judicial Department, whereas the three, the Deliberative Judicial and Executive, ought to be altogether separate. The permitting our Judges to sit in the Assembly, is I think very improper and has a natural Tendency to introduce a Confusion of Departments.

This my Dear Sir I hope will be deliver'd you by the Son of a late Worthy Friend Mr. John Edwards, who was prisoner with me at Augustine, a Gentleman who by his Industry, had with great reputation, acquir'd a very handsome provision for a large Family, but by lending great part of it to the public, and other common Accidents of the late Times his Fortune at his Death was much reduced. My youngest Son married one of his Daughters, Sister to the Young Gentleman. Any Countenance You may shew him, I shall be oblig'd to you for. I believe you'll find him a very modest well inclined Youth.

With regard to myself, having been as active as most Men in America for near Thirty Years, I have now taken a passive Turn, and indeed it is high Time, as I am pretty well advanced in Life. I am entirely the private Gentleman, endeavoring to repair, the amazing damages done me during the late Struggles, No man in this State having Suffer'd more in proportion to his Fortune. However I rejoice that Heaven has bless'd us with Success, and only wish our

---

[2] Gadsden referred to John Adams' *Defence of the Constitutions of Government of the United States of America* (1787). Adams undertook the work in answer to the statement by the French political thinker, M. Turgot, who in a public letter to Richard Price asserted, "he [Adams] is not satisfied with the constitutions which have hitherto been formed for the different states of America." He further said that Adams, in general, did not believe that government in America was "simple" or centralized enough. More specifically, Turgot was critical of the Massachusetts Constitution. His strictures on American government had been given in response to Richard Price's tract entitled *Observations on the Importance of the American Revolution, and the Means of Making It a Benefit to the World* (Boston: Powers and Willis, 1784). Price's work has been wrongly attributed to Gadsden by Robert Turnbull, *Bibliography of South Carolina* (Charlottesville: University of Virginia Press, 1956), I, 275. *See* Adams, *Works,* IV, 299.

July 24, 1787

American Friends may make a proper Use of it. I am With Sincere Esteem Yr. most obed. hble. servt.

CHRIST GADSDEN

To Thomas Jefferson

Thomas Jefferson (1734-1826) author of the Declaration of Independence, Secretary of State, third President of the United States, was minister to France at the time this letter was written. In 1785, he had concluded negotiations with the French Privy Council to open the ports of Havre and Orleans to the commerce of the United States.

This was a part of the Jeffersonian ideal of free tade with all of the world, and was especially a counter-move to British mercantilism from which South Carolina and other American states were suffering. Gadsden, long in agreement with such a program, also viewed the new Constitution in its international economic application. See Merill D. Peterson, "Thomas Jefferson and Commercial Policy, 1783-1793" William and Mary Quarterly, XXII (October, 1965), 595-6; 598-9.

Chas. Town 29th October, 1787 [1]

Dear Sir:

My Friend Mr. Izzard [2] favor'd me with a Sight of Yours to him of the 18th November and first of August last together with Mr. De Calonne's and Les Srs. Jean Jaques Berard and Co. Letters to you, the first dated 22d October 1786 encouraging from authority the Opening and fixing a General Trade with the United States, the other proposing a Plan of Mutual Commerce between this place and France, particularly respecting Rice, which I have read with great

[1] Papers of Thomas Jefferson, Library of Congress. Published in *The Papers of Thomas Jefferson*, Julian P. Boyd, *et al.*, ed. (Princeton: Princeton University Press, 1955), XII, 296-7.
   See also Walsh, "Letters of Morris and Brailsford to Jefferson," *SCHM*, LVIII (July, 1957), 129-44. Berard headed the French House of Orient: *ibid.* Charles Alexandre de Colone was comptroller general of France, and was favorably inclined toward Jefferson's proposals. Dumas Malone, *Jefferson and the Rights of Man* (Boston: Little, Brown & Co., 1951), pp. 36ff.
[2] Ralph Izard (1742-1804) was a planter who became Senator from South Carolina under the new government: Rogers, *Evolution of a Federalist*, p. 29 *et passim*.

pleasure and Attention, wishing it to be carried into Execution. From this Opening and the Honor I had to labor with you formerly in the political Vineyard, I take the Freedom to congratulate you on the noble Constitution agreed upon by our late Convention, and farther, on its seeming to give general Satisfaction, from whence tis hardly doubted it will be adopted; if so, and it is firmly atnd efficiently carried into Execution, a new and important Epocha must arise in our Affairs; The Apprehensions Strangers were under for some Time past, discouraging them from dealing with us so largely as many wish'd, will then diminish greatly and in a short Time cease altogether, as our Trade wou'd soon be on a safe, proper and respectable Footing, unsubjected in future to Frauds from Paper Tenders, and other too common unjustifyable Practices from Unprincipled Debtors very prejudicial to their Creditors. Besides this Advantage a Diminution of that pernissious partiality to the British Trade will in my Opinion follow of Course. The Number of Foreigners that will from other than interested Mercantile Views frequent us, will soon tend to open the Eyes of our Countrymen thoroughly to their own Interest, and to see with astonishment to what a paltry Customer we have been so long and losingly attached, and that maugre all their sophistry, that the trade of France and Germany are ten times the Consequence to this State than theirs, and therefore ought by prudent Traders to have ten Times more attention. All the States may be said to be Shopkeepers, and what Folly for any, to give the Preference to that Nation that is of the least Importance to them, that consumes the smallest Quantity of their Produce, which with regard to our chief Staple Rice, is the Case of Gt. Britn. who tho' they have made Peace, are manifestly far from being cordial Friends with us. If France at this Crisis, continued her Encouragements, fix and support proper shifting [i.e., shipbuilding] Ports similar to that at Cowes attentively dispatching our Rice Ships, she will in no long Time, from the advantage of her being so almost infinitely a greater Consumer of that article than Gt. Bn., thin the Business to that Harbor, and in a few years dwindle it to nothing. But Attention and Patience in Commencement is every Thing. From what I have learn'd, the French Merchants we have had here, have been as impolitic in their method of introducing a Trade with us, as most of our People in trying the like with the new markets open'd to us since the Peace. We, besides the Infatuation of giving the British the Preference of our direct Consignments to their Island, have as stupidly, or more so, even in our few Essays to other markets suffer'd them to be conducted under their Auspices. Tis natural and commendable for all Powers to give a preference to their own Subjects, but on new Trials, of Trade especially, quaery whether the End wou'd not be sooner, more effectually and generally come at and fixed, by employing Men of the Place of establish'd Character and experience unsuspected of any improper Bias to the British Interest, well acquainted with the Nature and Quality of the Articles most suitable and wanted, for a few Years than for a new Adventurer, speaking a different Language to conduct it himself through the Medium of such an Interpreting Clerk as he can pick up, but this has been the method generally used here by the French Merchants and tis thought the Cause of many Losses and Disgusts they have experienced. Few People, ours particularly, like to close their Bargains but with Principals; This City does not want for many Houses of this Character, mentioned among others Messrs. Brailsford and Morris are well establish'd here, both Natives of the united States the first of this City the other of Philadelphia. Mr. Morris I am nearly connected with as having married my Daughter and shou'd be happy to be the Means of recommending that House to any unengaged Friends.

I make no doubt the Phylosophic part of Europe will admire the Constitution recommended by our Convention, the Trading part of Gt. Bn. perhaps, many of them, may be jealous of it consider'd in a commercial View in its probable Consequences to them by increasing the means of opening the Eyes of America and exposing many rooted prejudices to them particularly. I have little doubt *[3] that part of the Island who so generally and pointedly hung upon our Skirts during the whole War will not be less busy on this Occasion. For my Part I bless God to have lived to see this important Point in so fair a Way to be accomplish'd, and if I live to see it compleatly so, I shall be apt to cry out with old Simeon: Now may thy Servant depart in Peace for mine Eyes have seen thy Salvation.

I beg your pardon, my dear Sir, and the Publics for trespassing so much on that Time which I am sure you wish to devote to the common Interest of the united States, and am with Sincere Esteem Yr. most Obedt. Hble. Servt.,

CHRIST GADSDEN

* These subtil, dextrous, long-train'd Systematical opponents well knowing the Constitution recommended must be approv'd of in toto, or not at all, therefore wou'd seem to approve of it as highly as any the most Zealous for it, only with an *All But,* which *But* alter'd wou'd gain they wou'd pretend universal Satisfaction, that it may be defer'd for that mighty reasonable *But* to another Convention hoping that will never happen and so the Bubble burst of Course.

---

[3] The asterisk represents an insertion by Gadsden, given here at the end of the letter. The original has every appearance of having been hastily constructed, presenting a general carelessness which is surprising in view of the eminence of Jefferson.

To Mrs. Ann Timothy

Ann Donavan Timothy (1727-1792) was the wife of Peter Timothy. After her husband's death she revived the Gazette of the State of South Carolina, willing the business to her son, Benjamin Franklin Timothy. He published the paper until 1802. Cohen, The South Carolina Gazette, pp. 247-8.

May 5, 1788 [1]

Mrs. Timothy,

The enclosed, copied from a paper sent me by a friend, seems so peculiarly adopted to our present situation, that I cannot forbear selecting it from the crowd of publications since the appearance of the proposed federal constitution, and recommending it thro' your paper, to the most serious attention of all our fellow-citizens, but previously a few HINTS, by way of introduction, will not, I hope, be impertinent.[2]

New Hampshire and Georgia are the two extreme barriers of the United States, if the latter can with any propriety be called a barrier without this state in conjunction; and both together, we know, are not in point of force, ready for any sudden emergency, to be compared to New Hampshire.

---

[1] *Gazette of the State of South Carolina,* May 5, 1788. This essay, in support of the ratification of the Constitution of 1787, was written by Gadsden, not Charles Pinckney. Gadsden's pseudonym was too well known, especially from the Gillon controversy, for the essay to be anyone's but his. Wolfe in *Jeffersonian Democracy in South Carolina,* pp. 33-34, 63n, gives credit for the essay to Pinckney, and Paul Leicester Ford erred originally in his collection *Essays on the Constitution of the United States* (Brooklyn: Historical Printing Club, 1892) by attributing the work to Pinckney. The newspaper which Ford used, from the files of the Charleston Chamber of Commerce, contained within its pages a slip of paper on which was stated by an unknown person that it was Pinckney's authorship. Ford asserted that the note was in a handwriting contemporary with the newspaper, and, because of that, labeled Pinckney the "Steady and Open Republican." Ford compounded the mistake by saying that Pinckney was the only one who gave any original thought in the South Carolina newspapers to the Federal Constitution. (pp. 409, 416.)

[2] The article written in the *Connecticut Courant,* March 3, 1788, is headed "Landholder No. X," and was addressed to the citizens of New Hampshire. "Landowner" was Oliver Ellsworth. "Landholder No. X" was also published in *Essays on the Constitution of the United States,* pp. 189-91. It is an exhortation to New Hampshire to ratify the Constitution in view of her dangerous proximity to the territory of Great Britain.

248

It cannot be doubted that Great-Britain has her busy emissaries throughout the states, and not a few amongst us, and should the constitution be rejected, how long can we flatter ourselves to be free from Indian cruelties and depredations, some time since begun in Georgia, and if at this moment warded off from us, 'tis principally owing to the dread of an efficacious union of the states by the adoption of the federal constitution. The three southern states particularly, we have had for several years past, good grounds to think Great-Britain wishes to separate from the rest, and to have reverted to her if possible.

Mr. Martin's [3] long mischievous detail of the opinions and proceedings of the late general convention, (already occupying a large space in six of your gazettes, and still unfinished,) with all his colourings and uncandid insinuations, in regard to general Washington and Doct. Franklin, may suit the short-sighted selfish wishes of an *individual* of a state, situated almost in the centre of the rest, and much safer by that means from sudden alarms. But the generous, manly *and truly federal sentiments* of Maryland are well known, and 'tis not doubted will be unequivacally shewn at her convention very shortly to be held—and that New-Hampshire, early in her first meeting on that important subject, has only by consent taken farther time to consider of it, and will at her next meeting adopt it, is the general opinion.

What a pity the salutary caution of Doct. Franklin, just previous to his signing the constitution recommended by the convention, had not been strictly attended to. If we split, it will in all probability happen in running head-long on the dangerous rock he so prophetically (as it were) warned us from, "That the opinions of the errors of the constitution born within the walls of the convention, should die there, and not a syllable be whispered abroad." *This Hint* is full

---

[3] Luther Martin was a Maryland delegate to the Philadelphia Convention of 1787. The reprinted essay to which Gadsden refers was Martin's *The Genuine Information . . . Relative to the Proceedings of the General Convention . . .* at Philadelphia (Philadelphia: Eleazer Oswald, 1788). Martin opposed the ratification of the Constitution. He admitted the necessity of increased power for the national government, although he believed this should not have been granted at the expense of the states. He therefore would not sign the Constitution, although in a negative way he had contributed much to its framing. Mrs. Timothy apparently reprinted Martin's *Genuine Information* as an antidote to the *Landholder* essays, giving the antagonists over ratification equal space. Martin called upon Franklin and Washington as witnesses to the veracity of his statements (p. v.). *See also,* E.D. Obrecht, "Influence of Luther Martin in Making the Constitution of the United States," *Md. Hist. Mag.,* XXVII (September, December, 1932), 173-90; 280-96; H.P. Goddard, *Luther Martin: Federal Bulldog, Maryland Historical Society Fund Publication,* No. 24 (Baltimore: Maryland Historical Society, 1887).

of that foresight and the penetration the Doctor has always been remarkable for.

When the general convention met, no citizen of the United States could expect less from it than I did, so many jarring interests and prejudices to reconcile! The variety of pressing dangers at our doors, even during the war, were barely sufficient to force us to act in concert, and necessarily give way at times to each other. But when the great work was done and published, I was not only most agreeably disappointed, but struck with amazement. Nothing less than that superintending hand of providence, that so miraculously carried us through the war (in my humble opinion) could have brought it about so compleat, upon the whole.

The constitution recommended, in all respects, takes its rise, where it ought, from the people; its president, senate, and house of representatives, are sufficient and wholesome checks on each other, and at proper periods are dissolved again into the common mass of the people; longer periods would probably have produced danger; shorter, tumult, instability, and inefficiency, every article of these and other essentials to a republican government, are, in my opinion, well secured; were it otherwise, not a citizen of the United States would have been more alarmed, or more early in opposition to it, than

A STEADY AND OPEN REPUBLICAN

Charleston, May 2, 1788

To Thomas Morris

Thomas Morris (1753-1829) of Philadelphia was the husband of Gadsden's daughter, Mary. Morris apparently came to Charleston immediately after the Revolutionary War to establish himself in business. In 1783 he was a correspondent of the Philadelphia firm of Alexander Nesbitt; and later, forming a partnership with William Brailsford, he took part in the new trade with France. By 1791 he was a member of the Board of Directors of the National Branch Bank of Charleston. Thomas Morris Letters, Ms, South Caroliniana Library; SCHM, XXXII, 73. Charleston Wills, Book G, 1826-1834, p. 305; Inventory Book G, 1824-1834, p. 327, SCAD.

Columbia 30th May 1790 [1]

Dear Morris:

Yesterday I received yours of the 21st am glad to hear you left all well at Spring Farm, and think you are right in intending to remove them to Town in a day or two. Yesterday morning the Committee of the whole finished their Business and reported to the Convention, some particular matters, the most material, that of the adjustment of the general Agreement of reducing the representation to one half as near as cou'd be, being left to a select Committee of 14 to prepare and report to the Convention which is adjourn'd to to Morrow 11 o'Clock (two Hours later than our Usual adjournments) in order to give that Committee sufficient Time properly to range and digest that Business. The Outlines of the Constitution as far as agreed upon, I am far from thinking a Bad one. The fixing of the Seat of Government is rather a matter of Conveniency, which I am sorry the last Assembly lost the most favorable Opportunity of bringing it back to Charleston. The two Laws respecting this matter which I had never read a Syllable of till I came here, being clearly in their Favor. However that being a matter of Conveniency only, if the Constitution in other respects is satisfactory, I shall not complain. I was in hopes when the Committee of the whole broke up, that we were in a fair way of compleating our Business by Saturday next, and in good Humour or of not encroaching at most above a Day or two on the following Week, but am now apprehensive from a Conversation last evening with one of the select Committee, that a most unreasonable advantage to the Back Country in regard to representation will be reported to the Convention and attempted to be carried. This must throw us back, occasion Heats, and take up no little Time, and in the mean Time the Impatience and Desertion of our lower members, as it has already given them the first Ground, so it will I am afraid compleatly place us at their mercy in that Point. I wish'd to take off ¾th of the representation, ¼th being in my Opinion fully sufficient to begin with; however was well satisfy'd with the General agreement for One half, but I must Question whether before we have done, there will be even One fourth struck

---

[1] SCHS. Printed in *SCHM*, II (January, 1901), 44-45. Gadsden's letter to Morris in Charleston—in which he also enclosed one for his wife—is datelined Columbia, site of the new capital of South Carolina. The fight to move the capital from Charles Town to the center of the State had begun in 1780, a movement which was resisted by many Lowcountrymen. Their resistance came to naught and, in losing, they sought to have two capitals, one at Charleston and the other at the more central location that had received the name of Columbia. Inasmuch as the old State House had been burned in 1788, the legislature met for the first time in Columbia in January 1790, in the unfinished capitol building. *See* Wallace, *A Short History*, pp. 342-4.

off. No Body to blame but ourselves for all this.[2] What remains of us will endeavor to do the best we can. Inclosed is a Letter for Mrs. Gadsden. My Love to Polly. Where is Tom? I have not had a Line from him since I left Town; I am uneasy about him; is he unwell? My Love to him and his Children, I am Dr. Morris Yr. Affecte. Father,

CHRIST GADSDEN

P.S. Thank you for the papers.

To Le Roy and Bayard

Herman Le Roy (1758-1841) and William Bayard (1761-1826) formed a New York mercantile and counting house in 1786. Charles McEvers (1749-1808), a cousin of Bayard, became a member of the firm about 1802. The firm dominated the commerce of the city from its quarters at No. 66 Broadway for nearly forty years.

Herman Le Roy, a son of Jacob Le Roy, received his commercial education in Holland, becoming president of the Bank of New York, 1799-1804. His partner in the mercantile firm, Bayard, was one of the directors of the bank. Bayard was a son of a wealthy Tory merchant who, because he raised a loyalist regiment, was forced to quit New York after the Revolution, leaving his son William behind.

William Bayard was an associate of the secretary of the Treasury, Alexander Hamilton; and it was at the Bayard residence, 6 State Street, that Hamilton died of the wound he suffered in his duel with Aaron Burr.

The mercantile firm was the agent for the speculations in the state debt for many prominent South Carolinians, notably Ralph Izard, Gabriel Manigault and William Smith. Le Roy, Bayard and McEvers held $395,386.11 of the State's debt. Henry W. Domett, A History

---

[2] In the State Constitutional Convention, the delegates from the Upcountry pressed for increased representation in the House. The Upcountrymen outnumbered the voters of the Lowcountry by more than four to one, but the older section gave ground grudgingly. Gadsden here agreed to the reduction of one-half the number of representatives from the Lowcountry parishes, and he might even have consented to more. The final result was that in the new government, the House was controlled by the Upcountry and the Senate by the lower division. William A. Schaper, *Sectionalism and Representation in South Carolina: Annual Report of the American Historical Association, 1900* (Washington: American Historical Association, 1901), I, 378-9.

of the Bank of New York (Now York: G. P. Putnam's Sons, 1844) pp. 61-62, 122; Henry Wysham Lanier, A Century of Banking in New York (New York: George H. Doran Co., 1922), pp. 94, 118, 121. See also, Rogers, Evolution of a Federalist, pp. 58-59, 205-8; DAB, II, 72-73; John Austin Stevens, comp., Colonial Records of the New York Chamber of Commerce 1768-1784 (New York: J. F. Trowe & Co., 1867), p. 149.

Charleston 19 June 1790 [1]

Gentlemen:

Through the recommendation of our mutual Friend Mr. Thomas Simms we have taken the liberty of introducing to your acquaintance Henry Middleton Esq. a gentleman of Family and Fortune in this Country and shall feel ourselves particularly obliged for your Civilities and attention to him. In our letter of this date put into the *Maria's Bay* we have enclos'd the Invoice and bill of lading of one hundred and sixteen whole and fourteen half barrels of rice, this ship to your House on Account of Mr. Middleton and which we will thank you to dispose of as soon as possible, as we will shortly after his arrival have occasion to call on you for part of the proceeds. We Remain Gentlemen Yr. Hble. Obdt. Servts.

CHRISTS. GADSDEN & CO. [2]

Charleston 30th August 1790 [1]

Gentlemen:

Your favors of the 1st and 15th of last month have been duely received and agreeable to your desire we have carried to your debit the proceeds of the rice sold on Account of Mr. Henry Middleton. We shall be obliged to you for the earliest notice of the advances you may take to either Mr. Manigault or Mr. Middleton as it is our intention to reimburse you from the very first of the Crop that comes to Market. We beg leave to trouble you with forwarding the inclosed letter to Mr. France by any American vessel that may offer for any part of England. We remain Gentlemen Yr. Hble. Obedt. Servt.

CHRISTR. GADSDEN

---

[1] Clements Library.
[2] Gadsden went into partnership with his sons, Thomas and Philip, as advertised in the *South Carolina Gazette and General Advertiser*, August 30, 1783.
[1] HSP.

To Ann (Gascoigne) Gadsden Lord

The following entry in the Alice Mighells family Bible cryptically reveals information relevant to this letter: "Thomas Gadsden and Ann Gascoigne Gadsden [d. December 6, 1808] were married 31st July, 1766 in London. Their first child was born in So. Carolina, 26 May 1767 at ½ past 12 in the morning and was christened 22nd September following James William [?]. His Godfathers were Christopher Gadsden, Andrew Rutledge proxy for James Gadsden, Mary Gadsden (ditto) for Elizabeth Hall as Godmother. Thomas Gadsden died the 6th of March 1768 at 8 o'clock in the evening and was interred the 8th instan. Aged 31 years."

This sister-in-law of Christopher Gadsden was the daughter of an admiral in the British Navy. Later she married Andrew Lord, merchant of Charles Town, on December 22, 1770, and after his death was again married, to William Greenwood, also a merchant of the city. From her marriages issued at least eight children. SCHM, XX, 212, XXI, 94, XXXII, 309; Gadsden Genealogy, SCHS.

[Charleston] 24 Aug. 1791.[1]

Dear Sister:

I am sorry the papers you mention are mislaid. I have not a paper relative to my Brother's Estate in my Hands, nor can I inform you any Thing about them. Perhaps the papers regarding those Lands you mention may have been left in England with your Friends— the Trustees to your Marriage settlement. This is generally usual here. They ought to have been mention'd in the Marriage Articles. I can safely aver, I have always understood they were settl'd on you. If you have ever seen them here, they must I think be amongst Mr. Lord's papers. If you think they are among Mr. Andrew Rutledge's papers,[2] one of his Brothers shou'd be applied to. My Love to all yours, I am Yr. Affecte. Bro.

CHRIST GADSDEN

---

[1] Emmett Collection, NYPL.

[2] Andrew Rutledge, Elizabeth Gadsden's first husband, and Andrew Lord, whom she later married, had been partners in the mercantile business in Charles Town. The firm advertised in the SCG, July 27, 1769.

To Jacob Read

Jacob Read (1752-1816), attorney, officer in both the Revolution and War of 1812, was elected United States Senator in 1795, serving until 1801. Born at Hobcaw plantation, Read became active in the Revolution as captain of militia. He was sent as a delegate to the Continental Congress in 1783-1785, sat on the Privy Council (1783), and was a member of the Jacksonborough legislature. Read showed strong Federalist tendencies in the Continental Congress and voted for the Federal Constitution as a member of the South Carolina ratifying convention. As senator he greatly favored the administration. Read was one of President Adams' "midnight appointments," to a district judgeship, but never served because of the change-over to a Republican government. His friendship with Gadsden was formed during their imprisonment at St. Augustine. DAB, XV, 425.

[Charleston] Fri. Morng. 9 Sept. 1791 [1]

Dear Read:

Last Evening Mrs. Ferguson put the enclosed into my hands drawn and sent by Messrs. Parkers at the Request of Mr. Ferguson's Children that any of age, for her to sign in behalf of her Children. It seems to me, upon the Perusal, mainly relative to the Children, and in no manner to their Dower which you have in hand to obtain for her from the Court of Equity, but still, thoroughly sensible of my No-Reading in matters of law, I send it to you to judge of the Propriety of it, which you'll soon do. I am sure by a glimpse of it, and whether it contains any Thing interfering with the part you have to transact for her. My servant will wait till you have perused it. When I'll return it to her to be signed, if you judge it proper, that no time may be lost, for I assure you my dear Sir 'tis of the highest Consequence to the Estate that not a moment should be lost. I am in great regard Dear Sir Yr. most hble Servt.

CHRIST GADSDEN

P.S. You'll see tis already signed by all the concerned except herself.

---

[1] HSP.

To Major Thomas Pinckney

Thomas Pinckney (1750-1828) was educated in England at the Westminister School, Christ Church College, Oxford, and the Middle Temple. Admitted to the Bar on the eve of the war, he joined Gadsden's regiment as captain. He participated in action against the British in the Florida campaign, the Battle of Stono, the siege of Savannah, and the Defense of Charles Town in 1780, from which he escaped capture. Serving under General Horatio Gates, Pinckney was severely wounded and taken prisoner at Camden. After the war, he practiced law in Charleston, later serving as Governor of South Carolina during the critical years, 1787-88. Pinckney was president of the South Carolina ratifying convention of 1788. He received this letter just before sailing for England as American minister to Great Britain. Two years later he commenced negotiations with Spain, resulting in the Pinckney Treaty which opened the Mississippi River to the commerce of the United States. S. F. Bemis, The Pinckney Treaty (New Haven: Yale University Press, 1960), pp. 236-314. C. C. Pinckney, Life of General Thomas Pinckney (Boston: Houghton, Mifflin & Co., 1895).

Charleston April 17, 1792 [1]

Dear Major:

As you happn'd to be with me yesterday when I received a Letter from Messrs. McCredie and Co. and just before had read and told you every Thing that had pass'd antecedently between us, to answer you when you get to Sea, (for you must be too much hurri'd, I am sure at present) I enclose you Copy of their Letter received yesterday and then read to you, with my answer. I find these gents by themselves or Clerks as fully determin'd to construe every Thing their own Way, and Phill's reply to their Clerk (Mr. Philton) is just as much perverted, as my Letter to them and conversation with their Clerk. I am resolved to sacrifice my Plantation and negroes on Black River as soon as this Crop is made.[2] If I can't bring about by that Time what I hinted to you, which I am trying for, this

---

[1] Boston Public Library.
[2] Gadsden did retain his plantation on the Black River, as is shown in his will.

256

patience is all I desire. Not one has been the least pressing as yet but this House, but the Northern Lads generally act systematically, get one to begin, and then the rest like sheep soon follow. However, I know the worst and am determin'd to ask no Favors, and at the same Time will do every Thing that can be reasonably expected. God bless and give you a pleasant passage to Philadelphia and from thence to London, and every Success you can wish yourself. My best respects to all yours I am with Sincere Esteem Dear Major yr. affect. hble. Servt.

CHRIST GADSDEN

For the City Gazette 1793

The occasion for this essay was the Congressional election of February 4-5, 1793, in which the incumbent William Loughton Smith (1758-1812) was opposed by Thomas Tudor Tucker and Jacob Read. During the period, Smith's rivals accused him of speculating in war debts while the Assumption Bill was under discussion in Congress. Gadsden called the charges "flimsy insinuations." Rogers, Evolution of a Federalist, pp. 239-40.

Messrs. Printers:[1]

Through your paper, gentlemen, give me leave, as an independent elector of this state, to return my most cordial thanks to Mr. William Smith, our member at Congress, for his attentive, spirited, faithful and able services in Congress. My own feelings extort from me this gratitude, openly to defend, as well as my feeble pen can, a good public servant, from the most—flimsy insinuations, I ever saw put to the press, against any man in high public character, under too the doubtful signature of a Voter. Nothing but its appearance at the moment of a new election, makes it worthy of *any* answer.

Let us, my friends, be watchful, and down with an angel if he would betray us, but not without solid proof. Facts and dates are stubborn things; produce them and then (not from the dirty insinuations of, very probably snakes in the grass) expose the man who

---

[1] *City Gazette and Daily Advertiser,* February 4, 1793.

dares to betray his trust. But, I am persuaded, *like* our legislature upon a *similar* occasion, we will not let the activity of our active servants, formidable where most wanted, operate against themselves, through our own lachesse. The more active a man in trust is in our service, the more his actions ought to be candidly and cooly examined, or who worth having will serve us? Only such contemptibles as know most dextrously how to trim, according to our humours; and alas! we have too many thus inclined, and we ourselves are too inclinable to listen to them. Give me the man who can dare to throw out a moot, a momentary opinion which he may think useful and necessary, however eccentrical, but that as willingly resigns it when mooted to the decision of the majority, and never to cram his own opinions down.

A prophet is not without honor but in his own country; thus we find it with our national constitution; all Europe seems to admire it, (though as from man it must be imperfect) but ambitious and designing men, either hirelings *from abroad,* or would-be Caesars *amongst ourselves,* seem to be trying the *old state* trick of making it cheap, by first *designedly* treating it with disrespect and contempt, in order to carry their insidious or Caesar-like intentions of oversetting it *altogether.* Fellow citizens, these are the men most to be dreaded and guarded against; may heaven ever protect us from such miscreants, and may we in time be thoroughly convinced, that though it be highly salutary and incumbent upon us respectfully to point out what we apprehend of a hurtful tendency in the transactions of congress, yet to treat them with contempt, we should always recollect, it is like a bad bird betraying his own nest. I would rather now conclude with the common name of an Elector, but apprehending it a duty as a citizen, however Quixotly it may appear, to support a faithful public servant, thus darkly and insiduously attacked, I therefore sign my name.

CHRISTOPHER GADSDEN

February 2, 1793

To Messrs. Vanderhorst and Gervais

Arnoldus Vanderhorst (1748-1815) and John Lewis Gervais were the commissioners for settling the accounts of the state treasury. Vanderhorst was a prominent businessman and a director of the Charleston branch of the National Bank. He was also an important Federalist party figure, having been elected to the govership in 1794 over Jacob Read. SCHM, XXXIII, 73; XL, 132. Wallace, A Short History of S.C., pp. 347, 415, 704.

Charleston, 30th Augt. '93 [1]

Gentlemen:

As we understand you are now engaged in the Settlement of the late Mr. Bocquet's [2] Accounts as Treasurer of the State, we request you will be pleased in that Settlement to take particular Care to give him the Credit according to the Order in which he became entitled, so that those accounts which accrued during his first appointment, for which, and for which *alone,* we stand his Security, may not be blended with subsequent Transactions.

We also Request that you will prevent the Sales of his Property for the Payment of his private Debts, until those due to the Public (if any) shall be satisfied, as by an Act of the Legislature passed the 13th March 1789 those Debts due to the public have a priority of *all* others.

We will be much obliged to you to acknowledge the Receipt of this Letter. We are Gentlemen Yr. most hble. Servts.

CHRISTROPHER GADSDEN
PETR. FAYSSOUX [3]

---

[1] Morristown (N.J.) National Historical Park. The letter is addressed "Messrs. Vanderhorst & Gervais, Commissioners for Settling the Treasury Accts," and inscribed "General Gadsden & Doctr. Fayssoux."

[2] This is Peter Bocquet: *SCHM*, XL, 7, 23.

[3] Dr. Peter Fayssoux was a physician and one of the few out-spoken anti-Federalists of Charleston at this date. Fayssoux voted against the ratification of the Constitution. He was one of the founders and first president of the South Carolina Medical Society (1783), and a founder of the Public dispensary with Doctors David Ramsay, Alexander Baron and Tucker Harris. Fayssoux, also, in 1785 was a director of the Inland Navigation Company and one of the first investors in the Santee Canal Company. *SCHM*, XXXII, 75, 79; Joseph I. Waring *et al., A Brief History of the South Carolina Medical Association* (Charleston: S.C. Medical Association, 1948), pp. 5-6, 87; Jonathan Elliott, comp. *Debates in the Several Conventions* . . . IV, (Philadelphia: Fac. ed. 1937), p. 333; Rogers, *op. cit.,* pp. 156, 265-6.

To Robert Burton

Robert Burton (d. 1806), merchant of Richmond, Virginia, was said to be "respected" by "all that knew him." The Burton family had been prominent in the history of the capital city. Burton's business was conducted with many of the principal merchants and trading firms of the period, among whom were Samuel Pitfield Braddick, James Brown, James Hunter, Fontaine Maury, and Robert Rives and Company. Burton died February 12, 1806. Richmond (Va.) Enquirer, February 15 1806; Virginia Mag. Hist. and Biog., XX, 289; Francis Burton Harrison, Burton Chronicles of Colonial Virginia (Williamsburg: n.p., 1903); Robert Burton Correspondence, Mss., Virginia Historical Society.

[Charleston] 28 March 1796 [1]

Sir:

Your Favour of the 13th Instant, the 26th Instant [in care of] Post—Mr. Charles Freeman's Father[2] was my intimate Friend, and besides, his first Wife, a Lady of this State, and my first Wife being nearly related, I did Business for him to a large amount after his Departure from hence without charging him a farthing Commissions and had fully remitted him *all* his Effects here long before the American War. But the last Remittance in a Bill of Woodroppe and Cathcart, (as good a House reckon'd at that time as any in Carolina) came back protested with a number of others drawn by them for the Cargoes of several Ships loaded on Commissions.

These Gentleman being much esteemed here and much pitied on account of that unexpected Accident which occasion'd their Failure: in this situation being very intimate with Mrs. Woodroppe, you may suppose what Tenderness and Management I must have us'd to recover that money for my friend Freeman. In the mean Time having undertook a large and expensive Improvement to my Estate here, I wrote to Mr. Freeman to let me retain this money which he had readily assented to. After this, our War happen'd in which it was not of the least Service to me, but on the Contrary, a great prejudice,

---

[1] Charles Roberts Armstrong Collection, Haverford College. The interpolation "[South]" in the close of the letter is Gadsden's.

[2] An advertisement in *SCG*, February 2, 1751, indicates that Gadsden had been a factor for "George William Freeman, Esq."

CHRISTOPHER GADSDEN IN LATE LIFE
By Rembrandt Peale, about 1795–97

wire

for during that Time large sums owing to myself were paid in depreciated Money, of which great part lays by me at this Moment not worth a Farthing. This occasion'd the Agreement between Mr. Freeman and myself that no Interest at all shou'd be paid from 1st Jany. to 1st July 1783. My Estate in Charleston being Injur'd in an Extreme Degree by the British when here, it was not in my Power to make her a remittance till April and May, 1791, when I sent Mrs. Freeman two hundred pounds which with the Exchange at that Time say 7% advance amounted to £245. The Remittance woul'd have been follow'd very speedily with the full amount of her Demand. But that *same year* in November, I lost a very worthy Son, who by his generosity and Indiscretion had involved his Family very deeply. My affection for him and them oblig'd me to interfere immediately for several very pressing Demands to the amount of some Thousands. This unavoidably occasion'd the farther Delay. Now thank God I am very near in status quo; therefore n the growing Crop of this year comes to market, I shall then (but not before, barring extraordinary accidents) be able to commence remitting and compleat the whole soon after, say by about this Time, Twelve Month. In the mean Time I wish to receive the Necessary Documents and papers mention'd in my two last letters to Mr. Charles Freeman, directed according to his prescriptions and which I make no doubt he has received. Copy of both these Letters I now inclose for *your Government*. I mention this because as an old man in my 73d [year], I wish to leave my affairs with the least probability of Embarrassment to my Executors, having seen many suffer greatly and that from very honest and well meaning men (in case of Death) by doing Business imperfectly. I therefore give this early Notice not as an Excuse, it not being in my Power to make a remittance till as mention'd before, and there will be full Time in the Interim, to furnish me with the satisfactory Documents in every respect. This Demand on me is easily calculated and is rightly set off by Mr. C. Freeman in his letter to me, it the 13th July last which you inclosed Vizt. "£4353.12.3 [South] Carolina Currency whilst a Province of Great Britain, to run at simple Interest at 8% from the first July 1767 to 31st December 1774 and at 7% from 1st July 1783 until the Debt is discharged."

N.B. The well known Exchange between Gt. Britain and Charlestown in July 1767 was 700% which makes the original Debt reduc'd Sterling to be £621.18.10¾

I have now troubl'd you with as full and candid a Statement of this Matter as in my Power and am Sir Yr. Most Hble. Servt.

CHRIST GADSDEN

261

Charleston 8th April 1796 [1]

Sir :

Since mine of the 28th last month [in care of] Post, I have received two letters from Mr. Charles Freeman, one dated 30th Nov. the other the 8th January last inclosing all the necessary papers I mention'd to you [even?] proper for me to have, so that I hope now to finish this matter by the time I mentioned to you without fail.

In his of the 30th Nov., he mentioned that he had requested of you to appoint some Person in Charleston to "receive his claims upon me." If this be done, it may be in my power to make some payments before the Time I mentioned in my last. As amongst ourselves by Transfers, Orders, and a Variety of Methods, we often have it in our Power to make payments easy with one another. Should I meet with a good Opportunity I remit to Mr. Freeman himself, I suppose it will not be objected to. If I do it, I will inform you thereof. I am sir, yr. most hble. sevt.

CHRIST GADSDEN

A Few Observations on Some Late Public Transactions

This essay was written to support the presidency of John Adams, but it was not meant to be a mere polemic. It was composed after the election, so that Gadsden could write freely without the accusation of prejudice. His essay, therefore, contains excellent insight into the political practices and philosophy of the period. He deprecates unfriendly French policy and warns the Nation—but especially the newly-arrived yet welcome Irish immigrants—to beware of the demagogue.

[Jan. 30, 1797] [1]

Obsta Principiis. [Resist these principles]

Much Respected and Worthy Fellow Citizens of all the United States, Those who call to mind the dismal, gloomy state of despon-

---

[1] HSP.
[1] Pamphlet in the Charleston Library Society. The complete title: *A Few Observations on Some Late Public Transactions, in and out of Congress particularly, on the dangerous and seemingly Unconstitutional Manner the Late Election for a Chief Magistrate was conducted throughout the states of the Union. Most respectfully recommended to the serious consideration of the Citizens of all the United States.* By a Member of the Congress on the Stamp Act, held at New York in 1765, and the two first at Philadelphia, in 1774 and 1775. [January 30, 1797].

dency we were all in at the very time (and for a year or two before) our deputies were framing our new constitution the then very small hopes, from a variety of symptoms, that when met, any would be fixed upon, so as to be generally agreed to: the very long and warm disputes and opposite opinions that happened amongst themselves upon that most important occasion; the turn, notwithstanding, as it were *all at once,* of all the states present, *unanimously* to consent to recommend the federal form we have; that the states also should *separately* debate as warmly on the acceptance of this form; that at last all the states of the union should *universally* adopt it; and *above all,* that this form should contain in itself, extracted from the demo-cratical, the aristocratical, and the absolute systems, whatever is worth having from each, clear of, and guarded from, all the shocking and pernicious tendencies each of those systems are exposed to, and have at times been woefully felt by the subjects of either. I say, those who weigh these occurrences alone, (many more extraordinary might be adduced) and do not perceive a kind fostering hand of Providence leading the United States to the formation and *universal* adoption at last, of our therefore excellent, and let me add, almost miraculously-made constitution, must I think, be looked upon, if possible, as great unbelievers as Mr. Paine seems to make himself to be. And here let me notice, *en passant,* a clause in a letter of this Mr. Paine to our President, dated at Paris, *but in July last,* in which he styles himself an Anti-Constitutionalist, not wishing to be called an Anti-Federalist. "It was only (says he) the absolute necessity of some federal authority extending equally over all the states, that an instrument so incon-sistent as the federal constitution is, obtained a suffrage." [2] By this, 'tis plain, he seems to think our constitution ought now to be kicked out, being *in itself* so *"inconsistent"* and not worth "a suffrage." Whatever may have been Mr. Paine's private thoughts, as he well knew what was brewed and brewing in July last in Paris against us, this passage carries more the appearance of the malevolence of an insidious enemy wishing to stir up divisions amongst us to favour the views of France, than any glimpse of feeling, sympathizing affection of a cordial citizen, *what he affects still to call himself.*

An idea of perfection seems to be implanted in our nature, far beyond what the best man can attain to in practice. Our works are like ourselves; in the most correct, imperfections may be spied.

---

[2] *The Letter to George Washington,* July 30, 1796, was written by Thomas Paine while he was being held in Luxembourg prison. The letter's embittered tone was seized upon by the Federalists and other critics of Paine's *Age of Reason* not only as evidence of his disrespect for Washington and disloyalty to the country but also of his mental deterioration. *The Complete Writings of Thomas Paine,* Philip S. Foner, ed. (New York: Citadel Press, 1945), II, 690-91, 723.

> *Whoever thinks a faultless piece to see,*
> *Thinks what ne're was, nor is, nor e'er shall be*

—POPE

Some men of strange turn, fond of laying hold of the least slips, even in the best plans, to overset them, seem always pulling down whatever may be proposed, without ever attempting themselves to substitute anything in its place, however absolutely necessary that something should be done. Mr. Paine seems to be one of those pull-down politicians. His Common Sense is a capital work of this cast, acknowledged to have been well-timed, and of great service to us all in our struggle with Great-Britain; but, still, not so necessary by any means, that we should not have succeeded *without it;* however, for this we were much obliged to his pull-down qualities. But has he not now entirely cancelled all this obligation, by endeavouring to pull down our constitution, and by that means throw us back again into the same goomy, desponding state we were in before it existed? Happy for us, he was not here to be concerned in the *building* it, his talents not laying that way. *Pulling down* in his forte; *here,* in my opinion, while he kept to (*quid valeant humeri*) [what the shoulders are able to bear], his true *political* line, none exceeded him; but his Age of Reason has run his bark bump ashore, and made him appear in as odd a character there, as the bear in the boat, turned sailor.

I confess I should be glad to see something *built up* by a man so long employed only in *pulling down;* it must, I think, be a curiosity indeed; any strong arm, with (I had almost said *with-out*) *any* head, may be sufficient to pull down a fine building; but, to erect a tolerably convenient one, that may be indispensably necessary, in its room, a nice hand, guided by a head furnished with many data in the *building way,* that Mr. Paine has never hitherto possessed of, seems not to be dispensed with.

Hitherto, in Mr. Paine's various political works of pulling down, he has offered reasons; but his bare *ipse dixit* he seems to think sufficient to make us ashamed of our constitution. But my worthy fellow citizens, under his *"so inconsistent"* a constitution, not worth "a suffrage," according to Mr. Paine, we have not been more happy and flourishing since our existence, now eight years, than any of the best and most tranquil powers in Europe have been for ten times as long. Let us, therefore, be thankful for it; and *such as it is,* a work made by men, not by angels, be contented with it, and join shoulder to shoulder in its support: not doubting that the same over-ruling Providence that has favoured us under it hitherto, will not fail us in future, if we do not fail ourselves.

The closer, my friends, you keep to this our heaven bestowed constitution, (for let Mr. Paine think what he will, I confess I think it so) and the more you watch over it, the better and safer situation will you and your posterity find yourselves in.

> *Still with itself compar'd its text peruse,*
> *And let your comment be——*

The farewell legacy of our long tried, true and trusty friend President Washington. For, be persuaded, you will find his fatherly recommendation as good a comment to our constitution as "The Mantuan Muse," so much recommended by Pope, can be to old Homer.

This intrusion, my friends, on your patience, is occasioned by three late public occurrences appearing to me much to affect our constitution, and, if not properly and timely noticed, their consequences may be very distressing if not fatal. That I might not appear a party man, I kept designedly silent till all our elections were over.

They are, first, an assertion in the last session of congress, very pertinaciously maintained by a number of members, that congress had no right "to inquire into the merits of a foreign treaty." [3]

2dly. The manner our last election for a chief magistrate has been carried on.

3dly. The attempt of a foreign minister to appeal to the people at large.

With regard to the first of these, it will be sufficient, in my opinion, *to contrast* the power given by the constitution to the president and the senate united, with the general power, given by the same constitution, to the congress, (of which the representatives are a part) to see, not only the danger, but the weak foundation of that. However, a few remarks shall be added.

---

[3] Republicans in the House claimed the right to examine and reject, if they desired, the Jay treaty. They maintained also their right to refuse implementary legislation, chiefly appropriations, in support of the treaty. Irving Brant, *James Madison: Faher of he Constitution, 1787-1800* (New York: Bobbs-Merrill Co., 1950), pp. 433-40; *see also* Samuel Flagg Bemis, *Jay's Treaty, a Study of Commerce and Diplomacy* (New York: Macmillan Co., 1923).

Gadsden did not favor the treaty. In a public meeting at the Exchange in Charleston in July 1795, he declared that he would "as soon send a favourite virgin to a Brothel, as a man to England to make a treaty." Washington Papers, vol. 273, May 31-July 23, 26, 1795; *American Daily Advertiser* (Philadelphia), August 24, 1795. Gadsden was a member of the committee formed at the meeting to draw up a remonstrance to Congress against the Treaty.

The president shall have power, by and with the consent of the senate, to make treaties; provided 2/3ds of the senate present concur.	*The congress shall have power to provide for the general welfare of the United States.*

Nothing appears to me easier than that each of these powers may do the duty enjoined, without clashing or interfering in the least with each other. Let the President and senate *make* a treaty *as directed,* without the congress interfering. Let the congress, when a treaty is *made,* provide for it, if they think it not contrary to the welfare of the United States. Here we find the congress have nothing to do with the *making* of a treaty, (and very rightly, from the delay and variety of obstructions that would probably happen in so numerous a body) but, *when made* by the president and senate, and application is had to them to provide for it, can any person *then* think this business *excluded entirely* from the direction given them, "to provide for the general welfare of the United States;" but that they are *still obliged* to make such provision, even if they are persuaded that it is extremely dangerous to, if not destructive of *that general welfare?*

Many good reasons may be given for their not being concerned in the *making* of a treaty; but not one, I imagine, that *when made,* at all events, whether they think it for, or not, for the general welfare of the United States, they ought still to provide for it. This appears to me so plain a case, that there does not seem occasion to call in the spirit of our constitution as an arbitrator; but yet let us call it in, in settling this point, allowed to be of the *utmost importance.* We are all made to believe that the three departments of our government, are mutual checks on each other, and that in those checks lies our great security. This is what I call *the spirit of* our constitution, and accordingly, even in this business of treaty-making, the senate is a check on the president. But where is the check on the president and senate *united,* should they combine and act treacherously, if their *new* doctrine should take place? Is there no danger here? No need for any *farther check?* A treaty, *when made,* is a supreme law of the land. Some trading nations would very probably, to bring about a treaty to their liking with the United States, give very large douceurs. I hope our president and senate will always be an uncorruptible body; but history tells us that consuls and senates have clammy fingers: what has been, may be again. Thank heaven, our constitution does not desert us even here. We must be *all* rogues, *all rotten,* before we can be ruined: when that indeed is the case, there is no help for us; the body politic, like the natural body, must be soon after entirely dissolved. They are both past cure.

Here let me declare my concern, that the congress sent for the papers relative to *the making* of the British treaty. This step appears to me to have been *unnecessary,* as the treaty itself was before them, a sufficient ground to form their judgment upon. But the astonishment to hear it asserted, that they had no right to enquire into its merits, must have irritated many. Heat begets heat; and one part overstretching one way, often fires the other to do the like their way. This is human nature collectively as well as individually.

I confess myself one, though no favourer of the British treaty while pending, made very happy at hearing that so many members, who had expressed themselves against it in the house, had sacrificed their private opinions to the peace of the public. But, indeed, I never at any time thought that treaty of such moment, that it should be refused to be provided for by our representatives.

Farther, what is said here, is intended to prove the constitutional right the congress have to consider the merits of a treaty; not by any means to insinuate, that upon every bad bargain, they should deny to provide for a treaty. No! But upon the most glaring, trying occasions, like the British parliament (*fas est et ab hoste doceri*) [It is all right to learn a lesson even from an enemy] to exercise that right. This causes no interruption amongst them in making their treaties with foreign nations, who knew they claim such a right, and will exercise it when they find it absolutely necessary. What reasonable objection can they have to our doing it only on such occasions?

I am aware that foreign nations, as well as bad presidents and senates would wish to see no possibility of any *after* reckoning; but that the representatives of the people should be obliged to provide for any treaty laid before them, whatever may be its merits, duration or tendency. But our constitution provides an ample remedy in such cases, if the people do their parts. Send honest, firm men, of good common sense, that can judge when it will be absolutely necessary to apply that remedy; [or] when not.

Still pardon me, my worthy friends, for thinking the manner of carrying on the last election for our chief magistrate, very objectionable, and, if continued, seems in its tendency, not only calculated to foment and keep up heats and animosities amongst us, but in no long time, I am afraid, to overset our union, or split and shiver us into many different governments; and if we once begin to divide, no one can foresee the end of it.

Our constitution says,

Each state shall appoint, in such manner as the legislature thereof may direct, a number of electors, equal to the whole number of senators and representatives to which the state may be entitled in the congress: but no senator, or representative, or person holding an office of trust or profit under the United States, shall be appointed an elector.

The electors shall meet in their respective states, and [shall] vote by ballot for two persons, one of whom, at least, shall not be inhabitant of the same state with themselves; and they shall make a list of all the persons voted for, and of the number of votes for each; which list they shall sign and certify, and transmit, sealed, to the seat of the government of the United States, directed to the president of the senate. The president of the senate shall, in the presence of the senate and house of representatives, open all the certificates, and the votes shall then be counted. The person having the greatest number of votes shall be the president, if such number be a majority of the whole number of electors appointed; and if there be more than one who have such majority, and have an equal number of votes, then the house of representatives shall immediately chuse, by ballot, one of them for president; and if no person have a majority, then, from the five highest on the list, the said house shall, in like manner, chuse the president. But in chusing the president, the votes shall be taken by states, the representatives from each state having one vote; a quorum for this purpose shall consist of a member or members from two-thirds of the states: and a majority of all the states shall be necessary to a choice. In every case, after the choice of the president, the person having the greatest number of votes of the electors, shall be the vice-president; but if there should remain two or more, who have equal votes, the senate shall chuse from them, by ballot, the vice-president.

The congress may determine the time of chusing the electors, and the day on which they shall give their votes; which shall be The Same throughout the United States.

No person, except a natural born citizen, or a citizen of the United at the time of the adoption of this constitution, shall be eligible to that office, who shall not have attained the age of thirty-five years, and been fourteen years a resident within the United States.

Now, my fellow citizens, suppose we read the latter part of these clauses, thus: "But No Person holding an office of trust or profit under the United States, shall be appointed an elector." Do not the words, "no person," *in themselves,* as completely include the senator and representatives, without their being particularly named, as with? Therefore unless these words, *"senator and represenative,"* are taken distinctly and separately, as the characteristic of a legislative capacity, they are altogether nugatory and superfluous. Whoever attends to the style of the constitution, will, I believe find no where else in it, such an *unnecessary* redundancy. Therefore, as it appears to me, senator and representative being to be understood in the legislative character of each, and Only so, they are both excluded, by the intention of the constitution itself, from being electors; for, had it been designed that any assembly should have appointed the electors *from among themselves, precision required that the words from among themselves,* or others of like signification, should have been inserted; as no such are, when they seem so necessary, no claim, especially one of such moment, ought to be assumed from an, *at least, equivocal expression.* Besides, to a public body appointed to fix upon another public body, upon a business of the greatest importance, surely it must seem awkward and indelicate, for the first public body to chuse out themselves, the whole or ⅞th of the other, upon an authority so doubtful and disputable, as not precisely and clearly giving them leave to appoint *a single one.*

Again, the electors for a president being equal, in every state, to all the members in each of those states, (senators and representatives) taken together, the electors seem to be left to be appointed by the representatives Only, (they being *peculiarly* the public's vice-regents) in order that our three departments of government, the president, senate, and representatives, might be All of a piece, All the choice of the people; and, therefore, such electors, when thus chosen to fix upon a president, ought to be as free, unshackled, and independent, as the members of the assemblies themselves, who are chosen in each state, to represent their respective citizens at large. This, I think, cannot be denied; and, therefore, the elector, who antecedent to his appointment, has engaged to vote for any particular person, sins, in my opinion, against the *spirit* and *vitals* of the constitution; and, as far as in him lies, is sapping it, and introducing precedents of the most pestilential nature; preventing the choice of *the chief magistrate* from being as free, and as *equally* the people's choice, as that of the senate and representatives, when they ought, *all the three departments,* to be so, as nearly as the peace and safety of the whole United States will admit. If, in any state, it has unavoidably happened, through accident, their assembly's meeting, or other unpremeditated circumstances, that they have been obliged to strain upon the meaning of the constitution, and to chuse electors from among themselves; such obstacles ought to be removed against the next election, that so dangerous a practice may not be sanctioned by custom; and any particular state, not wishing to be suspected as unfriendly to the union, will cheerfully conform its actions, so as, if possible, not to interfere with the expectations of the constitution.

Mankind are, generally, so unwilling to submit to restraints or rules, that even such as are made by themselves, are strangely perverted, to gratfy the present moment; or essential parts of them often neglected, through mere laziness, or inattention; for instance, the constitution plainly expects a number of candidates of the president's place; or why the following injunction? "If no person have a majority, *then,* from The Five Highest on the list, the said house, shall, in like manner, chuse the president." Or why permit each state to take one of the two persons to be chosen, from themselves. Is it owing to mere laziness, perverseness, or the arts of intriguing, designing men, played upon you, that you have been diverted from attending to, and pursuing this excellent, salutary provision? Are you infatuated to your own destruction? I wish with all my heart, no state of the union would ever, in future, neglect complying with this important constitutional right. Had they done this, in the last election, there would have been sixteen candidates from among themselves; and, if each state, had besides, chosen the other citizens a different one from the choice of any of the other states, there would have been at least sixteen more; what then? We should have mortified the sly emissaries, *behind the scenes,* foreign and domestic, to see their *deep* plan, to set us all by the ears with one another, effectually defeated. But our delusion this year, (I cannot help calling it so) may have been permitted, my friends, to happen so early in our national career, as a warning to us in future presidential elections, to be more cautious, and tenacious of sticking as close as possible to the plain meaning and expectation of our constitution, and not take upon us again, to be wise above what is written. Such a true republican procedure, will not occasion, in my opinion, much if any more trouble to congress, or to any particular state. But supposing it does; let us not *again* be persuaded *out of our senses,* to shrink from it. Our happiness, our independence, our existence as a nation, depends greatly on our peaceable, but firm, *collective* exertions in this respect, for the time to come.

Some of the good effects probably will be,

First, greatly to diminish, if not to banish entirely, that too prevailing spirit of jealousy and party, from among us: those most formidable weapons, which we have so madly put into our enemies hands against ourselves; and dexterously do they know, we clearly see, when and how to wield them against us, to their own advantage. How distressing is it to perceive a number of our back citizens, too unhappily possessed with an opinion, that the citizens on the sea coast, or near it, having the opportunity, from their situation, to be soonest and best informed, take advantage of them, to deceive and blind them into the choice of men best suitable to themselves, and their purposes of trade and speculation. Whilst too many of these, on the other hand, as weakly and groundlessly, seem to distress themselves that the back country want to cram down their throats, by their numbers, whatever measures of government they may think proper. To banish this dreadful demon, by taking the sting, if possible, out of those sly, ambitious, mischief-making go-betweens, of *both town and country,* that raise and foment these jealousies, is the ardent wish of the writer of this paper. 'Tis a necessary, but Herculean task; and without your strong exertions, my friends, cannot be effectually done. For these men, deficient in no arts of effrontery or cajolement, can transform themselves, occasionally, into any characters; travelling up and down, backwards and forwards, like Satan, seeking whom they may deceive and pervert, to aid their treacherous or ambitious purposes. What mischief have they done in almost every state! But so far, happy for us, one wholesome, skilfully applied catholicon, will operate alike in all the states, and undoubtedly effect a radical cure.

'Tis this—Only let us all resolve to entertain no ungenerous sentiments of each other, (at least, not so as to affect the public at large) remembering that we are all citizens of one and the same great government; have one great Common interest, and that nothing but such unnatural, shocking, impolitic mistrusts among one another, can keep us from being as great a government as ever the sun shined on. Away, then, with these jealousies among ourselves; turn all your resentment, my fellow citizens, against these sly, political, pretending, bettering gents, these suspicious zealots for reformation; these mischievous propagators of innovation! It warms me beyond measure, when I think of their impositions; especially, when I see how easily you swallow them. Can you avoid seeing how these gents start themselves into consequence, merely by striving, underhandedly, to set us all in a flame? Their first step, after feeling their power of delusion, is generally to riggle themselves into our state assemblies; success here, prompts them, by means of the fluent tongues and pliant consciences, assisted by your own most unaccountable infatuation, to look up to a seat in congress; and often do they gain their ends. After so many instances of their treading the same *beaten* path, one after another, is it not astonishing that you *still* continue to countenance the breed? At least, if possible, in future, prevent their going to congress to spread their mischief there. That body hitherto, upon the whole, has given great satisfaction; too many of these ambitious dividers among them, will, if not prevented in time, probable overset us all. Here act like true, generous federalists; prefer the general, to your particular good, and keep them at home, though you dislike their company, if you can do no better, by all the means in your

271

power. If each state would only so far baulk such inimical citizens in their ambitious career, we should soon not only get rid of them, but demonstrate to all the world, that for a man to rise in the United States, was only by noble, manly, virtuous means; by sincerely and steadily promoting the general welfare; by overlooking small inconveniences; by treating small errors with tenderness, and by disinterestedly endeavouring to heal those of consequence, by fair, friendly and candid reasoning. But reasoning will have no effect upon the men just hinted at; they are callous to every noble, generous, tender feeling; *self is their all.* But our keeping close to the expectations of the constitution, will much lessen even their power of doing mischief, in many respects.

Another advantage is this: that no foreign nation would hardly attempt, *again,* to interfere in our elections, from the little prospect of success in corrupting sixteen states, chusing their chief magistrate *at one and the same time.* And suppose they found means to tamper with three or four, the rest would be fully sufficient to shelter us from the bad effects of their corruption. But, could our enemies, themselves, have wished for a finer opportunity, than that given them at our last election, to chuse a chief-magistrate for us; having them to manouvre with the parties of only two men, pitted against one another by *our selves.* This certainly was making fine sport for, and costing them less daubing and less trouble.

Again, out of the thirty-two citizens to be chosen by the electors of the sixteen states, only two, by the constitution, could be approved. This, far from occasioning any heart-burnings to the other thirty citizens, they would rather think it an honour (as it certainly would be) to have been *so far* distinguished by their fellow citizens in their different states, and held up as worthy of the most important offices; and though kept back for the present, would be like a corps of reserve against the next election, with this advantage to the public in general that in the interim, we may all grow better acquainted with the real merit of each; and if elected again by their own citizens, it would be a high sign of their fixed reputation.

Another advantage of this strict adherence to the constitution would be, that the nation in general, the United States themselves, could not be reflected on, as carrying even the appearance of countenancing parties; whereas, in the last election, the nation seemed to split itself into two parties, through *predilection* for two citizens, a long noted, dreadful rock, a Caesar and Pompey, a Scylla and Charybdis. We ought to have *no Predilection* for any citizen. 'Tis of no consequence to the nation, what citizen, *from one end of it to the other,* is at our head, so that he is rightly chosen, an honest man, a steady, firm federalist, no party man, of good sound common sense, and otherwise constitutionally qualified. And here, I hope, I shall be pardoned for saying, I always looked upon those as very weak friends, or artful, insidious, undermining enemies, who made the execution of our president's office so difficult, as requiring such extraordinary, uncommon talents. Plain Sailing suits our constitution best: tricks, twistings, jostlings, and deep laid, equivocal subterfuges in treaty-making, let European powers divert each other with, and welcome. Our thousand league distance from these cunning, double refined politicians, (with whom, the less we have to do, the better) is not among the least of the blessings we have to thank a kind Providence for—Capitulations or treaties, with either Great-Britain or France, we have experienced already, mean any thing, every thing, or nothing, at times, as may suit either. But let us mind our own business; take as much care as we can of ourselves; be a party in none of their wars, what treaties we may find it necessary to make with them, let them not be of long duration, and let us, on our parts, keep them faithfully. Honesty is the best and truest policy—I think we have hitherto observed this rule, and hope we shall always. Our president, in treaty making, has the senate to consult; without two-thirds of the members present, agreeing and advising him to make a treaty, he cannot do it. What great difficulty then, can arise to an honest man, qualified as just mentioned, with such assistance, that he can scruple to encounter?

No state, or number of states should, in my opinion, give the least reason to suspect, that they wish to set up or name, upon these occasions, directly or indirectly, any man or men, in a manner that may carry the most distant reason to suspect they wish to push him or them through the rest of the states; the more delicacy shewn, the better; let every state be left *entirely* to itself. Such a cautious, unmeddling behaviour in each state, will naturally promote harmony, and discard every degree of suspicion and jealousy amongst ourselves as separate states. Now, added to this, if men, ready at their pen, wedded to the constitution, of true, *vital* philanthropy, would, from the time the election notice to chuse another president is given out, 'till the very day of election arrived, be as pressing as their powers of language will permit them, to enforce to the constitutional electors of each state, the importance and duty of their appointment; the great dependence the public had on the faithfully (without predilection, favour or affection) discharging their trust, he himself not mentioning a single name, this might be of the greatest importance, and convince the errantest sceptic, that the republicans of the United States had nothing more at heart, than to find out and obtain, in the most direct and peaceable manner, the man (no matter of what particular state)

273

for their president, that the majority of the people at large had, by their constitutional electors, made choice of.

Finding that the import of the few minutes I had made, with regard to the insulting appeal of the French minister to the people at large, has been laid before you by much better pens, in the public prints;[4] I shall now content myself with observing, that a stranger phenomenon has hardly been heard of in the political world, than that an absolute monarch over one and the same people, should, for the manifest interest of that nation, assist another people to recover their liberties, and become republicans; that that very nation, but a few years thereafter, should guillotine that monarch, in order to become republicans themselves; and, when hardly fixed as such should, regardless of a solemn treaty with the people they had assisted, like free-booters, suddenly and unjustifiably fall upon their trade, and intermeddle with their government, in a manner they, themselves, have shewn all the world they would not suffer the least glimpse of an attempt. What can this proceed from, but a romantic giddiness of a restless power, setting itself *no bounds;* or, not unlikely, prompted besides, by a jealously of our rising importance among the trading nations of the world, and wishing to check it? And here, by the bye, we shall much deceive ourselves, if we imagine the other trading nations of Europe, are without the like jealousy; for, however they may differ in other respects, they seem not far from being unanimous in this. I only wish we were as firmly agreed, in pursuing our own common interest and supporting our constitution and government; harbouring no mistrusts of either of its departments; their management, for eight years past, having shewn them, upon the whole, not unworthy or incapable of their trust. We had it not in our power to send angels; as men, they have acquitted themselves to the admiration of all the world. Any political differences that may arise in *particular* states, should, like *family variances,* be kept *within* those states. Congress ought not to be affected by them; and indeed, will not, I think, if our elections are managed strictly, according to the letter and spirit of the constitution.

No foreign minister whatever; I think, has a right to make appeals to the people at large; but the French minister has done this. On such occasions *particularly,* my friends, every respectful mark of confidential affection, ought to be shewn to all our three departments of government, that it may be seen how ready the people are to give

---

[4] Affairs with France had disintegrated to the point of seizures of shipping, and the French Minister, Pierre Auguste Adet, had actively campaigned against Adams in favor of Jefferson in the presidential election. William Loughton Smith to Ralph Izard, November 8, 1796, *AHR*, XIV, 784; Alexander De Conde, *Entangling Alliance* (Durham; Duke University Press, 1958), pp. 456-500.

them every support in their power; and all foreign ministers be convinced, that any little, indirect artifices of that sort, only serve to unite the people, if possible, more firmly among themselves, to oppose all such attempts, and to shew, in the strongest manner, their strict attention to their own rulers.

I cannot laugh at my fellow citizens, I am sure, for their zealous, uncommon attachment to the French nation, on account of their aid in our struggle with Great-Britain; for, I believe, few have been more so than myself. That their interest, as a nation, induced them to exert themselves to make the diversion they did, I never had the least doubt of; their not doing it *before* Burgoyne's defeat, that *capital* turn of the war in our favour, shewed their *cautious* resolve to be on the sure side. Yet, still, they had a right to our gratitude, but, not that we should involve ourselves in ruin, or neglect our own pressing affairs as a nation. But now, my friends, we must have eyes surely that see not, if their *very great love and friendship* do not appear to us in their *genuine* colours, every atom, self-interested *to the extreme;* craftily intended to make us merely their puppets; to move by, and *only* by their wire. But, my fellow citizens be afraid of only *their intrigues,* against which, by what we have *already seen,* we must be well assured, we cannot be too much on our guard; their long, well-trained emissaries are but *every where* amongst us. Quiet resignation to the resolves of the government we, *ourselves,* have set up, is my *uppermost political* maxim. But, exclusive of this, I never thought I should have been brought to like the British treaty, half so well as I do now. Providence seems to have thrown it in our way, as the means to bring about our being weaned, *in time,* from our over-ardent, too rapturous French love-fit. But do not, my friends, surmise from hence, that I mean, indirectly, to persuade you to a relapse to your former flame; by no means; we cannot but, by this time, know them both right well; to divide you is equally their aim. Corruption, we all know, is the most powerful wedge of division; watch, therefore, all those subjects which seem to have a crack ready to receive this wedge; keep a strict look out here, and your political peace and happiness will, in all probability, be lastingly secured. On our sea coasts they may scratch us; but not much, even there, if our country and other friends are alert to assist us. But, in the end, I am fully persuaded, they will deeply wound themselves. For what can the French, *Themselves Alone,* bring very formidable against the United States? In what a number of ships and transports? And, *while bringing,* to how many accidents exposed, in crossing the Atlantic? And for what national purpose to them, *cui bono* [to what good]? We have been obliged to fight, and though all of us deprecate being reduced to that *unnatural* necessity again; yet, if compelled, there is not the least doubt that our citizens, from one end of the union to the other, will turn out again with the *like* spirit, and advantaged by *some* experience, against any invaders, however giddily and romanticly impelled; relying on the same providential assistance that has never failed us hitherto.

Numbers freely allow, theoretically at least, that all governmental power ought to spring from the people at large. But most of these very men again say, that practically, they, the people, have from all ages shewn, that they know not how to use power when they have it, or to be contended *long,* under constitutions that have sprang entirely from themselves. Our's is of this sort, in the amplest manner; it has not only sprang, but, *In Every Step,* proceeded *under* the people's auspices; and, at last, has solemnly received their consent.

You may, perhaps, think me, my follow citizen, a very great enthusiast to our constitution, when I give it as my sincere opinion, that the world never had so good a one manufactured by man. Let all of us, therefore, join heart and hand to make it as lasting as possible, and have the honour to super-annuate such assertions, so extremely derogatory, disgraceful and mortifying to human nature. To countenance no tamperers with it, will much forward such an animating resolution. As the Israelites were ordered to have the words which Moses commanded them, in their hearts, and to write them on the posts of their houses, and on their gates; so let us imitate this injunction with our constitution, that excellent, (I think) heavenly gift *also,* by having it hung up in the most conspicuous places in our houses; and, if the farewall legacy of our worthy friend, President Washington, was joined with it, our rising generation, in my opinion, would want nothing farther, compleatly to understand, admire and love it. I always was, and very early, in congress, shewed myself against any irregular predilection of a citizen to any office whatever; but, when regularly elected, and he has served with reputation to himself, and done the public every service that could be expected from him in his station we must have had value received, and ought, in our turn, from gratitude, as good policy, to shew him, in his retirement, all the respect and honour we can, suitable to the station he has held. The thus joining President Washington's farewell address, to our constitution, which he hath so long, so honestly, and firmly supported, will have a *particular* propriety in it, and I think, be a greater mark of honour to him, than if his statue was set up in every state.

Like true republicans, my friends, whatever is once constitutionally carried, whether by a single, or number of votes, the very nature, the foundation-spring of our constitution, call upon you to submit quietly to, and to support it, if necessary; otherwise, as far as is with you, you seem to turn tyrants, determined to carry, at all events, your own opinion, joined with *the fewest,* against the constitutional resolve, though attended with *the greatest* number of votes. Is not this a strong imitation of the *sic volo, sic jubeo,* [so I want, so I order] of a tyrant? Will you not, by thus acting, *lessen* your right of being a republic? And, if you still indulge such an overbearing spirit, can it be long before you *lose it altogether*? The congress, unless an extreme bad choice is made, if wrong, will soon rectify their error themselves. Publications in the papers too, decently managed, often have, and may again, by giving useful hints, be of great service; but tumultuous opposition answers no end, but to disgrace the promoters, to cause us to be laughed at by anti-republicans, to create confusion, and to make ill-blood amongst ourselves.

The calling conventions of the people, on general governmental affairs, I confess, I am now no friend to. During our struggle with Great-Britain, they were sometimes unavoidable. The least objectionable instance, seems to me, is when the president, after having duly consulted the senate about a treaty, *still* appears to be (as it were) at bay, and therefore defers putting his fiat thereto, as if wishing to know the general opinion without; here, if conducted with propriety and decency, they may, perhaps, be sometimes of use.

Members, sent from each particular state, when met in congress, belong, certainly, *to the whole nation at large,* to consult for their general welfare, *as one body.* They ought, therefore, to go unfettered. That member who will suffer himself to be fettered, in my opinion is not worthy of his seat. He cannot be a true, firm, staunch federalist at heart: for, as the poet says, truly,

> Man, like the gen'rous vine, Supported lives,
> The strength he gains, is from Th' Embrace he gives.

So a single state, the more strongly it *embraces* the whole general interest united, the more it will find, in the end, its own real importance promoted and *strengthened,* and on the most solid basis. And the particular member, who *uniformly* acts on this principle, will find his own reputation, not only in the state that sent him, among men of true worth, fixed upon the most reputable and lasting footing; but, among the rest of the states, he will always be mentioned with the highest esteem.

No man has more heart-felt joy than myself, to find our young nation, but of yesterday, already become the asylum from tyranny, wherever shewing itself. Let our fellow men come and welcome, from any where and in any numbers, we have room enough for them all The only dread to be apprehended *to them, as well as to ourselves,* is

277

the mischievous use, artful, wicked men, (and too many such we have) may make of the long fixed habits and biases they may bring with them; by cunningly playing and practising upon them these habits, to pervert them to their own diabolical purposes, before we have time to get thoroughly acquainted with each other.

Men devoted to particular, ancient families, having had famous names, from their infancy, Sounded in their ears, and applauded like demi-gods, in the sports and songs of their native country, I say, men of this cast, are too apt to be taken in by designing, watchful waylayers. In the beginning of our struggle with Great-Britain, we had a formidable number of Scotch, in North-Carolina, so infatuated to the race of Stuart, as to cause much trouble to themselves and us. From some items, not very long since in the papers, with regard to an ancient, famous Irish family, some reason is given to suspect, there may be some dust attempted to be kicked up amongst those of that nation, to put them upon that, or some other family track. But, my Irish friends, be on your guard. I take the liberty to give you this hint, as being of Irish extract myself, by the mother's side, whose father was a native of Ireland, whom I am named after.

Your open, manly, generous, unsuspecting spirit, is well known; so is the tincture of credulity, naturally springing therefrom, as well known. Here you have *often* been, here you will still often be played upon, and your greatest caution is necessary to prevent it. Your distresses in Ireland, we have heard of; have felt and sympathized with you on that occasion. We are happy to know our country can relieve you; and you will soon find yourselves, in all probability, actually relieved, if you do not suffer yourselves to be cajoled into parties to distress us, and, in the end, distress and disappoint yourselves of that assistance you wish for. You are now in a land, that with half the industry and prudence you were obliged to use in Ireland, you may gain a landed property, all *really your own*, sufficient to support yourselves and families decently and independently. Let this very heart-chearing prospect add spurs to your industry; strive to rise gradually, peaceably and honestly, and pay no attention to foreign emissaries, or to restless, designing, ambitious men, amongst ourselves, wishing to come country or family over you, or, in some other artful manner, to draw our now Common country into confusion, for their *selfish* ends. Take this in good part, my worthy, unsuspicious friends, however impertinent and officious you may think it; in whatever light it may appear, or be made to appear to you, I am conscious it comes from an undesigning breast, that loves you, and wishes for nothing more than to see peace, harmony, and universal philanthropy promoted, not only from one end of the United States, but from one end of the world to the other.

I am persuaded, from what I have seen, that more than half the misfortunes of any consequences, that have happened amongst us, has been caused from the precipitation of honest men, not aware of, or giving themselves *time* to guard against the secret, deep-laid, round-about ambushes of crafty knaves, indefatigably labouring to have no body credited but themselves; and most of these men, so deceived, have been convinced too late, as well for their's, as the public's peace, of their own hasty, infatuated credulity, being the sole occasion of all the mischief.

My reader, still permit an old man one small disgression. Little things, mere names and sounds, have sometime considerable effects. I have often wished the name of our nation was Columbia; and, more than once, took, when I had a right, some pains to have it so. One of our citizens calling himself a Columbian, would sound, I confess, more *honestly* in my ear, than now, as in common, calling himself an American, and, I am sure, more harmoniously than *an United States man;* or than, by an awkward periphrase, (that few, if any, can bring themselves to) *a man of the United States.* From hence, it seems to me, the word *American,* is so, continually by foreignors as well as by ourselves, applied to our person, trade customs, *etc.,* scarcely ever, I believe, *an United States* ship, *etc.* Again, the word American, (citizen being *understood,* seldom *expressed*) stands alone, which, every time I hear it named, methinks I hear the shade of the great Columbus reproaching us for abetting and continuing the cheat upon him, who, though like Horace, he might say *exegi monumentum aere perennius* [I demanded a monument that would withstand time]; yet, that republicans seem to wish, and even to take pains to destroy it; for, is it not full as easy for one of our citizens to say abroad, I am a Columbian; which too, if adopted, would be peculiar and precise, than to say, as they do *indistinctly,* I am an American; merely to avoid, as it seems to me, this uncouth expression, I am *a United States man;* or, this roundabout one, I *am a citizen of the United States.* This shews what pains is taken amongst us, and how much out of the common road, to countenance injustice. Pardon this sensibility in favour of the fame of a man, dead several hundred years since.

The writer of this paper is an old public servant. No citizen, high or low, in or out of office, from one end of the United States to the other, was earlier than he, in the British struggle. He, like the widow with her mite, put his all into that cause, his person; his services to the utmost of his power; his property of town and country, were all, from the first to the last of that struggle, at the public service, and made by them, at times, very free with, for which he never demanded, or wished to demand, one farthing compensation; excepting in the three first congresses, to which he had the honour, unsolicited, to be called out by his fellow citizens; of the provision for that service, he partook.

Besides, indeed, when his country property was sequestered, and his town, though under protection of a capitulation, taken from him, was in very little better situation; himself sent and made a close prisoner at Augustine; his family shipped off to Philadelphia, and in distress there; he then shared part of some public assistance, which he afterwards *repaid* to our public treasurer, with interest. Not improbably, it may be said, vanity is the impulse here; be it so, my reader. But I intreat you to believe it forced out from a wish to procure attention to the Very Important Hints in this paper, as coming from a well-known, independent, friendly fellow citizen, devoted to our constitutional union, and therefore,

A Steady Federalist.

Charleston, January 30, 1797.

P. S. I am glad to hear the President has recommended a national university; I am persuaded it will tend to what we want most, a compleat union and general acquaintance with each other, throughout the United States.

To the Citizens of South Carolina
April 21, 1798

In this essay, Gadsden is outraged at the French Nation for the X.Y.Z. Affair. No such independent spirit as that of Gadsden could fail to respond to what he believed was an insult to national honor. Nor was he alone. His terse piece typified the popular feeling in South Carolina, a feeling made more intense because one of its Revolutionary heroes, Charles Cotesworth Pinckney, had suffered affronts by the French Directory. Page Smith, John Adams, 2 vol. (New York: Doubleday & Co., Inc., 1962), II, 952-65. David Duncan Wallace, History of South Carolina 4 vols. (New York: American Historical Society, 1934), II, 355.

It appears by the Dispatches received from our Envoys in France, which the President has delivered to Congress, that the French require of us [1] a Donceur of 50,000 [livres] ! for their Ministers of Foreign Affairs, and nearly 1,500,000 for their Directory, before they will hear of an accomodation of the differences between the two nations. The conclusion naturally drawn from these premises, is, that the United States must either reject these demands, and prepare for resistance or submit, to this and other contributions, as tributary to France. As the will and power of France is aimed only against the government and commerce of the United States, and not against the Land-holders, who we are told by the French and their partizans (for unfortunately there are still among us some Jacobins) advocate her outrages upon us, we may expect that our planters and farmers, will get in readiness their tobacco, cotton, rice, pork, corn and pease *etc.,* to satisfy her demands and avert the vengence of the Terrible Republic and an appeal to arms for the protection of our Independence and our property. It is time now every American should take his stand, and be known to be either for or against his country. If the French rulers and Jacobites here have belied the American people (and I hope and believe they have) in the charge of division and disaffection to the government chosen by themselves, it is a call loud and strong upon us to inspire it with energy, by an avowal of a firm confidence in those who excite it.

My fellow Citizens of South Carolina, you have been basely traduced; you have been called inimical to the Federal Government, jointly with all the Southern States; wipe away the stain and offer a glorious example to our Brethren of the North; come forward, and demonstrate whether your independence, be now as dear to you, as at the time you struggled to gain it, and that whatever measures may be judged necessary by your constituted authorities, will be manfully and warmly supported by you. Give to the French for their Motto of, *"Divide and Conquer,"* United we are and we will stand.[2]

A NATIVE

[April 12, 1798]

---

[1] *South Carolina Gazette and Timothy's Daily Advertiser,* April 23, 1798. The essay was identified from Gadsden's letter to Jacob Read, July 16, 1798.

[2] Gadsden also delivers a blow for his Federalists. Minister Talleyrand attempted to separate the envoys along party lines, declaring that he would treat only with Elbridge Gerry, the Republican, and not with the two Federalists, Pinckney and John Marshall. Gardner W. Allen, *Our Naval War with France* (Boston: Houghton Mifflin Company, 1909), pp. 25-26.

To Jacob Read

Charleston 16th July, [1798] [1]

Dear Read:

I am much obliged to you for your favor inclosing Our Envoy's correspondence with the French Fraternity, their first and last, this accompanied with the Presidents Message of the 21st June to both Houses of Congress, it does him great Honor and confirms the opinion I gave to a Friend asking what I thought of him some years since; my Reply was that a better and firmer piece of live Oak was not to be found in the United States. I ever had this opinion of him from my first acquaintance and every day since has established it. Pray my best respects to to him.

I am glad Marshall is safe with you, I wish Pinckney was so with us, and Gerry altogether done with the monsieurs, I am still afraid of some delusive diplomatic Slobberings and Patchings on their Side, to gain time to repair their shattered perfidious dividing Scheme against us.

Two measures you are about I have long wished to see completed, *a constitutional* Renunciation of our Treaty with France (not gratifying her with our Declaration of War, let her infer that, if she please, herself from the defensive proceedings she has at last necessitated us to adopt) and a safe and proper Alien Bill. In this whatever our Wishes may be to afford an assylum to all Mankind, yet, we must have an Eye to what the other Nations of the World do, especially G. Bn. and France, for it, as by their actions it plainly appears, they will give up the Allegiance of no quondum Subjects of their citizens amongst us since our Independence; we must of necessity imitate them, as near as we can, or upon a trying Pinch we shall find ourselves in a very precarious situation surrounded with Members we can plan little or no Dependence on.

As to Foreign Treaties, my opinion ever has been if possible to have nothing to do with them; with France we could not help it. Now thank God she has given us a manifest justifiable Opportunity

---

[1] South Caroliniana Library. The date line of the letter is barely legible and transcripts of it in the Library have been set at 1796. However, because of the issues discussed—the X.Y.Z. affair, defence, and the Alien Bill, the letter can have no date other than 1798. The presidential message referred to is in James D. Richardson, ed. *A Compilation of the Messages and Papers of the Presidents* (Washington: Government Printing Office, 1897), I, 266.

to take leave of her's. I Hope we shall go on with all the rest when a proper occasion offers in the same Manner. I am fully of opinion that the United States will always be on fairy ground, a very slippery footing, till the Law of Nations become their only trading Intercourse with the rest of the World, and here, I can by no means join (as in the Alien Bill) with those who think we *must* in this respect also *follow* other Nations. I see not the least necessity for it. I am besides thoroughly satisfied, that proper, honest, and liberal Relations on this Plan, would in general give Satisfaction to the Commercial Powers; even G. Bn. herself the greatest opposer to be excepted, would soon, by a steady firmness on our Side, and making use of the Means undoubtedly in our power, find herself obliged to acquiesce. The United States are her best customers (and how inestimably and progressively so are they in her present gloomy trading Prosperity) not she theirs and With regard to Carolina and Georgia, I am sure I am not out when I aver, that we deal with her for £100 when she does not deal with us for more than One, so vast is the Disproportion, and yet she like the Fox permitted in extreme Distress to warm his Nose under the Henrook, soon found means to wiggle himself wholly in, and carry everything before him. As to convoying our Vessels self Interest dictates it, as (amongst others) a natural prudential Consequence of their insuring them and Cargoes. Would she be contented with that very large present share of our Trade, and the immense additional Prospects besides, before her. No man would be better pleased with a renewal of our Friendship in the trading Way (but none of your dangerous Expedients, your offensive and defensive Treaties with her, or any other European Nation whatever, where coming off second best we may be sure will be our Lot). All I want of her is to be honest, to abandon the unjustiable arrogant Liberties she takes in searching and capturing our Vessels (Except when attempting plans actually beseiged). This even by Way of Bargain not favor, supposing she had an undoubted Right to what she here assumes, (against the Laws of God and Nature), wou'd be then but a Trifle, a mere drop in the Bucket, as a *Quid* for the very advantageous *Quo* she has for us. But the superlatively selfish G[reat] B[ritai]n will still directly or indirectly, prevent or embarrass our Trade with every other Power but herself, as much as she possibly can. A Variety of Instances have occur'd since the printed scribble I sent you. For one Instance, we have a large growing Hamburgh Trade here, all, every Farthing clear to the Rice planter, a Total Customer, as we may say to us and Georgia. A Single Merchant here Mr. Schutt [Schultz] [2], who settled amongst us as a Citizen soon

---

[2] Casper C. Schultz (or Schutt) was a merchant at 87 Broad Street, Charleston. *Charleston Directory, 1790.*

after the Evacuation, has for these three years past shipt himself (I am, sure I speak within Compass) at least 20,000 Barrels of Rice each year, besides many other articles of our Produce, and has been the principal Means of keeping up the Price of Rice. No Man since we shipped a Shingle or a piece of Scantling from this Country has ever been better supported, but the extensive Trade he has introduced from Hamburgh which may be called the Tunnel through which our Rice passes into Germany *etc., etc.,* for G. Bn. appears extremely jealous, and through this Man, in conformity to obsta Principiis, if possible to put an end to it, His Vessels have been particularly aim'd at, besides the goods etc., which he loaded; there is no end to his Embarrassments from the same Quarter; another Vessel of his lately from the Havanna with about 1200 boxes of sugar has been captured by Capt. Cockrane off our Barr, when at the same time he let a Vessel of Muir and Boyd's pass, more plausibly in my Opinion to have been objected to.[3] But this Hamburg Trade, I say, so extensively carried on and circuitously promoted seems to stick in the Gizzard of G. Bn., wanting not only to *sell* her goods at her own Price, but to buy our Rice, without Rivals, at her own Price also; here the shoe pinches with her, and if she succeed, we must rarely expect to see Rice in future above Six or Seven Shillings. This is a very serious matter, particularly to this State and Georgia, being the only Rice planting States, and from Maryland North they may be almost all of them said to be mere Carriers with regard to our Rice; therefore in point of interest the lower the Price of Rice here, the better Prospects of Freight for their Vessels. Virginia and North Carolina as concerned in Tobacco and no Carriers, may find it a little their Interest on a Pinch to give us some help, having an Intercourse with Germany in that respect. But all the rest of our States have a very triflng Trade indeed to Hamburg excepting a new Carrier.

---

[3] Gadsden refers to the capture of the *South Carolina* by Sir Alexander Forrester Inglis Cochrane who, as captain of the flagship, *Thetis,* commanded a squadron at the British North American station. He was not only a thorn-in-the-side of the francophiles but an embarrassment to the pro-British Federalists for his frequent violation of American neutral rights. *Naval Documents, Quasi-War with France* (Washington: Government Printing Office, 1935), February 1797-October 1798, pp. 250-1; *DNB,* IV, 615-6; Marshall Smelser, *The Congress Founds the Navy* (South Bend: University of Notre Dame Press, 1959), pp. 168-9; Alexander Hamilton to Rufus King, June 6, 1798, H. C. Lodge, ed. *Works of Alexander Hamilton* (Washington: G.P. Putnam's Sons, 1904), X, 292.

William Boyd was a "respectable" merchant of Charleston, residing at 134 King Street. He died in 1811. *SCHM,* XXXVI, 23. His partner appears to have been master cooper, William Muir (or Moer), a prominent mechanic who was vice president of the Master Coopers' Society and secretary of the Union Fire Company in 1786. Muir was born in Aberdeen, Scotland, and immigrated to Charleston in 1764. *Charleston Directory, 1790;* Papers of the Master Coopers' Society in SCAD; *SCHM,* XXX, 247; XXVI, 26.

Cochrane's Captures off our Barr and Blockade of our Harbor, you will soon hear a particular and from our Merchts. Your adjournment being expected I did not write you sooner. The printed scribble you received were sent to the Press the 12th April and published Eight or ten Days after, when I had neither seen nor heard *a Syllable* of our Envoy, first representation, however it required at that Time no Conjuration to perceive how our Matter with France would turn out. To conclude, (and I am persuaded you must be glad of it, and besides my Paper will not let me proceed farther) I am dear Read for no See-saw Work, now this Favorite now that; for risking No Openings or tendencies to preferential Jealousies, but in our open *Country* I hope to give a kindly Welcome Sir to every Friendly popp-in Customer.

I am not without Hopes that the general, I may almost say Universal Spirit, shown by the United States on this Occasion when disseminated, since their almost infinite addresses, through the Powers of Europe will be attended with some good common effect of Revivification there. My best regards to Mrs. Read.

P.S. The 18th July Since writing and directing the within, this minute, I have seen our Fellow Prisoner Capt. William Hall. He is very inclinable to engage in our Sea Service and intends he tells me to bring up his two Sons therein. He was very active last War, both in the Continental and in our State Service, in this he commanded several Vessels. No man knows our Coast particularly better. He is a very deserving Man. I have long known him and his Father before him;[4] he is in very good circumstances having been pretty fortunate for several Voyages past, so that only an Inclination to serve our Country I am well persuaded can be his Motive. If you [have] an opportunity to mention him to the President, I am *sure he* will give you no Occasion ever to repent your Recommendation. I am Sir yrs.

C. G.

---

[4] The father, also William Hall, who died in 1768, had been a gunsmith, a partner of Tunis Tebout, and one of the mechanics of the Liberty Tree Meetings. He also advertised himself as a carpenter. Charleston Will Books, 1767-1771, B, vol. 12, fol. 348-54; *South Carolina and American General Gazette,* July 1, 1768.

For the State Gazette
July 15, 1800

Gadsden, the Federalist, regarded the electioneering and maneuvering of the New York and Virginia Jeffersonian Republicans in South Carolina as an interference in the private political affairs of the State. Although he wrote in favor of Adams, he expressed a fear of "party" and "cabals" which might end in national disunity and tumult. Like many of his contemporaries, he harbored great suspicion of party organization. For the election of 1800, see Wolfe, Jeffersonian Democracy in S. C., pp. 135-65.

Numquam reponam perpetuo . . . vexatus? [After I have been perpetually annoyed, shall I never respond?]

—JUVENAL

Are we never to see an end [1] to the noisy electioneering cabals of two or three self important, turbulant, *meddling* states? To have our ears grated with the infamous party abuses of our President and Vice-President? Are we to be everlastingly duped by, and pestered with their insolent and assuming Dictates, whom at the approach of every revolving election, we are to choose as President?

To warn his fellow citizens of the pernicious tendency of listening to these turbulent, *meddling* gents will not surely be taken amiss from an old native of South Carolina, no party man, no popularity seeker; and who hath no attachment in this world superior to what he owes his country, *the United States of America.* One ever averse in foreign alliances, and hath constantly held it as his opinion that Great Britain and France equally wish to distract and divide us, and have their numerous artful emissaries thickly scattered amongst us to catch at, promote and make the most of every thing tending to that sly purpose, men of this suspicious cast, we cannot at this, their harvest time, be too watchful of.

Long riveted in their sentiments and having ever scorned, in dangerous or very critical periods like the present, to forbear doing

---

[1] *South Carolina State Gazette and Timothy's Daily Advertiser,* July 15, 1800.

his duty as a citizen by giving his opinion plainly and roundly, he therefore now in his very declining years cannot too earnestly endeavour to persuade his fellow citizens to to turn a deaf ear to even *the least* symptom of interfering or dictating from Any of the other states. Laugh at all or any such officious intrudings, put on your considering caps my worthy friends, and *in the very momentous choice of electors* soon to come before you, dare to judge (surely you are of age) for yourselves, keep as close to the constitution as possible, and let no improper man, that you can prevent, riggle himself into that appointment, think *again and again* whom you are about to vote for, that this most essential body may be composed of well informed men, of known integrity and firmness, and not be again packed, and antecedently bargained with, as was said to be too much the case at the last election for a President.

The electors have a very plain instruction in the constitution how they are to conduct themselves; it runs thus *"That they shall meet in their respective states and vote by ballot for two persons, one of whom at least shall not be an inhabitant of the same state with themselves."* This instruction though as well and cautiously expressed as its nature would admit, yet has one uuavoidable and not very pleasing consequence as supposing each state choose as permitted, one of its own citizens, then that state sending the greatest number of members to congress, of course having the greatest number of electors, can *always* secure to one of its own citizens the Vice-Presidentship. This appears at first sight a plausible objection to adopting strictly the permission in the first part of the instructions, that each state may choose one of its citizens. Pride and ambition have not failed to step in, perplex and cause here all the confusion they can, in order to prevent each state throughout the Union from adopting this salutary Union Saving permission.

A few cursory remarks on its objectionable part will I hope not only dispel all the dreads we have hitherto been infected with, but cause astonishment how any such could ever happen. For

1st. Had the commissioners on the constitution not permitted any state to choose one of its own citizens on this occasion what would have been thought of such constitution makers?

2d. Then if any one state had this permission, each of the rest must have it of course.

3d. This being the case it follows unavoidably (without any reflection on the foresight of the commissioners who seem here to have laboured under a choice of difficulties) that the state having the greatest number of members in congress, and consequently the greatest number of electors must, if unanimous in its votes for the same citizens of its own state, carry his election for the Vice-Presidency.

Admitting this, it concerns us then to know what power the vice-president as such has from the constitution, by which he can, if mischievously inclined, do any injury worth notice, and upon enquiry we may be soon perfectly easy in this respect.

But here is the rub, he steps into the president's seat upon his death, which by the bye, is a contingency that has not happened in the last twelve years, and may not for that or a greater time to come but in the interim what terrible *may-be* dreads, what continual vexatious alarms are we exposed to, spread *intentionally* to prevent each state from adopting strictly the permission to elect one of its own citizens at every presidential election. Such insidious suggestions have already brought many real and poignant evils upon us, and that of occasioning the many mischevous, turbulent, *meddling* cabals amongst us, cannot be numbered with the least, and where these evils will end, God-alone knows. An illiberal, ill-founded jealousy endeavours to lay them all at the door of the out-voting state (permit the expression) when, at the same time tis will known that this preference (if it can be called so) her proportionable rightful situation with regard to the other states alone manifestly and *unavoidably* entitle her to, yet she alone is still made the scarecrow, that if, truly this constitution permission is kept strictly to, it must in time put the rest of the states greatly into the power of the out-voting state, it will not only promote, but invite a combination therein, bring about a division, end in our ruin and what not! Now for a moment suppose such a combination to take its rise in that state *from the cause just mentioned;* let us paint it as strongly as we can, and endeavour to discover, how it will probably begin, the concerned therein, and the manner of their management. When this is done, so far from being under the least apprehension in future, I am persuaded we shall rather much be mortified and astonished at our own folly, in having stupidly submitted so long to such a flagarant imposition.

Now let us come to the Combination itself, where it seems:

1st. Absolutely necessary that not a few of the leading men of this out-voting state, long hackneyed in political villany, must not only be privy to, but principal secret directors thereof.

2d. Till the wishd for event comes about, it will be as necessary that a continued succession of such men, of the like dark abilities and steady rascality, be kept up.

3d. Tis also indispensible that all the sets (few or many) of contingent electors be of the same kidney, and here not a little of the prophetical discernment of spirit seems necessary.

4th. The choosers too of the electors must, in constant succession, be warily parked, lest any weak conscience should get in betray and spoil all.

5th. The heads of the combination and all concerned therein must be always extremely attentive and careful to preserve as strict an unanimity as possible among the whole body of voters, in order to be sure of the citizen they wish for, otherwise they may be disappointed, and the state having the next greater number of votes, may by better management, carry the election for the man of their own state, they must prefer, by which means this so much laboured visionary combination of the *then might have been* out-voting state is taken all a back, for the next four years at least. But should even such an unlucky stroke not quite damp their spirits and put an end to this strange combination, the majority of the concerned in this plot in their forlorn plight, quite chop fallen, and on the brink of despair at this not unlikely event must want.

6th. A true thorough bred disciple of Jonathan Wild the Great, to restore to life the half dead combination; a man completely equipt for a plausible disguise or pretence to cover his insidious designs, of short, a hero above all compunction, and entirely void of every spark of what *common* minds call your nice tender feeling, never at a loss for a plausible disguise or pretence to cover his insidious designs, ot a fixed persevering disposition, not apt to be discouraged by difficulties and disappointments. Let us suppose such a much wanted choice personage is found at this critical pinch—that all hands, by his encouragement, are again put in motion, are more careful than before; let him be set up at the next quadrenrial election, and then carry all before him.

7th. Now let this, or as many equally accomplished personages be always ready, and not again meeting with any untoward accident worth notice, till one time or other, as it may happen; very uncertain when; one of these meritorious heroes be inaugurated into that long anxiously wished for succession to the highest post for the Vice-Presidency, by the death of a President, possessed with every inclination, and watching for every opportunity to gratify the supposed ambition of his out-voting state, and so staunch, trusty, and fearless a conspirator as to be regardless of any dangers arising from his own responsibility for his abuse of power as president.

8th. As the last supposition, and most difficult of all, we must suppose our senate and congress for the time or times during the whole rise and progress of the infernal combination to be asleep, and entirely inattentive to its mischievous consequences; corrupted we will not suppose, for were that the case, we must all be irretrievably lost—President, Senate, and Congress all rotten! The people who choose such men cannot be expected to be in a better situation.

Pardon me my friends, for having been so lengthy and tedious, in endeavouring to expose the ridiculous *ficticious* causes for the groundless frights, by which you have been so long kept from the unanxious and serene enjoyment of as much political peace and happiness as ever came to the share of any nation under the sun: Depend upon it, an enemy hath sown these baneful tares *while we were asleep*. If these remarks tend to turn your thoughts maturely to consider the importance of the constitutional permission here dwelt so much upon, and of the free unlimited power you have to elect the second person from any of the other states, not suffering any state to meddle or interfere in the least with you on these occasions, the writer of them will then have gained all his well meant feeble efforts, were intended to bring about.

I have rather chosen to make us of the *general* name, *out-voting* state, than to apply it particularly to the state now possessing the greatest number of votes, as time may and probably will give this further a rotation, so that the first may be last and the last first; but whichsoever may be the out-voting state in future time and similar suspicious of a combination should be trumped up against that state too—the foregoing hints, if worthy of notice, may be equally applied to that state likewise, and farther the out voting state, whichsoever it may be, having it always in its power, acting unanimously, to secure the Vice-Presidency to one of its own citizens, for that reason, neither such a state or its so elected citzen, can reasonably expect that *therefore* a rise from that post after any number of servings therein, is to proceed to the first—this seems to be an allay (if it may be called so) naturally and reasonably attending the out-voting state. But this is not by any means, intended to affect any gentleman from such a state, originally voted for by a majority of electors as President, and who has discharged that arduous trust with integrity and ability a first time, from having the common reasonable expectation not to be overlooked by the electors, at the next Presidential election.

What have we got my friends, by deviating from the plain easy peacemaking and peace guarding instruction so carefully provided for us? Have we not flounced from one deviation to another, continually blundering on, every succeeding step worse than the first, till at last the elective instruction itself is become a mere nose of wax, and the down looking, sneeking thing called cunning is at present wholly resorted to; but her sly ladyship herself seems now to be put to her last trump, and at her slippery wit's end to out cunning and trip surrounding counteracting cunning, and no doubt at last, her cunning voteries will cunningly learn to out cunning themselves, the never failing consequence of harbouring such a treacherous guest. Where this will end is not difficult to judge but very disagreeable, if not dreadful to think of, and what is the cause? Why, like our mother Eve we have presumed to be wise above what is written and recommended. By our constitution (as cannot be too pressingly inculcated) each state may choose one of her own citizens, and the other at large as it pleases. Can any rule be more plain; more salutary; more equal?

Yet 'tis not a little to be apprehended still, that if each state do come thoroughly to their senses, and henceforward steadily choose one of its own citizens, the ghost about the Vice President that so long and vexatiously has haunted us, being entirely laid—that yet another and another will be started up, dressed in various shapes to plague and terrify us. For the last part of the instruction clause giving unlimited power to choose a member from any of the states, will not perhaps, be relished by many of our cabaling gents. What! Shall we choose a President from Kentucky? I say, why not? If a majority of honest, penetrating inspectors, anxiously desirous to discharge the important duty they have undertaken, should spy out the man of most merit and most fit for President there, when the honour and integrity of the rest of the state are no way pre-engaged, let us have him by all means; he is the very man we want; let it gall the pride of our insolent caballers. In other words our *hitherto election dictators* ever so much, the more the better. Our envied constitution means and wishes that every state should be maintained in its independency and dignity, as safest and best for the honour and lasting political interest and security of the whole, and seems plainly to shew this is its intention, as by no means insinuating that the political management of our general state affairs is so perplexing (or need be made so) that one honest firm man, of good common sense, cannot be found in each state, able to guide them with honour to himself, and with satisfaction and security to the union, and here without pretending to the spirit of prophecy, unless each state keep strictly its own constitutional check upon the whole, at Presidential elections, the most proper, if not the only times for doing it with effect, never suffering any interference secretly or openly, that it can prevent from any other state whatever, the dangerous jealousies and quarrels that at those times particularly have arisen, and have been always craftily fomented by our enemies, intramures et extra, will probably encrease so much more at every future election, till at least they burst out into a fatal much to be dreaded separation.

Greatly to prevent this shocking evil, may each state be instrumental, if it never cease to hold up at these elections that citizen whom for his own intrinsic merit it most delighteth to honour; though for the electors, the greater honour will certainly be done him and his state too, for their discernment and persevering good sense. Should he prove to be a man of real solid merit, and when a proper time comes after having been frequently introduced to public notice, he will have an equal chance with any other for the Presidency. Such a proceeding would soon cause the States to be better acquainted with each other, and the characters of their distinguished men would then be in a train to be enquired into and generally known; very important concerns are these to the whole union, to find the number of able men encreasing continually, in every quarter amongst us, and the field to choose our President from, of course more ample and spacious; and whosoever chosen, from whatsoever state it may be, if he discharge the important duty uprightly and properly, it would be greatly in my humble opinion, for the interest as well as the honour of the union to elect him a second time (as has been already hinted), and nothing would more probably please the emissaries both of Frances and Great Britain, then to see such a man baulked of his so natural and reasonable expectations, as hardly anything would tend in future more to discourage our best, ablest, and most amiable characters from venturing to serve in that most conspicuous and important station. You cannot but have heard my friends as least so much of the many artful intrigues, and underhanded interferences, daily practiced in Europe by the different powers at elections there, as not to dream that Great Britain or France will be idle on such occasions here. But let me not to be understood to mean that a President should be elected a *third* time successively, least any tendency towards a perpetuity be too jealously surmised; and I have been often led to think this had a place among the reasons for the steadily virtuous and penetrating Gen. Washington's, resigning when he did giving thereby his suffage to this wholesome republican principle.

Every state carefully attending to its own duty in this point, so very material, the election for a President, and to that only, leaving all the other states to do the same, without the least meddling, directly or indirectly *any where,* would soon restore peace, harmony, good humour, and good mutual confidence amongst us all, upon a firm and lasting footing, and prove the best and most effectual gag to stop the mouths of those turbulent and dangerous cabals that have never ceased to spread misunderstandings and jealousies at every Presidential election.

That epidemical itch for meddling, that ruinous diabolical curse to the whole union, our southern states have too much reason to suspect the *Ancient Dominion* too guilty of; her intriguing meddlings have been too notorious amongst us not to be perceived. Thank God, we have happily got rid of one Truly Ancient Dominion for its unconstitutional meddlings; surely the meddlings of its derivative shadow will never be countenanced, much less submitted to lest we may too late find, that we have jumped out of the frying pan into the fire. 'Tis strange that so many of our settlers here from that state, more than from any other in the union, still *awfully* look up to Virginia, more than even to the whole union besides, and their loftiness scarcely seem to condescend to think themselves settlers of the state of South-Carolina. No man wishes to see all invidious distinctions at an end more than the writer of these remarks, but while separate names and the state governments do exist, it cannot be deemed either fair or honest to act in this manner, by no means calculated to promote that harmonious union not only of each particular state, but of the whole nation, as one body politic, so ardently to be wished for, but quite the contrary. The true spirit of South Carolina has always led them to judge for themselves, and see through their own eyes their own business; and the like prudent and generous spirit has always prevented them from *impertinently* intermeddling in the duty and business of any of the other states.

Nothing perhaps has invited meddlers, and subjected mankind more to crafty, designing men, than that fondness for novelty and change so epidemical among them. This common foible, your cunning politicians, like the Devil of old, well known when and how to turn to their insidious purposes.

Without some such diabolical peace disturbers, could it have been possible that such incredible ridiculous false alarms as have been played upon us, should not have long since been seen through, hissed and exposed, especially when our private as well as public happiness so essentially concerned, pressingly required it. The good man enjoys and blesses God for the plainness, simplicity and sameness of the directions he is to govern himself by; but the designing man, quite on the contrary, cannot bear simplicity and sameness, they disgust him, as not by any means suiting his purpose of imposing and always lying in wait to deceive.

Let the recollection of what we have suffered from our past inattention and folly keep us my friends more watchfully on our guard in future. Our having so long thoughtlessly suffered ourselves to be carried away by such wild, incoherent, insolent impositions, will not unlikely encourage others to feel our weak *inviting* nerves again.

Our election for a President carried on in the plain, independent, uninterfering manner just mentioned will have besides the many good tendencies already noticed that of causing the President to be chosen with more ease, safety and general satisfaction, not only to the electors but to the citizens at large throughout the states, than has been of late experienced.

My friends, you who know and feel when you are well, you who dread changes, and by no means wish to speculate with that happy political tranquility you have by the blessing of God for so many years enjoyed under our envied constitution, and its worthy directors, exceeding any experience of the sort in the known world, B'e Awake, exert yourselves at the present crisis, believe me, *'tis a most important one,* and as far as your influence can possibly reach, contribute your endeavours (pardon my being so repeatedly pressing) to have honest firm men chosen electors at the ensuing election, and in this choice forming your judgement by the general tenor of a man's actions not, by any means by his oily flippant knack of speech making or speech-writing. Choose men who will not go to that duty shackled, and who when there will not risk the interest, honour and independence of our state, to the sly insinuating ambitious views of any state in the union, or to any other considerations whatever.

Whatever fate these well meant strictures may meet with, and however the writer of them may be handled, the six following beautiful lines of Mr. Pope, so applicable to our situation, he is sure his reader must be pleased with, and therefore with him he leaves them without a comment.

> *Man like the gen'rous vine, supported lives;*
> *The strength he gains is from the Embrace he gives,*
> *On their own axis as the Planets run,*
> *Yet make at once their circle round the sun;*
> *So two consistent motions act the soul*
> *And one regards itself and one the whole.*

> —Pope

C. G

Charleston, June [July] 12, 1800

For the State and Federal Carolina Gazettes
August 29, 1800

Gadsden comes out openly for a second term for John Adams and denounces the "party spirit" which threatens the union, the constitution, and defames the candidates.

In different circumstances a different conduct is necessary.

At our first setting out [1] upon our Constitution, we had all held off and were all electrified at one and the same wire. It pleased heaven to give us Gen. Washington and to preserve him a sufficient time, to shew the world what a real great man ought to be, always ready to serve the public cheerfully, and at once without any parade, when his service is wanted, and conscious he is able. On various other occasions thus acted our great man, as well as when called upon *twice* to serve as President. Nor did he shew himself *less great,* when he desired not to be chosen a *third time,* a seeming wish to continue in office *more than two elections* he would not countenance.

But can we now our friends, say that we are all electrified at one and the same wire. The fact alas! is glaringly otherwise, therefore a different conduct is now absolutely necessary in voting for our future Presidents.

The many dreaded consequences from the violent parties at our presidential elections, cannot but be very alarming to our worthy peaceable citizens, and a few more such must unavoidably be fatal to our union, but thank heaven we have a plain, easy and constitutional method of putting all to rights, if we will but set about it in good earnest, with any tolerable degree of unanimity, firmness and candor. The following hints if fostered with the assistance of better pens, may be of some service to promote this desirable end. They may not be if left at our next election, though so near at hand, but in the election after that; if in the mean time, they are worthy of the public notice, the writer is not without hopes, that they may be instrumental towards effectually ending the evil.

1st. Then it is not undeniable that no state has a right to dictate to any other in the union, who is to be chosen President, much less the whole.

[1] *South Carolina State Gazette and Timothy's Daily Advertiser,* August 29, 1800.

2d. That all the states having all the same political happiness and security at heart and the constitution to guard, 'tis certainly not *very modest* for any one, or more states to dictate to any of the rest, as by that means seeming to insinuate that those other have not (*each of them*) as much love for the constitution and as much understanding and prudence as themselves; that they do not use as much diligence and precaution to look about them, nor have penetration to discover so well as themselves the man in all the states most capable of that high office.

3d. Suppressing then all such unwarranted self important insinuations and dictates and allowing them all Equally solicitious in the momentous common concern, let us have each state to take its own way, choose *uninterfered with* the man it likes best.

4th. To clear out prospects and affix our judgements let us give no opportunity to over arch enemies, within or without or to both united, to succeed in their endeavours to perplex our governmental affairs, but let us keep close to, and mind our own business and situation attentively, avoiding alliances, and keeping to plain treaties of trade, such as every man of common sense may understand, and let them when [made?] be observed carefully and honestly, and in this respect, no directions can be preferable to these in Gen. Washington's farewell address, which can not be too much attended to. Our safe and advantageous distance from the powers of Europe ought also never to be lost sight of, or left unimproved to the utmost.

5th. Being now in the 25th year of our independence, and on the verge of our 13th of our constitution, it cannot be doubted that in this time, among our zealous and patriotic citizens, many have endeavoured so far to acquaint themselves with our public affairs [illeg.] as not to be unqualified if called out to serve their country even in the high station of President, with honour and credit to themselves as well as with general satisfaction to the union—Which

6thly. Must be in a shocking situation indeed (inhabited by millions) if five hundred men *at least* are not to be found Equally capable of being set at the head of our affairs—But

7thly. supposing only fifty (not exceeding about three in each state) are not only *equally* capable, but fired with a Washingtonian, disinterested union spirit are also Equally Ready and Willing to risk all and attempt whatever their country may request of them. Then

8th. Fifty such men so found *equally* capable of serving as President, let each man in the state he has a right to vote (neither directly nor indirectly trespassing upon or interfering in any other, for ☞ here is our lasting happiness and security) choose that man amongst all the states, he has reason to think in all respects, to be the best of his judgment and information best qualified without favour or affection, for the station; not suffering the man himself, but his well established good character and proper qualifications *alone* to direct his choice—now.

9th. If the voter thus divests himself (as he ought on this grand essential common concern) of all personal attachment and attend only to the necessary sought for qualifications in *whomsoever* or *wheresoever* found, will it be of any moment to the public, which of the fifty men is chosen? Or *of what state?* And here—

10th. By the bye, no method seems better calculated to keep all in good humour, nor better accommodated to the dignity, equality and even to the delicacy of each state in the union; strictly following this method I am persuaded we should soon hear no more of the self-important, caballing, meddling states we have been so long and so much plagued with.

11th. Another great advantage of this method will be no longer serving as pioneers to our foreign enemies by removing all out of their way, excepting two or three candidates left to amuse them—without squabbles helped on and promoted by themselves as we know was greatly the case at the last Presidential election.

12th. The Union now consists of six-teen states, and if it were (as probably it will be) increased to twenty, with a respectable territory to each, our safety from foreign meddlers would still be greater if, and only if we keep steadily to this harmonizing all-peace-making and peace-keeping solution of never interfering with each other in elections, and if each state, as soon as made one, would insist on being of age, and not suffer itself to be kept in leading strings by any other state whatever, whether taken off originally from that state or not; such a number, such a band of brothers, thus cemented, all powers in the world would not be able to corrupt; nay, it can hardly be thought they would be so mad or Quixotical to attempt it.

13th. Under these restrictions the election of a President would be carried on with the greatest satisfaction to the public in general. The man *of the public* would then *certainly* be chosen and each voter having not at setting out attended to the man, but only to the necessary qualifications wanted, and convinced that each state had an equal right to vote as it pleased, would no doubt cheerfully acquiesce and the cant names of federalist, anti-federalist, aristocrat, democrat, jacobin, *etc., etc.,* be heard of no more. Who can think without rapture and extacy of such a political happiness as this, and you may early make it your own, my friends. It is far from being European, for by every plain and practical compliance with our constitution, on our parts, there is no doubt of its being accomplished.

For our encouragement, we might then with some probability hope that the United States of America would be able to shew after ages Not Only that they had given birth to a Washington, a great statesman, and as good and honest a man as ever was at the head of any rising people; but that Also, all the United States themselves, taken together might be produced as an example of at least one great nation having *at last* existed in the world (*raisima avis* indeed) altogether at unity with itself, knowing and feeling when it was *politically* well, and not giddily aiming at more than became a mortal situation, but contented with a comfortable constitution and stopping in time, without striking their real comforts, in pursuit of a chimerical, unattainable political perfection.

The Poets' rule;

"To make each day a critic on the last" is a very good one and very suitable to an individual, but it will by no means apply to a great nation in possession of a peaceable and comfortable, though not a *perfect* constitution, whose defects may be seen and *theoretically* wished to be amended, but it may be often too dangerous and very [rash?] *practically* to attempt it, and I confess my opinion, that the alterations already made in our's, might have been let alone, and you cannot, my friends, be too much on your guard in this respect. We have a very good constitution with as few defects as any; let us be content with it and listen no more to your bettering mongers. The boasted constitution of Great Britain, with ten times more faults than our's and some of them so gross and unequal, as cannot be seen; yet still being thought a very comfortable one upon the whole, and the risk and danger of throwing all into confusion, by attempting to amend it, seems to be the grand parliamentry reason why Mr. Fox and his adherents have never been able to succeed in their long attempted bettering views.

Hitherto we have endeavoured to confine ourselves to the choice of a President to *abstract qualifications and abilities* for our own national political purposes *with as little attention as possible to the per-*

son possessing them but when we have actually called out these abilities into our service and they have answered the end wished for upon a trial of four years, then gratitude requires we should make some return to the possessor; we cannot make that return *abstractedly* therefore must do it, or not at all, [in propria person?] and thank him for his services, and how can these thanks be *unequivocally* given in a political way but by electing him a second time. The first time we were clouded with uncertainty, prudence directing us to make the best inquiry we could about certain necessary abilities and qualifications we stood in need of, before we could justifiably fix on the man, but after having had the value looked for and have actually received the use and advantage of those abilities to our satisfaction, 'tis but fair here to think of the person (very rightly and properly kept out of sight before) to make him some compensation personally, we do not *now* act in the dark as then; in choosing him the *second time,* we may with confidence join Now person *and abilities together,* sure in a manner that both will be employed to our benefit. These thoughts oblige me to declare my wishes that Mr. Adams may carry the election now pending, more on account of the public interest and honour, than for his own sake, for nothwithstanding all the idle nonsense and abuse of Mr. Jefferson, in the papers, which every man of feeling must be disgusted at, yet was Mr. Jefferson in Mr. Adams' situation, I should certainly be sorry to see him over looked at a *second Election.* The Constitution is the grand concern of all and for the greater part of the citizen of any state that can be named, [who] I am persuaded feel too well the *political* happiness they enjoy under it to risk a change, but a few restless individuals imposing on the ignorant and unguarded, whose habits of idleness, fickleness and total disinclination to any steady useful business, or to any employment whatever but of their mischievous tongues, often ridicule themselves to disagreeable situations; your ambitious and disappointed men also whose extraordinary merits no person but themselves is quick sighted enough to discover; and such as have involved and perhaps ruined themselves by gaming and extravagance, and other speculations; these and such like men are the common disturbers of the peace in all our states; nay, we may go further, and in all countries whatever; such as these our industrious quiet citizens cannot be too much aware of— but above all, my friends, don't let your gents escape your notice, by far *the most mischievous of all,* your Pseudo Orators, among whom where you find one Cicero, one true lover of his country as he was, you will find twenty at least that care not what confusion they throw things into, provided they can bring about their own ambitious selfish purposes. In the course of a long life, and of much public business, many such *respectable personages* have, I met with, and have

299

often heard them talk charmingly like angels who but thought of virtue, honor and true public spirit, when from the general tenor of their actions, whoever had the misfortune to have anything to do with them was to be pitied, *and the public,* as far as what lay with themselves for years and years together was left to support itself, against such as these, some of them not difficult to be detected, we cannot be too much on our guard.

The art of oratory with fire and water are good servants, but terrible masters. These, we can not do without, but that, thank God, we may, and perhaps would be better without than with it. Among some of the discerning, far-looking nations of antiquity, this enchanting sorceress did not make so pretty a figure, and was far from being so idolized with us; its *too generally* poisonous tendency and prostitution of its talents were so well known, as to incline them to wish rather for its room than company. Our common father, General Washington has strongly recommended a national university,[2] and one properly conducted would certainly be of great use, particularly in making us better acquainted with each other throughout the Union. No citizen wishes or has longer wished for one more than myself, and 'tis to be hoped we shall not be long without one. The growing resources of the United States, put it in their power to have a university equal in all respects to any in Europe—but, whenever this happens, the rhetorical professors in particular can not be too attentive to the weight of their charge. Eloquence confessedly is a powerful weapon in the hands of a truly virtuous man, but in those of the unprincipled slippery wretch, what mischief has it not actually done in the world! — The proportion, or rather disproportion, between the number of steady, virtuous, persevering lovers of truth and their country, and the unfeeling abandoned sycophants who gave these cardinal virtues a place no where but on their tongues, who can tell is it one to ten? Or alas! one to——? This, though a melancholy consideration, ought not to be forgotten by such as wish to make a proper estimation, of that fascinating accomplishment called eloquence.

Now my candid reader, (the writer of this paper, all who know him know that he is no party man) thus purely lays before you his sincere thoughts at this crisis, on a most important *common* concern to the whole union. He wishes to draw out yours, and those of many others on this same subject, the more the better, that it may be fully canvassed, according to its great importance acknowledged by all.

---

[2] In Washington's "First Annual Message to Congress," John C. Fitzpatrick, ed. *The Writings of George Washington,* (Washington: Government Printing Office, 1939), XXX, 493-4.

Vive, vale, Si quid rectius istis,
Candidus imperti: si nil his utre mecum

[Live long, farewell. If you know something better than these precepts, pass it on, my good fellow. If not join me in following these.]

P.S. The writer wishes to refer his reader to a piece published under the same signature (his name not desired to be concealed) in both Charleston papers, the middle of last month dated 12th June, but should have been 12th July.

N.B. Reading this paper always first.

Charleston August 26, 1800

For the State Gazette
October 8, 1800

Gadsden continues in the same vein as the previous essay. He thanks the mechanics for their "firm and steady" support in the trying days of the revolution and now asks their votes for Adams. To those who have proposed his candidacy for the Assembly, he pleads his inability to serve because of advanced age.

[October 8, 1800][1]

Mr. Timothy:

In the City Gazette of the 2d instant I am proposed as a representative for Charleston, in the next assembly by A.B. I should have tho't it a compliment had a proportional part of our mechanic citizens been joined therein, but not a single one being inserted, gives it rather the appearance of an electioneering manoeuvre to hold the persons inserted in A.B.'s list in an invidious light to that useful body of citizens, whose work, no man, perhaps, in the city is better ac-

---

[1] *South Carolina Gazette and Timothy's Daily Advertiser,* October 8, 1800. A.B. was possibly Aednus Burke, the Jeffersonian Democrat. He excluded the mechanics because they were Federalist and drew out Gadsden's statement in favor of Adams, not Jefferson. Wolfe, *op. cit.,* pp. 144-5, 169.

quainted with than myself. From the first of, and throughout the revolution, none have shewn themselves more firm and steady in the most dangerous and trying occasions, in short, had it not been for their assistance, we should have made a very poor figure indeed; many of these worthy men are gone, but still, thank God, there are some of them left in health and strength, who will not I am sure, be wanting to their country, if called upon at this critical moment. Observing also, my name mentioned in other lists where I am sure only the kind attentions of my fellow citizens must have been the cause. These, I trust, will believe me when I declare to them how extremely distressed I am that it is not in my power to serve them on this occasion. My age, now almost 77, and the long and fatigueing journey to Columbia, to a man that has not been five miles from Charleston for near ten years, I should not regard, if when there I could be of service. The same infirmity that prevented me from accepting the honour offered me at Jacksonborough in 1782, which I had begun to feel about two years before, having encreased upon me ever since, I dare not speak in public for in an instant I am lost, forgetting entirely what I have said or intended to say, and am obliged to sit down immediately. I am so fully persuaded that the honour and interest of the union is so much concerned in the re-election of Mr. Adams, that were I as sure I could, as an individual be of any essential service to bring that about, provided I lived to see the business done, I should be very happy and resigned whether I returned alive from Columbia or no. The respect I owe my fellow citizens of Charleston, having thus again necessarily drawn me into print, let me entreat them to bear with my adding a few hints, that in my opinion are of the greatest moment to the union at large.

I confess I am most anxious for Mr. Adams election, for I cannot bring myself to think that our directors will so much forget their own state as not to choose one of their own citizens, and what citizen has done more honour to the state, whose established good character, firmness and abilities, as well as whose long and important services are more conspicuous than General Pinckney? Let us run no risks my friends, whether Mr. Adams had three thousand votes, or only three more than Mr. Jefferson is nothing to the purpose, he has served us faithfully one four years and (as I have more fully said in another place) he at least deserves our thanks, which cannot be unequivocally given but by a second election. Which among you [illeg.] in your private affairs, having experienced the faithful and prudent services of an overseer over your whole estate, for four years, would discharge him for another man but had never served in that character, merely for the *sake of a change,* or for a general recommendation of his great knowledge and experience in another way?

The important use of a second election with regard to our President I have never yet seen fully discussed. On the one hand, if given to the deserving it will spur their successors to be so. On the other, it is a rod not to be parted with, but kept to make bad Presidents feel your power, by dismissing them with contempt when their time is out, and shew them, *by not electing them a second time,* that you are glad to have got rid of them. But a generous public *above picking holes* will use these powers discreetly, not expecting [a] more perfect president any more than a perfect constitution; it is an arduous trust, full of severe trials, and whoever may be Mr. Adams successor, numbers I believe, would gladly compound that he should gladly discharge his duty equally as well as Mr. Adams has. 'Tis lessening this great and almost only check we have upon a President, in fact, reducing it to none at all, causing no distinction between the good and the bad when it is improperly and capriciously used, as seems to be the mention of many at present. The arbitrariness, the *sic Volo sic Jubeo* [so I want, so I order] lie with the tyrannical imperious people who wish to act in this manner.

All the disagreeable events and notorious insolent inferences of our pretended foreign friends, that we had to struggle with at the last presidential election, seem to be forgotten, and a repetition of the like, or worse, it is much to be dreaded, will happen soon again, and be continued until it end in the ruin of our union, unless each state will emancipate itself from the alarming dictates of two or three of their sister states. We must get through now in the best manner we can; 'tis perhaps too late to make the alteration wished for, but by all means beware of *the third issue,* you have four years before you, think in time my friends. Of what consideration can two or three, or twenty men be of, pick them as you please, when set against the peace, harmony and safety of the millions the union contains. Besides, we want two of these millions capacitated as president; a very insignificant paltry nation indeed, must we be, if we have not instead of the two *only wanted,* five hundred at least to choose *these two* out of, and four years hence the greatest probability is, for the numbers encreasing than otherwise. Surely the states will not suffer any of their haughty sisters to domineer or dictate any longer, and set the whole union in a blaze, from one end to the other, as they have done now the *second time.* But let each state dare to think for itself, and permit no other to interfere with them in the least in their presidential elections, in the choice of *the two only wanted:* but should, notwithstanding such a wholesome union-saving resolution, any attempts be still made, even under the pretended *soft* name of a recommendation, look upon it as an insidious manoeuvre, and leave the persons named, be they whom they may, entirely out of your votes. Such a pointed neglect would effectually cure this terrible, growing evil, and restore peace, harmony and good neighbourhood amongst us; besides, adding insuperable difficulties to the never failing foreign intermeddling upon such occasions. Be assured by friends, unless some such step is taken, 'tis impossible the union can much longer exist. But our Government must prove *an abortion,* or smothered in its earliest infancy, will afford to anti-republicans and future historians the strongest example ever heard of, of the instability and very short duration of such kind of government. Never was or could be a fairer trial than ours, *every step* in its formation taken in the most deliberate manner by the people, if such a republic should be self-destroyed (the only way such governments ever have been destroyed) and the few trustless desperados, disgraced, joined to an ambitious, artful, indefatigable Cataline amongst us, should they succeed in their designs, which God forbid, then adieu (in all probability) to any attempt for such governments in future.

Our turbulent and foreign emissaries seem to depend on our new comers [the Irish] to help to carry on their schemes, sparing no pains to alarm them with groundless apprehensions of dangers to their liberties, giving into their national prejudices, and imposing on their ignorance before they have time to look about them, and be thoroughly acquainted with the happy country they have got into; some worthy discerning men amongst them, see and despise the artful and laboured attempts to deceive them, I wish there may be a sufficient number to repel their insidious designs, before both new and old inhabitants are involved in irretrievable ruin.

A pamphlet entitled, "The Philanthropist, or political love powder for *honest* Adamsites and Jeffersonians," [2] dedicated to General Washington, and strongly recommended by him not four months before we lost him, fell accidently into my hands about three weeks since, which, the instant after I read it, hoping that it might tend to put us into better humour with one another, I sent to Mr. Young,

---

[2] The pamphlet is Mason Locke Weems, *A Good Twelve Cents Worth or Political Love Powder* (Charleston: W.P. Young, 1800). Gadsden commissioned W.P. Young to reprint it. In 1799, the essay had been published in several states including Virginia. In content, the essay was Federalist, generally debunking the equality clause of the Declaration of Independence, pointing out that there was a natural inequality in men and things, and applying this socially and politically. Men, it asserted, attained equality only by serving and remaining in their stations in life. Weems even used the ancient quote as maxim in that election year: "Honor *all* men—Love the *brotherhood*—Fear God —Honor the King!", pp. 1-27.

and is now published. If it would not be too persumptious, after Gen. Washington's recommendation, to add mine, I would take the liberty to do so to my fellow citizens.

To conclude, I court no man, nor wish to offend any of my worthy *well meaning* fellow citizens, or any true lover of the constitution and union, Adamsite of Jeffersonian by any thing said here, and should any person think proper to make any stricture on what is mentioned in this paper, not the least notice, unless he signs his name, will be taken of it by

Christopher Gadsden

Charleston, 6th Oct. 1800

To John Adams

Charleston, 11 March, 1801 [1]

My Dear Sir:

For five or six years past, at least, very rarely have I been seen from home, (or wished to be,) excepting at church or funerals; but my duty to my country and to our old standbys, though now in my seventy-eighth [year], compelled me in our late election to take up my feeble pen again, at least to show my good will and inclination; and though many able hands were not wanting, yet sorry am I to say, all our efforts failed.

Many well-earned honors have the United States conferred on you. Had they added one more, a second invitation to the Presidency, it would have been not only what your long, faithful, important, and useful services might have reasonably expected, as a public acknowledgment and concurrence with all the world in your able and successful discharge of your first appointment, and of all your many other important trusts, but also what, in my humble opinion, sound policy seemed to dictate. God grant that the recollection of your ungrateful treatment may not deter truly firm, virtuous men from venturing their names to be held up to the public on such elections! I am not without my suspicions, that foreign meddlers must have had this deep political slyness in view.

---

[1] Massachusetts Historical Society. Adams, *Works,* IX, 578-80.

Many of our new-comers cajoled and imposed upon by emissaries from without, and egged on by a numerous or rather innumerable tribe of young law-followers amongst ourselves, especially in the circuits, have brought on a strange reversement in our State. Our oldstanders and independent men of long well-tried patriotism, sound understanding, and good property, have now in general very little influence in our public matters. Our too easy admittance of strangers has entangled us in this evil, and when or where it will end, God only knows!

But here, my dear Sir, I must confess my own credulity and short-sightedness, who was amongst the most zealous in that overhasty and not sufficiently guarded step, which we now have great reason to lament as big with innumerable mischiefs. Our worthy deceased friend John Rutledge, looking farther, was for giving them every reasonable protection and encouragement, but for admitting only their sons born amongst us into such complete citizenship as to vote either at State or Congress elections; and when unsuccessful in this point, was then for extending the time to ten years at least. Had even this been carried, it would have given new-comers full time to look so deliberately about them, as greatly to have deterred and hindered all designing tamperers and deceivers in most of their infernal views and mischievous suggestions; and much better, in all probability, would this have been for the peace, safety, and lasting political security of both.

You must have heard of and admired the open, honorable behavior of General Pinckney in our State election; that he would listen to no proposals of composition whatever, but persisted, from first to last, to stand or fall with you. I know you cannot want any consolation in this matter beyond your own breast. The firm, well-grounded complacency there, is, I am sure, amply sufficient to dispense with any thing exterior.

Long have I been led to think our planet a mere bedlam, and the uncommonly extravagant ravings of our own times, especially for a few years past, and still in the highest rant, have greatly increased and confirmed that opinion. Look round our whirling globe, my friend where you will, east, west, north, or south, where is the spot in which are not many thousands of these mad lunatics? But not a few strong symptoms seem now loudly to proclaim that this terrible, catching epidemic cannot be far from its crisis; and when arrived there, our all knowing, unerring Physician, always mercifully producing good from evil, and setting to rights the mad, destructive freaks of mortals, will, it is to be hoped, in the present forlorn distresses interfere, and give such a favorable turn to the crisis, as to make this bedlam-commitment end in the cure of all its miserable captives. More and more happy, I bless God, do I every day feel myself to find that my passage over this life's Atlantic is almost gained, having been in soundings for some time, not far from my wished-for port, waiting only for a favorable breeze from our kind Savior to waft me to that pleasing and expected land for which I cheerfully and humbly hope.

Since our country will have it so, that Mr. Jefferson may discharge his four years' duty with as much faithfulness and steadiness as you have done, and as much to the public benefit; that in so doing he may have the constitutional assistance and countenance of every citizen of the Union; and that his public actions may be judged of with candor and generosity, without any captious hole-picking; and above all, that every tendency to our reharmonizing and keeping so may be cordially embraced and zealously forwarded by all ranks, and happily effected, is the constant, sincere, and heartfelt prayer of him who is with great respect and affection, dear Sir, Your most obedient, & c.

C. G.

To George Simpson

George Simpson (1759-1822) of Philadelphia was cashier of the Bank of the United States (1795-1812). Later he helped to organize Stephen Girard's bank. Although not strictly a policy-maker in the first bank, Simpson, nevertheless, gave executive continuity to the organization. His decisions and reputation among world bankers greatly influenced early American banking practices. James Wattereau, "New Light on the First Bank of the United States," Penn. Mag. Hist. and Biog., LXI (1937), 261-85. John T. Holdsworth, The First Bank of the United States (Washington: Government Printing Office, 1910), p. 103. Kenneth L. Brown, "Stephen Girard's Bank," Penn. Mag. Hist. and Biog., LXVI (1942), 29-55. Henry Simpson, Lives of Eminent Philadelphians (Philadelphia: W. Brotherhood, 1859), pp. 890-93.

Charleston May 4th 1801 [1]

Sir:

We take this liberty of inclosing you Crocker and Heckborn['s] first bill of this date in your favor, on John Welsh for One Thousand Dollars at 30 days sight which when paid you will be so obliging as to forward to the credit of Col. Lewis Morris in the Bank of the United States, and to be held subject to the order of John Rutherford Esq., Trenton New Jersey. We are Respectfully Your most Obd. Sevt.

CHRISTR. GADSDEN & CO.

To John Adams

Charleston 24th June, 1801 [1]

My dear Sir:

Your highly esteemed Favour of the 16th April made me happy to find my Letter of the 11th March was taken so kindly. This moment hearing of the Departure of my Friend Mr. William Crafts our late Navy Agent, I wou'd not any longer omit the acknowledgement of yours. He is a gentleman of Boston [,] has resided here many years, has a family and lately lost his Wife. He can let you know all about us here, as well as any gentleman I am acquainted with.

I am endeavouring to be resign'd with Regard to Politics and 'tis Time I shou'd. But one Misgiving haunts me much. Heaven forbid that a Casar and Brutus ambitiously aiming at the same point, to take advantage of the loose philosophic Principles of the Times, and the Natural Confusions they may occasion, shou'd arise and *both* seize on such a critical Moment perhaps all along promoted and forwarded by themselves, and shake to the foundation all our promising Hopes and Expectations, of seeing the Blessings, we with the

---

[1] HSP.

[2] "Crocker and Heckburn" was a merchant partnership of Charleston. Crocker had been in business with a Mr. Sturgis in 1790, but Heckburn apparently was a newcomer, as he can not be found listed in business in any of the early directories of Charleston. *Directory of 1790.*

[1] Massachusetts Historical Society. Microfilm in the Library of Congress.

favor of the Almighty, have so dearly earn'd, to our latest Posterity. I am wth. Sincerest Esteem My. dear Sir Yr. most obedt. hble Servt.

CHRIST GADSDEN

To Le Roy, Bayard and McEvers

Charleston, October 23, 1801 [1]

Gentlemen:

We have the pleasure to acknowledge receipt of your favor of 22d Ultimo, and are thankful for your attention in forwarding the Several Articles to Rhode Island for Mr. Middleton.[2] We must beg your attention to the small box for Mrs. Middleton upon the return of the vessel we sent it by, which we beg you will forward to us here should Mr. Middleton and Family have left New York before you receive it.

Several letters for young Mr. Gadsden having been forwarded to him, which will not probably arrive before his sailing, we beg in that case you would have the goodness to send to the Post Office and take them up, and forward them to us by the first water conveyance. We understand some letters were forwarded to the care of Col. Barclay, which we will thank you to inquire of that Gentleman about the request he would deliver them to you to be returned.

We are with Great Respect and Esteem Yr. Most Obt. Servts.

CHRISTR. GADSDEN & Co.

---

[1] Morristown Museum.

[2] He was Henry Middleton (1770-1846), a member of Congress, a United States Senator, Governor of South Carolina, and Minister to Russia during his political career. He was a leader of the lively society of Newport, Rhode Island, and married Mary Helen Hering of Bath, England, in 1794. "Middleton of South Carolina," *SCHM*, I (July, 1900), 245-7.

Charleston January 7th, 1802 [1]

Gentlemen:

We have the pleasure to acknowledge receipt of your favour of 4th Ultimum and to thank you for the trouble you have taken in inquiring for letters for our relation[s] on board the Boston Frigate.

The Lady of Mr. Middleton was a Miss Hering of Bath, or near that City and we regret with you, that your Mr. McEvers had not an opportunity of seeing them when they passed through your Place, as we are persuaded he would have been highly gratified with the pleasing manner of that Lady.

It will always afford us pleasure to render you any services in this Place. With great respect I am your Most Obt. Servt.

CHRIST GADSDEN & Co.

To George Simpson

Charleston, October 19th 1803 [1]

Sir:

We take the liberty to enclose you Captain Sweetser's Bill of Loading for one Thousand Dollars, shipped on account on Col. Lewis Morris [2] (at present at Morrisania in the State of New York) which we request you will have the goodness to receive, and to place to his credit in the Bank of the United States, giving him advice of the same. We are with great Respect your Most Obt. Hble. Servts.

CHRISTR. GADSDEN & Co.

---

[1] South Caroliniana Library. Added to the text of the letter was the following: "Rice 14/1/per hundredweight/: Cotton Sea Island 2/c 2/1: Most Staples and so on 22. cents = Pound."

[1] SCHS. The date line of the letter is inscribed "arr [*arrival*] 1 November."

[2] Colonel Lewis Morris was a member of an influential New York family. He came to South Carolina with General Greene's army, and met and married Miss Ann Elliott. He remained to become one of the State's powerful Federalist party leaders after voting for the Constitution in 1788. Rogers, *op. cit.,* pp. 141-2, 155; Elliott's, *Debates,* IV, 339; "Letters from Col. Lewis Morris to Miss Ann Elliott." *SCHM,* XL (October 1939), 122-36.

Will of Christopher Gadsden

June 5, 1804

Christopher Gadsden, from his Writings, accepted philosophically in his late years the fact that his earthly tenure was soon coming to an end. Following his own advice that wills were important, in mid-1804 he drew up the document which was probated a little over a year later.

14TSNO14.[1]

I Christopher Gadsden Citizen of Charleston in the State of South Carolina, now in the 81st Year of my Age, and blessed be God of sound mind, do make and ordain this as my last Will and Testament, revoking and disannulling every other last Will and Testament heretofore made. My Soul with humble submission and confidence in the merits of my blessed Saviour Jesus Christ, I hope in the last trying moment to resign with chearfulness, to that Almighty and Merciful being who gave it. My body I desire may be put into a plain unornamented Coffin and interred in a frugal manner without any plate upon it, excepting of my Age and when it is removed from the place that is to know it no more, let it be conveyed to St Philips Western Church Yard, to the burial place of my parents, and the Earth be leveled over it immediately. My plantation on Black River with my Negroes thereon, my lot in George Town, my lands on Peters Creek and at the Cheraws, may be sold to pay my just debts; these I am persuaded will be full sufficient for that purpose. And to give as follows, to the two Grand Children of my last worthy friend George Gabriel Powell Esquire deceased, vizt to Mrs. Mitchell widow of the late Mr. Mitchell of St John's Parish deceased, and to Powell McCrae Son of Mr. McCrae, six hundred pounds sterling each, annually without interest, till the whole is paid. **Item** all my lands, houses, wharfes and stores in Charleston, or any of them, I wou'd not have disposed of by any means, nor divided in any manner till full seven years after my decease, but kept entirely together during that period, but when that time is fully elaps'd and gone, then I direct

---

[1] Charleston County Court House, Probate Court. Transcript in "Will Book, 1800-1807," Book D, p. 594 ff., S.C.A.D.

my Executors hereafter mentioned to divide My Estate real and personal as well my Negroes as otherwise into nineteen equal parts or shares, being the exact number of Grand Children I now have, giving to my daughter Mary Morris six shares, to my daughter in law Catharine Gadsden nine shares, and to my late Son Thomas Gadsden's Children four shares, N.B. to the two former this is given in trust.

The nett income arising from my whole Estate real and personal, till the seven years before mentioned is expired, and the division takes place, I direct may be annually divided into three parts and the nett amount of one third part over to Martha Gadsden my late Son Thomas's Widow, for the use of herself children and family. **Item** the nett amount of another third part to be paid over to my daughter Mary Morris in trust for the use of her family, but totally at her own disposal, in no manner subject to any interference of her husband, and whose receipt the Executors are only to take for the same. **Item,** the remaining third part to be paid over to my worthy daughter in law Catharine Gadsden the Wife of my Son Philip in trust for the use of her family, but totally at her own disposal, in no manner subject to any interference of her husband, whose receipt the Executors are only to take for the same. **Item** in like manner and under the same restrictions I give to my daughter Mary Morris and to my daughter in law Catharine Gadsden in trust all my Town Negroes, male and female, to be divided when the before mentioned division is made, by lot among my Grand Children, excepting my faithful Servants Nanny and George. Nanny I then give to my daughter Mary Morris, and George to my daughter in law Catharine Gadsden. Again at the expiration of the seven years already mentioned, I then direct my real and personal Estate, remaining after my just debts are paid, to be divided into nineteen equal parts in the manner herein expressed, and after such division is made, the four parts that fall to my late Son Thomas's Children to be divided among them equally, and in case of death or deaths where children are left, the children to inherit their parents share accordingly and duly. **Item** I give to my Son Thomas's Widow, Martha Gadsden, to my daughter Mary Morris, and to my daughter in law Catharine Gadsden two hundred and fifty pounds sterling each pr. ann. to commence after the aforesaid division is made and the seven years expired, and not before, and to continue during each of their lives no longer. Whatever monies may be advanced by me for my Son Philip and actually accounted for by me (for I am largely accountable for him) antecedent to my decease, I remit to him and will not have him called upon for, being convinced and satisfied that he has acted in the management of his late Brother Thomas's Estate, with all brotherly affection and with the greatest integrity and superlative generosity, meriting every degree of gratitude from his Brothers Widow and Children. **Item** four of the five lots that have fallen to me from Mr. John Wraggs marked D and painted blue in the Wraggs borough plan being the four the most Westward, after the expiration of fifteen years I give to my Wife Ann Gadsden and to her heirs for ever, to dispose of after that time, to any of the relations of the said John Wragg as she may think proper reserving to my Estate the most Easterly lot marked also D bounding to the Southward on Chappel Street together with all the Marsh annexed to said lot and fronting it on both Sides of a Creek, adjoining it. **Item** I also give to my said Wife four hundred pounds sterling to be paid her in quarterly payments of one hundred pound sterling pr. quarter during her natural life and no longer, these two gifts are given as full and compleat satisfaction for her dowry and all claims and demands for and concerning all the Bonds particulariz'd in a Marriage settlement a little antecedent to our Marriage in April 1776, she well knowing that any and every part of those bonds received by me was in extreme low depreciated money, and that one of those bonds of considerable amount is now on hand not worth a farthing. **Item** I give to my said Wife during her natural life and no longer, the use of the house and land whereon we now live, butting and bounding to the Westward on Front Street about one hundred and seventy feet, to the Southward on Washington Street two hundred feet to the Northward on other lands of my Estate two hundred feet, and to the Eastward on Water Street about one hundred and seventy feet, but on the decease of my said Wife, the said house and land to return immediately to my Estate and to the care and charge of my Executors herein after mentioned as part thereof.

Item I give to my said Wife the use of my Negroes Molly and Charlotte and Charlottes two daughters and my Negro Joe during her natural life and no longer. **Item** I give to my said Wife all my house furniture and liquors, my cows, my grey horse and chair. **Item** I give to my dear and kind Brother James Gadsden of London Fifty pounds sterling which I hope he will accept to lay out in some Memorandum of his Affectionate Brother. **Item** I also give to my three Nephews James William Gadsden, Thomas Gadsden and James Hasell a handsome ring which I wish their Acceptance of. **Item** all my books and pamphlets in Hebrew, Greek and Latin I give to be divided among my Grand Sons Christopher Edwards [,] John and James Gadsden, together with the proper books of Grammer etc., appertaining thereto. **Item** all my English books I give to my Grand Sons Christopher, Thomas and James Morris. **Item** I gvie to Mrs. Ferguson her note of hand dated 1st August 1798 for five hundred pounds sterling. I conjure my children not to forget the faithful services of the descendents of old Nanny and Elsy, Nanny's Offspring to the fifth generation are now with me, having never parted with one, Ned the Son of old Betty is a faithful Servant and deserves regard, so does old helpless Strephon. I leave my Son in Law Thomas Morris, and my Son Philip Gadsden, Mr. William Drayton and my Grand Son Christopher Gadsden Junior true and lawful Executors to this my last Will and Testament, as also my Grand Sons Christopher Edwards Gadsden and Christopher Gadsden Morris when they shall attain the Age of twenty one years. In witness to this my last Will and Testament I hereunto set my hand and seal this 5th day of June in the Year of our Lord one thousand eight hundred and four, and in the twenty eighth Year of the Independence of the United States.

CHRISTOPHER GADSDEN (L.S.)

Signed, Sealed, published and declared by Christopher Gadsden the above mentioned Testator as and for his last Will and Testament in the presence of us, who at his request and in his presence, and in the presence of each other have subscribed our Names as Witnesses thereto, this fifth day of June 1804.

William Hall — Frederick Hall — Joseph Pritchard Proved before Charles Lining Esquire O.C.T.D. September 18, 1805. At same time qualified Thomas Morris, Philip Gadsden and William Drayton Executors. June 17, 1807 Qualified Christopher Gadsden Executor.

Examined
1746 Co. Sh. } *C.L.*

Appendix

Notes on the Illustrations

PAGE DATED AUGUST 23, 1764, IN THE JOURNAL OF THE SOUTH CAROLINA COMMONS HOUSE OF ASSEMBLY *(endpapers)*.

Judging from the aggressive and provocative nature of the committee's reply, the Answer to Council appears to have been written by Christopher Gadsden who was named among those to act in rebuttal. Others were the Messrs. Thomas Bee, Gabriel Manigault, John Rutledge and William Henry Drayton.

The Answer refutes the right of Council to amend the Tax Bill to add £7,000 currency, or two years' salary, for the unpopular chief executive, Thomas Boone, whom the Commons had petitioned for removal. Boone had returned home May 14, 1764, virtually driven from office in South Carolina; and Lieutenant Governor William Bull had summoned the Assembly to meet as the summer was nearing its end.

Council's attempt to amend the Money Bill was responsible for the message issuing from the Committee which stated: "The Sum Annually inserted in the Schedule for the Governor, is not a Salary—but a Gratuity from the People; which it would be stupid in them to bestow upon a Governor, who has endeavoured to deprive them, of what ought to be valued by every Englishman [their rights], more than even life itself."

CHRISTOPHER GADSDEN AS A YOUNG MAN *(frontispiece)*.

Controversy over this portrait has arisen. From the collection of George D. Shore, Sumter, South Carolina, the painting of Gadsden is attributed to Sir Joshua Reynolds, and in the opinion of art experts in the South, it can be none other than a Reynolds' portrait. The Frick Art Reference Library of New York lists the portrait among the works of Jeremiah Theus, colonial artist of Charles Town;[1] Margaret Middleton, author of *Jeremiah Theus, Colonial Artist of Charles Town,* disputes the attribution.

[1] Letter to editor, July 27, 1966, from Mrs. Henry W. Howell, Jr., who stated: "Mr. Lawrence Park and Mr. William Sawitzky, both authorities in the field of colonial portraiture, considered the portrait [Gadsden] to be the work of Jeremiah Theus." But Mrs. Middleton, author of *Jeremiah Theus,* (Columbia: University of South Carolina Press, 1953), p. 132, states: "The compiler has seen only a photograph of this portrait of the Revolutionary patriot and regrets that she has been unable to locate the original. The photograph is used as one of several photographs making up the frontispiece of John J. Dargan's *History of South Carolina* [*School History of South Carolina.* Columbia: The State Company], published in 1906. Efforts to locate this portrait have not been successful. It is possible that it is a miniature."

315

ADVERTISEMENT FOR GADSDEN'S WHARF AT CHARLES TOWN *(facing page 4)* and GADSDEN'S "NOTICE" FOR BUSINESS AS A FACTOR *(facing page 36)*.

Christopher Gadsden, enterpreneur of the first magnitude, was an early sponsor of advertising. His wharf in Charleston, and his other business ventures, made him wealthy, and he brought notice of these in newspaper media, especially *The South-Carolina Gazette*.

DRAWING OF GADSDEN'S WHARF *(page 90)*.

On April 19, 1758, John Rattray sold to Christopher Gadsden a portion of land lying north of Laurens Street, south of Calhoun and east of Anson. Gadsden's energy and enterprise caused the marsh to be filled, and six wharf lots devolved, adding a large area to Charles Town. Christopher Gadsden's wharf, said to be the largest in America, occupied a conspicuous spot. From it the British embarked in 1782.[2] This drawing was made by Vernon Bailey Howe in 1906 for Ravenel's *Charleston: The Place and the People*, p. 333. Possibly Bailey did it from remains of the old wharf still existing after more than a century; today the wharf no longer exists.

DRAWING OF GADSDEN'S FLAG *(page 110)*.

When John Paul Jones hoisted a flag over the *Alfred* for Eseck Hopkins, first commander-in-chief, the American Navy was born.[3] The flag was not the Stars and Stripes, but a curious banner of yellow silk bearing a coiled rattle-snake and the words: Don't Tread on Me! Christopher Gadsden, Charles Town, South Carolina, delegate to the Continental Congress, was a member of the Committee on Naval Affairs, and had helped formulate the American Navy. Shortly after the colonies had unfurled their banner, Gadsden in February 1775 had presented such a standard to Congress, which had tendered its appreciation. Newspaper accounts of the period indicated that there was some contemplation of the adoption of the flag as the colors of the American Navy. An English writer of the period noted: "A strange flag lately appeared in our seas bearing a pine tree with the portraiture of a rattlesnake coiled up at its root, with the daring words 'Don't tread on me.' We learned that the vessels bearing the yellow flag had a sort of commission from a society of people in Philadelphia calling themselves the Continental Congress."[4]

When Gadsden returned to South Carolina from Philadelphia, he brought with him "an elegant standard such as to be used by the Commander-in-chief of the American Navy [,] being a yellow field, with a lively representation of a rattlesnake in the middle, in the attitude of going to strike, and these words underneath, Don't Tread on Me!" Upon Gadsden's presentation of the standard to the South Carolina Provincial Congress, it was ordered that it be carefully preserved, and suspended in the Congress room.[5]

The South Carolina Navy later adopted for its use a red and blue striped flag, emblazoned with a rattlesnake and the words "Don't Tread on Me!" However, the Grand Union flag later supplanted all other standards, and on June 14, 1777, [later to become American Flag Day], this statement was entered in the Journals of Congress:

---

[2] De Koven, *The Life and Letters of John Paul Jones,* Vol. I, 91. See also, pp. 81, 85.
[3] Ibid., p. 91, 1n.
[4] Hemphill and Wates, *Extracts from the Journals of the Provincial Congresses of South Carolina, 1775-1776,* p. 183.
[5] *Life and Letters of John Paul Jones,* pp. 206-7.

Resolved, That the flag of the United States be thirteen stripes, alternate red and white; that the union be thirteen stars, white in a blue field, representing a new constellation.[6]

TITLE PAGE OF GADSDEN'S COPY OF THE *JOURNAL* OF THE CONTINENTAL CONGRESS *(facing page 132).*

Interleaved *Journal* of Christopher Gadsden sheds further light on the proceedings of the Continental Congress, information not found in modern editions of the *Journals.*

PAGE OF GADSDEN'S SHORTHAND *(facing page 164).*

Christopher Gadsden's cryptic shorthand was a variation of the Weston System, employed by seventeenth and eighteenth-century writers. Gadsden made the system his "own," however, by omitting virtually all of the punctuation marks, except for paragraphs. Symbols were frequently distorted—especially if he were angry—when he made heavy brush-like strokes. The shorthand is found in the interleaved *Journal* of the Continental Congress, owned by the College of Charleston, Charleston, South Carolina. See *Manuscripts* (Spring 1964), pp. 17-24, for translations.

PLAT OF "MIDDLESEX," GADSDEN'S PROPERTY AT CHARLES TOWN *(facing page 228).*

A plat in the Charleston *Yearbook* of 1880 shows that Gadsden had laid out the Village of Middlesex on his land. How much this land had been increased is revealed in Purcell's plat of a later date. In addition to the six wharf lots, there were one hundred ninety-seven back lots, and the creek between Gadsden and Mazyckboro had been straightened, through digging a canal for the use of both properties, from Anson's landing on the creek to the river.[7]

CHRISTOPHER GADSDEN IN LATE LIFE *(facing page 260).*

Lines of character are etched into the face of Christopher Gadsden, who appears in this photograph as a man of old age. He gave everything he had to the making of America, not the least of these being his heart and his pen.

---

[6] Ravenel, *Charleston the Place and the People* (New York: Macmillan Company, 1906), p. 333.

[7] Smith, *The Dwelling Houses of Charleston, South Carolina* (Philadelphia: J. B. Lippincott Company), pp. 283-4.

Bibliography

1. Manuscript Materials

ADAMS, JOHN: Papers. Massachusetts Historical Society, Boston, Massachusetts. Microfilm transcripts in Library of Congress.

ADAMS, SAMUEL: Papers. New York Public Library, New York, New York.

BANCROFT, GEORGE: Transcripts, containing Francis Marion and Christopher Gadsden transcripts. New York Public Library, New York, New York.

BEE, THOMAS: Letters. Charleston Library Society, Charleston, South Carolina.

BURTON, ROBERT: Correspondence. Virginia Historical Society Richmond, Virginia.

CARNES, SAMUEL: Letter, October 12, 1780. South Carolinana Library, Columbia, South Carolina.

CAULKINS, FRANCIS: Manuscripts. New London County Historical Society, New London, Connecticut.

CHARLESTON WILLS: 1760-1805. Charleston County Court House, Charleston, South Carolina. Transcripts in South Carolina Archives Department, Columbia, South Carolina.

CONTINENTAL CONGRESS: Papers of; Record Group II. National Archives, Washington, District of Columbia.

DEARBORN, FREDERICK M.: Collection. Houghton Library, Harvard University, Cambridge, Massachusetts.

DUANE, JAMES: Papers. New York Historical Society, Albany, New York.

EMMETT, THOMAS ADDIS: Collection. New York Public Library, New York, New York.

FORD, GORDON LESTER: Collection. New York Public Library, New York, New York.

FRANKLIN, BENJAMIN: Papers. American Philosophical Society, Philadelphia, Pennsylvania.

GADSDEN, CHRISTOPHER: Letters. Historical Society of Pennsylvania, Philadelphia, Pennsylvania.

—————: Letter to Herman Le Roy and William Bayard, June 19, 1790. William L. Clements Library, University of Michigan, Ann Arbor, Michigan.

————————: Letters. National Historical Park, Morristown, New Jersey.

————————: Letter to Thomas Pinckney, April 17, 1792. Boston Public Library, Boston, Massachusetts.

————————: Letters, South Carolina Historical Society, Charleston, South Carolina.

————————: Letters. South Caroliniana Library, Columbia, South Carolina.

GERVAIS, JOHN LEWIS: Papers. South Carolina Historical Society, Charleston, South Carolina.

———————— and OWEN, ROBERT: Letterbook, 1783-1787. Library of Congress, Washington, District of Columbia.

GREENE, NATHANAEL: Papers. William L. Clements Library, University of Michigan, Ann Arbor, Michigan.

GRIMBALL, BERKELEY: "Commodore Gillon of South Carolina, 1741-1794." Unpublished Master's Thesis, 1951, Department of History, Duke University, Durham, North Carolina.

HOPKINS, ESECK: Correspondence. Rhode Island Historical Society, Providence, Rhode Island.

INDIAN BOOKS: Vol. VI, 1757-1760. South Carolina Archives Department, Columbia, South Carolina.

IZARD, RALPH: Papers. South Caroliniana Library, Columbia, South Carolina.

JEFFERSON, THOMAS: Papers. Library of Congress, Washington, District of Columbia.

JOURNALS: Commons House of Assembly, 1750-1775. South Carolina Archives, Columbia, South Carolina.

————————: Continental Congress, n.p., 1775, Gadsden Annotations. College of Charleston Library, Charleston, South Carolina.

————————: Council, 1754-1767. South Carolina Archives Department, Columbia, South Carolina.

————————: House of Representatives, 1783-1780. South Carolina Archives Department, Columbia, South Carolina.

————————: Senate, 1783-1800. South Carolina Archives Department, Columbia, South Carolina.

KENDALL, HENRY P.: Collection of Papers of Henry Laurens. South Caroliniana Library, Columbia, South Carolina.

LAURENS, HENRY: Papers. South Carolina Historical Society, Charleston, South Carolina.

LAWRENCE, MARTHA MORRIS: Collection, 1684-1759. Historical Society of Pennsylvania, Philadelphia, Pennsylvania.

LLOYD, JOHN: Letter to T. B. Smith, December 7, 1784. Charleston Library Society, Charleston, South Carolina.

LYTTLETON, WILLIAM HENRY: Papers. William L. Clements Library, University of Michigan, Ann Arbor, Michigan.

MANIGAULT, GABRIEL: Papers. South Caroliniana Library, Columbia, South Carolina.

MARION, FRANCIS: Correspondence. New York Public Library, New York, New York.

MORRIS, THOMAS: Letters. South Caroliniana Library, Columbia, South Carolina.

PAINE, THOMAS: *Common Sense,* n.p., n.d., Gadsden Annotations. College of Charleston Library, Charleston, South Carolina.

RECORDS, BRITISH: In British Public Records Office Relating to South Carolina, 1754-1767, Microfilm, South Carolina Archives Department, Columbia, South Carolina.

ROBERTS, CHARLES: Autograph Collection. Haverford College, Haverford, Pennsylvania.

ROOSEVELT, FRANKLIN D.: Collection. Roosevelt Library, Hyde Park, New York.

RUTLEDGE, JOHN: Letters. Library of Congress, Washington, District of Columbia.

SMYTH: ELLISON ADGER: Collection, of Miscellany, Presbyterian College, Clinton, South Carolina.

WARING, THOMAS: Papers. South Carolina Historical Society, Charleston, South Carolina.

WASHINGTON, GEORGE: Papers. Library of Congress, Washington, District of Columbia.

WILSON, ROBERT, JR.: "Christopher Gadsden: South Carolina's Revolutionary Leader." Unpublished Master's Thesis, 1958. Department of History, Princeton University, Princeton, New Jersey.

2. Newspapers

American Daily Advertiser (Philadelphia, Pennsylvania), 1795.

Annual Register (London, England), 1762.

City Gazette and Daily Advistiser (Charles Town, South Carolina,) 1793.

Gazette of the State of South Carolina (Charles Town, South Carolina), 1777-1780, 1783-1785.

South Carolina Gazette (Charles Town, South Carolina), 1732-1775.

South Carolina and American General Gazette (Charles Town, South Carolina), 1764, 1766-1772, 1774, 1776-1780.

South Carolina Gazette and General Advertiser (Charles Town, South Carolina), 1783-1784.

South Carolina Gazette and Country Journal (Charles Town, South Carolina), 1765-1775.

South Carolina Gazette and Timothy's Daily Advertiser (Charles Town, South Carolina), 1798-1800.

3. Articles and Documents in Periodicals

Bancroft, George. "Christopher Gadsden to William Samuel Johnson, April 16, 1766," *Historical Magazine,* V (September, 1861), 260-62.

Barnwell, Joseph W. and Jervey, Theodore D. (eds.) "The Correspondence of Charles Garth," *SCHM,* XXVIII (April, 1927), 79-88; (October, 1927), 226-35; XXIX (January, 1928), 41-48; (April, 1928), 115-32; (July, 1928), 212-30; (October, 1928), 295-305; XXX (January, 1929), 215-35; XXXI (January, 1930), 46-62; (April, 1930), 124-53; (July, 1930), 228-55; (October, 1930), 283-91.

Barnwell, Joseph W. and Webber, Mabel (eds.) "Correspondence of Henry Laurens," *SCHM,* XXVIII (July, 1927), 141-68; (October, 1927), 207-25; XXIX (January, 1928), 26-40; (April, 1928), 98-114; (July, 1928), 193-211; (October, 1928), 280-94; XXX (January, 1929), 6-26; (April, 1929), 90-104; (July, 1929), 134-67; (October, 1929), 197-214; XXXI (January, 1930), 26-45; (April, 1930), 107-23.

Barnwell Joseph W. "Hon. Charles Garth . . ." *SCHM,* XXVI (April, 1925), 67-92.

Barnwell, Joseph W. "Correspondence of Hon. Arthur Middleton . . ." *SCHM,* XXVI (October, 1925), 183-213; XXVII (January, 1926), 1-29; (April, 1926), 51-80; (July, 1926), 107-55.

"Death Notices from the South Carolina Gazette," *SCHM,* XXIV (January, 1933), 55-61; (April, 1933), 88-95; (July, 1933), 149-56; (October, 1933), 211-17.

"An Early Fire Insurance Company," *SCHM,* VIII (January, 1907), 46-53.

"Gadsden, Christopher to Thomas Morris," *SCHM,* II (January, 1901), 44-45.

Gibbes, Robert. "Robert Howe to the Continental Congress, August 28, 1777," *Historical Magazine,* IV (September, 1860), 262-6.

"Gillon, Alexander, Commodore, letters from, in 1778 and 1779," *SCHM,* X (January, 1909), 1-9; (April, 1909), 75-82; (July, 1909), 131-5.

Greene, Jack P. "Bridge to Revolution: the Wilkes Fund Controversy in South Carolina, 1769-1775," *Journal of Southern History,* XXIX (February, 1963), 3-52.

Greene, Jack P. "The Gadsden Election Controversy and the Revolutionary Movement in South Carolina," *Mississippi Valley Historical Review,* XLVI (December, 1959), 469-92.

"Hayne, Isaac, Colonel, records kept by," *SCHM,* X (July, 1909), 145-70; (October, 1909), 220-35; XI (January, 1910), 27-38; (April, 1910), 92-106; (July, 1910), 161-70.

Jervey, Ellen H. "Items from a South Carolina Almanac," *SCHM,* XXXII (January, 1931), 73-80.

Johnston, Christopher. "The Tilghman Family," *Maryland Historical Magazine,* I (September, 1906), 280-84.

Jones, Newton B. (ed.) "Writings of the Reverend William Tennent, 1740-1777," *SCHM,* LXI (July, 1960), 129-45; (October, 1960), 189-209.

Keen, G. B. "The Descendants of Jöran Kyn . . ." *Pennsylvania Magazine of History and Biography,* V (1881), 335-42.

"Marriage and Death Notices from the City Gazette," *SCHM,* XXV (January, 1924), 36-46; (April, 1926), 101-12; (July, 1924), 148-57; (October, 1924), 179-92; XXVI (January, 1925), 45-58; (April, 1925), 128-35; (July, 1925), 162-71; (October, 1925), 228-36; XXVII (January, 1926), 42-50; (April, 1926), 95-103; (July, 1926), 172-80; (October, 1926), 219-30; XXVIII (January, 1927), 44-54; (April, 1927), 132-7; (July, 1927), 198-205; (October, 1927), 236-45; XXIX (January, 1928), 49-54; (April, 1928), 151-63.

"A Maryland Loyalist," *Maryland Historical Magazine,* I (December, 1906), 317-23

"Mazyck, Stephan, letter from, to Phillip [Peter] Porcher," *SCHM,* XXXVIII (January, 1937), 11-12.

"Middleton of South Carolina," *SCHM,* I (July, 1900), 228-62.

"Miscellaneous Papers of the General Committee, Secret Committee, and Provincial Congress, 1775," *SCHM,* VIII (April, 1907), 132-50; (October, 1907), 189-94; IX (January, 1908), 9-11; (April, 1908), 67-72; (July, 1908), 115-7; (October, 1908), 181-6.

"Morris, Lewis, Colonel, letters from, to Anne Elliott," *SCHM,* XL (October, 1939), 122-36; XLI (January, 1940), 1-14.

Namier, L. B. "Charles Garth and His Connexions"; Charles Garth, Agent for South Carolina," *English Historical Review,* CCXIII (January-October, 1939), 443-70; 632-52.

"Officers of the South Carolina Regiment in the Cherokee War," *SCHM,* III (October, 1902), 202-6.

"Order Book of John Faucheraud Grimke, August, 1778 to May, 1780," *SCHM,* XIII (January, 1912), 42-55; (April, 1912), 89-103; (July, 1912), 148-53; (October, 1912), 205-12; XIV (January, 1913), 44-57; (April, 1913), 98-111; (July, 1913), 160-70; (October, 1913), 219-24; XV (January, 1914), 51-59; (April, 1914), 82-90; (July, 1914), 124-32; (October, 1914),

166-70; XVI (January, 1915), 39-48; (April, 1915), 80-85; (July, 1915), 123-8; (October, 1915), 178-87; XVII (January, 1916), 26-33; (April, 1916), 82-86; (July, 1916), 116-20; (October, 1916), 167-74; (April, 1917), 78-84; (July, 1917), 149-53; (October, 1917), 175-9; XIX (April, 1918), 101-4; (October, 1918), 181-8.

Peterson, Merill D. "Thomas Jefferson and Commercial Policy," *William and Mary Quarterly,* XXII (October, 1965), 584-610.

Phillips, U. B. "The South Carolina Federalists," *American Historical Review,* XIV (April, July, 1909), 529-43; 731-43.

Rankin, Hugh F., "The Naval Flag of the American Revolution," *Willian and Mary Quarterly,* 3rd Series, XI (July, 1954), 339-53.

Renick, E. I. "Christopher Gadsden," *Publications of the Southern Historical Association,* II (January, 1898), 243-5.

Renick, Edward I. "Letters of Christopher Gadsden," *American Historical Review,* III (October, 1897), 83-85.

"Revolutionary Letters," *SCHM,* XXXVIII (January, 1937), 1-10.

Rossiter, Clinton. "Richard Bland: The Whig in America," *William and Mary Quarterly,* X (January, 1953), 33-79.

Salley, A. S., "The Diary of William Dillwyn," *SCHM,* XXVI (January, 1935), 1-6; (April, 1935), 29-35; (July, 1935), 73-78; (October, 1935), 107-10.

Salley, A. S., Jr. "William Smith and Some of His Descendants," *SCHM,* IV (July, 1903), 239-57.

Smith, D. E. Huger. "The Luxembourg Claims," *SCHM,* X (April, 1909), 92-115.

Smith, H. A. M. (ed.) "Entries in the Old Bible of Robert Pringle," *SCHM,* XXII (January, 1921), 25-33.

Stoesen, Alexander R. "The British Occupation of Charleston, 1780-1782," *SCHM,* LXII (April, 1962), 71-82.

Walsh, Richard, "Christopher Gadsden: Radical or Conservative Revolutionary?" *SCHM,* LXIII (October, 1962), 195-203.

——————. "Christopher Gadsden: the Challenge of His Diary," *Manuscripts* (Summer, 1957), 132-9, 187.

——————. "The Gasden [*sic*] Diary Deciphered," *Manuscripts* Spring, 1964), 17-23.

——————. (ed.) "Letters of Morris and Brailsford to Thomas Jefferson," *SCHM,* LVIII (July, 1957), 129 44.

Webber, Mabel L. "Josiah Smith's Diary, 1780-1781," *SCHM,* XXXIV (January, 1933), 31-39; (April, 1933), 67-84; (July, 1933), 138-48; (October, 1933), 194-210.

Woody, Robert H. "Christopher Gadsden and the Stamp Act," *Proceedings of the South Carolina Historical Association,* (1939), 3-12.

Zarnow, Frank. "Tariff Policies in South Carolina, 1775-1789," *SCHM,* LVI (January, 1955), 31-44.

4. Collections of Documents

ADAMS, CHARLES FRANCIS (ed.) : *The Works of John Adams.* 10 vols.; Boston: Little, Brown & Co., 1851.

BECK, ALVERDA S. (ed.) : *The Correspondence of Esek Hopkins, Commander-in-Chief of the United States Navy.* Providence: Rhode Island Historical Society, 1933.

——————: *The Letterbook of Esek Hopkins, 1775-1777.* Providence: Rhode Island Historical Society, 1932.

BIGELOW, JOHN (ed.) : The Works of Benjamin Franklin. 12 vols.; New York: Houghton, Mifflin & Co., 1904.

BURNETT, EDMUND: *Letters of Members of the Continental Congress.* 8 vols.; Washington: Carnegie Institute of Washington, 1921-1936.

Butterfield, L. H. *et al.* (eds.) : *Diary and Autobiography of John Adams.* 4 vols.; Cambridge: Harvard University Press, 1961.

CHARLESTON DIRECTORY: *Directory and Revenue System for 1790.* Charleston, 1790. [In Charleston, S. C., Library Society].

CLARK, WILLIAM BELL (ed.) : *Naval Documents of the American Revolution.* Vol. I. Washington: Government Printing Office, 1964.

CONWAY, MONCURE DANIEL (ed.) : *The Writings of Thomas Paine.* 4 vols. New York: G. P. Putnam's Sons, 1894-96.

COOPER, THOMAS and McCORD, DAVID (eds.) : *The Statutes at Large of South Carolina.* 10 vols. Columbia: A. S. Johnson, 1836-1841.

CUSHING, ALONZO HARRY (ed.) : *The Writings of Samuel Adams.* 4 vols. New York: G. P. Putnam's Sons, 1904-1908.

FONER, PHILLIP S. (ed.) ; *The Complete Writings of Thomas Paine.* 4 vols. New York: The Citadel Press, 1945.

FORCE, PETER (ed.) : *American Archives.* 4th Series, 9 vols. Washington: U. S. Congress, 1837-53.

FORD, PAUL L.: *Essays on the Constitution of the United States.* Brooklyn: Historical Printing Club, 1892.

FORD, W. C., *et al.*: *Journals of the Continental Congress.* 34 vols. Washington: Government Printing Office, 1904-1937.

Niles, Hezekiah: *Principles and Acts of the Revolution in America.* Baltimore, Md.: W. O. Niles for the author, 1822.

5. Works by Contemporaries and Gadsden

ADAIR, JAMES: *History of the American Indians.* London: E & C Dilly, 1775.

BLAND, RICHARD: *An Inquiry into the Rights of the British Colonies.* Williamsburg: Alexander Purdie & Co., 1766.

CASSIUS [BURKE, AEDNUS] *An Address to the Freemen of South Carolina.* Philadelphia: Robert Bell, 1783.

DEANE, SILAS: "Diary." *Collections of the Connecticut Historical Society,* II. Hartford: Connecticut Historical Society, 1870.

DRAYTON, WILLIAM HENRY: *Letters of Freeman.* [Gadsden on the Association, 1769]. London: n.p., 1771.

[GADSDEN, CHRISTOPHER] : *A Few Observations on Some Late Public Transactions.* Charles Town: Freneau & Paine, 1797.

——————: Philopatrios. *Some Observations on the Two Campaigns against the Cherokee Indians.* Charles Town: Peter Timothy, 1762. [In Library of Congress].

MOULTRIE, WILLIAM: *Memoirs of the American Revolution.* 2 vols.; New York: D. Longworth, 1802.

QUINCY, JOSIAH: *Memoir of the Life of Josiah Quincy.* Boston: Cummings, Hilliard & Co., 1825.

RAMSAY, DAVID: History *of the Revolution of South Carolina from a British Province to an Independent State.* 2 vols.; Trenton: Isaac Collins, 1785.

——————: *History of South Carolina.* 2 vols.; Charleston: David Longworth, 1809.

SABINE, WILLIAM H. W. (ed.): *Historical Memoirs of William Smith.* New York: n.p., 1956.

WEEMS, MASON LOCKE: *A Good Twelve Cents Worth of Political Love Powder.* Charleston: W. P. Young, 1800.

WELLS, [JOHN]: *Wells' Register and Almanac for 1775.* Charles Town: John Wells, 1775.

WOOD, JUDSON P. and EZELL, JOHN S. (eds.): *The New Democracy in America; Travels of Francisco de Miranda in the United States.* Norman: University of Oklahoma Press, 1963.

6. General Histories and Biographies

ALDEN, JOHN RICHARD: *General Charles Lee: Traitor or Patriot?* Baton Rouge: Louisiana State University Press, 1951.

——————: *John Stuart and the Southern Colonial Frontier.* Ann Arbor: University of Michigan Press, 1944.

ALEXANDER, EDWARD P.: *A Revolutionary Conservative: James Duane of New York.* New York: Columbia University Press, 1938.

ALLEN, G. W.: *Naval History of the American Revolution.* 2 vols. New York: Russell and Russell, 1962.

BASS, ROBERT D.: *Swamp Fox, the Life and Campaigns of General Francis Marion.* New York: Henry Holt and Co., 1959.

BECKER, CARL: *History of Political Parties in the Province of New York*. Madison: University of Wisconsin Press, 1909.

BEMIS, SAMUEL F.: *Jay's Treaty: A Study of Commerce and Diplomacy*. New York: 1923.

——————: *The Pinckney Treaty*. New Haven: Yale University Press, 1960.

——————: *The Diplomacy of the American Revolution*. Bloomington: University of Indiana Press, 1957.

BRANT, IRVING: *James Madison, Father of the Constitution, 1787-1800*. New York: Bobbs-Merrill, 1950.

BRIGHAM, CLARENCE S.: *History and Bibliography of American Newspapers*. 2 vols. Worcester: American Antiquarian Society, 1942.

BROWN, RICHARD MAXWELL: *The South Carolina Regulators*. Cambridge: Harvard University Press, 1963.

BUTTERFIELD, L. H., *et al.*: *Autobiography and Diary of John Adams*, 4 vols. Cambridge: Harvard University Press, 1961.

CLARK, GEORGE L.: *Silas Deane. A Connecticut Leader in the American Revolution*. New York: G. P. Putnam's Sons, 1913.

CROCE, GEORGE C.: *William Samuel Johnson: A Maker of the Constitution*. New York: Columbia University Press, 1937.

COHEN, HENNIG: *The South Carolina Gazette, 1732-1775*. Columbia: University of South Carolina Press, 1953.

DABNEY, WILLIAM and DARGAN, MARION: *William Henry Drayton and the American Revolution*. Albuqerque: University of New Mexico Press, 1962.

DECONDE, ALEXANDER: *Entangling Alliance*. Durham: Duke University Press, 1958.

DICKERSON, OLIVER M.: *The Navigation Acts and the American Revolution*. Philadelphia: University of Pennsylvania Press, 1951.

DOMETT, HENRY W.: *History of the Bank of New York*. New York: G. P. Putnam's Sons, 1884.

FRANKLIN, JOHN HOPE: *From Slavery to Freedom*. New York: Alfred A. Knopf, 1961.

GIBBES, ROBERT W.: *Documentary History of the American Revolution*, Vol. I, 1764-1776; Vol. II, 1776-1782; Vol. III, 1781-1782. New York: Revised Edition, D. Appleton & Co., 1855-57.

GIPSON, LAWRENCE HENRY: *Triumphant Empire, 1763-1766*, Vol. IX: *The British Empire Before the Revolution*. New York: Alfred A. Knopf, 1956.

GREENE, JACK P.: *The Quest for Power*. Chapel Hill: University of North Carolina Press, 1963.

HEITMAN, FRANCIS B.: *Historical Register of Officers of the Continental Army.* Washington: Rare Book Shop Publishing Co., Inc., 1914.

HENNIG, HELEN KOHN: *Great South Carolinians.* Chapel Hill: University of North Carolina Press, 1940.

JENSEN, MERILL: *The Articles of Confederation.* Madison: University of Wisconsin Press, 1948.

JOHNSON, ALLEN, *et al.*: *Dictionary of American Biography,* 20 vols. (1st ed.) New York: Charles Scribner's Sons, 1928.

JOHNSON, JOSEPH: *Traditions and Reminiscences Chiefly of the American Revolution in the South.* Charleston: Walker & James, 1851.

JOHNSON, WILLIAM: *Life of Nathanael Greene.* Charleston: A. E. Miller, 1822.

LABAREE, BENJAMIN WOODS: *The Boston Tea Party.* New York: Oxford University, 1964.

LAND, AUBREY C.: *The Dulanys of Maryland.* Baltimore: Maryland Historical Society, 1955.

LONN, ELLA: *The Colonial Agents of the Southern Colonies.* Chapel Hill: University of North Carolina Press, 1945.

McCRADY, EDWARD: *The History of South Carolina under the Royal Government, 1719-1776.* New York: Macmillan Co., 1899, 1901.

——————: *The History of South Carolina in the Revolution, 1775-1780; 1780-1783.* New York: Macmillan Co., 1901, 1902.

McDONALD, FOREST: *We the People: The Economic Origin of the Constitution.* Chicago: University of Chicago Press, 1958.

McMURTIE, DOUGLAS C.: *A History of Printing in the United States.* 2 vols., New York: R. R. Bowker Co., 1936.

MAUNCEY, ALBERT C.: *History of Castile de San Marcos and Fort Matanzas.* Washington: R. R. Bowker Co., 1955.

MERIWETHER, ROBERT L.: *The Expansion of South Carolina, 1729-1765.* Kingsport: Southern Publishers, Inc., 1940.

MILLER, JOHN C.: *Samuel Adams, Pioneer in Propaganda.* Boston: Little, Brown & Co.

MONTROSS, LYNN: *The Reluctant Rebels.* New York: Harper Bros., 1951.

MORGAN, EDMUND S. and HELEN: *The Stamp Act Crisis.* Chapel Hill: University of North Carolina Press, 1953.

PORCHER, F. A.: *A Memoir of General Christopher Gadsden.* Charleston: South Carolina Historical Society, 1878.

QUARLES, BENJAMIN: *The Negro in the American Revolution.* Chapel Hill: University of North Carolina Press, 1961.

RAVENEL, MRS. ST. JULIEN: *Charleston: The Place and the People.* New York: Macmillan Co., 1912.

ROGERS, GEORGE: *Evolution of a Federalist: William Loughton Smith of Charleston, 1758-1812.* Columbia: University of South Carolina Press, 1962.

REYNOLDS, EMILY B. and FAUNT, JOAN R. (eds.): *Biographical Dictionary: Senate of South Carolina.* Columbia: South Carolina Archives Department, 1964.

SALLEY, A. S., JR.: *Delegates to the Continental Congress, No. 9: Bulletins of the Historical Commission of South Carolina.* Columbia: South Carolina Archives Commission, 1927.

SCHAPER, WILLIAM A.: *Sectionalism and Representation in South Carolina: Annual Report of the American Historical Association, 1900.* Washington: American Historical Association, 1901.

SCHLESINGER, ARTHUR M.: *The Colonial Merchants and the American Revolution.* New York: Facsimile Library, 1939.

SCHUTZ JOHN A. and ADAIR, DOUGLASS. *The Spur of Flame.* San Marino: The Huntington Library, 1966.

SELLERS, LEILA: *Charleston Business on the Eve of the American Revolution.* Chapel Hill: University of North Carolina Press, 1934.

SINGER, CHARLES GREGG: *South Carolina in the Confederation.* Philadelphia: University of Pennsylvania Press, 1941.

SMELSER, MARSHALL: *The Congress Founds a Navy.* South Bend: University of Notre Dame Press, 1959.

SMITH, ROY W.: *South Carolina as a Royal Province.* New York: Macmillan Co., 1903.

SMITH, WARREN B.: *White Servitude in Colonial South Carolina.* Columbia: University of South Carolina Press, 1961.

STILLE, C. J.: *Life and Times of John Dickinson: XIII, Memoirs of the Historical Society of Pennsylvania.* Philadelphia: Historical Society of Pennsylvania, 1891.

THAYER, THEODORE: *Nathanael Greene: Strategist of the American Revolution.* New York: Twayne Publishers, 1960.

U. S.: Bureau of the Census. *Colonial Times to 1957: Historical Statistics of the United States.* Washington: Government Printing Office, 1960.

WALLACE, D. D.: *South Carolina: A Short History.* Columbia: University of South Carolina Press, 1961.

————: *The Life of Henry Laurens.* New York: G. P. Putnam's Sons, 1915.

WALSH, RICHARD: *Charleston's Sons of Liberty,* Columbia: University of South Carolina Press, 1959.

WARD, CHRISTOPHER: *The War of the Revolution.* 2 vols., New York: Macmillan Co., 1952.

WARING, ALICE NOBLE: *The Fighting Elder: Andrew Pickens.* Columbia: University of South Carolina Press, 1962.

WARING, JOSEPH I., *et al.*: *A Brief History of the South Carolina Medical Association.* Charleston: South Carolina Medical Association, 1948.

WOLFE, JOHN HAROLD: *Jeffersonian Democracy in South Carolina.* Chapel Hill: University of North Carolina Press, 1940.

ZEICHNER, OSCAR: *Connecticut's Years of Controversy, 1750-1776.* Chapel Hill: University of North Carolina Press, 1949.

Index

Feb. 23 of Aug.ᵗ 1764 — Public, which we have provided, and have a constitutional right to provide for. So we cannot discern any Dilemma you can on that Account be reduced to.

That your Honours stand greatly in need of Instruction cannot be denied, but we much Question if any such Instructions as you hint at, has been sent ~~~~~ from the ministry, in either of the Capacitys, you or take upon your-selves to Act in. And we are very sure, there can be none from our most Gracious Sovereign to warrant your extraordinary Threat in that Character, in which alone you have already, very lately declared you would Correspond with this House. —

We readily allow, that no such Omission as that you mention, has been been made in any former Tax Bills, which clearly evinces the Readiness and Chearfulness, with which the People of this Province, have always provided for his Majesty's Governours. Nor is the Omission upon this Occasion, by any means so extraordinary, as the repeated insults and attacks upon the rights and Priviledges of the People that Occasioned it. The sum Annualy inserted in the Schedule for the Governor, is not a salary, but a gratuity from the People; which it would be Stupid in them to bestow upon a Governor, who has endeavoured to deprive them, of what ought to be valued by every Englishman, more than even life itself. —

That we may not be wanting in Justice to your Honours, we most highly applaud your profound Sagicity in discovering the Great abilities and merit of a Governor, who (in our opinion) has not been exceeded by any of his Predecessors in the arts of Haughtiness and Despotism Arts! which when known to be principles of a man in power naturally create the utmost attention and Suppleness, in all his immediate dependants, who cannot but be Solicitaous to avert that suspending Rod, which the least Refractoriness would inevitably bring upon them. We therefore highly commend your extreme prudence, and Officiousness, in so Zealously inlisting Yourselves, as Volunteers in the Governours Cause, not doubting that such uncommon pains and forwardness will in due time, meet with an uncommon Reward. —

ASSISTANCE FOR IMPAIRED MEDICAL STUDENTS

Dartmouth Medical School

ASSISTANCE FOR IMPAIRED MEDICAL STUDENTS

Impairment in one's personal and professional life, whether the result of substance abuse, emotional difficulties, or unaddressed physical deficits (for example, Alzheimer's dementia or poor eyesight), is an area of increasing concern for state and national medical societies, as well as medical schools. With respect to the first two areas, there is research to suggest that as many as 14% of all practicing physicians will become impaired at some point during their careers, and as many as 10% of medical students may qualify as "problem" drinkers, according to the AMA's Primer on Medical Student Impairment. In addition, a number of studies have found high incidences of depression, anxiety, psychosomatic disorders, and suicide among medical students due to the stress of training.

Most individuals experiencing personal difficulties will seek out solutions or professional help on their own, but there are some who do not seek help even when it is in their own best interests and even though they may be endangering their patients or their colleagues.

In order to handle such situations in a compassionate and respectful way, Dartmouth Medical School has established a Committee on Impaired Medical Students, consisting of students, faculty, and staff. The purpose of the Committee is to handle problematic situations that may arise and to organize educational programs around issues of impairment. Specifically, the goals of the Committee are: (1) to protect patients, hospital staff, and other medical students from the harm that impairment may cause, (2) to provide assistance to impaired students, (3) to protect their privacy, (4) to enable them to progress through their medical school curriculum without penalty or delay, and (5) to serve in an advocacy and supportive role as they address their difficulties.

Committee Membership

The Committee on Impaired Medical Students consists of two student representatives per class and one faculty/staff member for each class. Students serve for the duration of their education at Dartmouth Medical School and are elected during the second half of their first year. (Second Year representatives assume responsibility for the First Year Class until the first year elections take place.) The professional faculty or staff member for each class is an individual who has a teaching responsibility or other special relationship with a given "year" in medical school. Thus, someone who teaches in the first year is the faculty member for the First Year Class each year. There is also a permanent chairman for the Committee who is an individual knowledgeable about substance abuse and mental health issues. A list of the Committee members is provided at the end of this brochure.

Faculty members who serve on the Committee on Student Performance may not simultaneously serve on the Committee on Impaired Medical Students.

Identification of Impaired Students

Anyone, including faculty, staff, residents, or students, who believes that a medical student may be impaired can enlist the assistance of the Committee by contacting any of its members in confidence. The class representatives, the faculty member for that class, and the Committee chair will discuss the information, evaluate the case, and establish if it is serious enough to take to the whole Committee. This procedure is consistent with practices followed nationwide.

If these four Committee members establish that the case should be presented to the full Committee, then a meeting is called and the case is discussed. The Committee will then decide if there is a need for a formal, professional evaluation. In this process, the Committee will collect as much information as it can about the student and the situation. If the Committee decides on a formal evaluation, it will choose an outside professional to make an objective evaluation.* If the student would like to have a second opinion after a first evaluation is made, this can be arranged.

*Neither the evaluation nor the treatment will be conducted by Committee members except in special cases where it would be advantageous to the student.

2

Treatment and Confidentiality

When treatment is recommended by the outside evaluator, the Committee will present recommended treatment options to the student as well as a list of approved treatment providers.* The Committee will then monitor compliance. Non-compliance (including a refusal to engage in treatment or premature termination of treatment) may result in information about the impaired student being communicated to the Associate Dean for Academic and Student Affairs. However, no information will be reported to the Dean if the student cooperates with the requests of the Committee. In such a case, the records will be held confidential.

The Dean's office is not ordinarily involved in the Committee's work unless a student refuses to work on his or her own behalf by cooperating with the Committee. The purpose of involving the Dean's office in the event of non-cooperation is twofold: (1) to provide some incentive for the student to get help, and (2) to allow the Dean's office to choose an administrative course of action if there is serious impairment which goes unaddressed or continues to be out of control. This is standard practice followed by impairment committees around the nation.

In the case of a graduating student, the Committee will report a "continuing" case to the impaired physician's group of the state medical society where the student decides to practice and/or undertake residency; as another alternative, the Committee may report a continuing case to the impaired physicians committee at the hospital where the student chooses to practice. These groups generally operate with the same concerns for privacy and confidentiality as our Committee. If a case is "closed" before graduation (i.e., not a continuing case), no report is made to any agency. A continuing case is defined as one where the student has not yet completed evaluation and treatment along with a year of abstinence in substance abuse cases. The one-year period begins at the point where the student engages in a recommended treatment program and establishes abstinence. Where it is appropriate and in the student's best interests, the Committee may modify the one-year requirement.

Residency programs will not be notified by the Committee except with the express written permission of the affected student.

3

Your Ethical Responsibility

As physicians in training and later as practicing professionals, you will be required to make painful but ethically and morally correct decisions throughout your career. Such decisions may include reporting the impairment of a colleague, friend, or fellow medical student. We recognize and fully appreciate the fact that this can be a difficult task. But please also note that the AMA has established it as a physician's responsibility to identify and intervene with impaired colleagues.

With respect to Dartmouth Medical School, you should recognize that impaired students are best served by enabling the Committee to direct them toward treatment, and then having the Committee serve in an advocacy role as those students go through their training. In addition, you should be aware that the Committee has gone to great lengths to build checks and balances into its system and to remain flexible in considering possibilities, alternatives, and options for treatment. Information brought to the Committee is always handled carefully, and if there is reason to evaluate further, the Committee will do this. However, if the information presented to the Committee does not warrant further action, no action will be undertaken.

Educational Programs

Another aspect of the work of the Committee is the presentation of educational material on the topic of physician and medical student impairment. Formal programs which are organized each year supplement those impairment topics (substance abuse, emotional difficulties) which are already built into the curriculum in a number of different disciplines.

Counseling Resources

We hope that medical students will make use of the counseling resources on the Dartmouth campus and in the larger community, when needed. A number of resources are available, whether or not the difficulties are serious enough to qualify as "impairment." In fact, the earlier an intervention can be made, the better.

These resources include the office of Counseling and Human Development (646-5442) at the Dartmouth College Health Service,

4

the Department of Psychiatry at the Medical School (Dartmouth-Hitchcock Psychiatric Associates, 646-5806), The Treatment Center at Alice Peck Day Hospital in Lebanon, New Hampshire (448-6380), and numerous mental health professionals in private practice in the community. On campus, those indivduals with a specific concern about substance abuse issues may contact Dr. Philip Meilman (646-5442), Mr. James Platt (646-5855), Mr. Rahn Fleming (646-2738), Dr. John Severinghaus (295-9363), and Dr. Donald West (646-5855). Referrals can be made to providers and facilities outside of the Hanover area when needed.

Resources other than the Dartmouth College Health Service generally charge fees for the services they provide. For this reason, medical students should make sure that they can pay for such services or that they have adequate insurance coverage. An insurance policy available for purchase from the Dartmouth College Health Service (DSGHIP) provides 100% coverage for mental health services in the Hanover area, up to a maximum of $7500, provided the condition being treated is not defined as a "pre-existing condition." The policy regarding reimbursement is somewhat different outside of the Hanover area. In order to activate DSGHIP coverage for counseling services, a referral must first be obtained from a staff member at the Counseling and Human Development office at the Health Service. Enrollment for the policy year must be completed by September 1. Call the Health Service Business Office (646-5438) for further details.

In the case of a referral from the Committee on Impaired Medical Students, the individual student will likewise assume all costs associated with evaluation and treatment. Every attempt will be made to keep costs within reasonable limits.

Committee on Impaired Medical Students

James Bell, M.D.
Joseph Franklin, DMS II
John Severinghaus, M.D.
Kim Urban, DMS III
Nancy Wilson, DMS IV
E. Jamie Wright, DMS IV

Fred Coler, DMS II
Philip W. Meilman, Ph.D., Chair
Charles Solow, M.D.
Carolyn Walsh, DMS III
Charles Wira, Ph.D.
DMS I students to be elected

DMS1.5M0889